Searcher Reaches
Land's Limits

Searcher Reaches Land's Limits

A reading commentary on

Tarthang Tulku's
Revelations of Mind
Chapters 1–35

Richard Dixey

Dharma Publishing

SEARCHER REACHES LAND'S LIMITS
A reading commentary on
Tarthang Tulku's
Revelations of Mind

by Richard Dixey

ISBN 978-0-89800-220-1
Library of Congress Control Number: 2020941159

Copyright © 2020 Dharma Publishing

Printed in the USA by Dharma Mangalam Press,
Ratna Ling, 35755 Hauser Bridge Road,
Cazadero, CA 95421

10   9   8   7   6   5   4   3   2   1

Contents

SECTION TWO

SECTION THREE

APPENDIX 1

APPENDIX 2

APPENDIX 3

Foreword
by Tarthang Tulku

Dr. Richard Dixey is a scientist who has spent a lifetime studying Buddhist philosophy. Holding a PhD in biophysics and an MA in the history and philosophy of science, he directed the Bioelectronic Research Unit at St. Bartholomew's Hospital in London before founding his own biotechnology company, where he served as the Chief Executive Officer for a decade. He is at present a senior faculty member of Dharma College, a position to which he brings his many years of experience working at the intersection of scientific thought and transformative Buddhist approaches to mind.

Having taught at Dharma College since its founding in 2012, Richard has dedicated himself to a close, careful study of *Revelations of Mind* over the course of the last eight years; his efforts have helped many new students creatively engage my work. Teacher and students alike have been passionate and deeply devoted to exploring the potentials of *Revelations*, working their way through the text several times together, year after year.

The depth of Richard's understanding of *Revelations* is apparent in this two-volume commentary. I greatly appreciate the effort and care he has put into bringing out the layered meanings of my book. His commentary gives readers many points of entry into the deeper levels of its significance, opening up fruitful lines of inquiry and encouraging the religious and scientific, the philosophical and the practical-minded alike, to take a profound journey of mind and spirit.

I wish to thank my wonderful son-in-law for having made such a meaningful contribution to the great encounter between Eastern and Western ways of knowing. May these volumes nourish and inspire all who read them.

Sarvam Mangalam, Jayantu Ho

Tarthang Tulku

Copper Mountain Mandala, Odiyan

May 30, 2020

Introduction

Revelations of Mind is an important and remarkable book. It seeks to explore how we understand anything at all.

My relationship with *Revelations* began ten years ago, when I first began to edit the book for publication. But real engagement began a few years later, when the first classes began at Dharma College. Working with the material released insights like flavors from a carefully prepared meal; slowly meanings became clear. It was exactly as Tarthang Rinpoche had said. Mind had begun to *work* with Mind, and meanings emerged that did not seem to be there before. The effect has been a gradual but continuous change, as if a new center of being was in slow but steady construction. In many ways I date events as either before or after 2012, when those first classes began.

In preparing this reading companion I hope I can offer some fruits from this journey. My hope is that others can approach *Revelations* assisted by some of the insights that came to me, but in some respects that is also my concern. *Revelations* is transformative, and I am sure each reader will have perspectives that open for them that are uniquely different from mine. I pray these words will encourage them to open the door to their own perception, rather than provide a wall of information that just acts as a further obstacle to true engagement.

The reading companion arose from two two-year classes where a group of us worked through *Revelations* word for word, chapter by chapter. Both classes were transcribed, the first by Barbara Korta, and the second by Richard Zeisse. I cannot thank them enough for all the long hours they gave to such an endeavor. Without those transcripts I would not have had raw material to work with, and certainly the participation of the students in those classes was as much a part of the process as I was, especially since working with *Revelations* is more about self-exploration than teaching any subject per se.

Having collated those transcripts, a long editing job was carried out, first by Julia Witwer, then by Howard Hertz and lastly by Zara Wallace, to finally prepare a script suitable for typesetting. I want to especially thank all of them for asking questions and seeking clarifications. Book preparation, and the print and eBook versions were prepared by the staff of Dharma Publishing.

But that is the process. The transformation has been remarkable, and *Revelations* has allowed me to constellate all the teachings I have received from the Khyentse lineage and before around this new and productive focus. This is a great gift, and I can only offer thanks and sincere appreciation to my father-in-law Tarthang Tulku, for revealing this masterpiece and allowing me such a relationship with it.

We live in times of unprecedented historical change, and the message of *Revelations* is both highly relevant yet also strangely outside history. This is the measure of its transformative potential. If readers are able to engage with *Revelations* more readily with the help of the reading companion, I am sure my work is well done.

Richard Dixey
Berkeley, June 2020

Searcher Reaches
Land's Limits

CHAPTER 1

The Central Importance of Mind

PAGE 1, FRONTISPIECE: *Normally, we do not think to question how mind does its job. Now we would like to take a more active role, to learn how mind designed the systems that have such significance for our lives and consider what modifications might work better for us today.*

PAGE 2, PARAGRAPH 1: *The study of mind is a vital and important subject, for mind is our life and the basis for our reality: its power is vast and its radiance illumines every aspect of our being. Active in every moment of our lives, mind governs our way of experiencing and influences how we respond to all that it presents. Wherever something is acting, creating, and energizing, wherever something is expanding or contracting, wherever there is suffering or pleasure, mind is revealing its presence. There is nothing in our experience that does not arise from mind, depend upon, and bear the imprint of mind.*

Mind is both our life and our reality. This statement is initially surprising to those educated in modern technological cultures, which uncritically accept a 'real' world 'out there'. When you consider it, however, the point is unassailable. All knowledge we have of anything is mediated through our mind.

While all our knowledge arises through our minds, the mind itself is hidden. But the mind is not a hidden component of our experience, as if it were some 'thing'. Rather than being something to be found, the mind is the transparent mediator of experience itself.

Objects are perceived through differences, the edges they make with their background. One of the principles of camouflage is to blur those edges so that an object becomes indistinct, but mind is not hidden in that manner. Rather like translucent shrimp, whose invisibility is based on their bodies being almost completely transparent, mind's invisibility arises from its very clarity and transparency. Mind is so clear that we cannot see it.

> PAGE 2, PARAGRAPH 2: *Whether or not we are attuned to its activity, mind does the minding that sustains the momentum of our lives. Every instant, mind manifests through a complex array of operations, many on subliminal levels to which we have no access. Since it is difficult to question these inner operations of mind, our ways of understanding how mind gathers, presents, points out, and draws meaning out of the elements of our inner and outer environments are limited. Without knowing how mind processes and interprets this input, our ability to appreciate, cultivate, and direct the power of mind is constrained.*

A major theme within *Revelations* is that of minding. The metaphor used again and again in the book is that our minding presents itself like a readout. A readout is the result you get by running a computer program, the output of an algorithm. You have a processor, a device that runs a program, and it reads out an answer. If the processor can be understood as our brain, and the data that is being processed arises from our sense inputs, the display that results can be understood as a readout; another word might be a display. All this processing is hidden from us, however; rather than seeing the display as constructed, we respond to it as if it were merely a passive reflection of a 'real' world.

Layer upon layer of unnoticed processing goes on in every aspect of our experience. When I look at an object and name it, as in saying, "Oh, there is a telephone," I don't consider that the statement I have just made is the readout from a lot of inputs, a lot of material provided by senses and memory. By exploring in depth the many operations that go into the making of that statement, *Revelations* invites us to open up our understanding of the elements of perception and further, to examine the 'I' that pronounces that the object is a telephone.

Neurophysiologists have studied the elements of perception extensively, and there is a large literature available on all aspects of this process. But for this information to be useful to us, we have to access it ourselves. We cannot have experience outside our own minds, so to understand the readout process in a way that we can use, we must access it from within the very readout itself. There is no other alternative. Even if our minds were a computer, there would be no way for us to look at the wiring at the back, because we take our readout with us when we do this. The idea that we are going to somehow discover the secret of humanity by merely studying the brain is an illusion. Our very studying of it is within the readout. We are going to have to turn in an unexpected direction.

> PAGE 3, PARAGRAPH 1: *If we do not understand our minds, how can we have confidence in our motivations and decisions? What can we stand on as real? How can we know who we are? Lacking the knowledge even to begin to answer these questions, we have no choice but to suffer, for we do not know how or why our problems come about.*

If you are unaware of how your experience is generated, you will lack a full understanding of the basis of your decision-making. The typical Western approach to this is to ignore personal experience and seek 'objective' knowledge as a guide for such tasks.

A small aside may be helpful here. This deep distrust of personal experience has its roots in the early period of the scientific revolution, which began in the counter reformation. In Galileo's famous dialogues, he makes fun of medieval scholasticism, which was firmly based on a personal and subjective perspective, pointing out that much of scholastic knowledge is mere naming rather than explaining. The Galilean ideas hardened into what we now call 'experimental philosophy'—more normally called the 'scientific method'. This new idea at the very beginning of the modern era was based on the view that personal experience is unreliable, something to be eliminated in generating 'objective' knowledge. Personal experience is regarded as mere opinion, as opposed to scientific results, which should always be expressed from a 'third person' perspective.

However, such a position creates an intractable problem. After all, personal experience is all we've got. If our system of knowledge eliminates personal experience as unreliable, then who are we? Are we always to be placed on the outside of our knowledge? Is there any other alternative? *Revelations* suggests that there is.

What if personal experience is not irredeemably unreliable, but merely untrained? There is hard evidence that this may indeed be the case. In earlier historical periods, written materials were rare and expensive, and far more emphasis was laid on the development of reliable memory.[1] The idea that human memory always changes over time is refuted by multiple ancient examples.

---

1   See Frances Yates, *The Art of Memory* (Oxford: Routledge, 1966), for a good description of techniques used in the late medieval period.

What about modern observers? Are they reliable? Not so much! Eyewitness accounts are often fallible, for example. The problem is that modern observers have been educated almost exclusively with respect to the 'external' world, and so have no need to rely on 'internal' faculties. We don't think internal faculties can be reliable because we have all been seduced by the Galilean perspective.

A second point arises from the very success of technologies discovered by scientific techniques. The fact that modern technology works does not mean that personal experience should be discounted, however. Indeed, one of the things that we will be doing in working with *Revelations* is trying to encourage ourselves to develop faculties which are reliable, so we can use those faculties to guide us in developing insight into the nature of mind. This will be an unfamiliar way of working with our own experience.

> PAGE 3, PARAGRAPH 2: *Over the past hundred years, much has been said about the conscious and unconscious mind, psychological archetypes, human behavior, the interaction of sense organs and brain, and the interaction of sensory data, mental concepts, and behavior. But even with the current interest in consciousness studies and the advances in neurology and imaging of the brain, our understanding of both brain and mind remains preliminary. Although theories abound, and science now has powerful tools for measuring aspects of mental activity and testing new insights, we are still working on the level of description, outlining the measurable operations of our neurological systems to gain a sense of what we could know from our own experience. But even this kind of knowledge remains one-dimensional and incomplete because it relies on perceptual and mental operations that themselves go unexamined.*

Relying on our normal 'scientific' perspective, we assume that scientific studies of the brain will somehow provide answers about our own experience. Alongside bookshelves full of advice on well-being written by neuroscientists, there is an extensive literature on the philosophical implications of this topic, which can be described as the 'mind-brain problem' or sometimes just the 'hard problem'. If all we can study are brains, what then are minds?

We need to cut through a deep confusion here. First-person descriptions of experience and third-person descriptions of observed events are different logical categories. Third-person descriptions are *about* things and events. But they can never tell you what it is like to be those things or events.

There is a wonderful article by the philosopher Thomas Nagel called "What Is It Like to Be a Bat?"[2] that directly addresses this issue. Given the emphasis on third-person 'scientific' descriptions in our education, this should be required reading at school. It deals with the question of what it is like to *be* something. The argument is simple and compelling. If you gathered together every bat neurology expert, bat physiologist, bat biologist, bat anatomist, and so forth, even if you knew everything there was to know *about* bats, you would still never know what it is like to *be* a bat. You have to be a bat to know what it is like to be a bat. In exactly the same way, if you want to know what it is like to be you, reading any number of scientific textbooks will bring you no closer to understanding yourself. Indeed, if such knowledge is predicated on the idea that your own experience is unreliable, then you can never know what it is like to be you. One hardly needs to look further if one wants to identify the personal alienation that seems to pervade our technological culture! The very engine of discovery that lies at the center of modernity excludes our own experience as essentially irrelevant.

---

2   Thomas Nagel, "What Is It Like to Be a Bat?" *The Philosophical Review* 83, no. 4 (1974): 435–50.

PAGE 4, PARAGRAPH 2: *We say that mind discriminates and judges; we say that mind alone knows and that mind is responsible for identification, recognition and decision-making. English has more than twenty different ways that the word 'mind' is used, and other languages may have yet other, different meanings. Each individual adds to this complicated brew a set of private meanings and connotations. The proliferation of meanings and definitions testifies to the archaic origins of words we apply to mind and raises doubts that we truly understand what we mean by 'mind'. We might wonder what deeper meanings have been lost through millennia of transmission, or ask what outmoded associations might be inhibiting a fresh perspective. If we could give mind a different name, might we open a new frontier for understanding?*

If you study language and you look at words for mind and being, you'll find they are highly irregular. Look at 'être' in French, or 'to be' in English. "I am, you are, he is!" This kind of irregularity may well be related to our struggle to understand what being is. Likewise, it is a simple matter to give a regular term to a clearly identifiable object or action, but it is extremely hard to find a word for mind. Are we a 'mind'? What does that mean exactly?

PAGE 5, PARAGRAPH 1: *Normally we rely on the conceptual apparatus that mind makes available. Now the time has come to enter the inner realm of mind and understand how it operates on all levels of our being. But where might we find a point of entry to this realm? We would like to question mind directly, but mind seems reluctant to show itself. For all our methods of rational inquiry, for all our treasury of concepts and philosophical systems, it seems that we do not yet have the tools we need to explore the mysterious territory of our own minds.*

It is extremely difficult to turn attention toward this readout maker—this "display-of-the-world" maker. When we turn, we suddenly realize that the maker behind the projector has just turned with us! We cannot walk around to the back to see the projection being made! We are still looking at the readout. It just follows us around, so there's no point of entry. We can't make a rational inquiry, which is why philosophy has never done so successfully. It is not as if the mind is some sort of mountain for us to scale; it is a lot more difficult than that! At least you can walk around a mountain.

PAGE 5, PARAGRAPH 2: *When we consider the difficulties of understanding exactly what mind is and what it does, when we attempt to look more closely at the structures that condition our knowledge of self and world, we begin to appreciate how little we really know. Despite pretenses to the contrary, at some level we sense the power of mind to override our intentions, dismiss our questions, and determine the outcome of every moment of experience. Usually unacknowledged or brushed aside as we deal with the more immediate pressures of life, this sense that we must endure whatever mind presents is an ongoing source of insecurity and fear.*

PAGE 6, PARAGRAPH 1: *However reluctant we may be to engage this topic, our own readiness to dismiss, deny, or reason our discomfort away should give us pause: Why do we shy away from exploring the insecurity that lies at the root of our being? Doesn't our fear tell us that at a deeper level we know that such fundamental ignorance is not acceptable?*

Now, this is a key point. Most of us do not accept that there is something about our own existence of which we know very little. We find ourselves shying away from the question, perhaps with an internal dialogue saying, "I don't have enough time for this. I have things to do, things to learn, and I'm going to be better at this and better at that, and I'm going be successful here." But this fundamental inquiry is universal. No matter how accomplished we are, if we don't understand the readout maker, we're always going to be going around in a circle. We will have no clear idea of the base of our own experience. It may be a good-looking circle, but it's going to be a circle. So, what are we going to do?

PAGE 6, PARAGRAPH 2: *The knowledge that this kind of disquiet affects every human on this planet can motivate us to re-examine what we do know of mind on the basis of our own experience. Perhaps we cannot look at the face of mind directly, but we can examine its processes more closely, asking how they were set up and how it is that within the infinite possibilities for human experience, we have so little choice in what we think and feel. In questioning the operations of mind, we might discover how to guide them in ways that ensure a better outcome for our lives.*

PAGE 7, PARAGRAPH 1: *This inquiry challenges us to strip away the veils of assumptions and denial so that we can see how our efforts to be free are undermined—not by others (as we so often think)—but by the orientation and operations of our own minds. The more honestly we can acknowledge the extent of our not-knowing, the more mind will open, allowing the light of understanding to illuminate what is not yet known. In the process, we may experience a most inspiring insight: there is more to be understood, and more to be revealed, by a mind fully engaged in understanding.*

These last paragraphs are a reference to a whole set of insights that arise in the later sections of *Revelations*. But let us not leave too quickly what was covered in earlier sections of this first chapter: the fact that we always, and without exception, ignore the universality of our own experience because we have been taught again and again that there is a real world 'out there' in which we live. This central element of our education causes us to ignore our own experience as unimportant. Religions then take over that experience and often express it in mystical language, but that leads to the strangely modern paradox that we can be dutiful when it comes to religion but blind when it comes to the world of experience in which we actually live!

Exercise 1
Quiet sitting

Sit quietly and look at the mind for brief periods of time (five minutes max) throughout each day. Keep a journal and record your reflections after each practice session, or at the end of each day. What did you see when you looked at mind?

After a week, answer the following questions: Has looking at the mind in this way led to an understanding of "exactly what mind is and what it does"? What don't you understand about mind that you would like to understand?

CHAPTER 2

Mind and 'I'

= mind is a different entity than self.

PAGE 8, PARAGRAPH 1: *If mind is central to all aspects of our lives, it is in our best interest to develop a satisfying rapport with mind and make it a good friend. With a clearer understanding of the nature of mind, how it operates, and how it communicates to our conscious awareness, we could be more consistently at ease with our thoughts and feelings, more comfortable in our embodiment, and more confident in exercising our capacities for creativity and meaningful accomplishment. Viewing our mind as a partner we might find it possible to direct its power into a mutually supportive relationship with our own being, a kind and nurturing relationship, a profound, perhaps even enlightening relationship.*

objective or self

In recognizing that what we perceive is a display constructed from primary cognitive events, there would appear to be a conceptual difference between ourselves as perceivers and our mind as the constructor of such perceptions. One could even talk about a partnership. Does this imply that there are two entities, a 'knower' within the cognitive structure, or is this apparent duality merely a function of how we describe our experience? *Yes!*

PAGE 8, PARAGRAPH 2: *Considering how language presents 'I' and mind as discrete entities and fosters distinctions between them, the notion of a partnership that called this separation into doubt would seem promising. But it does not appear that this potentially useful line of inquiry has been widely pursued.*

A fundamental consideration is the role language plays in formulating expressions of, and generating insights about, the nature of our experience. Grammatical construction requires a knower and a known; in this case, 'I' and 'mind'. It is valuable to deeply examine how language operates in this context, and examine how this structure emerges.

PAGE 9, PARAGRAPH 1: *We generally use the word 'I' to point to ourselves. Here we use 'I' in this same familiar, non-technical way to explore how concepts of mind and 'I' operate in the context of everyday experience.*

One often hears that the ego 'I' needs to be controlled or subdued in some manner. It might be more fruitful, however, to see how it is generated. The key point is that the 'I' is the grammatical subject in the sentence, "I did this," or "I was there." In describing any aspect of experience, the grammatical subject must always be present. The mind organizes information around the narrator or actor 'I'; it is inevitably going to be utilized any time information is displayed, remembered, organized, or communicated. If all these activities of mind require an ego structure to be expressed, it follows that you cannot escape the ego. The task is to understand it.

PAGE 9, PARAGRAPH 2: *In everyday dialogue, 'I' seems close and intimate, the voice of personal identity, an active agent that some disciplines refer to as ego or self. In contrast, 'mind' seems more general, perhaps more all-encompassing and remote, more difficult to point to and describe.*

We can begin by examining our everyday language. 'Mind' is like a spacious enclosure in common everyday use, whereas 'I' is an agent that acts within that enclosure. "I've got a problem on my mind . . . my mind's full of worries." This is the first thing to notice about the way we use these words.

If you think about this, it's quite common to say, "Ah, I've got a problem on my mind." What we never say is, "I've got a problem on my I." Mind seems important, yet also separate from 'us', as if it is the space in which we live.

> PAGE 9, PARAGRAPH 3: *But this is just a first approximation. The relationship between mind and 'I' is not fully clear. Sometimes mind is viewed as the thought-producing aspect of our being, the provider of ideas, comments, and interpretations that 'I' can then express.*

Mind can also be understood as something like a repository that you take ideas from. 'I' is the actor and mind is the receptacle where such actions are stored. Supported by this passive storehouse, the ego, the 'I', gets it, does it, works it out, is good with it, is bad with it, has successes and failures with it. The 'I' is the agent working with materials taken from this passive storehouse.

> PAGE 9, PARAGRAPH 3, CONT'D: *In this context, mind may be sensed as a presence that can criticize, demand, or warm the heart with good feelings.*

In Western thought the old Lockean empirical model was that the mind was blank when you were born: it was a 'tabula rasa', an empty slate. The idea was that over the course of your life the blank slate filled up with impressions and experiences. In this model the mind is essentially passive. I am there as the active person and the mind is merely a repository of memory and experience.

But the idea of mind as passive repository begins to break down when you start to realize that the mind itself is active. This is exactly what Freud proposed at the end of the nineteenth century. In his view the mind is active, but it is unconscious and thus active underneath our experience. This insight started the whole psychoanalytical movement a hundred and twenty years ago.

> PAGE 9, PARAGRAPH 3, CONT'D: *It can also be an annoyance, nagging about trivia when we wish to concentrate, sleep, or just be quiet. In darker moments, mind can become a source of pain, flooding the cells of body and brain with unpleasant memories and toxic emotions, inciting guilt, fear, rage, frustration and a stream of nightmarish thoughts and images.*

Here we have an observation very much in the mold of the Freudian idea that there is an unhealthy, seething unconscious that has been repressed by our education and upbringing.

> PAGE 10, PARAGRAPH 1: *Usually mind and 'I' function as natural complements to one another and protective of each other's interests. Often 'I' occupies the foreground of our consciousness, where it seems more powerful and assertive than mind; at other times, 'I' is more humble, more aware of its limitations and open to the deeper knowledge that mind may provide. Approached in this way, mind can act as a wise counselor, a kind of interpreter and facilitator for 'I'.*

These various views of mind and I deserve exploration. One way we can do it is to keep a diary to explore 'I' and mind. Initially this may feel artificial, but there are well-established techniques for journaling in this way: you can actually create a dialogue between you as 'I' and your mind.

A good example of this kind of approach is described in the autobiography of the famous psychoanalyst Carl Jung.[3] Diaries were a very important element of his work. It was as if he was discovering the inner landscape of his experience

---

3   C. G. Jung, *Memories, Dreams and Reflections* (New York: Vintage Books, 1989).

through keeping a diary. This kind of exploration can also be carried out in meditation if your concentration is stable enough. However, those new to meditation nearly always get swept away by random thoughts when they try to do this.

In keeping a diary you can ask yourself a question; for example, "How am I going to deepen my experience?" Just ask that question and see if you get an answer. The process is about activating a deeper relationship by asking for it, and being willing to wait for it to develop. Most of us live on the surface of our being because we are facing the world at the level of display. It is as if we are trapped at the gates of our being.

> PAGE 10, PARAGRAPH 2: *Most often we seem to experience mind as operating quietly in the background, while 'I' is the decider, the one in charge. But this decider-'I' can become detached and self-absorbed, paying little attention to mind and what it requires to operate efficiently.*

The grammatically constructed 'I', the subject in the sentence, "I did that," plays a central role in the organization of our experience. One could use the adjective heroic to point out this important element of our mental structure. We live our lives with this hero who is called 'me'. Somehow, it's 'me' against the world. Here, a second feature of the ego structure becomes apparent. The ego 'I' is embedded within a story of 'me'; it's the story of our life.

Consider this illuminating quotation from Leonard Cohen in an interview he gave in 2002. Besides being a famous musician, Leonard Cohen was also a Zen monk for thirty years. He said:

"Roshi [his Zen Buddhist teacher] said something nice to me one time. He said that the older you get the lonelier you become, and the deeper the love you need. Which means that this hero that you are trying to maintain as the central figure in the drama of your life—this hero is not enjoying the life of a hero. You are exerting a tremendous maintenance to keep this heroic stance available to you and the hero is suffering defeat after defeat. And they are not heroic defeats; they are ignoble defeats. Finally, one day you say: "Let him die, I can't invest anymore in this heroic position." From there you just live your life as if it is real, as if you have to make decisions even though you have absolutely no guarantee of any of the consequences of your decisions."4

This quotation highlights an important point. At the level of operation, the ego 'I' is the actor around which action constellates. There is, however, another level. The operant ego does not merely act as the locus for action or narration. The operant function is clothed in meaning. Instead of being a mere actor, the ego structure is cast within a story line as the central actor. This second level could be called the heroic ego—the figure at the center of being who is what it is like to be me. This heroic structure requires enormous maintenance, however, and faces the eventual inevitability of defeat, if only in old age and death. All of us are interested in heroes, how they rise and inevitably fall, and what we don't realize is that we are all living that same story in our own small way.

For example, we can do considerable damage to ourselves by taking heroic stances, such as jealousy or self-righteous anger. We get upset by some slight or event which we perceive as an insult to our dignity. That whole process of getting riled up happens almost independently of our own internal structure. Often it can be very damaging, as we have to deal with the toxicity that is released by our actions.

PAGE 10, PARAGRAPH 2, CONT'D: *This may be why the decider finds it hard to comprehend that, while 'I' cannot operate independently of mind, mind seems to be capable of deciding on its own. Even when the 'I' makes no*

---

4 Leonard Cohen, *Interview in Spin Magazine* (2002).

conscious decision to judge and evaluate a situation, it may experience subtle reminders of right and wrong, like and dislike, generated by the mind, that ripple through the silent field of awareness until some energizing thought or memory takes hold and sparks a response. Mind points, thoughts grasp, associations awaken memories, and emotions follow. This sequence can unfold so rapidly that we may not realize what is happening until we find ourselves seething with emotion, propelled into action, or frozen in confusion, uncertain which way to turn.

In certain schools of psychotherapy this is called a 'loaded vector'—a situation where some seemingly minor event causes a major upset. It triggers a whole chain of associations that you're not fully aware of, but you find yourself being upset by. This is an example of mind, completely independently of you, running through an association chain, as we will explore below. So, whereas we can upset mind, mind can also upset us. It goes both ways. Until we get a handle on this relationship, it's going to be an unstable one! If it's not based in any understanding, it's going to be purely reactive on both sides. This is clearly not the way to operate a partnership.

PAGE 11, PARAGRAPH 1: *In the role of 'I', we may sense ourselves as independent actors, yet upon closer observation, we may note that in fact it is mind doing the directing, focusing our energy, commanding not only 'I' but also 'me' and 'mine'—the labels that express our various roles as subject, object, and owner. Eventually we realize that mind has business with 'I', and 'I' in turn relies on mind to supply the assurance 'I' needs to exercise 'my' authority.*

Page 11, paragraph 2: *'I' says, "I am," and mind agrees, "Yes, you are. You are here, you are real, you are in control." So far, so good. It seems that 'I' am the owner of mind and all that comes up in mind. This is 'my mind', these are 'my thoughts' and 'my feelings'. 'I' have something 'in mind', 'I' think, and 'I' feel.*

The mind can't communicate conceptually without an 'I' there. There's no method for it to relate to anything without an 'I' there, even though the focus on the 'I' limits perspective. This inevitable narrowing is important to understand if we are to recognize the constraints on our own experience. An ego has always got to have a point, a line, a narrow slit through which it's going to operate. This is called a 'point' of view.

The ego says, "This is my mind. These are 'my' thoughts and 'my' feelings. I have something in 'my' mind. 'I' think and 'I' feel." This should be a stable relationship, yet somehow the mind has reactions that appear to be independent of what the ego wants. As a consequence of this independence, the heroic ego is defeated ignobly. Initially we bounce back from such setbacks, putting them down to inexperience. But over time we begin to see that we are being defeated continually, not in some great battle, but by nagging doubts and small things that eat away at our heroic authority.

It is very helpful to realize that this ego structure is always operating. When you carry out your everyday activities you are going to be the hero in the story of your own life. The hero is the person around which everything else revolves. The hero is the person who is making sense of it all. We run our lives like that—everybody does. We have reasons for our actions, goals and long-term ambitions. Seen like this many of us would agree that we have to have a heroic pose to make any progress or get anything done. For example we send our children off to school—to do what? To be heroes, of course! They play sports—to be heroes! When my child scores a goal in soccer, I applaud—he is a hero! When they act in a play or sing in a choir, we are all enthusiastic; heroes! You can see our education is predicated on this idea that somehow we are going to get somewhere. Who is going to get somewhere? The heroic ego is going to get somewhere, and be somebody.

It is valuable to really see this working, and realize that our everyday psychological structure is predicated on this relationship. Maybe the heroic ego is seeking enlightenment. Gautama Buddha, the hero, sits under the Bodhi Tree and determines to become enlightened! It's a totally heroic story. Jesus Christ on the cross—a hero. It's important to recognize the fundamental significance of the hero; this is not some trivial thing.

> PAGE 11, PARAGRAPH 3: *'I' might therefore assume that 'I' can command and direct 'my' mind to produce thoughts and stimulate feelings that 'I' find appropriate and satisfying. But this is not the case. 'My' mind does not always accept what 'I' want to do. It speaks through 'my' nerves and muscles; it aches, complains, and holds back. We may sense it murmuring silently in the background of experience, making comments that surface as 'my' own thoughts: "I am not happy. I am bored. I am tired. I really do not want to do this." As soon as these thoughts are voiced, they become 'mine'. 'I' take possession of the feelings flickering within body and mind. Mind signals, "I am bored," and without knowing quite why, 'I' find myself becoming restless and sleepy.*

It takes clear introspection to see this. But once you start developing an understanding of the hero, you realize that the things that the hero abrogates as his, or hers, are actually being given, sneakily, by mind. And then they become 'mine'. Unfortunately, we are focused entirely on the hero. Obsessed with our heroic struggle, we remain deeply unknowing of our actual situation. It's like a moth with a candle flame; we are just stuck in the role of a hero without realizing that there is this hand coming out and giving us stuff from behind. We only realize that there is a problem when our lives start breaking down. And often then, the hero says, "You are no good!" and tries to turn around and beat itself up, because it doesn't know how to deal with what is actually happening.

Even calling yourself an idiot is the hero being a hero: "You idiot, don't do this!" Self-criticism is very heroic. It's the hero who is being critical, because underneath, the hero has got it together! We have the hero saying, "You idiot, tie your shoe laces!" It is a strange structure, because the you it's referring to is itself!

For example, have you ever given yourself a telling-off in the mirror? You stand in front of a mirror and you say, "You! I am talking to you! I want you to listen to me!" Make eye contact with yourself. It's so interesting when you do that. It is a very strange sensation. It is almost as if the language structure of the mind resists it. Yet the language that is used makes sense, because it is what we use in our internal dialogue all the time. It's worth doing, please. Use a mirror!

We are not going to try and defeat the hero; that just plays into the heroic story. The goal of *Revelations* is to understand the hero. The first thing to understand is why the hero has feet of clay. No matter how heroic you are, there is always the suspicion that you are not legitimate, that you are not really heroic at all. Maybe we all know in our heart of hearts that this hero is a construct, totally reliant on its relationship with its big brother mind, a mind that has no voice of its own.

> PAGE 12, PARAGRAPH 1: *Usually, we would not think to question what is so clearly the case. Yes, I am bored, and so of course I feel restless and sleepy. Yet if we do pose the question, matters may take a different turn. If we ask, "Who is saying this? Who is bored?" the sense of boredom may lift. Such questions put the mind in an unusual posture. Mind seems reluctant to assert itself when challenged to take on the role of 'I' directly.*

Now, this is very characteristic of the approach taken in *Revelations*. When we ask "who," we begin to uncover the tacit structure that we have taken for granted. For example, one of the good moments to ask "who is sleepy" is when we are meditating. For meditators, sleepiness is an opportunity. Consider this: you are meditating; you are kind of dopey; and then you ask, "who is dopey" or "who is dopey right now?" Asking that question immediately breaks the lethargy. It's as if mind's attitude changes when that question is asked.

It's almost as if some hidden hand has been seen behind the scenes—and when confronted it slips back into its place. It doesn't want you to see it, it doesn't want you to capture it or catch it out.

This "attitude of looking" is very productive to begin to open up what initially seems like an impenetrable façade. Most of us are completely asleep in our heroic tale, but asking "who?" can wake us up a bit to the story. This is not meant to change the story but to see the hero in action.

Exercise 2
Watching the hero

Keep a diary that records the role of the hero in your life. Consider the story of your actions, and see how the central character is constructed. It is particularly visible when there is something upsetting, or something that did not go well. What narrative is the hero using to explain difficulties and failures? Write down a record at the end of the day.

CHAPTER 3

The Business of Mind

This is a short but very important chapter, because it introduces the term 'the regime of mind'. A regime has the connotation of an all-encompassing structure that governs everything we do. The term also carries a negative connotation in that the regime will always be against you.

This is not the intention of *Revelations* in using the term 'regime'. What *Revelations* is interested in demonstrating is that there is a regime that encompasses us, and this has good and bad consequences. This regime is not designed to wreck our life; on the contrary, rather the reverse; if anything, it is overprotective.

People who have lived in a totalitarian regime say that if you are born into it you can't imagine an alternative. There was a film entitled, "Goodbye, Lenin!" made on this topic by the German director Wolfgang Becker after the fall of the Berlin wall. It was about an East German woman dying of cancer who was so disoriented by the freedom that was suddenly on offer after the regime collapsed that her children recreated the regime for her by wearing the official uniforms of the old communist government and behaving as if nothing had changed.

A regime is like that. You can't imagine what it would be like to be outside it. When you fight a regime, you are fighting for an intuition about something you don't actually know anything about. You don't know what lies outside the regime, nor can you fully understand it from the inside. You just kick against it because you sense there must be something else. These are some of the connotations of the word 'regime' as it is used here in *Revelations*.

So, for us it's really important to be very clear about this universal structure we inhabit. Only with that clarity does the import of *Revelations* really become apparent. Without clear comprehension, *Revelations* can become a kind of yoga, a set of exercises to help us feel better for a little while—but the yoga is within the regime itself.

Along with 'regime', you could also use the word 'structure', and try to become familiar with all the operations that lie behind appearance. Sometimes the metaphor of a stage is also used, but the readout we live in is not only a stage, but also the props behind the stage and the actor in its center.

Indeed, the problem with the idea of 'structure', or any reference to the mechanism of mind, is the seductive appeal of learning *about mind*—the idea that there is a mechanism that we can understand somehow. The problem is that the one who is looking at that mechanism is also part of it. You can't just look at the mechanism and conclude: "I understand the mechanism now—I'm free!" You will be deceived if that's what you think you're able to do, because in actuality the *looker* is also part of the regime.

All metaphors break down here. Even our capacity to look within ourselves is formed and captured within this structure. In short, we have to recognize how all-encompassing it is.

Of course, if this were the former East Germany, there would be amidst the seemingly mundane, boring, and ordinary world actual Stasi members, part of the regime. The regime of mind also has such agents, but they are not necessarily working against us; they are image processors that process what we actually perceive with inhibitory mechanisms to give us a readout that we then call 'real'. That's how we're trapped and totally blind to our actual physiology. Some of these processors are instinctive, but most are learned. You might say that we have been civilized by suppression; our civilized self is a repressed subset of our actual self.

That Stasi member in your perceptual field is hidden, unnoticed, unless you poke at it; if you do you get an unexpected reaction without having had any idea you had a problem.

This is the so-called 'loaded vector' mentioned above; it causes much confusion. Things that seem perfectly banal become extremely annoying. The classic example in modern conditions is reactivity to traffic. Some people get strangely and inappropriately angry when they're cut off in traffic. For them, there are all kinds of memories and irritations that have been repressed but now arise as they are driving along. That's the regime. That's why we end up civilized, but trapped.

Of course, psychotherapy offers a partial relief. Those techniques can move you some distance toward freedom. But they can't get you the whole way because, ultimately, there are an infinite number of elements in our perception. In fact, our entire perceptual field is made up of more and more subtle traces of prior conceptualization. Psychotherapeutic concepts are fine in principle, but to be free you will have to find something to cut through all of these traces at once. You've got to be able to transcend the regime. If you can't transcend the regime you will never totally purify it—it's too complex.

This is why there is so much emphasis within *Revelations* on deeply understanding the operations of the regime. Until we're very clear about the extent and complexity of the regime itself we cannot make the necessary moves to transcend it. How can you transcend something you don't even see?

To do this, this chapter begins by talking about ownership, and it asks a very interesting question about who owns what in the mind. Now, remember, we all have a degree of confidence that we are actually here. But who gives us that confidence? Where is it coming from? We all seem to have a very good idea of what we are doing, but why and how? How do we know what is real? What is giving us the comfortable feeling that we are in a familiar world—where does that security arise from?

> PAGE 13, PARAGRAPH 1: *'I' by its nature tends to assume ownership of all aspects of our being. I, myself, my reality, my mind, my body, my feelings—all are mine, all belong to me. But in the very moment 'I' is firmly enthroned, mind comes forth to take an even more authoritative role. 'I' may be the owner, but mind expresses, points out, and establishes order. Dividing everything it perceives into right/wrong, useful/useless, good/bad, mind lays down laws like a king giving orders: "This is the right way to be and to act."*

When you look at anything there is always a judgment being made. You may not notice it because it takes a bit of introspection to spot a judgment. But every perception within ordinary mind is assessed by asking "is it good or bad, is it nice or nasty?" This continual flow of assessments is what gives you the feeling that you are safely in the world; your world is being constructed out of things that have been assessed.

You are legitimately the hero in the center of your world, because everything in that world has been assessed for you; it's been named and labeled up, given a judgment and in some cases even a score, like five out of ten. It's your world and you constructed it.

Try and observe this dynamic yourself. The obvious time to do so is when you are meeting other people. Don't tell me you don't do it! I don't care how many of you think you don't do it—everybody judges what everybody else looks like, particularly when they first meet. You know, the boys are saying the girls are good-looking, the girls are saying some other girl is badly dressed, the boys are saying the other boy is a wimp, whatever. It is happening all the time! And this is a very, very deeply programmed behavior pattern.

If you just sit on a street and watch people, and then watch yourself while you're watching them, you'll find that you are judging them the whole time. The judgment may not be malicious and you may not act upon it, but the judgment is there. It is important to know this because it is how the legitimation process works.

PAGE 13, PARAGRAPH 2: *As the king of our being, mind projects its power through operations that administer and coordinate all of our mental and physical functions. Operating as awareness, <u>consciousness, perception,</u> or through other <u>processes</u> called by other names, mind collects and distills input from our senses; it cognizes, identifies, and re-cognizes. It confirms and re-confirms what has been identified and recognized. It labels and spells out the meaning of everything we find conceivable. It points out and interprets meaning, then announces it properly in language we can understand. Together, these operations of mind set up a powerful regime that controls the nature of our experience from moment to moment.*

'Cognize, identify, re-cognize' is an important sequence. For example, in the judgment process discussed above, cognition is the first impression of the person you have just met; identification is your judgment of them as attractive, unattractive or indifferent; and recognition is that judgment confirmed as an internal opinion—something you 'know'. The person is recognized as well dressed/not well dressed, powerful/not powerful, rich/poor—all those dichotomies with which we structure our world.

This sequential process is operating at all times. Elements of it can be revealed using a device called a tachistoscope; by flashing images very rapidly, you can see how earlier phases in a visual processing sequence are reacting.[5] So when you flash an image at about one hundredth of a second, you can see the very first level, a level we normally do not notice because it is suppressed by later phases of the cognitive process. If you flash an image of a couple holding hands, many will have a fleeting impression that perhaps they glimpsed a couple fighting, for example. That's an insight arising from the first layer of cognizing and identification, before it has been cleaned up by recognition. We normally have no access to it because we are way behind the curve, living in the readout, so we never see these early events unless we have special training.

The time taken to make recognitive judgment has also been extensively studied.[6] It's just under one quarter of a second. So don't fight a rattlesnake, because in the time you say, "It's a rattlesnake," the thing has bitten you! This is a physiological fact.

We live within this reaction time, so we can't tell what it's like to be in reality; we are always between 150 and 250 milliseconds behind it, in our own model of reality. Events are going on in front of us in time, and we are always going to be that little bit late. We can go faster, of course, with appropriate training, as for example with athletes and sportsmen who

---

5   Morris Moscovitch, "Afferent and Efferent Models of Visual Perceptual Asymmetries," Methods in Neuropsychology (Oxford: Pergamon Press, 1986).

6   Eugenio Rodriguez, Nathalie George, Jean-Philippe Lachaux, Jacques Martinerie, Bernard Renault & Francisco J. Varela, "Perception's shadow: long-distance synchronization of human brain activity," Nature 397 (1999): 430.

train for years to sharpen specific reflexes, but there are—in terms of cognition, identification, and recognition—some hard physiological data with regard to the speed with which the regime of mind works.

Another way of gaining insight into the regime of mind working in real time is to look at optical illusions. One type confuses our framing mechanism, for example the famous Necker cube.

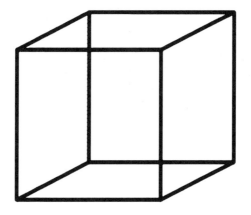

There are two ways of looking at that cube. You can look at it as if it is pointing down to the left and coming out of the page, or as if it is pointing up to the right and going into the page. As you look the image, it will alternate between one formation and the other, it will tick-tock back and forth as you land on one side or the other. You can never hold both perspectives, and actually if you watch yourself, you can feel your visual system re-framing. This is an example of visual processing. It's actually just a flat image on a piece of paper, but our visual system can't help but impute dimensionality to it, because it has never processed an image like that before that was not actually a cube. So, it automatically pops it in and out as if it is three-dimensional. And if you watch yourself as your system is doing that, you can get a sensation of the visual system making the adjustment from one framing to the other. The artist Escher famously made many pictures based of this sort of phenomenon.

A second example is a duck-rabbit. Here there are two ways our perceptual system processes a likely image. Either it is a duck facing left or a rabbit facing right.

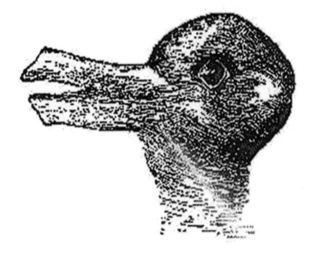

This is a similar phenomenon—is it a duck or is it a rabbit? It could be either. You can see how the system gives you a duck, and it's definitely a duck, looking one way, and it gives you a rabbit, definitely a rabbit, looking the other way. And notice that the duck comes not just with a duck face, but it comes with a duck looking in a particular way, with a particular expression, and the rabbit equally comes with a rabbit's face and a particular expression. You might see the duck as smiling and the rabbit as sad, for example. You even see the little rabbit's mouth in one direction, which is the back of the duck's head in the other. This is the regime of mind doing its very best to deal with what is presented to it.

Now, the third example is very significant—the famous Ebbinghaus illusion.

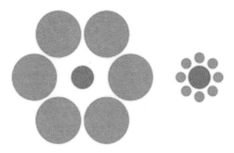

There are two images there, a central orange disc surrounded by grey discs. The orange disc surrounded by the smaller discs looks bigger than the orange disc surrounded by the larger discs. Actually the orange discs are of identical size. This illusion is why the rising moon looks so big on the horizon. It's because when the moon is framed against the horizon it looks bigger, and when it's in the middle of the sky and framed against nothing it looks smaller. Our visual system processes and makes judgments based on what it is likely to be seeing, not on what is actually there.

Technically one would say that our visual system is a highly sophisticated bio-computer providing sense input that is then cleaned up with higher order conceptual processing. Recently an astounding discovery was made that confirms this description, namely that only ten percent of the light-sensitive receptors in the eye actually connect to the brain![7] Far from imprinting an image, as one would with a camera, we are actually receiving highly processed data from our sense gates; it is a striking confirmation of the ancient Buddhist idea that each sense organ is also a consciousness. It seems we actually do have eye consciousness, ear consciousness, and so forth.

---

7   Kevin Hartnett, "A Mathematical Model Unlocks the Secrets of Vision," *Quanta Magazine* (August 21, 2019).

does a curve ball curve?
a "rising fastball"

The study of optical illusions gives us a demonstration of the regime of mind working in real time and coloring our actual experience. These illusions point to an interesting insight, namely that such processing is a very important evolutionary device. In matters of life and death, we don't have time to take measurements of our visual field; we have to make judgments, often in milliseconds, in order to survive. So, the regime of mind, in very large part, is the device that enables us to navigate an uncertain world. It's not an enemy as the regime metaphor might imply, but is more like a protector. Whatever you call it, it's nonetheless all-encompassing.

> PAGE 14, PARAGRAPH 1: *Throughout each day of our lives, the regime of mind continues to monitor, identify, interpret, and report on every feature of experience, substantial and insubstantial, concrete and abstract, internal and external. Mind processes all these diverse streams of input into a steady flow of meanings and associations, producing the thoughts and feelings that enrich our experience and bring it alive.*

The mind creates the world in which we live and think we own. A 'thought' is defined as an 'idea or opinion, produced by thinking or appearing suddenly in the mind.' So, thoughts can be opinions and ideas. And 'ideas' are defined as 'a thought or suggestion as to a possible course of action.'[8] These are somewhat circular definitions, but it is helpful to understand them because when we are walking down the street to our morning coffee we are swept up in thoughts—all those judgmental things happening, giving us ideas about what we are going to do next. It is not surprising that we are all talking to ourselves! Moment by moment we are making a world of words and thoughts, and having ideas about them.

Anybody who meditates knows that the moment you shut your eyes you hear this internal commentary going on. Ideas

8   Merriam Webster

and opinions produced by thoughts are going round in the mind. This is the regime. What is it doing? It's monitoring, identifying, interpreting and reporting on every feature or aspect of experience. Features of experience are being cognized, identified, and recognized: it's a sea of thought.

Then mind does something more extraordinary. It processes all these diverse streams of input into a steady flow of meanings and associations. Although this process is very granular at the core, it becomes less and less granular and more and more even as it rises into our conscious experience. It is evened out until eventually the readout is this beautiful, creamy continuity. This is what we think is real.

> PAGE 14, PARAGRAPH 2: *Mind also integrates and interprets input from 'I' and the senses, reporting on what experience means from the perspective of 'me'.*

The stage is set—we have things in a world that are identified, and now the hero emerges: "Is this good for me? Is this bad for me? What am I going to do about this?" This is where conscious dialogue begins.

> PAGE 14, PARAGRAPH 2, CONT'D: *"This is pleasing, this makes 'me' happy." "This is not good, this is painful, this makes 'me' miserable." The business of mind is multiple: it coordinates impulses and signals from the body and senses, it carries out its own internal 'minding' operations, and it empowers 'I', 'me' and 'mine' by interpreting experience in ways that affirm their various identities as subject, object, and owner.*

So, onto the stage that's been set, enter 'I', 'me' and 'mine'. And remember, 'I', 'me' and 'mine' are referents—they refer to the grammatical necessities of operating on a stage that's been created for them before they came into being. "Where were you when I laid the foundation of the Earth?" said God to Job out of the whirlwind in Book of Job 38:4. Where were you? You didn't even exist! How can the ego hope to understand the regime of mind? It wasn't even there when it was made! The stage is made, the backdrop is made, the conceptual frame is made, the words are made, and then 'I' turns up and says, "Oh, I am going to fix it all!" No chance! This creates the fiction that we all have, that we are in control of our lives. Actually we are the fruit of our lives. We have the illusion of self-control—but from the perspective of the full process it's hopelessly shallow. We have to come to grips with this. It's a fundamental truth.

> PAGE 15, PARAGRAPH 1: *As mind labels, points out meaning, monitors, and interprets, the constant flow of its 'minding' produces a seemingly solid matrix for our experience to take place. Rarely stilled, this 'minding' generates a sense of continuity that shapes the way our experience unfolds and reassures us of the reality of all we perceive.*

To study *Revelations* is to begin to see that experience is actually a stage. The stage of our conscious experience is made of known things. We are reassured that it is real. This reassurance, however, is based on the fact that everything within it has been assessed; it is like an actor who thinks that the play that he or she is in is actually happening rather than being staged. Now, of course, this makes for very good acting, because the actor is totally convincing within the role she or he is playing!

This is not to say that there are no facts; being the hero on a stage is not suggesting there are no external circumstances. But the heroic world in which we live is a construct, and it is a construct from the bottom up. There is no point where it is not constructed, from raw sensation onward, because in every single layer you look at you can see the construct happening—layer upon layer upon layer of construction, until finally, pop, we appear on stage, and we think we are real. And we are real and on stage, of course! So, you could argue we are real, because after all there's a stage and we are on it. But we are only real in that limited sense. In the absolute sense, we are just constructed, a product of a regime that is already there.

CHAPTER 4

Mind and Language

First, a review of the previous three chapters. The first proposition is that the mind is our primary reality. As such, it is all-encompassing and transparent. Although such an enveloping element of experience would appear to be beyond analysis, the second proposition is that an actor or narrator is operational in all activities. This leads to the third proposition, namely that the mind can be understood to be similar to an all-encompassing regime.

These three themes form the background for this fourth chapter, an examination of the role that language plays in our perceptual construct.

Although the centrality of language in the process of perception was recognized in early Indian philosophy, particularly in the Yogachara school,[9] the important role that language plays in object recognition has only recently been studied by modern cognitive psychology.[10]

---

9   William S. Waldron, "The Co-arising of Self and Object, World, and Society," *Buddhist Thought and Applied Psychological Research: Transcending the Boundaries.* Ed. D. K. Nauriyal, M. Drummond, Y. B. Lal. (Routledge Curzon, 2006), 175–208.
10   Daniel T. Willingham, *Cognition: The Thinking Animal* (New York: Prentice Hall, 2007).

The scene is set: the stage is created; the spotlight shines in the center; the actor enters, and then—he or she speaks! Many cultures recognize the deep importance of language, especially those ancient cultures that have preserved a creation story that begins with language, such as the cosmic sound within the Vedas, or the beginning as the word within the Biblical creation myth, or the talking of dreamtime into being in the aboriginal culture of Australia. In fact, there may be few ancient cultures that do not have a creation story that begins with language.

PAGE 16, PARAGRAPH 1: *If mind is the king of our being, language, its medium of expression, is surely its prime minister. Language gives mind a voice that communicates externally, with other people. But language also communicates within, mind to mind, mind to heart, and mind to psyche or soul. Through language, mind makes itself known to our conscious awareness and, through language we express mind's interpretations of our experience and observations. Language and mind are natural allies, intimately involved in operating our physical and mental processes.*

While language gives us the ability to communicate to other people, it is also a central element in our communication to ourselves. In our everyday experience, we talk to ourselves all the time. This inner dialogue is so unceasing that most of us don't realize we are continuously whispering 'the world' into being. And this process is absolutely universal—everybody does it. The moment children acquire language they start narrating their experience. Nowadays we've externalized a good deal of this activity into the World Wide Web, but the process is the same. If we are not on our mobile phones or computers, we are talking to ourselves. Recognizing this centrality of language gives us a tool with which we can start to work with our own experience.

PAGE 16, PARAGRAPH 2: *Because of the way mind gener-ates and applies language, we tend to accept as real all that mind identifies and pronounces, as well as all that mind presents to us as memories and recollections. Usu-ally this acceptance occurs subliminally, below the level of our conscious awareness. Only when we look more closely at mind's relationship to language can we appreciate how strongly this interaction impacts our lives.*

Language makes things real. A major reason to study *Revela-tions* is to question that word 'reality'. It is an irony that many people on a spiritual quest accept the physical as real and try to escape it. However, this is unlikely to be effective unless an inquiry is conducted into how the sense of the real is gener-ated. Without this understanding, there is a risk that either in pushing away, or in going toward, we are unconsciously repli-cating the very prison we are trying to escape. This is a reason why many attempts at self-transcendence ultimately fail—ei-ther totally, or by dissolving into mystical ideas about hidden doors that seem utterly secret.

The inquiry we are embarking upon here isn't just a matter of analysis. Here we are tasked with a more fundamental ques-tion—how do we know anything at all? This may sound like a rehashing of Descartes and his skeptical inquiries. However, the famous dictum "I think, therefore I am" is highly prob-lematic. What does one mean by 'think'? We began an explo-ration of this in the last chapter. Furthermore, who is this 'I'? It is only by examining language itself that one can get insight into such questions.

PAGE 17, PARAGRAPH 1: *From experience, we know that mind is acutely sensitive to sound, and that it responds to the subtle nuances that carry meaning directly from ear to brain. An image alone may not be sufficient: Mind requires a second kind of marker to con- firm an object's identity and distinguish it from all other possibilities. This is what sound provides.*

Sound plus meaning increases discrimination. This sounds surprising, but it's been clearly demonstrated.[11] When you look at something, you don't just look at it, you make a name for it, and that name increases your ability to recognize it. For example, actually hearing 'chair', compared to thinking about a chair, temporarily makes the visual system a better chair detector. When you pronounce the name of something you see, it becomes more real for you.

Most of us are unaware of this relationship between sound and meaning and have probably never even thought about it. It's actually quite hard to experience, but there is one way you can gain an insight into this connection, and it's by doing the reverse. Take any everyday object—say a clock. Say 'clock' out loud, but don't just say it once, say "clock, clock, clock, clock, clock, clock, clock, clock" until you exhaust the meaning of the word 'clock'. When you first say 'clock', there is a clock-like feeling and image that immediately pops up. When you say 'clock' repeatedly, the image fades and you are left with just the sound of the word—it could mean anything. You exhaust the association, and you can actually observe the association fading away.

In this manner, language plays a central role in the organization of our world. In recognizing its centrality, however, we meet two guardians that stand at the gate of self-exploration. The first one says, "There is no point in looking at this—the world is real." The second guardian says, "If you look at this, the world will disintegrate, because nothing will be real anymore." In other words, one says, "there is no point," and the other says, "Don't do it because it's too dangerous." To pass these two guardians we need to understand where their warn-

---

11 Gary Lupyan and Daniel Swingley, "Self-Directed Speech Affects Visual Search Performance," *Quarterly Journal of Experimental Psychology* (2012).

ings come from. We need to carefully study the ways we can keep in contact with our own experience as a primary reality, but at the same time be free from it.

The key to being able to pass the first guardian is to see that our experience of the world is methodically constructed. At the same time, to pass the second we need to realize that the statement, "the world is a construct" does not mean "the world is *only* a construct." That word 'only' is really important. If we conclude that the world is only a construct, we will end up going down the road of having absurd beliefs about experience that don't conform to actual experience. For example, believing the world is flat is not a helpful expression of personal liberty! To pass the second gatekeeper is to be attentive to our own experience, and that includes both the data of our senses and the data our extraordinary technological culture has given us.

> PAGE 17, PARAGRAPH 2: *Of all identifiers available to the human mind, sound registers most strongly and offers the broadest range of features. Mind combines the elements of sound—pitch, intensity, duration, and rhythm—into phrases capable of transmitting complex, highly differentiated meanings. These elements are the basic components of language; they give words the power to resonate like music at the core of our being.*

> PAGE 17, PARAGRAPH 3: *It is interesting to contemplate how perfectly eye, mind, and ear work together to shape sound into language, a vehicle of profound power and significance. When we pay close attention to the words that emerge through thought or speech, we can note that each word represents an internal marriage of sound and image. The sound comes, and the image is immediately available, because the mind has learned the shape that this sound represents: in merging sound with shape, mind has captured the meaning. Now sound, shape, and meaning are imprinted in mind, fused into a convenient label that can*

be pronounced and recalled in three-dimensional detail whenever the impulse arises.

So how do names or labels come to be ascribed to our perceptions? In the Western philosophical tradition, this question leads to an examination of universals, the classes of things which all have the same name. All words are universals. For example, no two sense impressions are exactly alike, but we seem to be able to effortlessly recognize in them features related to other impressions we have stored in our memory, and so ascribe to them a name.

Pick up a cup for example. It is certain you have never seen this particular cup, in exactly this particular light, in this particular position, with this particular perspective. But we know it is a cup—it's not 'the' cup. The universal term 'cup' has been applied to this individual complex of sense impressions. But each perception of a cup is particular and unique; there are big cups, small cups, light cups, heavy cups, cups made out of different materials, in different colors, in different places, against different backgrounds etc. How then do we know that this is a cup and not a one-off, unique kind of thing?

Overall, we can see this as a two-step process. Take vision for example. First, there is a unique visual input, doubtless cleaned up in the visual organ, with some judgments being made there such as we saw in our brief examination of optical illusions in Chapter 3. This is an extremely rapid process, taking between 20 and 100 milliseconds, perhaps the duration of a finger snap.

Second, that input is classified and named in its own two-part process of call and response. The response is of course the ascription of a name, but not a name in isolation. It is a 'name in the world'—a name in a world with me in it. That second phase takes a little longer, perhaps an additional finger snap.[12] The name—the label that is ascribed to that particular perception—is called a universal, because the mind has taken an individual perception and ascribed to it a label that could be universally applied to many such instances. This process of labeling-up gives us the known world.

Clock, tape recorder, keys: this is a process of taking an individual experience and giving it a name. So when I say, "My keys are on the table," we know what is being talked about, even if all of us see something slightly different.

This is the function of language. It is a central engine in our mental structure that takes raw perception and classifies it into things, and then pronounces them as real. The internal call and response happens with every element of sense data we receive. And so, when we see a 'table', our mental apparatus has decided that's a table, based upon all the other tables it has seen. It can be a small table, a long table, a white table, a black table, an oblong table. We are rapidly able to identify things even though they are seen at unusual angles or in a strange light. A human baby can recognize a face after about five exposures. So-called artificial intelligence requires thousands and thousands of exposures to achieve the same constancy.

In Indian philosophy, which is based upon the perspective of the first person—unlike our own philosophy, which is based upon the idea of an external world—there is a lot of interest in how universals are generated. They made discoveries that we will find useful in our own explorations. The early Indian philosophers concluded that universals were generated by negation, not by assertion, i.e. the way you get to 'table' is

---

12   Eugenio Rodriguez, Nathalie George, Jean-Philippe Lachaux, Jacques Martinerie, Bernard Renault & Francisco J. Varela, "Perception's shadow: long-distance synchronization of human brain activity," *Nature* 397 (1999): 430-31.

by eliminating all the 'not-table' entities it might be, which leaves one with 'table'. These ideas were famously expressed by the great medieval logicians Dignaga and Dharmakirti.[13]

PAGE 18, PARAGRAPH 1: *Strengthened by usage into words and concepts, labels merge into the structure of our language and gain certainty through repetition. They become the content of 'our' thoughts, thoughts that engage and re-engage our perceptual processes while accumulating additional nuances of meaning. Networks of associations develop that can then be activated instantly by the sound of a label. Mind continues to affirm their reality throughout our lives.*

Now, the word 'label' is the key here—it's the universal. Chair, clock—these are all labels. And the metaphor of the label is the idea that your mind is going around and posting names onto perceptual sets like little Post-It Notes.

Young children do this obsessively. They will spend hours naming the objects that surround them, and solidifying those names until they are certain of what they refer to. A four-year-old, for example, can't see the difference between white and silver. For a parent, afternoon walks will be full of 'white car', 'silver car', 'white car', 'silver car' until gradually they fully apprehend the distinction. It's hard for us as adults to imagine that we ever had any issue with white and silver, but we had to learn the difference. The repetition through language makes the labels more and more certain, and of course, more and more rigid. The regime of mind, which helps us make these useful discriminations, eventually ends up solidifying into an absolute prison, because the labels it uses to create the world make up a limited set with a fixed group of meanings.

The second important feature of labels is that they act as anchors for memory. We've worked out the label 'chair' and we

---

13   For example, see the entry for Dharmakirti in the Stanford Encyclopedia for philosophy.

have seen many chairs. Occasionally other experiences we have had involving chairs have created associations and nuances, so we say, "Oh, I like that chair. I don't like that chair. That's an ugly chair." We start developing all these other associations on top of the label, like barnacles clinging onto a ship, until eventually the labels are not only identifying a 'thing', but are linking us up to the whole network of memories we've had about those things. Now this network of associations is valuable in that it can help us recall lessons we have learned with regard to our experience, and doubtless this is why it has developed so strongly in the human species. But it is also problematic, because while some of the associations are useful, many are not—or at least, they are no longer relevant.

If we are not able to understand how we generate these nuances of meaning on top of the basic label, we become trapped by a thicket of associated meanings that we can't control or change. This process narrows perception into a highly colored and narrow slice of what is potentially present.

The network of associations does not stop there, however. Often labels are personalized, owned as part of a world view. We say, "This is my idea," and so the heroic ego appropriates the process and places it beyond analysis.

One can see how racial and religious prejudice feed into this process. Sunni and Shiite, Jew and Arab, Protestant and Catholic: prejudice demands that 'we' kill 'them', just because of the name we give them, because the name anchors so many other associations.

It has often been recorded that whenever people who are fighting actually meet, they like one another. A famous example of this is the Christmas truce of 1914 between English and German soldiers.[14] When the two sides facing each other

14   See https://en.wikipedia.org/wiki/Christmas_truce for an accounting of this event.]

in the trenches called a truce and started playing football together, the High Command had to stop it, because they realized that if this camaraderie spread, the First World War
would have been over. Once you are able to experience your
enemy rather than merely having a label for him or her, fighting becomes a lot less likely.

> PAGE 18, PARAGRAPH 2: *Once mind has a label prepared
> that applies to specific sensory impulses, that label carries
> significance that cannot be dismissed. When mind meets a
> similar perception again, it identifies it instantly through a
> process of exclusion: this is a chair, because mind has iden-
> tified a similar object as a chair before. Mind knows the es-
> sential character of that label, and no other label in its col-
> lection fits so precisely. Mind recognizes the object, stamps
> it with meanings previously assigned, and projects it back
> to the mind, where it is confirmed and enriched through as-
> sociations with past perceptions and experiences.*

This is the internal dialogue that's going on literally all the
time: tick-tock, tick-tock. And through this process we are
making the world.

> PAGE 19, PARAGRAPH 1: *This process—sensory vibrations,
> identity, labeling, recognition, confirmation, interpreta-
> tions, and associations—sustains a kind of auto-matic
> feedback system that plays out and rewinds within the
> mind like an endlessly repeating tape. In this way, mind
> bears witness to itself, confirming and re-confirming that
> the object has been accurately pointed out and the mean-
> ing correctly conveyed. If there are other interpretations
> and meanings, they belong to another category or situa-
> tion and apply to different purposes. Mind has already ex-
> cluded them. In effect, mind is reassuring itself, even as it
> reassures us: "This is the right interpretation, guaranteed
> to be accurate."*

Sensory vibrations manifest as the 'beginning sense impressions' of sense input, the first phase. *Identity, labeling, and*

recognition are the call-and-response of the second phase, which creates 'me' in a known world. *Confirmation, interpretations and associations* are all the associated judgments: "I like the chair, I don't like the chair. Oh, remember when I fell off a chair when I was a kid? This kind of chair is dangerous so be careful of it!" Most of this process is completely unconscious.

Such interpretations and assertions seem to carry some guarantee that they are accurate. Guaranteed by what? Guaranteed by previous experience. Human beings are almost unique in the animal kingdom with regard to the amount of learning they need to become operational, and the flexibility of behavior that can be displayed as a result. Human babies do not run straight out of their mother's womb, like horses; infants have to learn pretty much everything, but crucially, this labeling mechanism gives our species a means to learn directly from experience rather than just instinctively reacting to what happens to us. As a result, there can be little doubt that this process has high survival value; it is the basis of how we learn from our experience.

> PAGE 19, PARAGRAPH 2: *Through this process of exclusion, mind designs the frame of our reality. It determines all we can perceive, think about, and know. In determining the precise positioning of words and concepts, it shapes the rules that govern how objects are to be named and identified, the fundamental principles of exclusion and polarity, and the grammatical rules that enable us to understand, interpret, and communicate meaning to others.*

> PAGE 20, PARAGRAPH 1: *While based on standards shared by society and culture, language is also custom-tailored to fit each individual who uses it. Much as a contractor works from a blueprint to build a house, mind adopts the basic framework and patterns of language transmitted to it early in life, then integrates its store of names and concepts and associated objects and meanings into the*

structure already established. The 'house' built by mind suits us perfectly, because mind has adapted it according to our individual preferences, experience, and needs. It is truly custom-made.

This learning process creates for us a language that's quite literally a custom fit. We could look at what we have built as a house rather than a regime. But how can you be free if you are carrying your house on your back? You can live in a house, and you can project out from the front door a certain distance, but you are never going to go that far before you've got to come back, because everything is referred back to the house and its contents. This house of language is like a foundation. We need a foundation, but if you chain yourself to your foundation, you can never travel far.

In this custom-made language, the heroic ego is working. We now understand that the heroic ego is on a stage, conceptually constructed, labeled, named, and associated. The heroic ego is 'here'. The heroic ego is here because he or she is seeing a world understood and identified and confirmed by all our previous experience.

PAGE 20, PARAGRAPH 2: *It is as if mind has established a business whose principal product is language, with the 'I' as its primary customer.*

Here's another way you can look at it. You can say that the heroic ego is a customer and the mind has created a language-based shop, in which the customer can obtain all the things they want.

PAGE 20, PARAGRAPH 2, CONT'D: *Language conveys meaning not only to others but also to our own conscious awareness. Having pointed out and identified sensory impressions, mind uses language to label perceptions, to interpret and confirm them in light of previous experience, and to transmit them to us in ways that establish a sense of reality or truth. This mass of data feeds back to the mind, yielding meaning that can now be expressed. As mind agrees with the feedback it has received, we gain confidence in the reality of what we now 'know'. We buy the product that mind has produced.*

All the props on the stage, the backdrop, the actors, their lines—they are all universals, all names. However, the main label, the universal we really have to penetrate, is the universal label 'I'. 'I' is the label we use to locate ourselves in a particular scene in memory. 'I' is the basis of so many associations, so many memories that coalesce into 'me'. 'My' character, 'my' nature, who 'I' am. But is 'I' actually there while these events are going on? Of course it is not! It is the label by which those events are remembered as involving 'me'. This is where we have to look.

Go on, actually look! As you are talking, or as you are doing something, is 'I' doing it? Look! LOOK! Look while the activity, the conversation, the task is actually going on. Is 'I' doing anything at all? Indeed, is 'I' actually there?

The ego, the sense of 'I', appears in memory as a locator. 'I' is a label. But 'I' is not doing anything, any more than 'cup' is doing anything. The real thing that happened is remembered as 'I' in the sense of a feeling that we were there. That recollection, that knowingness is remembered as 'I'. But in the moment of action 'I' is not present. How on earth could a label do anything?

If 'I' is not present at the moment the action is happening, why does 'I' play such an important role in our experience? This is because when we remember the conversation, action or event, we use the label 'I' to locate it. "I was talking to so and so." The 'I' that is remembered is the subject that the rules of grammar require in order to make the sentence, "I was talking to so and so." But when we look as the talking is actually going on, we come to the surprising realization that

'I' is only a locator, a label, rather than a thing in itself. 'I' is always referred to in the past tense.

This is why 'I' never think I am getting any older. One can go through one's entire life with an internal 'I' that is still sixteen years old! This is not surprising when one understands this key point, for the 'I' is just a label, a name. Truly one could say the 'I' is immortal! 'I' is just the label drawn from memory that describes your being there when it happened.

Just like every other label, 'I' acts as an anchor for associations. The set of associations and narratives anchored by the 'I' is called the super ego in psychoanalysis—it's the narrative within which our life happens; it's the story. So, we've created the stage, 'I' is on the stage, 'I' has a backstory that informs 'my' actions, and then the drama will unfold. We will examine the backstory in later chapters, but at the moment we are just dealing with the stagecraft of knowing.

> PAGE 21, PARAGRAPH 1: *Once this process is set in place, the whole system operates smoothly. Mind has its sources and suppliers—our senses and awareness. It knows how to run its operations, how to please its customer, and how to enforce the rules of the system so they cannot be broken.*

> PAGE 21, PARAGRAPH 2: *It seems there is no ground for complaint. Mind serves its customer well, providing the words and meanings 'I' use to orient myself and identify everything in 'my' surroundings, as well as the content for thoughts, memories, and imaginings. 'I' accept without question what mind makes available, confident that it will serve the purpose. This process continues automatically through the course of our lives. The notion of an alternative simply does not arise.*

We can now see how 'I', 'me' and 'mine' are linguistic cloaks of this fundamental process of recognition. 'I', 'me' and 'mine' are remembered. When we realize this we see that there is a kind of mixing up—a mixing of what we remember to be the case with what actually is the case. This is a root cause of our confusion. We have experience that's identified, labeled, and confirmed, and that process is going on all the time. It is written into memory and recalled as 'I' was doing something, 'me' in the room, surrounded by 'my' friends, associates and possessions who are 'mine'. But the result is to confuse words with real things!

> PAGE 21, PARAGRAPH 3: *Because these products of mind accumulate, we tend to feel that our knowledge is increasing. Yet can we, as mind's customers, trust that these products are sufficient to advance our knowledge and deepen our understanding?*

Now, clearly you can see how the answer to this is "No!" This structure is potentially a prison. At best it is a very efficient survival mechanism, but we are a bit beyond survival. Our mind uses a mechanism developed to help apes live in caves surrounded by saber-toothed tigers, and here we are flying 747s—is this ancient system still going to help us now?

> PAGE 21, PARAGRAPH 3, CONT'D: *Depending on mind for structure and meaning, we may never have looked closely at how mind established the basis for this structure, how it makes and enforces the rules for its operation, how it interprets words and concepts and applies their meanings. In satisfying our needs, does mind exclude potentially productive lines of inquiry? Does its structure limit the products available to us, like the factories in a totalitarian state?*

So here we are, in the regime. And does the regime limit us? "Yes, it does!" Not because it wants to; it's not actually a totalitarian state, there is no evil commissar in the background trying to control everything, but mind doesn't have the data, because it's way of structuring reality has locked new data out. This is how the regime becomes a monolith that can actually block us from obtaining new information.

PAGE 22, PARAGRAPH 1: *Since the language of interpretation is established within the mind, it can be examined further. At any given point in the realm of mind, we can survey what we know and investigate what we would like to find out. Of course, everything that operates within this realm is part of the mind- business under investigation. This means that what we are investigating is ordinary knowledge—knowledge that relies on language custom-made for us and reinforced by every movement of our mind. For this level of understanding, our custom-made language serves us well. But it is not certain that mind can use it to recognize experience for which no label has been established.*

This is the limitation of philosophy. Philosophy works within language to clarify its meaning and explore its implications, but it is always within language. Language itself remains beyond analysis. Now of course, the philosopher who famously pointed this out was Wittgenstein, and the gnomic writings of Wittgenstein were often aimed at language itself. Language itself has implications that can't be explored in language, and you can see why—because language is custom-made by us to describe a constructed world.

As Wittgenstein famously said: "Philosophy is a battle against the bewitchment of our intelligence by means of language."[15] Indeed!

---

15 Ludwig Wittgenstein, *Philosophical Investigations* (Oxford: Blackwell Publishing, 2009).

Exercise 3
Looking for 'I'

Observe yourself as you are talking to someone. Look as the words are coming out of your mouth. Is there an 'I' that is talking? The words are coming out—but there is no 'I' inside making the sounds! If there was an 'I' inside doing the talking, there would have to be an 'I' within that inner 'I' doing the talking for it as well! And within that innermost 'I' there would have to be another 'I', and so on.

Observe yourself as you are doing something. Is 'I' doing it? Suppose you are brushing your teeth. Is 'I' doing it? If 'I' was doing it, there would have to be an inner 'I' inside the 'I' telling it what to do! To posit an internal actor leads inevitably to an infinite regress.

CHAPTER 5

Rules for Reality

We have been looking at how the mind makes the world. It's completely everywhere, and so presents itself as a monolithic experience. Once you realize that everything you do, see and are is mediated through mind, once you begin to understand the totality of our immersion, that realization becomes really tangible.

Then we looked at the roles of 'I', 'me' and 'mine' in how the mind operates. This started to give us a little bit of insight into how we might analyze the way the mind makes the world. We then considered the categories such as inside and outside, the conceptual categories that create the backdrop against which 'I', 'me' and 'mine' operate, particularly the heroic ego, the 'I'. And then we looked at the fundamental role that language plays in generating this structure.

This chapter considers the final element. It's a bit like making a soup. The mind itself is like a thin consommé, shimmering in the background; it's just the beginnings of a soup. But gradually, as 'I', 'me' and 'mine' appear, the conceptual categories added to this shimmering consommé begin to thicken it. Then it is enriched by language and associations, the soup thickening and thickening and thickening, until eventually we have a really dense experience, which we call 'reality'.

We only get to experience the soup as a completed event, as a readout. We only get the thick soup; we never get to see how the soup was made. We are like the customers in a restaurant who are served the soup, but we don't see what was going on in the kitchen. Nevertheless, our mission is to understand how that soup is made. We need to know that because when we are happy or sad, when we are satisfied or dissatisfied, when we feel free or trapped—all of that is part of the soup, the readout in which we live our lives. If we don't understand how that readout is made, we are just going to have to live with the results, whether we like them or not.

It is because of this aspect that one of the themes of the fifth chapter is inner peace. The final element in this soup is the fact that we never seem to be totally at peace. You would have thought, given the fact that it's a readout, that we would be satisfied with this thing, this nice thick soup—that we would be at peace. But we are not! We always seem to be agitated; there is never a feeling of stillness. And one of the greatest wishes that most people have is to be at peace.

Many people seek peace through meditation; and 'rest in peace' is a common saying in our culture. There is a definite recognition that peacefulness and clarity are worth having, but that peace is hard to come by. How many times have we set out to enjoy the beauty of a sunset and somehow have just not quite been there? It is as if we can't quite get there; we can see it, perhaps even buy it, but we can't have it; somehow we are just a little bit short of feeling peaceful.

Why is that? What is happening to cause that?

> PAGE 23, PARAGRAPH 1: *Mind's way of processing language reveals that it is capable of establishing strong dichotomies. We see this tendency in the cycles of recognition and confirmation that reverberate through mind over and over, like instant replays of contested plays in sports. This*

*ability to divide itself into two distinct, often contradictory
roles underlies the logic of the rules mind has established
for assigning names and labels.*

Imagine you are looking at the commentators in the commentary box watching a game of baseball. You might wonder,
"Are the commentators causal agents in this game of baseball?" "Of course not—they are merely observing the game,"
you respond. Is that what it is like for us? Is our chatter just
commenting on the world without being engaged with it? To
understand if this is so we need to understand the process by
which the commentator comes into being, because, as an aspect of the heroic ego, the commentator does not come first
in our mental process.

We always remember the commentator as being first. Naively we think, "Oh, I am watching the world." This is one of
the mistakes that many yogic traditions make. Realizing that
people are acting in the world without awareness, these traditions encourage practitioners to watch the world, become
the 'watcher', or 'the witness'. This advice hides a fundamental mistake—because the world comes into being before the
watcher does. The world the watcher is watching is constructed, not an actuality. But we don't remember that, indeed we
can't remember that because the watcher is like a geotag, a
locator in the process of perception. How can we remember
anything before the watcher came into being?

The way our memory works is a central element of the problem we confront in trying to work out how the mind is creating our experience. The world we experience is created
through a process of dialogue, internal dialogue. Remember,
something is identified and then it is presented to the knower
who says, "Yes, it's real." Now, that knower is clothed in memory as an 'I' or ego. So we remember the knower saying, "Yes,
it's real," as if the knower was already there and saw what was
presented. But the knower didn't see it; the knower just con-

firmed it. Whatever was there had already been constructed by the mind before the knower came on the scene.

PAGE 23, PARAGRAPH 2: *Activating reflexively in every instant of perception, this dichotomy serves to establish and maintain the dualistic perspective that separates self as subject from everything else in the objective, 'knowable' world. It comes up the moment an object presents itself for identification. Mind grasps, and instantly the sound of the label arises. Recognition that there is something 'out there' calls attention to what is 'in here'. This response activates mind's logical sense of positioning and gives rise to the roles of subject and object. With this, the concept of 'I' comes into play: I, as subject, am aware of the object (an image, form, transition, or action). On the most fundamental level, language enshrines this dualistic way of perception as its operating system and imposes it on all of mind's expressions. We accept and follow the rules because this kind of body/mind interaction is familiar and has meaning for us.*

Activating reflexively—that's a very important word, reflex. A reflex is where you have a stimulus and a pre-programmed reaction to it. Two events come as one. The doctor taps your knee and your leg kicks reflexively: that's why we use the term 'knee-jerk' for something automatic in someone's response. In every instant of perception this reflexive creation of a knower and known is happening. We are re-refreshing the ego, reflexively activating it in each moment of perception.

So, just to be clear about the way the soup is thickened: beginning sense impressions arise, these impressions activate the sense organs—the ears or the eyes, the touch or whatever—and a sensation arises. Immediately there is the labeling event. It's got to be understood—what it this thing? That is happening before 'we' are happening, but once the initial label has been assigned, immediately 'we' are reflected as the one who knows that label—"Yes, it's a clock."

At that point, we have 'me' and 'the clock' as a perfect pair, seamless, then all the likes and dislikes, "what time is it," "am I late for work"—all those kinds of associations pile on top. But right at the very beginning, before we've got to 'me', the initial impression of the clock was already there. I wasn't first; the beginning sense impression was. I came after!

This is a complete inversion of how we remember it. We always remember "I saw the clock"—we can have the clearest recollection of seeing the clock. "I am absolutely certain that I saw the clock, I was the viewer, I as subject saw the clock as the object." Actually, it's quite the other way round. The clock as the subject made 'me' as the object, in the actual event as it happened. It's only in memory that 'I' as the subject saw the clock as the object. Right at the very beginning the 'I' was reflexively constructed in the process of recognition. The external world we project is projected from an internal process that creates us as the knower of it. That's how the illusion is made. That's why we think an internal 'me' is seeing an external 'world'. Actually sense impressions create 'me' in their knowing of themselves.

For example, you get attracted to beautiful things before you know why. Beauty is really interesting. Why is beautiful, beautiful? What is it about a beautiful thing that makes it beautiful? You get attracted to it, and then you say it's beautiful, but you were already attracted. The natural world is exquisitely beautiful; its exquisiteness is an interesting point to examine, to examine what that actually is. Arguably that natural world is just neutral, just the way it is. Yet that experience is exquisitely beautiful. This is something really, really important. Is there something we are seeing about ourselves that we do not realize in our appreciation of beauty?

PAGE 24, PARAGRAPH 1: *As mind points out sensory impressions and characteristics, it distinguishes shapes, colors, right-ness or wrong-ness, likes and dislikes, and pain*

*or pleasure, and associates them with labels previously as-
signed. According to rules it has received or created independently, it makes judgments: this is right, this is wrong;
like this, don't like that; this is real, this is true; that may not
be real or true. While there are various shades in between,
mind's interpretations follow the same basic pattern: agree-
able/not agreeable, acceptable/not acceptable, and so on.
These pronouncements imprint strongly on consciousness,
where they shape our attitudes and ways of thinking.*

We annoy ourselves with our own judgments. As we are continuously receiving impressions, each one acts as a focus for
recognition and association. As a result, we keep making
judgments. We might well think it's the impressions themselves that are disturbing, but it's our own reaction that is the
cause of our disquiet. This is why we are never at peace.

We all experience this. For example, as was mentioned in the
last chapter, when you meet people for the first time there
is immediate judgment. This is illustrated by the difficulty
many of us have in remembering names in social situations.
When we are introduced, there is so much judgment going on
that it drowns out the name. There are various ways of overcoming this problem, old tricks known by business people
and politicians. For example, one way is to say at the end of
the conversation, "Remind me of your name again?" At that
point you'll be better able to retain the information. By the
end of the conversation your judging facility will have sub-
sided and the name can be imprinted without all the internal
noise obstructing it.

But it is this noise that makes the world. The world of right
and wrong, good and bad, happy or sad, success or failure is
constructed by judgment. This is what finally solidifies the
thin soup of initial experience into something like cement.

PAGE 24, PARAGRAPH 2: *Since the features of mental activity are closely interconnected, with no gaps in between,*

perceptions are immediately sealed and accepted as 'how things are'. Once this process begins, it establishes the framework for our view of reality. Accepting this mind-created framework as real, we can only act within it.

PAGE 25, PARAGRAPH 1: *Having established patterns that sustain its sense of rightness and order, mind continues to monitor perceptions and thoughts. Now subtly, now more firmly, mind shepherds us continuously: "This is the correct way; this way is not." "Yes." "No." "Maybe." Mind has already scoped out the territory and claimed it—now it is exercising its power to direct everything we think and do. Constantly vigilant, mind creates, monitors, and maintains the inner environment of our lives through inner dialogues that continue day and night.*

Now, of course this mechanism had great evolutionary value back in the time we were wandering on the savanna, because the lessons mind learns from experience and from parenting are survival lessons. As long as the environment is fairly regular, having experience that's partially pre-digested in this manner allows for faster reactions to what is going on around you. But as you can see, it becomes of decreasing value in our current situation where little is actually a threat and our environment is much more complicated. We become distracted from distraction by distraction, as a famous poet[16] put it.

Internal disquiet is the fruit of the reflexive structure of mind. Events arise, they are labeled, and reflected back with a 'me' as a knower—that fundamental internal exchange is going on all the time. Every arising perception triggers this positioning.

PAGE 25, PARAGRAPH 2: *Mind's reliance on dichotomy tends to invite indecision, misunderstandings and confusion that agitate mind and cause us needless suffering. Conflict*

---

16   T.S. Eliot, "Burnt Norton," *The Four Quartets* (New York: Harcourt, Brace and Company, 1943).

creates blockages that invite 'second thoughts'—opinions,
doubts, and uncertainties that activate both sides of the
dichotomy simultaneously.

All the noise comes along with a sense of self. You have an idea
of who you are and what you want, what you like and what
you don't like. The 'me' is a product of your own construction,
a locus around which all these opinions constellate.

You might conclude naively, "This 'me' is the culprit here. If
I could just kill the ego it would all be nice and peaceful!"
But without understanding why the ego comes into existence,
that endeavor is completely pointless. Indeed, you will never get to the bottom of the problem because the ego itself is
not its origin. The ego is only a reflection of a deeper process.
Once you know that, then perhaps there might be a door, but
until you know that, you have no chance.

PAGE 25, PARAGRAPH 2, CONT'D: *The need to maintain the*
positions of both sides causes perceptions, thoughts, and
feelings to reverberate back and forth like echoes from the
walls of a deep and narrow canyon, while mind vacillates
from one to the other at great speed, working toward res-
olution. But this zig-zag, back and forth movement can
also escalate inner conflicts into frustration and anger,
perhaps even rage.

As mentioned above, it's not the upsetting event that causes
our reaction. What we are experiencing is our reactivity to
the event. For example, you are in the car and the guy ahead
brakes suddenly. The 'braking suddenly' is just an experience,
it's an arising event. But on top of that comes our judgment
about it— like a Stasi agent of the regime of mind inserting
itself! It's not the brake lights coming on that makes you angry; it's your reaction that makes you angry. With on-coming
brake lights the reflexive reaction is "Emergency!" The instinctive need to stop the car sets off a chain of associations
linking to emergencies that happened in the past. Memories

flood in of other emergencies, troubles; pressure builds . . .
Rage! But this is a secondary reaction.

If you slow down the chain of events enough, you'll realize
that the on-coming brake lights weren't what made you angry; not even having to react to the brake lights made you angry. What made you angry was the associated web of memories that were triggered by that event— that's what made you
angry.

To understand how anger arises, consider the metaphor of
the mind as a canyon where echoes are reverberating back-
ward and forward. Anger comes on fast and furious, just like
all the negative emotions—regret, sadness, feelings of use-
lessness, envy, jealousy, greed, lust—all of them triggered by
the associations triggered by an arising event, not the arising
event itself.

In Buddhist teachings these reactions are called kleshas. The
nearest English words for the Sanskrit word 'klesha' are 'negative emotion'. More precisely, one might say a klesha is a colo-
rant, a pollutant of perception. If we think of klesha in the
context of our driving example: the brake lights coming on
was a neutral event; it reflected back to mind, another neutral
event. Reactively we braked, another neutral event. But the
judgment to that braking triggered the associative web, and
memories of previous emergencies flooded in and colored
the perceptual field, and anger arose. That was the klesha.

Suddenly the entire field has become distorted and 'we' are
angry. We are forced by that anger into action, because emotions do that—they move you, they emote you into activity;
we are almost obliged to act. Reactivity causes us to act in
ways that inevitably cause suffering, and once that happens,
we lose our freedom. From something that started as neutral,
we are triggered into action that we may well regret. That's
how a klesha operates.

Karma and klesha come as a pair. Klesha colors experience; then we act. Karma refers to actions taken because of that colored-up experience. Those actions leave residues that get recorded in memory as impressions waiting to be associated with a future event. Karma creates klesha; klesha predisposes us to create more karma. It's a reflexive loop.

While this happens at the coarse level, it also happens at many, many subtle levels to which we don't have ready access. This is why attempts to simply reprogram reactivity don't work. At a shallow level they can be effective, but at more subtle levels a more radical approach is needed.

PAGE 26, PARAGRAPH 1: *When mind becomes agitated, pressure builds up and thoughts demand some sort of action. While one part of mind has a powerful urge to move on, a second aspect of mind may insist on resolution. Struggling with contradictory thoughts and feelings that flash back and forth, we can find ourselves at the center of a situation that is difficult to control. Once mind is caught up in this dynamic, its energy accelerates so strongly that we may be unable to stop it or change its direction.*

In the light of this analysis, what is the difference between a conscious pacifist and a master of awareness? The conscious pacifist may have this agitation building up, but through an act of will says, "No, I will not do that. I will overcome it." So, through the act of will, they are able to suppress their reactivity. This is admirable restraint, but it's not the action of a master of awareness.

Like a martial artist, a master of awareness does not react to events, but is completely calm when a threat arises. He or she sees the situation with clarity and without reactivity toward it. In martial arts, it is the ability to see someone else's reactivity that enables the artist to be so effective. Seeing what the opponent is preparing to do, the master artist can effectively counteract it. No effort is required to suppress reactivity, because reactivity is not present.

PAGE 26, PARAGRAPH 2: *The need to accommodate mind's nearly continuous back and forth motion interferes with the clarity necessary to sustain inspiration or make important decisions.*

The word 'clarity' should be stressed here. This is what we long for when we are sitting on a hilltop watching the sunset. What if we could just watch the sunset without thinking, "I like it. I don't like it. Oh, I am late. Oh, this is going to happen. Oh, I forgot about that." If we could just see the sun setting without any internal dialogue, wouldn't that be a wonderful experience? Just to have that clarity! Extreme sports invoke this feeling because at the end of an extreme experience there's a moment of clarity. A person may dive off a mountain or do a bungee jump, and just for a moment at the end of that extreme experience there is clarity. This is because the perceptual apparatus has been completely overwhelmed by the intensity of the experience. It's as if the internal dialogue has been interrupted—and there is a moment. Then it's gone.

Another example is what happens at the end of a great performance. Think of how the audience reacts at the end of a symphony. Just for a moment there is silence. The inner dialogue has stopped—and then, crash, applause! Normality has reasserted itself.

PAGE 26, PARAGRAPH 2, CONT'D: *While everyone understands that indecision can be painful and result in the loss of valuable time, the alternative—pushing ahead without focus and insight—may not be the best or only alternative.*

PAGE 27, PARAGRAPH 1: *Could we use these experiences as opportunities to appreciate how this one-dimensional back and forth pattern of mind restricts our intelligence and creativity? What fresh insights could be realized by a mind able to penetrate the contradictions inherent in its patterns? What vision might be awakened by a mind unburdened by duplication of effort, the useless baggage of past perceptions, the need to follow rules that overlap and conflict, and the inner uncertainties that shadow all we do?*

We are continuously ignoring the openness of mind. It's not that we are 'in' a kind of prison and have to escape. The enclosure we are in is being re-created moment to moment and we are not going to be able to bash a hole in the wall, break out, and be free on the outside. Even if we could do that, we would just take our prison with us, because we are making and re-making it all the time.

PAGE 27, PARAGRAPH 2: *The power of mind operates subliminally and pre-verbally: its gathering momentum flows through patterns that find expression in thoughts, feelings, and actions. By thinking, acting, and doing, we activate this power, expand it, and project it to others, who in turn pick up the same patterns, copy them, and feed them back to us. The momentum expands and accelerates, exerting a powerful impact on body and mind, on the attitudes of others, and on our entire environment.*

This word 'momentum' is akin to the thickening of the soup. Experience becomes more substantial as it gathers associations and relationships. We are not alone in this; we are all in this together. Whether we are sitting on a mountaintop or mixing with people, this thickening is happening. Society is an important element in all of this, because everybody is brought up in a society, and that society models us. This whole thing is a communal process, wherever we eventually go off and live.

We may be living with a comfortable assumption that everything is normal—but that's also a prison. However we express it, there's an enclosure within which we live.

PAGE 27, PARAGRAPH 3: *Because of the way mind perceives and interprets experience and uses its power to convince us of the truth of what it proclaims, we accept what is happening and everything associated with it as real. This sense of certitude merges with our sense of self and the meanings mind produces. Mind knows for sure that an object has been accurately identified, and the ongoing momentum of its minding process removes any residues of doubt. With no independent way to discriminate reality from illusion, whether mind operates in a way that leads to resolution and clarity, or embroils us in confusion and conflicts, we have to engage our surroundings in the way mind interprets and presents them to us. Such is the power of mind, power that we draw upon continually in making sense of our experience.*

You could say that we have become like passengers in our own boat. There are events going on that need to be understood but we end up passively riding in the boat. When things happen to us, all we do is react to them. As passengers, we will always be subject to where the boat goes; we will always have a sense that we are out of control. Things will arise that we can't explain, things will go wrong that we can't fix, and life will seem to have little meaning because we are not responsible for it. That is the power of the regime of mind. We need to learn how to sail the boat, not just be passengers.

PAGE 28, PARAGRAPH 1: *We speak of consciousness, conscience, desires, regret, anger, love, and more, and identify a wide range of emotional and psychological patterns. But these are all specific manifestations of mind—products that we give different names, buy into, consume, and incorporate into our way of being.*

PAGE 28, PARAGRAPH 2: *Everyone manifests emotional and psychological patterns, but which ones surface most strongly or readily seems to depend on environment, circumstances, and genetic or other factors. One individual may tend to experience anxiety more often than anger; another may be more inclined to avoid than to confront, to become hesitant or insecure rather than over-confident.*

We may think we have complete freedom in our thoughts and feelings but actually we don't. Our range of emotional responses is quite predictable. We are in a sense in a recurring drama that keeps going around in a circle. It's not going around in an identical circle, but it's going around in a similar circle all the time. History does not repeat, but it rhymes!

Different things may trigger different reactions, but they stay within a certain range of reactions that are often referred to as 'character'. You can be pretty certain that someone who has a tendency to anger is going to blow up if you poke him or her a particular way. Knowing this, kids love playing with this kind of reactivity with adults. They know exactly what will make someone blow, and they like pushing button A and standing back and watching the reaction happen! We should consider this and realize that our much-vaunted freedom is in fact quite constrained. We are tethered as if by a peg in the ground: we can only graze in a circle. We can graze to the edge of the circle, but we can't go any farther because that peg in the ground limits our responses. Everything is stuck there.

PAGE 29, PARAGRAPH 1: *At some point, individuals identify themselves with particular products of mind, in much the same way that people are drawn to certain brands of products that support their self-image. They may shape their fantasies and desires accordingly, or identify with certain kinds of music, or take up concepts or forms of language that enhance characteristics they admire. Doing this can provide a sense of personal empowerment. Accepting the products of minds as their own, they become strongly convinced of the reality of whatever it is they identify with. "This is the way it is, this is the way I am, this is the way I should be."*

One of the most common ways you see this kind of 'branding' is in political affiliation. People have very strongly held views about matters that are not really their own, views they have adopted and then made personal. "This is the way it is, and this is the way I am, so this is the way it should be."

When you meet people who hold these sorts of positions, they are very hard to argue with, because their affiliation is completely tied up with their sense of self. This is why people go to war over beliefs, more than over anything else. What one side thinks is the case is different from the other, and they both get locked together in a temple of righteousness. You get this absurd situation in which two sides are clashing, and both are praying to God. They may even be praying to the same God!

Exercise 4
Just listening

Sit with your eyes closed next to an open window or on a park bench and listen to what is going on around you. Don't try to identify sounds, just let them happen. There is just sound— there is not even inside or outside; there is no you, there is just sound. Then, after a minute or two, turn on your process of identification, locating where the sounds are coming from, and what they are. Do this very intently, as if you are a detective on the job. Suddenly you are there, it is there and there is a world—the whole structure clicks into existence. Do that for a few minutes, then switch back to just hearing sound without identification. Experience that contrast.

CHAPTER 6

Customer Mind

This chapter deals with self-confidence. We shouldn't take this word in the standard way, however. Here we're examining why we are so confident in what we believe. No matter whether people are shy or outgoing, they are absolutely sure that 'they are'. This is all part of the 'I' illusion that's so important to understand. This chapter is talking about how the regime of mind creates the confidence of 'me'. And remember, if I think I am a meditator, if 'I' am mindful, then the 'I'-illusion has taken hold. Mindfulness is not about 'I'; mindfulness can see 'I', but mindfulness isn't 'I'.

But why am I so sure that 'I am'? How am 'I' so sure that I am here doing this? What is the basis for this self-confidence?

Realizing that the mind is all we've got is a fundamental precursor to mindfulness. That's to say, when you really accept the pre-eminence of mind, you finally overcome the illusion that you can inhabit an external world. With that realization one comes to a deep acceptance: "Yes, this is literally it—I am never ever going to experience anything other than my own mind." That's a very important precursor for mindfulness.

Not realizing that your experience of your own mind is primary is a consequence of our unconscious positing of the real. Most of us have been educated to believe that there is a real thing that we live within—a universe or cosmos, whatever one calls it. Overcoming the metaphysical assertion that there is a real world that is external to us is a central element of truly engaging in personal transformation.

This process of defining our world starts early. Preschool children populate their experience obsessively with words until they feel they've got a full dictionary. They build up words that correspond to known objects in their world. They then go to school and are taught that they are actually part of a real world that is external to them. There is a world 'out there' and a picture of it 'in here'. This is where the problem starts, because in the end the question arises: "Well, there is this huge world, so what am I? I am just irrelevant." Children start out populating the world with their own experience, but by the end of their education may feel alienated, looking at this vast thing that apparently exists but to which they are almost completely irrelevant.

PAGE 30, PARAGRAPH 1: *Mind relates to the whole of our being, and its qualities manifest in all we think, feel and do. Since mind pervades every aspect of our reality, we might say that mind is our entire reality. But for most of us it seems more natural to think of reality as being 'out there', somehow apart from our selves, consisting of objects and events we can define and categorize.*

PAGE 30, PARAGRAPH 2: *We tend to objectify and define mind in the same way. For instance, we may state with some certainty that the brain is a physical organ that relates to the body's nerves and senses, while mind is more associated with the psyche, which is less localized and more diffuse. But what is the basis of this certainty?*

Objectification is another consequence of our education. It is like a three-card trick. This is the trick where you are asked to follow a card hidden under one of three mugs, and if you have a skilled operator, you never find where the card is hidden.

Let's play the first card: we start by living in our own experience. Our experience is primary; we are at home. Then the second card is played: we infer an external world as real. Then we play the third card. If the external world is real, then my mind and my experience—let's call that the mind/body complex—must be just another object in this real, external world. With that third card I have lost my nice, warm subjectivity and have become an object in the universe of objects, a thing in a world of things, a stranger to myself.

PAGE 30, PARAGRAPH 2, CONT'D: *A closer look might reveal that the process of definition is in fact ongoing and open-ended, suggesting that our understanding of these concepts is far from conclusive. Instead, we unthinkingly apply labels and categories, confidently pointing out what purpose each one serves. Analyzing the aspects of mind intellectually, much as we would point out the names and functions of the components of a computer, we distance our sense of 'I' from mind.*

This process of objectification is not to be underestimated. Remember, our labels are applied to phenomena on the basis of a hidden framework of assumptions. Labels may impute objects, but what they are actually applied to are experiences. In chapter 3 this was laid out in some detail—sense input, cognition, recognition. We even know how long the process takes. So when I say 'gong'—you think 'that object over there', but what we are doing is labeling the experience of the shiny ball thing as 'gong' and placing it in a construct that is named 'place and time'. But this fundamental metaphysic is hidden, completely invisible—you can't see it in the term 'gong'. Once you stick the label on it, you've adopted the metaphysic by default, and you've adopted the system in which the metaphysic operates.

It follows that everything you name, everything you label, is actually generated from an experience. We label up experiences as objects to create the world. And in exactly the same way, the mind is an experience, not an object. And so, all we have is our own experience—there aren't any 'objects' here.

You can see how seductive it is—this shortcut from experience to label. This is not to suggest there is not an external world by the way, but it is not to assert it either. With this understanding, mindfulness is not mindfulness of things; mindfulness is of experience itself. Things are already inferential. Things contain already an unmindful set of assumptions that has inserted itself. We try, for example, to be mindful of 'here' and 'now'. To even use those terms is to accept important elements of which we are not mindful. There is an exercise concerning this at the end of the chapter.

> PAGE 31, PARAGRAPH 1: *Without inquiring how the mind-system was set up, 'I' am content to take charge of its operation. The truth is that we cannot separate ourselves from mind and observe it directly, so we cannot verify what mind really is. Yet, convinced by a false sense of resolution, 'I' can assume charge of mind's operations because mind has become familiar, an object that 'I' can name and relate to as real.*

> PAGE 31, PARAGRAPH 2: *Comfortable with our conclusions, we may see no reason to investigate further. Like an architect drafting the plans of a building, we move on to compartmentalize and define all aspects of experience, including the functions of mind. Everything has a label, and every label has a story, complete with its purpose and meaning. The meanings assigned to the labels take care of all the specifics.*

'I' the hero has now objectified myself as an object that 'I' can now know. In so doing, the actual ground of my experience has disappeared—'I' have become an object in the world of objects. 'I' have inferred 'myself'.

What follows from this act of self-alienation? Endless ennui. Something is wrong; we don't feel right; we are not at ease in our own skins. The reason? We have become an object of our own knowledge.

> PAGE 31, PARAGRAPH 3: *Thinking we know, we rely for meaning on our concepts and the stories that accumulate around them. We act on this basis, and our actions have consequences through the operation of cause and effect.*

Having become an object of knowledge for ourselves, we can only rely on concepts and stories as a source of meaning. The ground of our experience has been covered over. We have eaten of the tree of knowledge, and left the garden of Eden. Added to that, our actions have consequences. We conclude that the conceptual structure we have set up must be real because what we do has tangible results. Our sense of the real arises directly from our ability to ascribe causes to events and to see the consequences they have. We now conclude, "Yes, of course that's correct, because when I do this, that happens. When I do that, this happens. There are consequences. I am in the real world."

We are acting on the basis of a misconception, but because the misconception has consequences, we think it is right.

> PAGE 31, PARAGRAPH 3, CONT'D: *By the very way it operates, mind maintains the conditions for cause and effect and develops the patterns that perpetuate disappointment and pain. But, unless we understand how mind produced these patterns through identifying, labeling, and recognition, our concepts and stories have no real basis. This means that we lack access to the full significance of our actions. We do not fully understand why we do what we do, we cannot foresee the effects of our actions, and we do not realize what patterns we are establishing for our lives. We can only learn by trial and error, a method guaranteed to be wasteful and potentially destructive.*

It's often said that first impressions never lie—but how often do we notice first impressions? Often we are misled into mak-

this ~~this~~ is an assumption.

ing bad decisions because the shiny bubbles of our own ambitious preconceptions cloud our ability to appreciate what is happening. This is how we get sucked into mistaken decisions. The first impression is often accurate, but we miss it. We miss it because we are not in direct experience—we are in a sea of judgments based on our concepts. We neither realize the patterns of behavior such concepts generate, nor have a way not to be ruled by them.

PAGE 32, PARAGRAPH 1: *To examine more deeply, we need to know what lies behind this system: who set it up? Who is receiving this information, who is the user, and who is monitoring and updating it? There does not seem to be much clarity on these issues. Instead, patterns of thought become so habitual that we rarely notice them in operation.*

This is the attitude of questioning. It's not the same as actually asking a question, with a subject-questioner and an object the question is 'about'. When we are in a conceptual structure, it's really difficult to see it working—because we are in it. But we can ask, "Well, why do I do this? Who set this up?" These questions are useful in terms of generating mindfulness of our own process, even if it is hidden from us at present.

PAGE 32, PARAGRAPH 2: *Mind participates in this process as both creator and 'customer'. It creates the timing and continuity that enable cause and effect to take place; it initiates actions and renders them automatic through the processes of identity and recognition. As 'customer', mind also receives the product—consequences that are welcome or unwelcome, depending on the clarity that informed the actions. Participating in both cause and effect, mind perpetuates patterns that leave us vulnerable to confusion, frustration and pain, and it enforces these patterns by convincing us that they are real and 'right'.*

The timing and continuity that mind creates enables the inference that 'causes' happen before 'effects'. We make sense of our lives by remembering previous events and relating them to current events in a continuous chain. That chain of causation, the 'because' of our experience, is nonetheless a construct. It is enabled by an internal clock, and the placing of 'I' in a remembered place. Using that clock we are able to say, "This happened before that, so it was the cause of it." Furthermore, we can recognize continuity; we can say, "This relates to that." That's how we construct our world.

The heroic ego is constructed out of this process of assent, and we remember the part of the mind that says, "Yes, that's right, it's me." It is an interesting thought to realize that while this was going on, the label 'I' was not even present! If you introspect mindfully your own process, you are not present as it's happening, but you will find yourself saying, "I did this, I did that." As mentioned above, such statements are always in the past tense.

This metaphysical framework is totally buried underneath naming and framing, so we never see it. But because of the metaphysical framework we become aliens to our own incarnation—we are like visitors inhabiting our own skins. This is our fundamental dislocation.

> PAGE 33, PARAGRAPH 1: *This question is worth careful consideration. Only mind knows how to spell out the features, the names, and the qualities of everything we can perceive. Mind is the anchor of the news show put on by our inner broadcasting system, the one who collects data from our organs and senses, compiles and interprets it, then broadcasts it, laying out our reality in forms we can act upon.*

> PAGE 33, PARAGRAPH 2: *Like a chef, mind presents the menu and the schedule for preparing and producing it. Mind selects and combines the ingredients it deems necessary, then places before us the completed meal. All we need to do is accept it and take it in. Whether we enjoy the meal or suffer indigestion afterwards depends upon*

the quality and wholesomeness of the ingredients mind has provided.

PAGE 34, PARAGRAPH 1: *Similarly, for everything we do, mind sets up the framework and we fill in the details. We expect mind to do its job, and we are expected to do ours. Normally, we do not think to question how mind does its job. But now we are ready to take a more active role, to learn how mind designed the systems that have such significance to our lives. Only then can we determine how these systems might be modified or if entirely different systems might work better for us today.*

If we follow this idea of doing our job, being mindful is the first step. How can we take control of our mind if we are not even aware of what it is? Clearly, we can't! The very first thing we've got to be is mindful—otherwise we have no chance. Only when we are mindful of the first event as it happens have we any possibility of penetrating it further and, if necessary, making changes.

PAGE 34, PARAGRAPH 2: *If we look inward and contemplate how experience takes shape and form, at some point we may realize that reality is established by mind-telling and mind-dialoguing, mind-feeling, and mind-interpreting, all on the basis of a dualistic perspective that sets us up for problems. Perhaps mind developed this system in ages past to communicate meaning to consciousness. But since we are the ones who have accepted it, we may have the option to consider an alternative.*

PAGE 34, PARAGRAPH 3: *As unique individuals who have each matured within a certain array of physical, social, emotional, psychic, and environmental conditions, each of us must investigate for ourselves the specific system that governs our reality and determine how best to improve it. But below the specifics of individual identity flows a deeper, more universal current that connects us to the qualities we associate with human being. Reflecting on the beauty that*

*mind is capable of transmitting, we may recall moments
when love, joy, and gratitude have broken through the fog
of our mind-created stories and illuminated every cell of
our bodies. Surely we can transform the regime that now
blocks our voluntary access to this power. Surely mind can
become more generous with its riches and end the games
that set us up for disappointment and despair!*

How?

What is striking about this is the realization that our individuality is the most irrelevant part of us. That's truly important to think about. After all, our individuality is a series of constructs based on accidents—accidents of birth, of education and experience. Indeed, one could conclude that what makes me, me is actually blocking me from my actual potentiality.

Being an individual and proudly 'doing it my way' may not be very wise because those characteristics are really quite banal if you think about it. Yet it is our individuality that we are so proud of! All the while what really matters is potentiality because our potentiality is truly unlimited; when we are confronted or inspired we are capable of wonderful things.

Yes

PAGE 35, PARAGRAPH 1: *This is our very own journey, a journey that leads to the heart of our being. It begins with making friends with our mind and observing what it reveals in the context of our own experience.*

How do we go about being mindful? We may need to be smart about it—remember, we are not prison guards looking at prisoners when we're trying to be mindful. Our mind is our friend! Think about being mindful as if you were just hanging out with a friend. If we have that attitude we might be able to hang out right at the beginning, where it is all happening. But often we take mindfulness as an instruction to observe, as if we are observing a prisoner. This wrong view leads to the attitude of "I am mindful" because I am watching the watcher, which of course is not what mindfulness is.

Exercise 5
Here and now

Try to be mindful of the 'here and now': watch a clock, preferably with a second hand, and try to be mindful of the exact
present moment. Really concentrate hard. Do this for a period—say one minute, then relax the concentration. Rest. Then
repeat. Then rest again. Ask yourself, are you more mindful of
the present moment when you are concentrating or when you
are resting from concentration?

To be mindful of the present
moment is to objectify it,
rather than being one with it.

Watching a clock to become
mindful of the present seems
well, not useful.

Perhaps the present moment
is a creation of mind,
as much as time is.

CHAPTER 7

Mind on Automatic

This chapter deals with another unexpected aspect of our experience. We live a lot of our lives on automatic pilot, effectively unconscious of what we are doing. Whenever we read about consciousness, there is an implicit assumption that we are continually conscious during our waking hours. Evidence indicates that we are only conscious for short periods of time.

It's worth considering that in general when we learn to do something we tend to only do it well when we are unconscious of it. Consciousness seems to be an obstacle to doing anything well. *"self-conscious", yes*

Remember your first experience of learning how to drive? You were totally conscious of the steering wheel, the pedals and everything else. Driving required being painfully cautious and slow. Then gradually, as you became familiar with what you had to do, there was no longer the need to be conscious of each process or movement. You could be unconscious of driving but still be aware. Even race car drivers on the knife-edge of what is possible can hold conversations over their team radio.

So, what is the purpose of consciousness? In reading philosophical texts on consciousness you might have thought that consciousness is a prerequisite that makes aware experience possible, but that is clearly not the case. It's not a central feature of being in a body at all.

The fact is that we are on automatic most of the time. We do things we are not conscious of continuously. To use the metaphor from the earlier chapters, we are on the stage but we just don't know it. This is one of the reasons why our behavior is quite predictable. Since this is happening all the time, understanding how our autopilot works is a valuable insight.

> PAGE 36, PARAGRAPH 1: *Mind accommodates feedback from the senses as well as from its own operations. As it does so, it automatically imposes its processes on whatever input it receives. Mind moves instantly to respond to questions, situations, and challenges and to deal with all variations of experience, while also coping with the push-back from its own patterns. Since its nature is to respond, it cannot avoid engaging whatever presents itself, even when engaging them activates patterns of denial or drives them deep into our subconscious, where they foster resentment, fear, and negativity.*

Our normal mental functioning is highly reactive; it rarely lets anything be without imposing 'views' on it. When something arises it has to do something with it. It's like a manic filer that can't stand clutter, so everything has to be sorted. That reactivity is very characteristic of mind.

In the classic descriptions the mind is likened to a monkey that's forever swinging in the trees—it simply can't be still. But obsessive reactivity has important survival benefits. It's easy to understand why that would have been useful back on the savanna. You can't afford to relax when you've got lions in the bushes. You've got to be reactive, you can't just be relaxed or you'd get eaten pretty quickly. And this is where we've come from. Human beings evolved in an environment where many things were dangerous.

For prey animals, relaxation is not an option. The stronger urge is to be reactive, and reactivity happens whether they want it or not. We all experience this ancient system, where reactivity can drive us into stress or feelings of disquiet generated by seemingly everyday events. In many people, particularly those who are shy, there is a lot of reactivity going on which can overwhelm them in social situations, making them seem and feel awkward. In such cases, alcohol can break the ice because it is a depressant—it actually depresses reactivity.[17] For precisely the same reason, you shouldn't drink and drive; you drink to become less reactive at a party, but you need that reactivity when you drive a car.

> PAGE 36, PARAGRAPH 2: *This process is dynamic and inclusive. Impressions flow in from all directions, stimulating interpretations and mingling with commentaries and emotions already in progress. So much can be happening at once—seeing, hearing, tasting, touch, scent, thoughts, images, happiness, pain, terror, guilt trips, anxiety, passion, and aggression. With all these streams of data competing for attention, mind is fully occupied from moment to moment.*

This is one of the main reasons why mindfulness can be so effective: there is so much going on in so many directions that something completely unexpected can push us into reactivity.

There is a wonderful exercise in Tai chi called "pushing hands" which is a play on this. Someone puts their hand out, you lay your hand on top, and the idea is that you keep moving with their hand. That's it— it's that ability to move anywhere without any muscular effort. Tai chi masters can just move in a relaxed way. Unless you've had training, it's hard to follow the motions of your partner, because most of us are unable to stay in relaxed contact. Our mindfulness should be like Tai chi

---

17   https://www.healthline.com/health/alcohol-and-anxiety

pushing hands—flowing like water. But unfortunately, events happen and we lose contact with our own experience and our own process.

Our mental environment is very complex: there are many inputs coming in, not just seeing, but hearing, tasting, touching, smelling, and thinking—the so-called six gates. On top of these primary sense inputs there are associations and reactions they link to, all the images, happiness, pain, terror, guilt trips, anxiety, and passions. In terms of our mental processing we can think of it like an inner sensorium that is as much a part of our sensory apparatus as our external senses. We can consider thought itself like an organ of sensation, in that the associations that come from thoughts trigger a response just as external sensations do. Indeed, if we just had external sensations without any internal responses, it would be quite easy to be mindful. It's those responses that seem to arise as if from behind us that push us off our perch of mindfulness.

> PAGE 37, PARAGRAPH 1: *Self-imposing and self-projecting, mind allows all manner of expressions to manifest, then repossesses and recycles them back into its systems, where they become the bases for new cycles of projections, interpretations, judgments, and feedback.*

This is a description of the associations that link to our primary perceptions. The first layer is the primary cognitive exchange: beginning sense impressions of a watch or something and the recognition—"Oh yes, it's a watch." That "Oh yes, it's a watch," then acts as a peg for all the watch associations to hang onto. Without the peg of "Yes, it's a watch," there is no basis for association; but once the pattern of sense inputs is identified as a watch, then all the watch links activate; nice watch, not nice watch, big watch, small watch, new watch, old watch. This is true of any sensory object. This process of recycling associations is a central element of learning. However, it is fundamentally based on making judgments as its primary feature.

PAGE 37, PARAGRAPH 1, CONT'D: *It is mind that says 'yes' or 'no', or hesitates in between, perhaps listening to its own echoes. From time to time, it may get caught up in negotiating with itself, as if questioning its own interpretations. "It could be this, or it could be that. If it is this, that could happen, and I don't think I want that. But if it is that, this will happen. That might be all right. But what if it isn't?"*

In learning to remain quietly present with mental functions it is quite common to discover this inner intuitional self and think, "Oh, this is it, I've come to the ground." But you haven't, you are in the first phase of 'I' making. The Tibetans call this the defiled basis of mind. It's a basis, so it feels like the bottom of the bucket, the primary moment of cognition, but it is not, it's an initial reaction. This hidden self demands judgment. As long as you are located at the level of the defiled basis of mind, you are still making judgments. In meditation we catch a glimpse of this when we get the feeling of, "Oh, I am meditating well. What a good meditation I've got. How well I am meditating!" or perhaps, "I am not meditating well—how badly I am doing!" In either case there is judgment. That is a sign that the 'I' that is doing well or badly is itself a reaction to something deeper.

One of the reasons why our initial attempts at mindfulness get knocked off their perch is because first attempts are normally based in this subtle self, and this subtle self has a position or view. Any position or view you have will make you rigid in one dimension or another. It's only when you have no positions at all that you are completely able to move with events. As long as you've got a position, the pushing hands master can elude you, because you are rigid in that dimension.

PAGE 37, PARAGRAPH 2: *The mental traffic that results from all this activity can jam the flow of thoughts and images, so that very little else can get through. Even when the traffic runs more smoothly, it still occupies the mind continuously, clouding the open clarity of our mental environment and setting the stage for distraction. This is mind as we know it, and we have to live with it.*

The possibility of clarity and peace that we so desire is clouded over with all our mental activity. Because our mind is reactive, we think the only way we can achieve clarity is to shut down input, so we have less to react to. This is to become still and closed. Here Revelations is talking about something quite different, however—a mind that is open yet not reactive, still yet open. In an open and non-reactive mental space, there is the possibility of true clarity.

Consider meditation. When we meditate we normally close our eyes. We are trying to shut down the noise, to find some inner peace. When we are more familiar with the practice, however, it's interesting to meditate with all senses open. Discovering clarity there is quite different from being shut down.

> PAGE 38, PARAGRAPH 1: *As mind takes in whatever is presented, interpretations come up instantly, almost magically, with great sharpness and immediacy. As questioner, mind asks, "Is this ok?" As responder, mind verifies, "Yes, that is right," giving its seal of approval. Having no way to join in this dialogue, we can only accept what mind decides.*

Although our internal dialogue is readily apparent to us, we rarely see the deeper level where assent is being given. Sensations are neutral in themselves—they don't actually have value judgments included with them; they are just inputs. The first value judgment happens as a sense array is identified as being of one form or another. Before that, it's all neutral. The first point where a judgment is sealed, the first point where your freedom is being curtailed by judgment being made, is at that subtle moment of, "Yes, you are right"—that first level of assent.

This process of association can be seen as the beginnings of the regime; the subsequent reactions are like a retinue. When phenomena are arising, they are being identified and then judged. And the moment that judgment has occurred, a complete retinue is triggered, a retinue of associations that contextualize identified phenomena within the realm of our own memory and our own experience. So judgment creates the link for the retinue of associations to come along. That retinue can be very, very rich. It thickens the initial judgment into a real thing. Even an identified object without the retinue doesn't have much impact—things only get real when the retinue has put its stamp on them. Then you really have a feeling of, "Yes, I want it," or "No, I don't." In other words, that very strong sense of 'thingness' arises after the initial sensation has provided a link to the retinue that associates with it.

> PAGE 38, PARAGRAPH 2: *Mind's regime of associations, interpretations, and commentary takes over automatically and immediately. If we look closely, especially when mind is quiet, we can sense mind's retinue approaching:* . . .

A quiet mind is important. Every sensory input triggers a retinue, so there can be multiple retinues happening at the same time. It's literally like a busy shopping street with lots of different conversations happening all at once. This is why one starts meditating with one's eyes closed and tends to avoid noisy situations. You've got to quiet things down so you can see what's happening.

> PAGE 38, PARAGRAPH 2, CONT'D: *a few thoughts, then feelings, perhaps a sudden surge of anger as memory recalls how someone took advantage of us a few days before, or a brighter outlook as ideas or urges take our thoughts toward daydreams and the anticipation of pleasure. Within an instant, we are completely immersed, already responding to whatever scenario the regime has imposed. There is little we can do to distract it—mind will keep going, identifying*

and commenting according to its own rhythms, according to what it has learned to interpret as 'right'.

This is a description of the point at which we lose our mindfulness. Initially we are watching everything happening, but unbeknownst to us, we are standing on a subtle sense of 'I am'. Then the retinue comes, and suddenly we are pushed off into reactivity. It's like a surfboard that just took off, and suddenly we are lost in reactivity—memories or reactions take over and then it can be a long time before we wake up again. Sometimes half an hour or more will pass! "Oh, my God, what happened to my mindfulness?"

Try sitting on a park bench with closed eyes and listen. It is not long before associative fantasies take over. You hear the rumbling sound of a truck, and of course the fantasy arises that it's on the pavement about to run you over. You can experience the retinue coming up really easily when your primary sense input, vision, is interrupted. You might even produce a complete scene in which an out-of-control dump truck is plowing down the pavement toward you. It is very hard not to pop one's eyes open to check!

We have a protective regime and within it there are associations, interpretations, and commentaries that quickly take over. We sense mind's retinue approaching—sensation, identification, association. With association come all kinds of memories and internal commentaries. Those are the waves that wash us off our ledge of mindfulness. That's the thing that takes us down— it's the retinue. But the reason we are so easily distracted is because we are not truly mindful. We have assented to a hidden 'I" at the foundation of our mindfulness.

This is very slippery terrain and something we are going to have to work with. As long as we have an idea of mindfulness and a little voice that says, "Yes, this is it" or "Here I am, being mindful," we are perched on an unstable foundation where we can be swept away easily by any association that comes along. It's only when our mindfulness is based in direct experience that it can become stable.

> PAGE 38, PARAGRAPH 3: *While this kind of automation speeds processing and offers convenience, when it takes over our consciousness in this way, we might well question the cost. What price might we be paying for this ever-expanding accumulation of patterns and the proliferation of an ever more efficient automation?*

We are unwitting passengers in this extremely efficient vehicle that is operating very nicely, but it is a prison at the same time. Automation has its advantages, but it's extremely difficult to escape it.

> PAGE 39, PARAGRAPH 1: *Accustomed to the rhythms of thoughts and dialogues that direct an inner chain of reactions, we tend to notice very little of what is going on around us in real time. What we experience are the thoughts and feelings prompted by the recycling and interpretation that follow upon identity and recognition.*

It seems that we live one step back from actuality. The first 100 milliseconds are what it takes for a sensation to even be experienced. But in the next 150 milliseconds all the assents are given. So we are a long way temporally but also a long way structurally from the thing that's actually happening. We are in a bubble of *"thoughts and feelings prompted by the recycling and interpretation that follow identity and recognition."*

> PAGE 39, PARAGRAPH 1, CONT'D: *We react, but the primary perception is long past: we are experiencing echoes of the original, presented in our custom-made language, as interpreted and revised by mind's regime.*

The echo metaphor is important. In a canyon, for example, an original sound occurs, then bounces off the wall on the other side. That's that little voice that says, "Oh, yes, that's true," and echoes back assent—the basis of all the associations. And that's where we are, that's where we are living.

As mentioned earlier, music is fascinating because it's so non-conceptual. The listener can actually get through the thought bubble into a direct relationship with the sound itself. Whether it's modern or classical, formal or folk, there can be moments when we enter a kind of heightened awareness. Because music has no conceptual content it can take us to a point of awareness beyond language and words.

> PAGE 39, PARAGRAPH 1, CONT'D: *While we may be fully connected to the elements at work in the regime, we are out of touch with the actual experience that gave rise to the regime's activity. This disconnection leaves us vulnerable to forgetfulness, mistakes, and misinterpretations, all of which feed uncertainty and confusion back into the mechanisms of mind.*

Imagine you are in an argument. Whatever you say, your partner hears it as something else. We have all had this experience. How about a political discussion? You quickly realize that communication is really, really difficult. This is because the other person is receiving an echo of what you are saying, lensed through his or her own conceptual apparatus.

This is happening all the time to a greater or lesser extent. That's where confusions and misinterpretations are rooted. And often it's really, really difficult to break through to actually communicate anything at all. The phenomenon is just a symptom of a far more general issue, which is that we live in a bubble, a casket of concepts, a box made up of concepts which we call the world. This box is both temporally and experientially behind the curve of events. Experientially it limits our capacity to react in a spontaneous way. It's colored, conditioned, and limited by preconceptions, judgments, memories—the entire retinue. The efficiency of this kind of automation has limited our range of responses.

PAGE 39, PARAGRAPH 2: *Throughout our lives, we live within this mind-created realm, cut off from the immediacy of experience and subject to the dictates and interpretations of mind's regime. Within this realm, the regime holds sway. Everything mind presents—even the most toxic feelings and emotions, even extreme anxiety and physical pain—is acceptable, because on a very fundamental level we have empowered mind to feed back to us the regime's interpretations and meanings.*

It is a strange fact that the regime of associations, the actual bubble we are in, can be quite toxic. Because it is built on the unconscious process of confirmation, the foundation of "Yes, that's right," we don't change it.

People can be living in really quite hellish constructs and yet not want to change them. This is one of the enigmas of the human condition. We can have unhappy lives yet, because assent is at the basis of our experience, we think our lives have a sense of rightness. Unless you can get down beneath the level of the assenter, it is virtually impossible to change.

You hear this when people say, "It's the way it is" or "I am a victim of circumstance, I can't do anything, I am stuck." "If only this or that changed it would be better." Actually, it's an inside job; that little assenter who has given us a sense of rightness is the false friend who has entrapped us.

PAGE 40, PARAGRAPH 1: *Mind recognizes and interprets continuously, but it appears that we are missing out on much of its activity, for at any point during our day we can remember very little of what we were thinking during our prior waking hours. Perhaps this lapse in recall indicates that we are not always consciously directing our minds in purposeful activity. At best we might say that our periods of purposeful activity are continually interrupted by less focused mental operations.*

Now, that's putting it very politely! If we are honest, we will have to admit that our situation is a little ridiculous. It could be that as little as two percent or perhaps even one percent of our time is truly purposeful amidst this huge morass of unconscious processing.

That this is so widespread is a cause for compassion. Virtually all of us, with very few exceptions, are wasting most of our lives—that's really the truth of it.

> PAGE 40, PARAGRAPH 2: *If we suppose that this is true not just for us, but for every human being, then it is fair to say that the minds of seven billion people are churning more or less without direction for at least five or six hours every day, and probably much more, generating thoughts, making decisions, and motivating actions. This would amount to a total of roughly forty billion mind-hours lost in generating idle thoughts, planning for the future, indulging fantasies, chewing on resentments, coping with desires, fretting over worries, awash in emotionality, obsessing over concerns, frozen in fear, or spiraling into depression and despair. This amounts to some 60,000 entire human lifetimes each day that are not engaged in productive activity. Assuming that thoughts tend to manifest in ways that influence others, such erratic mental activity must have far-reaching effects.*

This is a properly quantitative description of samsara. Sixty thousand lives a day wasted on unconscious processing and then all the incalculable consequences of that unstructured activity. It is not surprising that history is so enigmatic; it is largely unconscious! We are in this terrifying free-spinning wheel of association.

> PAGE 41, PARAGRAPH 1: *Seen in this light, a simple question takes on much greater weight: Does mind really know what it is doing? Mind monitors our internal processes; it calculates, plans, and initiates with some efficiency. But it does not seem so intent on revealing the source of our*

difficulties or removing obstacles that prevent us from transcending them. (Why is so great about transcendence ?)

Mind only gets what we give it. Mind is very efficient—very! But it is undoubtedly working with a limited data set. So, if you ask a question, "Does mind really know what it's doing?" the answer is no. Mind, our whole mental apparatus, is conditioning our experience so we can operate as efficiently as possible. It is doing a good job, but in a limited way. In the bigger picture, if we ask, "Do we really know what we are doing?" it's difficult to give a positive answer.

Our inability to answer this question with a positive answer shows us that the price of efficiency is very high. This is not to suggest we should be inefficient, but it is to suggest that perhaps we can improve in specific ways because unexamined efficiency is a prison. There is a certain totalitarianism about the regime of mind in its efficiency.

Exercise 6
Conscious timer

Take a stopwatch, or the timer on your phone, and make an intention to be totally conscious. Go about your activities. Try to be aware of every action as it happens. It would be impressive if your effort to remain conscious lasted more than a minute. Normally we remember the stopwatch many minutes later, and have no idea when we lost contact with it. Keep a record of your efforts. Can you recall what events cause you to lose contact with your awareness?

CHAPTER **8**

Identifier Mind

The first seven chapters have set up the structure of mind. Now, we are going to talk about its consequence, suffering.

Suffering is a universal element of human existence. Although our physical circumstances are improving dramatically, people still feel that they are out of control and suffering. Surveys indicate that general levels of happiness haven't changed much under modern conditions—if anything, they are slightly worse. We need to understand why this is.

On April 1, 2019, an Indian television presenter came home after presenting the news on a local station, opened the window in her seventh story flat, jumped out and fell to her death. She left behind a suicide note that said, "My brain is my enemy."[18] That's really significant language. When you talk to depressed people, they often say, "I've got this war going on inside." It's like somehow their minds are attacking them and making them feel miserable. And on occasion, they take their own lives.

Suffering and unhappiness have three general categories. The first is the suffering of suffering, like pain. You have a

---

18   *IBT Times*, April 20, 2018.

disease or injury; you don't have enough to eat or you don't sleep enough. This is suffering caused by damage to the physical body, the most obvious example. Even without physical intervention, this can be mitigated, as any meditator can tell you.[19]

The second major category of suffering is the inability to get what we want or to get rid of what we don't want. The possessions and relationships we have never seem to provide the lasting happiness we thought they would.

The third form of suffering, perhaps the most interesting, is the sense of pointlessness that many people experience. Even when our lives are going well, it is almost like we live on automatic pilot. Life doesn't really mean anything. There is a sense of ennui, hopelessness or pervasive meaninglessness.

If you were able to take someone from the eighteenth century and put them into our current circumstances, although for weeks or perhaps months they might be ecstatic about all our new technology, how much there is to eat and all the television channels, gradually these three types of suffering will take hold. Within a couple of years, they would not feel quite as happy as when they first arrived. In the same vein if we look at science fiction projecting forward 100 years from now, it's as if human circumstance doesn't really change even though people have much better technology. Or, if we explore the past and read what people have written hundreds of years before us, again it's as though human circumstances haven't changed even though technological and cultural differences can be quite large.

The conventional understanding of most politicians, scientists and commentators is that the problems we suffer from are physical and if we can overcome them, either politically or

---

19   See https://www.zeidanlab.com/UC San Diego, Department of Anesthesiology, 9500 Gillman Drive, MC 0898, La Jolla, CA 92093.

technologically, then we will be happy. This is demonstrably false, as these examples show, even though this idea dominates discussions of what to do. It's as though we spend our entire lives trying to improve our circumstances so we can be happy and free of suffering, while at the same time failing to recognize that our circumstances and our suffering are not fully connected to one another.

This chapter deals extensively with this issue. The point we will examine is that these three categories of suffering are all the inevitable consequence of our reaction to impermanence, the fact that things change.

Our standard reaction to impermanence is to try to categorize our experience into arrays of labeled things. Because we name things and the names don't change, this strategy means that we are by and large unaware of change itself. It is this fundamental misalignment that is the root cause of our problems.

> PAGE 42, PARAGRAPH 1: *Mind retains impressions of everything it has learned to distinguish and name from prior perceptions and experience. These serve as models for identifying and naming all that comes up later, both externally and internally. As the senses present impressions from instant to instant, we may feel their subtle vibrations as the stirrings of perception or imagination. There may be a sense of something pushing toward recognition, but not yet manifest. At some point, what was 'not yet' becomes 'now': An object has presented itself. Immediately, it is grasped and matched to a store of pre-cast impressions. A name comes up, and the mind says "Right!" The stages of this process flash to completion instantaneously.*

We humans have an ability to learn. This is what makes *Homo sapiens*, the knowing human, so unusual. Actually, many animals also have a limited ability to do the same thing, but our capacity, our versatility, is undoubtedly greater than that of any animal on the planet.

The ability to learn from experience is hardwired into our process of perception. When we see and recognize something, what we're experiencing is a memory. It is a recognition of a primary event that has been identified, confirmed and named. It is identified and named based on prior perceptions, and this process creates a map of known things. This map making is automatic and makes it very difficult for us to see things as they actually are. What we see is a memory of what impressions have been identified as being, along with pre-digested behaviors toward them, projected like a map of things in the world. That's how we can identify them; that's how we know what they are.

Once things are recognized and named they are then projected forward. The next round of experience is also recognized and named—so we live in a cycle of recognition and naming. It is as if we are in our own little bubble that we call 'the world', a bubble of recognition and naming. People have different bubbles; that's why they disagree. The deepest disagreements seem to occur when two people have different memories and associations generated by the same events. That's exactly how real conflict develops.

This naming process is the anchor for the mind's retinue. Most of the time we are operating within that retinue—we could call it the 'story of our lives'. But before the retinue manifests, underlying sense-impressions have to be recognized. That process of recognition occurs very early on in our mental process, so we usually miss it. By the time something comes into view, it's already been recognized and we are in the readout of that recognition.

It would actually be quite scary to have something in view that was totally unfamiliar. Most of us never have this experience. But imagine sitting at the kitchen table and suddenly there is an object in front of you and you don't know what it is. Furthermore, you have no idea where it came from, so you cannot even fix it in time. Your immediate re-action is likely to be fear. "What is that!" Fear will cause you to tentatively reach out and try to identify it. "Where did that come from?" you might ask. That first phase acts as the basis for subsequent naming and the arising of a retinue of responses.

A really good example of how this works occurs in advertis-ing. Advertisers are always trying to make you identify with what they are selling. There's a lot of stuff in the world, so how do they get you to buy their watch, their car, perfume, clothes or whatever? They use a 'hook' to get your attention and make you identify with their product. One well-known hook is to have a very pretty girl hold something. "Oh, what's that she's holding?" Once you've identified with that something, you're hooked. A lot of advertising is about providing hooks that will get your attention.

The study of body language—the use of posture and gesture to communicate intention—demonstrates this principle. Postures come in sets. One of the most famous sets frequent-ly used in advertising is called a 'courtship cluster'. It is put in motion when a girl turns toward the camera with a flick of her hair and her hand open beside her face. The male equiva-lent is a handsome man with a big belt buckle, often with his hands in his pockets or cupping the buckle. These poses are designed to grab your attention.

This attention-grabbing happens completely subliminally; you don't realize your attention is being manipulated. Once attention is captured, the next thing that the mental process will do is grasp. "What is that? Oh, this person is holding a packet of Marlboro cigarettes." That's what the advertisers are trying to evoke. The process of getting attention and then fix-ing a name happens early on in the process of perception, and is recorded as the retinue engages.

Normally we don't see this process. We live in a mental map of the world and the retinue pushes us this way and that. If we are sitting in our kitchen, we know exactly what this kitchen looks like. We don't have to look at and grasp every single object. If something changes though, we'll notice it. You must have had this experience. You walk into a friend's house. It all looks normal. Then they move the sofa or take down a picture. They change something in the layout of the room, and next time you visit you immediately notice it. It's what's changed in the room that you notice, not the room itself. The reason for that is that you are walking into a memory of the room, and if the room doesn't conform to the memory then you notice it.

If you look closely at advertising strategies it's obvious that they are trying to get to your map. Perhaps there is a picture of a cowboy on a horse with one hand on his big Texas belt buckle and the other smoking a Marlboro cigarette. The caption says, "America, the Land of the Free." Now, that is a complete set of entrapments. We are likely to notice and identify with that image. In so doing we give it a place in our retinue of associations.

This is important to understand. Once we are in the world with an object, all the associations around that object become activated. We have been primed for what comes next. Take the image of the Marlboro man sitting on a horse in a huge open space with all its connotations of power and freedom. He's a good-looking guy on a fantastic horse holding his cigarette. What's the retinue going to make of that?

Well, that depends on who is doing the making. Perhaps the maker is a miserable guy in some small town thinking, "I don't like my life." The mind's retinue is going to suggest, "Oh, Marlboro cigarettes, maybe I should get some of those. That's exactly what I'm looking for." The retinue has been primed. All it takes is a small trigger and suddenly we are buying a pack of cigarettes. Advertising works by manipulating this process of perception. What we don't realize is that this is happening all the time.

> PAGE 42, PARAGRAPH 2: *Once we have a specific orientation, there is a need to take a position, to stand on what we 'know', to add reasons and interpretations to perceptions and responses. This need calls into play the mechanisms of mind's regime: identity leads directly to interpretation, and positioning excludes alternatives. Mind leads and we follow. As its regime unfolds and envelops us, we may find ourselves bonded to the position we have taken, holding it fast, defending it with reasons grasped out of nowhere, perhaps without understanding why.*

We can think of this activity as a 'tagging' process, a way for the mental apparatus to identify sense objects, which are inherently impermanent, and fix them into a permanent structure of named, identified and associated things. This is a continuous process going on all the time. The brain activity of someone asleep and awake is almost the same, it's only plus or minus five percent. Whether you think you are doing nothing or not, the process keeps churning along. And what it's doing is making a fixed world out of a fleeting world.

Grasping at appearances and clinging to our names for things is the foundation of the linguistic categories of 'I', 'me' and 'mine'. These categories require grasped things to be present in order to give them meaning. What does 'I' mean if there are no things for 'I' to own or interact with? Without things, what can be 'mine'?

But once sense impressions are labeled in this manner then the referents 'I, me and mine' have meaning and arise as the actor, knower, or owner of those things. In turn, the whole associative structure we talked about in the earlier chapters comes along—the whole structure of outer-and-inner, the structure of time, the structure of reality—all of these constructs become possible because of this fundamental mechanism that's given them a foundation. These associations make a strong bond. It's as if one's sense of self is bonded to the specific circumstances in which it arose.

Furthermore, there is a need to defend such associations because they are fundamental to our being. We become bonded to positions without knowing why. Even though the circumstances of their arising are almost always accidental, what gives them their power over us is the structure of the regime of mind.

> PAGE 43, PARAGRAPH 1: *This process unfolds instantly and automatically, but it carries a certain tension that is amplified by the quantity and variety of sensory impressions that mind identifies and processes moment to moment. Some of these relate to 'I' as subject; others relate to 'me' as the object, and still others pertain to 'mine' as the owner. Each perspective may have its own set of associations, all of which bear directly on what this experience means to 'me', as if there were three or four personas with competing interests involved in each perception. Behind this complex network is the dualistic mind, weighing pros and cons, likes and dislikes, acceptance and rejection, relating them all to 'I', 'me', and 'mine'.*

'I', 'me' and 'mine' are referents based upon clinging to the labels that have arisen from sense impressions. Because every sensation is a potential hook for 'I', 'me' and 'mine', it gets quite noisy and turbulent. There are multiple 'I', 'me' and 'mine's happening depending on what's going on. All these different elements are generating metaphysical bubbles, little universes of meaning, each one organized with the heroic ego in the middle, and each one dissolving in its turn.

If you go out walking on the street, there are sights and sounds, there are feelings, there are smells, there are all kinds of activities happening—all of which are generating these subliminal impressions. We just don't realize it because it's all down at the level of subconscious formations. As we become more sensitive and used to working with our impressions, we can become aware of this process and the important role it plays in the generation of our awareness.

It doesn't matter what moment of stimulation comes to the sense gates—mind will always produce the same structure in response to it, the steps required to create the stage for 'I', 'me' and 'mine'. It doesn't matter what the vector is—whether it is sound, thought, smell, sight, taste or touch. Some are easier to work with than others; for example, it is hard to introspect arising thought because for most of us the act of introspection is itself a thought. It is much easier to listen to a sound coming to our ears than to sense a thought popping up. But if you become really skilled, you can see this structure triggered by your own thoughts as well.

> PAGE 43, PARAGRAPH 2: *The interactions of these operations nearly guarantee that we will be faced with problems of one sort or another, each of which will add new layers of complexity. The instant mind identifies a problem, recognition triggers the whole mechanism of response. If we have no way to 'un-recognize' the problem, the responses it arouses can hit us in the head and the heart, arousing our feelings with great force and throwing our whole being into turmoil. Mind becomes blocked, with no clear path to resolution.*

There is a wonderful teaching in old Persian culture called the 'blue roses of forgetfulness'. It is the recognition that though we can try to remember, it is much more difficult to try to forget. We are invested once the ego has arisen in response to something. We are invested in the recognition: 'I' cannot forget it. 'I' arose in response to it. If only there were blue roses of forgetfulness we could say, "aaah, that wasn't me!"

There are many times when we wish we could say, "Can't you just forget that? Do you really have to be hung up about this?"

But we can't forget. It's like someone with a grudge: every time the object of the grudge comes into view the problem is there.

Not very long ago, in many cultures, it was commonplace to have a highly developed sense of honor. When someone insulted your honor, you literally could not co-exist with them; one of you had to die because the psychological mechanism had no other way of dealing with it. You literally had to fight a duel to the death—for the psyche, there was no other way out.

Interestingly, there is a sutra about this. The Buddha's disciples were shocked when he did not react to someone insulting him. But why should one react if the very mechanism that creates an insult is no longer functioning?

For *Revelations*, the immediate goal is to become aware of what was formerly an entirely unconscious process. This unconscious process does not offer us choices; it just leaves us with its fruits, which are always poisonous. It doesn't matter whether the fruits are good- or bad-looking, because even the best fruits, like our aspirations or ambitions, carry the seeds of suffering; either we cannot achieve them or we will lose them once we have finally obtained the results we were looking for. The bad fruits are suffering in themselves, and bring additional suffering because we wish to avoid them.

Although the blue roses of forgetfulness is a beautiful idea, an even better one would be the 'white light of awareness'. Seeing would give us choices.

> PAGE 44, PARAGRAPH 1: *At this point, attempts to deny the problem may only increase the pressure; on the other hand, acknowledging the problem tends to validate it and perpetuate its effects. Holding on to the position of 'having a problem', we have to endure the mind-created anxieties and emotions that go with it, for mind is now operating in its 'problem' mode. The more we try to suppress*

these reactions, the more we re-cognize and re-validate them, and the more persistently they return.

If something is identified as a problem we are already set up for difficulty. Wouldn't it be more useful to be rid of that feeling of difficulty? If we could get rid of that baggage it would be transformative. We would have a much greater degree of ease and freedom. But unfortunately, the blue roses of forgetfulness are unavailable.

Understanding this process we realize that our own existence is predicated on a process of recognition; yet recognition sets us up for disappointment. No matter how good everything else is, like medical care or the food or possessions we have, this problem will never go away because it's built into the mechanism of mind. So no matter what utopia we imagine for ourselves in the future, no matter what diseases of the body we eventually conquer, this process will still be occurring unless we can fix it. It can be fixed, of course, but not by some new technology or political system. It is baked into the structure of mind; it's the psychopathology of suffering.

PAGE 44, PARAGRAPH 2: *Later, when mind calms down, we may wonder what all the upset was about. But this insight is momentary. The pattern is likely to repeat, and residues of confusion and unresolved emotions accumulate with each repetition. This kind of inner struggle opens the door to self-doubt, insecurity, and anxieties that lurk in the background of mind like enemies awaiting their opportunity to attack.*

There is a common misconception that the mind is a sort of a computer. This makes it very easy to slip into the metaphors of processes and processors as if we were silicon chips. But we should not forget that our mental apparatus is chemically based and every time problems occur there are chemical residues. These residues color the next arising event until eventually the environment becomes so polluted and colored that there seems to be no solution, even if we were able to identify the problems we create for ourselves.

Many of us have a highly toxic inner world, full of residues from experiences that have happened before. It's as though we build a city with huge walls to protect our well-being but are continually assaulted from all directions. Eventually something gets over the walls and we react in ways that we will regret.

It is because of this situation that we can never succeed in transforming ourselves from the perspective of 'I'. But the 'I' is not the cause of the problem. Remember what God said to Noah: "Where were you when I laid the foundations of the earth?" We are born into the world. It's not our fault! But what we don't realize is that we are being born into the world moment to moment to moment. The world is always there before we are. Attacking ourselves with words like, "Oh, it's my fault. I could have done better. I'm no good. I've got to get a grip," isn't going to work. They may work temporarily to push the retinue away but the retinue is going to come back until you finally feel that your brain is your enemy.

If we can understand and accept how this process works, we can effect change, but it may require us to eat a bit of humble pie. We are educated through and through to feel that we are in control of our lives. We are responsible and are told again and again that life is our business. But when we truly look at our lives, moment-to-moment, not looking back in memory but looking at our lives as they are happening, we realize that we are not in control. We are in a readout.

PAGE 45, PARAGRAPH 1: *While most of us prefer to think that we are calm, balanced, rational, and 'can hold it together', even the most intelligent mind is vulnerable to this kind of agitation. Ignoring this vulnerability, or erecting walls around it, will not prevent agitation from arising. At some point, most likely when we are least able to deal with*

*it, a situation will penetrate whatever defenses we have
erected, and we may be unable to respond effectively.*

Most of us have this vulnerability. Even the well organized
and rational are vulnerable to this problem because it's built
into the mechanism itself.

> PAGE 45, PARAGRAPH 2: *Even in good times, much of our
> life is lost to the ups and downs of mind's distractions and
> its black holes of worry and depression. Knowing this, we
> know as well that we have a precious opportunity to un-
> derstand the foundations of our doubts and fears and free
> ourselves from needless suffering. Can we try now, before
> we meet with problems so overwhelming that they could
> seriously impact the course of our lives?*

Can you remember when you were sixteen? Can you remember when you opened the curtains and it was a bright new day
and you were excited to do something? Where has that feeling gone? Why does it seem so completely out of reach?

Most of us settle into stoic self-denial: "Life is a heap of problems, but I get on okay." That's pretty much the universal attitude. Every now and then a populist leader comes along and
sells people a dream of something or other and they believe
it for a while. Of course, it's all fantasy and goes away; then
we are back to the same stoic resignation. And stoicism is a
quite rational response to our situation, in that the process by
which we are navigating our lives is generating toxicity that
we can't control.

We may tell ourselves such things as, "that's just the way it
is." From that perspective the best we can hope for is a modest level of contentment. Of course, we can give ten percent
of our income to charity; we can help other people. That is
considered a life well lived, and that's how most people see it.

But was that really what we had in mind when we looked out
of that window at the age of sixteen and thought, "Wow, I've

got things to do!" It is really good to let that realization sink in a bit; that this is really the situation we are in. This is the psychopathology of suffering.

Normally we think that the best response to the recognition that life isn't going to work out is to do something different that might make it work this time. Maybe we get a new car or impulse shop, or get involved with a new charity—we are always looking for something new. Instead, what we really should do is address our own minds.

The trouble is that our colleagues, friends and family think that addressing our mind is avoiding the problem rather than solving it. "Look at your own mind?" they say. "What are you, a feeble, pathetic, self-indulgent person sitting in the corner looking at your own mind? How weak is that?" This is a common response when you admit to doing this. You can dress it up, of course, maybe saying, "Oh, I am learning to meditate"—but how does that make it better?

Because of the workings and influence of culture we too can have the idea that just looking at our own minds makes us weaklings who can't fix anything. But when we look more closely, we can sense that it's the mind itself that is the real problem.

> PAGE 45, PARAGRAPH 3: *There seems to be a certain shyness in the West about connecting problems too closely to the workings of the mind. The general tendency is to assume that most problems come from an external source. "I don't have any money." "I don't have the knowledge I need." Even sophisticated and accomplished persons tend to trace problems to events beyond their control. It is as if everyone has been somehow manipulated into looking in only one direction and thinking in only one way, applying a knowledge mass-produced and sold to each individual mind as the sole standard for functioning well and exercising control.* Capitalism creating demand.

Can you imagine a politician getting on TV and saying, "The reason why we have a gun problem is because it's an unexamined psychological necessity?" Or, "The reason why we have poverty and thirty-six percent of students at the university can't buy food is because it's a psychological problem within all of us." They would be laughed off the TV. The audience would say, "This is a physical problem. We've got to fix it." But so many of our problems are psychological problems because we're looking at the wrong thing, and we live in constant and ubiquitous denial of that. We reinforce our impulse to create a world of opportunity that doesn't deliver happiness.

There would, of course, be no purpose in looking if 'I' actually did come first. But if 'I' comes third, then what? Once we start looking at that we might get nearer to actual solutions.

Here we have to underscore the final point: 'I', 'me' and 'mine' are embedded in a super narrative, called 'my character'. It is who 'I' am, the backdrop against which 'I' live 'my' life. The labels 'I', 'me' and 'mine' are the labels that anchor a set of associations called 'my life'. We then mix our stories with those of our friends, our family, our job, our country, our religion— and a shared identity is formed. That's why when you are with your friends you feel so comfortable: you have a shared story. And not surprisingly, that's why your friends might get upset when you begin to examine your perception, because you are threatening to leave the story. They don't like it. They want you to be part of the story so they can have fond memories of you. "Remember when we went fishing? Wasn't that fun? Go back to being that fun guy again. That's what we want you to be. We're not interested in what you discover working on yourself!"

> PAGE 46, PARAGRAPH 1: *Even when we see the value of changing this situation, it can be very difficult to relax our hold on what we believe—or want to believe—is right and real. This can be especially true if we think that doing so*

might affect how others judge us. People who care very much how others feel about them tend to cultivate and present a particular image, even if that image is a negative one. Unexamined, even a negative self-image can become the anchor for an individual's personality and sense of empowerment to the extent that losing it would leave him or her with no sense of place or position.

The narrative of our life is literally the most important thing we have, this set of associations in which our ego, our hero is embedded. Now let's look at something that's really fascinating here. We go to a party, dress up and put on our best face. That's our superego manifesting. But there are people whose story has them as awkward, difficult, nasty and a curmudgeon. Amazingly, they'll hang on to that as who they are. They'll say, "Oh, I'm a bad-tempered person. I don't like doing that. I don't have any friends." The story does not have to be nice. It can be nasty and work just as well.

What's important is not the specific contents of character but rather the narrative in which the ego is embedded. What counts are not the details but the structure that both shelters and constrains. That narrative is more than a possession, it's who we are. Consequently, when we try modifying it, we find it very heavily defended.

PAGE 46, PARAGRAPH 1, CONT'D: *Even when struggling in the worst of circumstances, such persons may go to great lengths to uphold their image, thinking, "I cannot lose my position, I cannot lose my dignity!" Anything—even physical or psychological pain—might be endured more easily than humiliation.*

Here's another way of thinking about this. Consider the nation-state as a collective superego. We hear such things as, "You have insulted the dignity of my country," as if it were a real thing. That is the collective superego at work. Nobody challenges it by questioning its basis in reality. Indeed, looking at our current circumstances we appear to be pouring more and more energy into the superegos of nation states. The result is nations fighting like children.

We all have a strong sense of our own dignity. "I've got this far. I know who I am. I'm not going to change. This is what it is." Indeed, that might be fine if it would make us happy. But we're not happy. When we have occasion to know more about the lives of people who appear to be doing well externally, we often find that they admit to being unhappy. The superego has cemented their ego into this walled city that is under continual attack.

> PAGE 47, PARAGRAPH 1: *Preoccupation with this kind of 'dignity' isolates us from our own experience. It makes us strangers to ourselves, reluctant to look too closely at what lies inside. When we cling tightly to this perspective, it becomes nearly impossible to look meaningfully at the workings of mind. Ignored, allowed to continue without intervention or guidance, the mechanisms of mind will become more rigid and oppressive over time. As patterns intensify and residues accumulate, mind will present us with problems that are ever more crippling and painful.*

Many recognize that they have problems and even demonize the ego as the cause. Some, recognizing that 'I' is isolated from their own experience, get religion, put on a hair shirt or try to kill the enemy 'I'. In Eastern religions some try to meditate 'I' out of existence. It's a remarkable achievement to be able to sit without thoughts—no 'I'! Many seem to think that if you sit like a statue long enough, that leads to enlightenment. Why? Why is that a good thing at all? Because we have the idea that somehow if we sit like a Buddha and then get up after half an hour we've done something useful. But by definition, we have done nothing at all.

The secret door that gets us out of this prison is that 'I' comes third, so 'I' am not the problem. 'I' was not there when the problem first manifested. 'I' am not responsible. 'I' am like the guy who turns up after someone has been murdered but is there when the police arrive, so they think, "He did it." But 'I' wasn't there! If you understand this you can become a friend to yourself.

If, however, we can't find a way to do this we remain trapped in the psychopathology of suffering. We're not facing some unnatural, artificial, external problem—it's hardwired into the process of perception. Because of the way mind works it creates a structure that, in turn, is the foundation for what is described here. It's a natural occurrence, which is why people have been suffering since records began; and they are going to be suffering as long as we continue on into the future. It's never going to change no matter how good our mobile phones are, how long we live, how fast our cars drive, how fast our spaceships are; nothing will change it unless we come to grips with the process of perception.

CHAPTER 9

Victimizing Mind

This chapter discusses success, failure, self-hatred and integrity. These are complex subjects but central to our culture. You can see them play out in fundamental differences between the biographies of successful people in Western culture and those in the East.

In the West the successful person is often a tortured genius who had some difficult problems to overcome, or someone who came up from the gutter. Beethoven, for example, was deaf but overcame his condition to continue his career as a successful composer. The idea of overcoming obstacles to become successful is a common theme.

In Eastern cultures, it's really very different. If you look at Chinese culture, for example, a successful person is considered someone who is in harmony with his or her surroundings and expresses themselves spontaneously. Success has a completely different connotation.

In the West you have to force yourself to do well. If you don't you won't be anyone of any importance. We see this in the Western attitude toward almost anything: you've got to have grit.

There was an article about school sports recently pointing out that instead of being enjoyable but challenging, sports have become a matter of highly disciplined work.[20] As a result, participation in sports is dropping because kids no longer enjoy it. Playing sports should be the part of the day that is fun and carefree, but clever advertising and helicopter parenting are driving kids to specialize in one sport and go professional from a really young age. It's as if you can't do anything without setting yourself up to be either a success or a failure. The national obsession with 'winners' and 'losers' is characteristic of our culture.

This has much to do with the regime of mind and a clear manifestation of our mental apparatus. Once we identify a target the regime of mind can become quite ruthless in driving us to achieve it. If that target is not achieved, the regime of mind can take people into very dark places.

If we are going to develop a path that goes beyond the regime of mind we'll have to try to do so with eyes open. We'll have to work out the qualities that matter to do this successfully. But we can't just abandon the regime of mind like the hippies tried to do in the 1960s. "Tune in, turn on and drop out" was the mantra then—but it didn't work. It did not work because the regime just reconfigured itself in new ways. In short, we need to be clever and systematic in going beyond the limitations that the regime creates for us.

> PAGE 48, PARAGRAPH 1: *Nearly everyone assigns great importance to business, career, and family, and builds his or her life around these central features of our society. Some are successful, others have to struggle to find their way; some experience strong ups and downs, and some fail to get anywhere on their own. Everyone is vulnerable: Life is unpredictable and offers few guarantees.*

---

20   https://www.parenting.com/activities/sports/are-kids-sports-too-competitive/

This is particularly true in a culture like America. In Scandinavia, it would be slightly different, because they have more of a social structure. In America and in similar countries, if you mess your life up, it's your problem. This is a typical Western capitalistic response: your job in life is to either succeed or fail.

Many Western parents encourage their kids to adopt this attitude toward virtually every aspect of their lives. These pressures are pushed on us when we're young. Although we may resist them, they are constantly reinforced. For example, advertising relies on images of successful people having a good time. But these images aren't reflective of anything real. Even the actors in the commercials often turn out to be unhappy!

So we have to question what makes a good life as well as how to deal with our desire to be successful in a sensible way.

> PAGE 48, PARAGRAPH 2: *Successful or not, some people may end up lonely and hopeless, their truest thoughts and feelings sealed deep inside. Finding it difficult to inspire themselves or take encouragement from positive advice, they may have no one they trust to counsel them. Eventually they may see nothing of much value, not even in themselves. Their self-esteem weakens; they withdraw more and more. As their inner environment darkens and takes on a quality of mourning, the senses draw in, and pressure builds internally. Thoughts and memories turn negative and become sources of pain. They cannot trust and they cannot reach out for help. Finally, there is nothing they can do.*

The regime of mind is a self-referential structure. Things that arise in your experience are identified and processed in a construct in which 'I' know 'it'. That construct is then used as a framework for associations that are attracted to it.

Part of the net of associations is what you tell yourself, and that can be a very strong influence. If you say, "I am a failure" or "I'm no good," it feeds back into the network. That internal language becomes a further attractor for other examples to be drawn from memory by this process of association. All of the feelings of being no good, of being a failure, start piling in. One can end up in a very unfortunate spiral in which failure creates an internal commentary that creates more failure. This can undermine confidence and performance and create real feelings of hopelessness. In this way it matters what you say to yourself.

Images and suggestions, either positive or negative, are food for our mind. The protective mechanism becomes polluted. This is how moods work. For example, if things are going badly, we can be attracted to the gloominess and start feeding it back. When the protective mechanism picks it up and amplifies it, all those gloomy associations become projections that influence our decisions and ultimately determine our future.

PAGE 49, PARAGRAPH 1: *All of us have some experience with these ways of being. When we hear expressions of self-doubt and discouragement—"I am unhappy," "I'm not doing the right thing." "This doesn't seem worth it." "This is not what I wanted to do, but I have no choice"—we understand what they mean. We may not use the same words, but we can relate to the feelings behind them because we have felt something similar.*

We are constructed by our mental apparatus. It matters what we say because what we say reinforces the association network that is already in place. Because the association structure attaches itself to 'I, me and mine,' what 'I, me and mine' do is an important element in the secondary associations that come in and attach. What we say to ourselves makes a difference to how we feel. The narrative that one has in one's own mind is important.

PAGE 49, PARAGRAPH 2: *How can we respond? There are powerful medicines for physical illnesses, but our ability to reverse such a drift into hopelessness and depression remains limited. Some use drugs to ease their pain and turn their minds in a more positive direction, but these may provide only temporary relief or have unforeseen outcomes. Surely we would like more lasting and reliable solutions that benefit the whole of our being.*

Large numbers of people are suffering an opioid epidemic today, and it is serious. A slow-release version of morphine was developed and licensed for the treatment of pain, and it has turned thousands and thousands of people who were depressed into addicts. Numbers vary, but there are large numbers of middle-aged Americans who are now essentially junkies. They've turned to drugs because they were depressed. They may have been depressed because of their economic conditions, but what's happened now is they've become addicts.[21] Of course, the drug can never remove the problem—that's the point.

The great pharmaceutical myth is that you can medicate away anything. In the opioid epidemic, we can see very clearly how that myth has failed us. Is there another way? That's the question we have to ask.

Whatever the political situation, we can be pretty confident that the future will not improve for us if we are not able to get hold of our own psychology. Furthermore, new stressors are on the immediate horizon, because mass automation is coming. Many people feel helpless in the face of these changes. If your self-worth is entirely predicated on your economic circumstance, what is initially a problem becomes an inevitability. Without the ability to understand our internal commentary, our situation is literally hopeless. So, the question is, is there any way that we can address our own protective mecha-

---

21   For a good review see: https://en.wikipedia.org/wiki/Opioid_epidemic_in_the_United_States

nism, the mind, so it doesn't drive us down an inevitable road toward self-harm and failure?

> PAGE 49, PARAGRAPH 3: *The root cause for this kind of suffering is a lack of understanding what mind is and what it needs to fill us with the joy and beauty that can be realized in even the most humble surroundings. Even people who have invested time and energy in exploring various routes to inner knowledge may have given little thought to how our minds process input from our senses and feelings. Yet this kind of understanding seems crucial. Sensitive to our feelings, our minds pick up resentful, distrustful, even paranoid images and project them back into the ongoing streams of perception. They build up and intensify negative input, providing labels that appear to fit our frustration and emotions.*

A lot of people seek inner knowledge through denial. In fact, almost everybody on a spiritual path starts off doing that, because we have a very strong image that comes through many, many religious traditions—that somehow self-denial and beating oneself up are important elements of inner exploration. There are all sorts of stories of holy men who go off and live in sackcloth and ashes and really, really suffer. It's hardly surprising that that's what we try and do, even if we are seeking inner knowledge.

In the light of the associative web that structures our inner life, we need to be aware of the diet of mental images we are feeding ourselves. In the 1950s the great cause was 'Ban the Bomb' and people became obsessed with images of nuclear devastation. It seemed like a good thing, but actually, it was profoundly unhealthy, because what these people were doing was filling themselves up with awful images of nuclear destruction. Now Islamic fundamentalism has become a similar obsession. The regime of mind, trying to make sense of the world, gets all this negative input, and does what it always does, which is to provide relevant associations, to make a story out of it. Suddenly we become convinced that we are under attack by crazy people in SUVs who are going to mow us down, because that's what the regime has amplified as an image.

To address this tendency of the mind, it is helpful to have an idea of how we are predisposed to react. Having that idea means that when we do react, it has much less of an impact. On the other hand, if we spend time with people who feel they have failed or feel they are no good, we will realize that the language they use to describe their life is absolutely reinforcing the feelings they are having. It is a loop, and just looking at that language is really striking. By looking at examples like this we can see how people become very attached to negative language that impacts their ability to function.

> PAGE 49, PARAGRAPH 3, CONT'D: *We discriminate in all the ways the mind has learned—unfair, unjust, right or wrong, real or unreal—and we act them out. The words associated with these reactions are spoken through the mouth and taken in through the ears; mind hears and responds, setting into motion new cycles of cause and effect. Words have consequences: once spoken, they imprint meanings and images on the mind that are difficult, possibly impossible to erase. Their effects can ripple through consciousness for a long time.*

Our internal commentary and emotions can trigger associative imagery and significantly distort our experience, so we end up in a feedback loop—darkness making more darkness. The image of the loop can be a helpful way to visualize the operation of the kleshas. Once emotions have been triggered, they have a very long-lasting effect—and this loop is why.

The regime in itself acts like a scenario planner, helping us navigate through life. If we introduce into our internal dialogue a degree of self-knowledge, we can take advantage of that functionality. Instead of having the attitude of being fated to something inevitable, as in, "This is just the way I am. There's nothing I can do about it," suddenly there is the possibility of choice: "Okay, so I'm using this language because I'm used to using this language. But that's not really all there is."

Emotions are learned phenomena; we learn to emote in particular ways. Emotions are also highly motivating. Something will happen in our experience, and the emotions that are attached to that event will trigger more emotions. Those emotions will amplify the response. Emotions trigger a cascade, an entourage, a retinue of mind.

> PAGE 50, PARAGRAPH 1: *Yesterday we may have felt as though we were in the hell realms; today, perhaps we are in a happier place. Tomorrow, we may be somewhere else. Mind makes available all the realms accessible through human experience, from the frozen and burning hells to celestial realms of continuous delight.*

The same event can have many different meanings depending on people's predispositions and their emotional makeup. These differences reflect this process of association.

We can create positive feedback and that in turn creates positive experience in life, or we can be in a bad mood and see only bad things happening. This experience is what creates this metaphor of living in heaven or hell. We have constructed a world and provided it with meaning based on our association networks. If we don't understand how these association networks operate, we are left thinking this world is real. Stuck with this belief, we naturally fight to defend our world, and the pain we experience ends up justifying the sacrifices we make. That experience reproduces itself: we react to it as though it is real, when in fact it is being in large part constructed by our own association networks themselves.

One can see the same thing in one's own psychology. Many of us have gone through periods of intense self-criticism and judgments about our performance, and to heal that takes reconciliation. We have to go through a process of befriending our own psychology.

One of the most important things to do, once we realize that there is a mechanism that we can influence, is to take responsibility for it. We can't just run away from it. A lot of people think, "I'm not feeling well. I think I'll take a holiday. When I come back, I'll feel better." The trouble is that this approach is completely passive. It's as if deep down, we're convinced the association set can't be fixed, and all we can do is leave it for a while and then come back and hope it's gotten better. But it is possible to do much more than that. We really can understand the association set and see how it's made.

> PAGE 51, PARAGRAPH 1: *Reflecting on this, we might find it difficult to believe we have the power to choose what realm we wish to experience. But since experience comes through the mind, the flavor and quality of our experience largely depends on the way we use our minds. Identity, labeling, validation, and interpretation form the mind-regime that structures experience, and this regime is the reason we have problems. How we view this regime and relate to it has important implications for all aspects of life.*

Once you feed negativity into your mind, it's quite surprising how rapidly negativity manifests. If you feed relentless positivity into your mind, then positivity begins to manifest. This of course is the whole positive thinking idea and it's remarkably effective. And indeed, a lot of psychotherapy is based on the understanding that we suggest failure or success to ourselves hypnotically, through words and thoughts. A lot of sports psychology is concerned with trying to eradicate failure thoughts in athletes.

PAGE 51, PARAGRAPH 2: *Up to now, we could always blame our problems on others, on the way things are, or on causes and conditions outside our control. Now we may see that we have a choice: We can continue to play this game with our minds for the rest of our lives, assuring that we will remain insecure, vulnerable to problems that can pop up at any moment. Or we can make a better choice: understanding.*

We can use our knowledge of our cognitive apparatus to understand ourselves. By reflecting on our memory of events, we can begin to identify association sets and generate a better idea of how we're going to react to certain circumstances. When we don't react in those ways, it gives us a strong sense of reassurance that real understanding of ourselves is possible.

PAGE 51, PARAGRAPH 3: *To determine the value of understanding, we have only to observe what happens when we do not understand how our minds produce and process our thoughts and attitudes. We all regularly plant and cultivate fantasies, posturing, excuses, and denials. However harmless they may seem at the time, the games we play in this way plant thoughts and images in the mind. When this kind of planting, cultivation, and re-seeding is repeated over many years, it can be difficult to separate ourselves from the convoluted images and attitudes that these games perpetuate.*

This is about honesty. If we are to see real change, if we are to get some real distance from the controlling influence of our regime, we must commit not to lie, to ourselves or to others.

In truth, there is no such thing as a white lie. All these ideas like, "reality is malleable. I can fix it," are destructive to personal development because what it tells our own psychology is that everything is adjustable. If we start saying everything is adjustable, then how stable is our intention going to be? The regime is dedicated to our protection. To go beyond its protective shield requires the demonstration of both sincere

(GOP!

intent and reliability. This requires honesty in all our actions. There is no such thing as private—we are being listened to! Lying to ourselves or others in private merely tells our regime that we are not to be trusted.

> PAGE 52, PARAGRAPH 1: *When we see someone in distress and disoriented, unable to play the usual games in the usual way, when we see such a person falling victim to whatever thoughts and imaginings his or her mind projects, we witness first-hand the helpless vulnerability, the nightmarish fantasies, and the anger and hostility they have to endure as mind wanders in confusion, drifting from happier realms to the hells. Once mind has gone to those dark places, it can be very difficult to pull it back.*

One of the things that we see when interacting with people who have emotional problems is the extent to which they fool themselves. Telling stories and not facing up to our situation multiplies our problems. There is a sense of vulnerability that then creeps in because there is no firm foundation on which we can stand. If at the base of our psychology there is fundamental dishonesty about our circumstance, we become a victim to ourselves. Relying on external experts isn't going to help much either. Having someone else saying we have this or that problem won't make much difference.

At a deep level we know how to fix ourselves. All we have to do is get serious about it. We need a degree of sobriety to go down this road which amounts to crossing a sea of mirrors in which most of what we see is a reflection of who we are. That means if who we are is not sober and truthful, we are never going to get anywhere. The sea of mirrors is going to become so confusing that we'll just get lost.

This is an important theme in *Revelations*, because if we are going to transform our minds, we have to have the self-discipline of being straightforward. If we are not straightforward, we run a serious risk of getting lost in fantasy. The risk arises because in order to transform ourselves, we've got to be willing to disconnect from society, and in that disconnection, we are responsible for ourselves on our own. There is no societal pressure on us anymore, and this can become dangerous if we are not willing to be responsible. If we are not willing to have a code of honor that we live by, it's better not to try doing this at all, because if we try to do this, we could end up infinitely worse off than we began.

> PAGE 52, PARAGRAPH 2: *When we get into difficulty, we tend to rely on experts. But experts are human beings too; their knowledge is limited and they have similar human problems. Ultimately, for some situations, there is no solution. We are in the realm of the conditioned, dualistic mind, responding to whatever arises from moment to moment and vulnerable to misunderstanding, conflicted feelings, and emotional pain. Not knowing where our choices are leading—or if we even have choices—we participate in cycles of cause and effect and become caught up in them. Even if we have not intentionally caused a situation, when the results begin to manifest we can only endure whatever happens.*

Our choices have consequences; what we do in the world has effects. If we're lying to ourselves then we'll have to endure the effects. In an emergency, when events become serious, perhaps even dangerous, people start getting sober. Often, however, by the time we get sober we are so far down the road that we can't pull out from the consequences of our actions. We need to get sober while times are good; that way we are prepared.

> PAGE 53, PARAGRAPH 1: *When we observe the suffering that mind can inflict, when we realize we are ultimately helpless to control our own responses or to ease the pain of loved ones lost in confusion, we understand that this is not a happy situation. Seeing this, we have the knowledge we need to question, "Does it have to be this way?"*

For us, the consequence of inner toxicity can be seen as a choice—it was just a wrong choice. We need to be willing to take ownership of bad choices and resolve that we are not going to let them happen anymore. If we really wish to go beyond the protective mechanism offered to us by the regime of mind, we've got to take care with our inner lives, because if we don't treat the regime correctly, it will provide us with all kinds of wrong feedback and distorted views and before we realize, we are off down the wrong road, a hopeless road. It is very, very important to get this message clear.

> PAGE 53, PARAGRAPH 2: *If we ask why we feel anxious or have low self-esteem, now we may understand, "Mind is telling us this, and we have accepted it. We have obeyed its rules, and it is confirming that this response is the proper one." For example, suppose your mind says, "You are a failure. Others were depending on you, and you let them down. How can anyone trust you again?" What choice do we have but to go along? Consciously or subconsciously, we embrace the image of 'failure'. As mind continues to re-affirm the reality of this label, 'failure' becomes our reality. If someone challenges us by pointing out why this is not true, we might find ourselves actually defending the image of failure: "This is just the way it is. This is what I am." Mind has pronounced judgment and we have accepted it.*

Here we have a good example of wrong feedback. A super-narrative of failure can be generated and confirmed through association and suggestion. In reflecting on this, it's valuable to generate a personal history. Events that happen to us are always put into a narrative, particularly those that happened to us when we were powerless in childhood.

> PAGE 54, PARAGRAPH 1: *Certain this is so, we take on the identity assigned to us, resentful of the unfairness of it all. Mind listens to our pain, then identifies and reinforces it, making certain that we fit the definition of whatever label has been assigned. Perhaps we can muster the confidence*

to reject the label in a way that mind will accept, but if not, this identity becomes strongly fixed. The processes of our own minds—our way of identifying and recognizing, our history and associations, the memories that tell us mind is right—convince us to hold on tightly to the failure role. Our own mind has now become our enemy.

If we never take our internal life seriously or make a commitment to be totally honest in looking at the regime, eventually it becomes toxic. That's sad, because the regime was never intended to be toxic. It was intended to help us get through the world. But if we generate an internal dialogue of resentment and victimhood, our innate sense of rightness will convince us to hold on to what is poisoning us.

PAGE 54, PARAGRAPH 2: *Now our inner environment may become more hostile: Mind continues to dictate: "Yes, you are this, and this, and this. Yes, you have done that and that and that." It pounds on the same theme, sealing off one escape route after another until there is no way not to fail. When our intelligence and energy become demoralized in this way, we cannot exercise good judgment or make good decisions. If we have no way to put this process on hold, failure will indeed become our reality.*

Mind pronounces, and we accept. Where can we turn? In more extreme situations, even the senses are blocked—we cannot see the light, we do not know what to do. Others may sense our pain and reach out, but we are alone, locked into our own inner environment. Without some support for calming this downward momentum, thoughts can go to desperation, self-destruction, even self-annihilation. The mind is so powerful that it can crush us completely.

Here, we can see how this protective mechanism of the regime of mind can get distorted into something self-destructive. When suggestive people get into this negative cycle, it can be very, very difficult to pull them out of it, because everything they do is being reinforced by a mechanism saying,

"Yes, there we are, you are a failure, you are no good!" This is how it happens, how the feedback goes wrong.

> PAGE 55, PARAGRAPH 2: *Nearly everyone experiences similar cycles from time to time, even if they deny what is happening, and many people live this way much of their lives. If we wish to be free from frustration and emotional upsets, free from the painful situations that come up unpredictably and make life so difficult, we need to cast off the victim's role. We need to question why we participate so willingly in the tyranny of mind's regime.*

The most seductive idea is that we are a victim of circumstance. A victim does not have to do anything, essentially. So thinking we are a victim of circumstance is somewhat lazy, but we can get away with it as long as our circumstance remains completely uninteresting. But the moment anything goes wrong with our circumstance, it's a disastrous attitude to take.

If we can understand this message and take responsibility for our own experience, then we allow ourselves the possibility of transformation. But if we don't take responsibility for our own experience, when we hit problems we will have no way of dealing with them. The entire idea of transformation is that we are looking for another way of life that's not merely given to us by our place in society, even though every society is shot through with mechanisms to hold people in place. This is how societies endure through time—they have institutions within them that ensure that people don't go too far off the rails. But if we are going to try and move on from those safe beaches into deeper water, then we've got to take personal responsibility for how we react to what is happening in our lives.

Exercise 7
Personal history

Start to make a personal history. We have all lived a long time, and much of our experience is lost to immediate memory. However, with effort, considerable details can be re-collected, and the result is an important tool to understand who we are. To make a personal history, start by setting out major dates on a timeline that can be verified. Use school reports, tickets, diaries, catalogues, photographs, any record that can be validated. As you begin to arrange these events on your timeline, you will find memories being evoked, which you can also record. Slowly you will be able to fill in considerable detail.

Pay particular attention to periods where there seem to be blanks. Often within them are important events that have been protected and locked away. Also it is valuable to see how patterns repeat themselves. It is not that there is some deep meaning in the personal history itself, but by making it we can get an understanding of the association set we carry with us. We can start to see where it came from, and how it enters into play in our life. This can be helpful precisely because we are beings with histories. We all carry all the experiences we've ever had from conception onwards. Seeing this allows real insight into how meaningful change can be made.

CHAPTER 10

Dependence on Identity

This first section of *Revelations* is analytical, laying out the groundwork for the study of mind. Having established the omnipresence of mind, we can start looking at possible approaches such as the central role of the storyteller in how we construct a meaningful life. This leads to the consideration of the central role the narrative structure plays in the creation of reality, as well as the importance of the heroic actor who animates the scene. Further analysis provides important insights into the pervasive disquiet so many of us suffer from, but to complete the picture we need to consider yet another factor—that of self-identity.

The function of a narrative structure is to provide an explanation of events. In so doing, it is intimately connected to the question of causation. Causation is what ties together a narrative, and without causation life would be just a series of disconnected events. Indeed, when faced with a natural disaster or some extraordinary occurrence, there is an eerie feeling of unreality, part exhilarating and part terrifying. This is because such unexpected events rupture the casual narrative in which we live our everyday lives. Without being able to say, "I did this, because of that," nothing would make much sense at all.

The Greeks classified causation into four categories. There was the material cause—what something is made of; there was the formal cause—how it is shaped; there was the efficient cause—what it does; and there was the final cause—what it's for. In contrast, modern culture recognizes only one of these: the efficient cause, or what something does.

Because we live in a technological culture, we tend to assume that if things do something they are real. In fact, our definition of reality is predicated on efficacy: 'It does something so it's there' is a very deeply held intuition. Scientific experimentation is predicated on this very fact: what things do determine what they are.

Does this mean that the existence of our identity is demonstrated by our actions in the world? Can we, for example, imagine acting in a world without an 'I' in it? That's an interesting thing to try doing. Is 'I' needed in the world? Could the world without 'I' make any sense?

These questions take us to the problem of self-identity. The metaphor that *Revelations* uses for self-identity is having and carrying an identity card. This is a provocative metaphor for many reasons, not least in that most of us really do carry things like credit cards, driving licenses, entrance cards, and so forth—and it is actually difficult to live without these forms of identification. In actuality, they are identity cards.

Two hundred years ago most people had no identity at all. They would literally have nothing to identify them: no passport, no credit cards, no driving license—no documents at all to identify who they were. Yet almost all of us now carry many bits of plastic that give detailed information about us.

PAGE 56, PARAGRAPH 1: *Identity is key to the reality-creating program that mind operates.*

How is our identity generated and why are we so confident that it's real? In fact, we are so confident that it's real that it's incredibly difficult to question it.

A feature of the identity-creating program of the mind is that it has no room for self-awareness. When you are self-aware you don't have a strong sense of identity. But when something grabs your attention you, as an actor, get sucked into it and your self-awareness shuts off. You literally get sucked out of self-awareness into self-identity. It's like an undertow that sucks us off the beach of awareness. How this transpires is extremely subtle—it's a kind of discontinuity: you are aware and then you are not aware. When you become aware again, it's like waking up and wondering what happened.

This process is extremely fast and the basis for ignorance in its true sense.

Often we can't remember what we were doing—long periods of the day are just blank, as if we were not present at all. It can be difficult to reconstruct what happened—we actually have to think, "Ok, so at ten past nine I was there, and then twenty past nine I was there, so . . . oh yes, I walked down that street." That's literally how we have to do it, reconstructing events in which we were apparently present by reconstructing what must have happened in a temporal sequence, event by event. We have to use our reasoning facility to reconstruct what we were doing because our self-awareness is discontinuous. It is being continuously disrupted by our self identity.

> PAGE 56, PARAGRAPH 1, CONT'D: *We believe in identity— our own and that of everything around us. It is as if mind has provided us with a card bearing our image and the label, 'I am'.*

Have you ever had a dream where you go to a party and you find you haven't any clothes on? You go to the party thinking you are part of a club. You have identification and you were invited—but you look down and you are naked or just in your underwear! This is a common but significant dream.

Being part of the group and being accepted by them is a deep social need. There was a very famous cartoonist in the United Kingdom called Baxter who was always making cartoons of these types of situations. He was working in the 1920s when people's social mores were even stronger than they are now, so even having a wrong number of buttons on your cuff could become an issue of identity.

Paranoid dreams in which your identity is being questioned are common because we believe in identity. Identity gives us a very strong sense of being here. If we think in terms of a map we need a point on that map indicating 'me'. "That's me, there."

We also use identity to remember what we were doing. If we didn't have a marker called 'me' how would we remember why we were here? This geotag is really important. But we should wonder about the territory that we are mapping so continually; do we have an identity there?

Despite the central role it plays, many of us have an intuition that 'I' is not real, that it's an elective identity, that we have elected to be a member of whatever club we claim to be part of. Yet we cannot leave this club and have no identity. People who drop one identity in an act of rebellion often just take on another—they are not breaking free of having an identity at all.

> PAGE 56, PARAGRAPH 1, CONT'D: *More fundamental than credit cards or the usual legal proofs that identify our names, addresses, and vital information, mind's identity card serves as our own special label: it validates our existence and confirms our sense of ourselves as unique individuals.*

It appears that our self-image is created by mind and provides us with a great deal of comfort. We are touching here on fundamental processes. In Sanskrit it's called 'I-making', a translation of the word *ahamkara*. This I-maker is reminiscent of the heroic ego. We are always the central actor in the drama of our life—the whole story constellates around 'I'. That actor must be unique and special, for he or she is on the center of the stage of life.

PAGE 56, PARAGRAPH 1, CONT'D: *It represents the qualities we wish to project to the outside world; it reveals the view we hold of ourselves and fits in seamlessly with mind's way of establishing reality.*

Why do we need to establish reality in the first place? Why do we need to prove to ourselves that we are actually here? Everybody does it—it's hardly a trivial issue.

The simple fact is that we are born into a world that was already in progress. When we come onto the stage everything is already in full swing. Given this disquieting situation there is a fundamental requirement that we establish a place in this reality for ourselves.

The world was in process when we arrived and the world will continue after we die. We've all seen people die and nothing changes, literally nothing. What is going on here? We don't seem to have any identity yet here we are in the world—wow, very alarming!

So, can we imagine a world without 'I' in it? How would we go about operating in a world without 'I' in it? We are here, obviously we are here. Yet the way in which we are here is the question. Self-identity is the solution our mind has come up with to answer it.

PAGE 56, PARAGRAPH 2: *Processing sensory data, identifying what is and excluding what is not, assessing right and wrong, judging what is desirable and what is undesirable, mind is constantly scanning and verifying the labels that convey the full meaning of its products. This is how mind sustains the identity of 'I' and supplies the sense of security we have come to depend upon in viewing ourselves as independent beings.*

The process we're exploring is that when something is presented to mind there is a label suggested and confirmed prior to the projection of a 'known' thing. To explore this, a good modality to use is sound, just listening. It's quite hard to explore with vision because the sense is too fast and impactful. If you listen attentively you can become aware of the internal process of naming and recognition.

Earlier in this section a practice of sitting beside an open window and exploring sound was suggested. We were exploring the contrast between working to identify all the elements in a soundscape, doing this intently for a period, and then dropping the identification completely. This exercise is helpful in exploring two ways of being.

Exploring sounds, however, can also go deeper. A state of non-identified calmness can be a gateway to explore how the process of identification actually works. When there's merely a sense impression—a sound—there is no identity. But once it has clicked into place as some 'thing' that has been identified, then a whole stage is there at once, all together: not just the object, but also 'I', 'me' and 'mine'.

Artists who have the skill and talent can take us out of our own identity for a brief time. We have already discussed music. The same effect can be found in great paintings. You can look at a Cezanne, Rembrandt, or a Vermeer and become transported beyond your normal frame of reference. It can happen in film if the director is skilled enough. Reading a wonderful poem or an expressive piece of writing, watching a play or live performance—all these events allow us to escape the enclosure of self identity, if only for a few moments.

PAGE 56, PARAGRAPH 2, CONT'D: *Identity gives us a sense of status and focus that our customer-mind views as essential. It is useful, it helps us fit in with others, and it generally appears to be working well.*

If something works well, is that proof that it exists? That is the normal assumption based on our understanding of the efficient cause mentioned above. Because our sense of identity helps us navigate the world, it's accepted by us as absolutely existing. Existence equals function in our understanding.

However, the equating of existence with function is wrongheaded. If something existed in an absolute sense it couldn't change, and would therefore have no function. If it actually existed without a relationship to anything else it could not do anything; in order for something to actually exist in an absolute manner, there can be no change. Our Western habit of concentrating exclusively on the efficient cause leads to a paradox of identity, a paradox with rich implications for who we are.

This idea was expressed in ancient Indian thought, and also in modern physical thinking such as Alfred North Whitehead's process philosophy.[22] Action involves change.

This is equally true of our identity. In creating our identity, what we do is name something that's actually changing all the time. The 'I' that we think drinks a cup of coffee is not the 'I' that we think looks out of the window. If that 'I' actually existed, it wouldn't change—it couldn't change, by definition.

PAGE 57, PARAGRAPH 1: *Because our identity depends upon it, carrying mind's identity card requires our full focused attention twenty-four hours a day, seven days a week. Coded into it are all the labels and associations that apply to every aspect of experience, as well as to our jobs, status, associations, education, and the qualities we wish to project.*

---

22 A good introduction can be found here: https://plato.stanford.edu/entries/whitehead/

Our normal process of memory is a location system. It's like a computer that has to tag or mark bits of its program. Without those markers the computer could not function. Similarly, 'I' isn't actually present right now, but 'I' is used as a tag, so a few minutes from now, memory can locate 'I' and remember what happened to 'me'. The memory might be expressed as, "'I' am here now because 'I' came up the stairs ten minutes ago," or something similar. Through the location of 'I', 'because' can operate as a connecting link, holding the narrative of our experience together.

> PAGE 57, PARAGRAPH 1, CONT'D: *With our card, we can present ourselves to others in ways that they can recognize and respect: we have the right qualifications, we can be counted on to behave in acceptable ways, and we are responsible. Now we can conduct business; we have the power and position we need.*

All of us transact life like this. However, it's unusual for people to do so with total strangers because it's very difficult. We want to know that people are in some respect similar to us. With strangers the difficulty arises because we don't know what they are expressing. We communicate because of a tacit acceptance that my 'I'-maker and yours are basically similar. How do we communicate if that's not the case? It requires a theory of other minds.[23] If those other minds are not known to us, communication becomes very difficult.

For example, how do I know the people who surround me are not robots? I have a theory of mind that says: if this guy raises his eyebrows and his mouth opens wide, he must be surprised. But why do I know that? Because when I do it myself, I am surprised. So I have a theory of other minds that tells me

---

23   Theory of mind develops in young children and allows communication, initially through exchange. It is thought that developmental abnormalities in this process lead to problems such as autism.

that they are broadly similar to mine. It's only on the basis of such a theory that transactions are possible at all.

What happens if you go to a foreign country for example? Then it's much more difficult to work out what people are doing and saying until you get an idea of how they express themselves. People in India, for example, say 'yes' with a head gyration that in Europe means 'no'.

This realization feeds into our identity. We exist and are surrounded by other embodied beings. We all have this continuous reality-creator that produces an identity for us so we can live in the world. However, the 'I' is a label, and the story in which we embed it, our identity, is in itself constructed from the events that happened to us. But we are ferociously loyal to it because if we're not loyal to our identity, our whole sense of reality would begin to disintegrate.

So identity comes with a big price tag: we must be absolutely loyal. We have a loyalty pledge that we give to our sense of self. This is one of the reasons why it is extraordinarily difficult to imagine a world without 'I' in it. I'm so loyal to 'me' that I can't begin to imagine how the world could exist if I'm not here. Even though we know that when people die the world keeps going, somehow we still hang on to that loyalty as central.

> PAGE 57, PARAGRAPH 2: *Of course, we need to be loyal to the identity the card confirms, and we need to fulfill the functions and obligations this symbol represents, regardless of how our feelings, aspirations, and situation may change over time.*

Perhaps the best example of this is the national flag. In many countries this symbolic object is treated with great reverence, both in honor of all those who have died in service of national ideals and because many of those ideals are taught in schools. Such unifying themes provide important cohesion and allow people to feel allegiances beyond familial or ethnic identities. But they also carry with them unexamined ideas, often invoked by politicians, such as Manifest Destiny or Exceptionalism. These ideas are powerful influences on the super narrative we all create for ourselves; they form part of our personal identity. We are born into the world, wake up in a crib and then gradually piece together a construct in which 'I' makes sense within the surrounding world. This is all identity-making.

> PAGE 58, PARAGRAPH 1: *Of all the functions of mind, the ability to establish our identity—the 'me', the 'I', the self—may be the most important, because without it we have nothing. What if we reached for our card and it were not there? Even the thought that it might be lost is threatening. Once we have it, however secure we may feel in our sense of 'me', 'I', and self, we need to protect, use, and be fully responsible for it. We need to validate it over and over again.*

Watch people walking down the road. As mentioned earlier, if they're not talking on the phone they are talking to themselves. They are validating their own identity, all the time. We live in a mental construct that is continually being made and remade around 'me' as a central actor.

Without that 'me', the construct has nothing to support it. So within the construct there is a sense of insecurity, a feeling that it is not completely solid, that it has to be continually maintained. This is why when you attack people's identity they get so upset and usually attack you back immediately. They are anxious about their identity. We are all insecure because who we think we are has to be maintained like a leaking boat.

> PAGE 58, PARAGRAPH 2: *Everything essential to experience as we know it, including consciousness, thought, and senses, is conveyed through the operation of identity. Invisible, it affects the course of every interaction. Interpretations take shape within its realm of influence. Mind points out and*

identity designates accordingly: this is right, that is wrong; accommodate this, reject that. All this is done from the perspective of an 'I', 'me' or 'self', in accordance with the rules for subject/object polarity that mind itself has established.

We spend most of our time as a concept in a world of concepts. That's essentially it: the 'I' is a concept that lives in a conceptual map. The 'I' and the map are a perfect pair; they fit together perfectly. This conceptual world functions, it exists; there is nothing wrong with it, except that it's a prison. Its very perfection is what imprisons us.

This again highlights the important function that artists play in our everyday situation. The world is boring, it's named, it's limited, it's day-to-day, hum-drum, nothing happens, everything is the same. That's the prison. Why is that the prison? Because we've labeled it up and are ourselves labeled within it. It's as if it's dead. It's closed up, clammed up. But a great artist can open it up for you. If you stand in front of a Vermeer or a Rembrandt self-portrait it's almost as though the painting is more than itself. It refuses to be labeled as just a painting.

In poetry we can find other examples. You read a great poem and it can have the magical effect of opening you up into something new. Somehow the words portray a meaning that cannot just be labeled and put away. One could say the same about all the arts—photography, sculpture, film, ceramics.

PAGE 58, PARAGRAPH 3: *But what is behind this operation? This is difficult to determine, because we cannot see into that space. Since identity happens and objects appear, we assume that these objects occupy some kind of space, but we cannot tell what occupied that same space before the objects appeared or after they are gone.*

Let's imagine that I notice a clock. What was that clock before I identified it as a clock? I've labeled it as a clock and that label sticks to it. What did I actually notice? What was captured in that label?

Now, back to Vermeer. One painting that comes to mind is 'The Milkmaid'. It's a seemingly mundane image of a woman pouring a jug of milk. Yet if you stay with it for a moment, it's as if you are seeing some primeval jug-pouring before you identify the woman pouring the jug. The painting is so alive and glowing with potentiality that it defies a simple label. That's it—the artist has captured something ineffable that you felt before a label covered it over.

> PAGE 58, PARAGRAPH 3, CONT'D: *We cannot know if there is an unoccupied openness behind the operation of identity that allows for origination to come about independently.*

From a conceptual perspective the world before we label it is unknowable. It is what Kant called the noumenal; we just cannot get there because we require our labels to identify it and our labels are a reaction to that initial process. From the point of view of 'me', 'I' will never know whether there was an unoccupied openness that came before 'me'.

Within traditions such as Zen this is a major theme: what is original mind? This is an important question because there is a recognition that we are all living in a reflection of something prior. What is the original thing before 'I' saw it? That's the repeated question that we find within the meditation traditions, arising as it does from the intuition that our display of the world is fully cooked, totally labeled up. What was there before? What was the unoccupied openness?

> PAGE 59, PARAGRAPH 1: *What we generally call 'mind' encompasses senses, perception, and all kinds of thoughts that arise and move in and out, shifting our view back and forth between subjective and objective orientations. All the while, identity is functioning, sustaining a continuous flow of recognition, associations, and interpretations. These interactions powerfully demonstrate mind, but the question remains: Behind the fabric woven by so much functioning, is there actually any director or boss? It does not seem*

possible that such a complex, multi-faceted process could operate without some kind of strong central director. But if there is one, we might well wonder: who assigned this person such an all-controlling role?

How come the mechanism of mind is able to bind our experience together into such an impressively seamless structure? Is there some controlling faculty that is putting it all together, this prison in which we find ourselves?

Behind this question lies the realization that the problem is somewhat akin to a mirror, in that self-identity and conceptual frames mirror each other. It is this mirroring that creates a unified whole which seems completely seamless. Within that seeming whole we are totally vulnerable to manipulation, to opinion, to fashion, to fantasy, because we are blind to its structure, to what comes before it is projected. Historians of culture can easily demonstrate that human society just veers around and around, being influenced unconsciously by concern after concern in this manner.

At the end of the previous chapter, there was an exercise to create a personal history for ourselves. This is a long project. What our lifelines show us is that despite our apparent sophistication and the complexity with which we live our lives, there are patterns that repeat again and again. Anyone who has access to our lifeline can see those patterns and predict certain behaviors. These patterns reveal the stories in which we live. When we were hunter-gatherers in the savanna this worked efficiently because there was a high probability that the pointy ears in the bushes belonged to a saber-toothed tiger. It was vital to have a model of such a world. Now our experience is totally different and much more complicated, yet this mirroring system is still in operation. But what happens when we are confronted with circumstances for which we have no prior conceptualization? Can we find a new way of being? It is time to find a new way to work with this operating system.

CHAPTER 11

Questioning the Foundation

This is the final chapter of the first section. It asks a question: "Why bother to do this? Is there something here that's really worth doing, or should we just get on with our lives?" We all know that our lives are full of problems. Many practically inclined people would say, "Well, this is just wishful thinking. You guys are just thinking that by working on yourselves it's all going to change for you. This is just fantasy. Just get on, raise a family and make your contribution to society. Why are you bothering with this self-serving nonsense?" This objection is worth taking seriously. If we cannot deal with such objections, our commitment to change is merely provisional.

It's undoubtedly true that for many of us who have an interest in a spiritual life, part of the attraction is that we hope that somehow all our problems will go away—that somehow we will get beyond suffering. Pretty much every spiritual text points to that possibility in one way or another. Another big motivation that many of us have is the potential to experience incredible things that are somehow like a special trip.

I think we need to realize how these motivations could look to an outsider, particularly a sober-minded outsider. They might say, "Well, both of those motivations are essentially indulgent." Self-indulgence is a great weakness of Western people—we get soft, essentially; spoiled. In this sense spirituality can be seen as the pinnacle of the consumer culture: having got the best clothes and the best cars, we are now after the best mind!

There is also the cultural mainstream to consider. The materialistic, scientific culture regards the mind as epiphenomenal. That is to say it is regarded as a sophisticated function of the brain, but it has no causal efficacy beyond the consideration of alternatives. Essentially the laws of physics rule, and beyond that the mind isn't particularly interesting or important. Alongside this is the religious or humanistic view. This view regards the mind as something to do with service to society. Humanists go so far as to say that the mind is a social construct and has no absolute meaning. Religious people will say it's in service to God and has no meaning independent of the Creator.

What neither position allows for is a direct engagement with the mind. That's not considered to be important, valuable or worth doing. What's more, personal experience is thought to be unreliable, particularly at the early stages. The reason it's not reliable is because it arises from the operation of layers of conceptual control, and, as pointed out above, is likely to change if one relaxes or alters the constraints under which it operates.

None of these three views—the hedonic, the materialist or the religious—seems promising. You could conclude that the situation is hopeless, and that one might as well fall back on scientific modeling, the inferential ways of knowing which the West has developed so effectively. After all, such techniques have given us considerable knowledge about materiality, along with phones that work and cars that work and houses and spaceships—surely this is everything worth having! Anything else is surely a diversion from this valuable activity, so trying to clean up the mind, while theoretically interesting to a psychologist, is clearly pointless and just a diversion from the real business at hand.

The humanistic objection is equally cogent. "Just get on with it and help people—that's the path!" The trouble is that our ability to be actually helpful will be severely hampered if our perception is not clear. It is genuinely quite difficult to help people, unless you've worked out what they really need. Human affairs are full of unintended consequences. We all know how often unforeseen consequences ramify out of what was a 'good thing'.

We need to consider these objections, otherwise we do run the risk of not fully engaging in self exploration. Even if we are able to overcome the materialist and humanist viewpoints, having a purely hedonic interest in spirituality is still a major obstacle. Hedonism is the idea that experience is worth having in its own right. Spiritual hedonism is a major expression of spirituality in consumer culture: yoga, meditation for stress reduction, spas that offer spirituality along with therapy and a healthy diet. Our culture is a master of hedonic consumerism, and we need to be careful that we are not going down that road either.

> PAGE 60, PARAGRAPH 1: *When we have problems, we usually point to an external cause or search for reasons. At a deeper level we may seek understanding by questioning our mental patterns and processes.*

So, this is Western culture, and we will normally point to external problems. At a deeper level, we might turn to psychoanalysis. The idea is that we are maladjusted and need to become well-adjusted and get on with a successful life.

> PAGE 60, PARAGRAPH 1, CONT'D: *What if instead we look more closely at the foundation of our being and question mind itself? We soon discover that we can only touch the*

thoughts and images that constitute the surface level of mind. What lies behind, above, beyond, beneath or inside this mind remains a mystery.

This is an invitation to recognize that we are unable to look at our own experience except from the perspective of 'I', 'me' and 'mine'. The question, "How is my mind working?" is unanswerable, because the looking mechanism itself is a construct. Just as a knife can't cut itself and a light can't light itself, there is no way 'you' can get behind the looker to see how the looking is made. From the perspective of the looker, the mechanism is all-encompassing. It's a perfect readout of mental functioning, totally invisible. The actual readout-maker cannot be seen from within the readout any more than you can see the internals of your computer by looking at its screen. The computer screen, the interface, is not the computer. It's a readout of the computer.

> PAGE 60, PARAGRAPH 2: *Mind may have designed its processes to fit its customer—the individual 'I', but it seems indifferent to the emotional turmoil its processes can inflict on that 'I'. We may be so frustrated that we can imagine smoke coming out of our ears, yet mind keeps grinding away, its inner workings concealed by a barrier we cannot penetrate.*

If we set out to be spiritual, we will find that our mind acts like an obedient servant in providing us with spiritual things. This is true of any intention. If you get obsessed with the number six, for example, you will see the number six everywhere. Equally if you give yourself the instruction that you are interested in spiritual life, that's what you are going to see in the world. It will be astonishing to you that other people don't see it. The mind selects from the enormous range of individual elements of perception it receives what fits for us as its customer, based either on our intent, or on its own associative memory.

Most of us can remember the teenage-angst years, and all the suffering that used to go on: girlfriends, boyfriends, always some thing or other, endless angst being produced by the mental process. And with maturity we can look back on that and see that the suffering was caused by us—we gave the instructions that caused the suffering, but we weren't wise enough to see it, so the suffering happened.

> PAGE 60, PARAGRAPH 2, CONT'D: *We feel the power of mind in the pressure building inside our heads and the surge of emotion within our bodies. Mind responds to what we feel; it may even be speaking to itself in ways we do not understand. But it is not necessarily giving us solutions. At this point, it is doubtful that we could trust what it says.*

We can also understand how people get themselves into positions where mind is sending all the wrong messages and we get hurt in the process. This problem is familiar in Western and other cultures and some have developed techniques to reduce suffering, but they only go so far. The only thing left to do is to look under the hood—explore the operations of mind itself.

The first thing we will need to look at is what could be called inner blankness. This often happens when meditators, for example, try to generate internal questioning for the first time.

> PAGE 61, PARAGRAPH 1: *Mind is rarely silent; its mumbling continues even in quiet times or during contemplation. Whatever thoughts and feedback mind presents are expressed in the phrases of the language mind has custom-made for us. But if mind should happen to lapse into silence after all, we come up against the walls of mind, the blind alleys and blank places that indicate there is nothing beyond.*

Blankness is a very common experience. In our meditation, we might sometimes find that the voices settle down but then there is just this cotton wool—like a 'nothing going on' experience. Many of us just go to sleep at this point. This seems like an impenetrable dead end, as if you finally get to the end of the island and there is just a wall of fog. What do we do now?

> PAGE 61, PARAGRAPH 2: *It can be easy to settle down in those quiet places. If we are following some kind of spiritual discipline, we may feel that we have attained the peaceful state we have been seeking. But however remarkable these places may seem, however welcome and refreshing, they too are within the realm of dualistic mind. We are not necessarily learning anything new: Mind is still mind, and the peace we are now enjoying may vanish in the blink of an eye. We might not even remember it.*

This is called 'false vacuity'. We are going to talk a lot more about it in the next section of this book, but it's the phenomenon of having peacefulness that literally disappears the moment you get off your meditation cushion. The term comes from Zen tradition. Zen is always looking for the 'original mind', looking for the true sense of voidness, but if you give that instruction to yourself, you are likely to get whatever mind thinks it is. That is false vacuity.

> PAGE 61, PARAGRAPH 3: *We want to make direct contact with mind itself. But we cannot. We have only the tools that mind has provided—the language and projections that mind can recognize and interpret. When we look for mind directly, we find nothing we can grasp or connect to. We can only engage the secondary level of perception, where the essential pronouncements have already been made. All the labels are already there, as if the knower has a dictionary ready to consult.*

It's important to know that unexamined experience is not primary. In that sense, the humanistic critique is actually correct. Remember, the experiencing self arises after the perceptual input has occurred. Though it seems to us that we're at the cutting edge of our own experience, it's not so. 'Experience as experience' is not primary, since the fundamental metaphysic of the 'knower' and the 'known' is already in place.

So how do you knock this house down? What method can we use? The house is built from the very language that we are trying to use to demolish it!

> PAGE 61, PARAGRAPH 3, CONT'D: *Even after the primary interpretation has been rendered and a name applied, the senses continue their urgings, as if marketing their wares to a hesitating buyer. "How about this one, or perhaps that one instead?" Sometimes we say yes and other times no, but the process continues, repeating the same cycles.*

Words are universals; they label individual things or events. 'I, me and mine' are examples of labeled events. In using them, all we can do is play around with them. This is why after thousands of years of philosophy we get more able to discriminate, but rarely does it feel that philosophers are engaging with their experience. The one exception to this was possibly Wittgenstein. He was definitely engaging directly with experience, and his students were terrified because he would pin them to the wall and demand that they answer in their natural mind without using complicated language.

> PAGE 62, PARAGRAPH 1: *This way of exercising the mind is circular; once it begins, it has no ending. Yet we keep going, led by hopes and wishes, trusting in mind's sense of right and wrong to determine what we should do. Fascinated by what might be coming up next, fearful of what might be chasing us from behind, our minds spin round like dogs chasing their tails.*

Those who care about the well-being of the world have to recognize that from the earliest times the human condition has essentially been unchanged. And there are no indications at the moment that it will change. We are spinning around chasing our tails and ornamenting our secondary percep-

Yes!

tions. Those ornaments manifest as better cars, planes and food, more efficient technologies and healthcare; but these developments are essentially ornamental in the sense that there is a basic structure underlying human behavior that goes unchanged. Though we have made technological advances it seems that human development has stalled. This is certainly the message gleaned from reading science fiction set in the future or the imagined past. How could it be otherwise if we're like dogs chasing our tails, running around with only secondary perceptions to guide us?

> PAGE 62, PARAGRAPH 2: *This ultimately aimless activity seems to characterize much of human experience. Whatever image or sound the senses present, whatever smell, taste, bodily sensation, thought, or emotion comes up, we generally go along with it, enjoying an imagined sense of freedom while following mind and senses like cows grazing on a hillside. Although time may pass pleasantly enough, if we pay close attention, we might sense a tiresome, dull quality clouding consciousness, depressing energy and eroding interest. Time slips away, and memory fades. Looking back, there may be very little we can remember.*

Consumerism does this brilliantly well—it creates a complete field of consumption within which we are free and are having 'a good life', but being manipulated by it. Not surprisingly, the regime of mind does exactly the same thing. You want stuff, it gives it to you, but it sets a boundary. The boundary is the regime itself. It can't give you more than what it has constructed. We could argue that this is not malevolent, it's just the way the machine works: you wanted this, I gave you this, there you are. You can't ask for reality, you have to temper your requests to what's on offer! If we are well-adjusted, we are happy consumers within a field of consumption that's been created for us. The good life comes and goes, and really, at the end of the day, there isn't much going on.

PAGE 63, PARAGRAPH 1: *From time to time, many among us do question the purpose of it all and wonder if there could be a better way. This question has inspired major changes in lifestyle, jobs, location, or partners. While such novelty gives hope that things will be different, without serious introspection and commitment to self-understanding, mind continues much the same. Attitudes and patterns regroup and new cycles of futility and discontent begin, with no clear path to lasting satisfaction.*

We might be thinking, "I'll get married, have kids and they'll go to school. That's the start of what looks to be a good life and I'll end up a serene grandparent on my porch surrounded by my children and grandchildren and horses in the paddock." Yet, in this projection there lurks an underlying feeling of futility, maybe even ennui, if that's all there is. With everybody having the same aspirations the whole setup looks like the product of a machine: your parents push you through high school, you get good grades, you go on to college to get a good job, have children, push them through high school to get good grades, go to college and get a good job, get married . . .

Does it ever end? There is no reason or set of conditions for it to end. There may be a variety of good and bad experiences, ups and downs, highs and lows, but if you look you'll see remarkable uniformity in the pattern.

PAGE 63, PARAGRAPH 2: *We like to think that we have the freedom to be and think as we wish, but it could be that all our responses have been prepared for us, and we are just acting them out. It is as if the gun is already loaded, perhaps with the wrong ammunition. Not knowing the proper target, we shoot at random, sometimes wounding ourselves in the process.*

The gun metaphor feels depressingly accurate. Historians have taken note of the sense of aimlessness that pervades the study of human life and development. There doesn't seem to be an inner logic to this history that points anywhere, so we have to ask if it's going anywhere at all.

> PAGE 63, PARAGRAPH 3: *Going along with the regime of mind, we may be unable to distinguish between what has lasting value and what is transient and unreliable, wasteful, enervating, and ultimately destructive. At best, we walk through life diminished, unable to access the full dimensionality of our human consciousness. At worst, we may find ourselves entrapped in a mind cut off from all sources of happiness, committed to patterns likely to produce hostility and paranoia.*

What the exploration in *Revelations* is fundamentally about is becoming fully human. It's less about escaping suffering and more about manifesting the fullness of human potential without becoming hedonistic consumers.

> PAGE 64, PARAGRAPH 1: *Just as each horse has its own gait, each person has his or her own way of thinking. But all thinking goes through the mechanisms of mind. So the question comes back, again and again: "Do we control mind, or does mind control us? Does mind own us or do we own mind?" If even raising this question is confusing, if our first impulse is to dismiss or invalidate it, it seems fair to say we do not know. Our language may not accommodate such questions well. But whatever the source of our confusion, it seems we need to act as though we are in control. Although the difficulties and dissatisfactions we experience reveal that our role is not always a happy one, we must maintain it for the sake of continuity.*

Far more satisfying than pretending to have control would be to actually exercise it: to take a fresh look at mind, study the nature of its regime, and open options for operating it differently. If we do not take this opportunity, mind will continue to build on patterns developed in response to conditions and absorbed into our sense of self. Relying on a regime invested in delusion, it will spin ever denser webs of interpretation, closing off alternatives and preventing us from savoring the richness of experience that is our birthright as human beings.

This is a call to arms, a call to take control. Ultimately, this is going to be a decision. It is a decision to part company with hedonic consumerism, which is essentially passive. What is being suggested here is that we make a conscious decision, with our eyes wide open, to take control and become active in a deep sense. It's not going to come about by accident, or because of some experience that we've had. At the same time, the decision that we make cannot be conceptual. When we realize that most of our so-called decisions have been conceptual, we eventually get to a point where we have to make a decision that moves in another direction altogether. This is a conundrum; an enigma. How do we do this? We will be carefully considering this point as we go forward.

> PAGE 65, PARAGRAPH 1: *Resentment, irritation, and agitation, anger, hatred, pain, agony and anguish—how often in our lives do such forceful negativities come and go? Their residues are deposited in consciousness and stored there like seeds that can sprout at any time. Between eruptions, they lie dormant, like fire under ashes, ready to burst into flame when the ashes are stirred.*

All the actions that we have taken create preconditions, predilections, and these can be likened to seeds. When the circumstances are right they will sprout and manifest. We all know what this is like: you have a bad idea about something, a prejudice about something, and then circumstances conspire to recreate exactly that circumstance. Our experience has this kind of rhythm, so although circumstances are changing all the time, events come around to give our preconceptions the conditions to manifest; and when they do, we get swept off our feet into action.

As mentioned earlier, we all have experiences that leave little residues inside us, whether it's getting into a fight in the morning and feeling bad all day, or whether it's a negative memory that gets triggered, and we end up getting into a conflict with someone without knowing why. These things persist, so as we get older there are more and more of them that have accumulated.

What we experience as 'reality' can be understood as the play of chance upon this accumulated history. We are often surprised by the 'turn' of events, unaware of this underlying structure. It gives us a sense that we're doing something with our lives.

In reality, we are cycling through incredibly rich, multifaceted and random processes with multiple karmic seeds, traces or preconditions generated by our previous activity that activate depending on the circumstances they meet. It's called secondary causation. We have predispositions to see things in particular ways, whether it's due to labeling or emotional residues, and then events trigger responses that we think are spontaneous, but actually are not. These days social media like Facebook track our predispositions and habits every moment of the day, reflecting back to us the products and services we are most likely to find attractive, capitalizing on the data collected to expand their business. With big data following our habits every moment of the day, they create an objective measure of who we are. If only we could know ourselves as well as they do!

> PAGE 65, PARAGRAPH 2: *Time has its own rhythm: there is a time to prepare the soil, a time to plant and to nurture, and a time to celebrate the harvest. In the rhythms of time, human beings are born and manifest, each one differently. Problems arise and become more complex; life fills with obstacles that we step around with caution and fear. We accumulate all kinds of baggage that we carry with us*

as deeply ingrained patterns. Unexamined and nurtured through repetition, these patterns imprison our lives and drain them of accomplishment and joy.

So, what's being said here is that living to our full potential means finding ways to be fully expressed as human beings. And what stops us from being fully expressed is our baggage of preconditions; we are full of loaded vectors. We are carrying all these seeds. As a result, most of us aren't uninhibited, and we don't want to be uninhibited because if we were we would be out of control—and with loaded vectors that is problematic. The fullest expression of human potential is about having the ability to purify and transcend this whole structure.

> PAGE 66, PARAGRAPH 1: *We are part of the human lineage; our genes reflect the way human beings have developed through the centuries. As participants in this heritage, are we content simply to repeat the same tired routines that have brought suffering to countless past generations?*

When presented like this, the need to understand the regime of mind can be properly set against human history, generation upon generation. If we don't arrive at an understanding of how we make our experience, the seeds that we are carrying will pollute the next experience—not only our own experiences, but those of the people around us, and those of our children.

> PAGE 66, PARAGRAPH 1, CONT'D: *While it may seem that we lack the knowledge and power to make a difference, it helps to consider that we have a duty, if only to ourselves, to recognize the misunderstandings that have slowed our progress and to acknowledge the extent of our ignorance. In doing so, we empower ourselves to shape our destiny in more positive ways. It might then be possible to manifest the full promise of a human birth and contribute this*

understanding to humanity. Is there a better legacy we could set in motion for the future?

So that's the call to arms. It is not to say we just need to have a good time, or that the answer is right there in front of us, that all we have to do is relax, it's going to emerge. We have to get a grip on our own psychology in order for this to be the case. If we don't do this, our hedonistic tendencies will precede us, and we will never see it clearly. It will always be a mirage—an image of what we want, shimmering up ahead in the distance.

Once we recognize that we are in a secondary readout, we realize that the primary events that shape our lives are happening before we are even on the scene. Because of that, human behavior always goes around in circles. It's not because we are bad people or because of some external factor. It's an internal factor. Recognizing that is really important. No external development will change what's inside. It can't. But we can change internally, and if we do so we are doing something really important.

> PAGE 66, PARAGRAPH 2: *At this critical juncture of time and opportunity, it is important that we understand how to manifest the joy of being. Sharing such rare and precious understanding could lead to a flowering of the human psyche that could foster inner and outer harmony for the benefit of all forms of life.*
>
> *Even if we do not presently recognize the true nature of our embodiment, we, as people everywhere, yearn to be free. We are born free, with no obligations; we are free to conduct our lives in the present, and we are going to be free in the future. This understanding is itself a kind of liberation.*

So the call to arms is really a call for freedom. It says that we are not truly free because we are trapped. All that we see and experience has already been processed. That is why we're not free. You can be the Marlboro man, get on your horse and ride across the Arizona desert. You're still not free. You can go on a spaceship to Mars. You're still not free. The display itself, however, can show us where freedom might lie. If freedom lies there, isn't it worth looking for? If it is, then it is worth exploring what *Revelations* has to teach. We will need a firm intent, and we will need to stop lying to ourselves. When we accept that there are problems, we allow the possibility that there might be solutions. As long as we don't fool ourselves into thinking that we're going to find those solutions overnight, we may be able to successfully develop a path toward a richer way of being.

* Can we improve the human experience toward Enlightenment, rather than toward "spiritual materialism," or is life on earth doomed to be what it always has been?

Did Buddha, Jesus, et. FAIL? Imagine how much life could be without them!

SECTION TWO

CHAPTER 12

Mirrors of Mind

PAGE 69, FRONTISPIECE: *Some of us have a meditation or contemplation practice to which we are committed. But if we practice without understanding the nature of mind, we may misinterpret what we experience, because mind is deceptive and does not reveal itself easily. This is what this section describes. But all of us can benefit from reflecting on this aspect of mind. Mind tends to give us what we look for, and following it blindly can entwine us in layers of confusion.*

In the second section of *Revelations*, we are following a classic path of study and practice. First there is study, here of the regime of mind, as laid out in the first section. Then there is meditation on what we have studied, which is the topic of this second section and the third section to follow. Finally there is the realization of what we have studied and meditated on, which will be the subject of the remainder of the book.

Another way of putting it is that the first section of *Revelations* is about 'the view'. In this case it's how the mind works; the fact that mind is universal, the fact that the ego is a linguistic construct—all that is view. Then the second stage is path. The idea is we take the view into practice and enter a system of mental development, bhavana as it's called in

Buddhist teachings. And then the third stage is fruit, the result of the mental development. View, path, fruit. So that's another way of analyzing this structure.

So here we are moving from study into practice by moving from the first to the second section of *Revelations*. There are a few things to say about practice that are very important. A path without a view is blind, obviously. A path without a fruit is pointless. However, the path itself is always misleading. Most religions get into fights over the path, rarely over the view. They fight over practice, and the problem is this: practice alters your perception. Obviously, it does—that's the point of it, isn't it? As a result, whatever we perceive the practice to be when we begin, the way we perceive the practice once we are on the path is going to be quite different. This means the path is always deceptive to us; that's to say we never quite know whether what we think we are doing is actually what we are doing. Because of this, it is wise advice to not get attached to what we think we are doing, because it will surely change. Actually, if it doesn't change, chances are we are not on the path at all!

We may think we know what we are doing when we start entering a system of mental development. But whatever we think we are doing will change if the system of mental development is effective. As a result, whether it's halfway along, or toward the end, we will look back at what we understood at the beginning and think, "That was wrong!" Best not argue with people about the path, because the chances are we will be fighting with ourselves at the same time!

This obviously makes the path very challenging. It's a bit like traversing the Taklamakan Desert, this journey between the view and the fruit. The Taklamakan is a 600-mile-wide trackless waste in central Asia near the Silk Road with almost no water. It literally means, 'go in, don't come out'. Like the Taklamakan it's extremely difficult to traverse the path, which is why so few people manage to do it. Because it's continuously deceptive, you end up having to rely on your view as a staff, a support, while at the same time accepting that you don't really know where you are going. You are relying on your foundation, your good roots, in order to traverse a terrain you don't understand. By definition you don't understand it, because you are developing your mind to understand it.

Nowadays the path is often assumed to be synonymous with meditation. This is actually a dramatic oversimplification. In Buddhist teachings at least, the path is a system of self-discipline that is combined with meditation, and within the self-discipline element there are also study, ethics and devotion. Because self-discipline, ethics and devotion feel a bit religious to Westerners, modern versions of Buddhist teachings tend to focus on the practice of meditation on its own and leave out the rest of the path. This is why Zen has been so superficially attractive to Westerners, because Zen appears to present itself as just meditation. But anyone who has studied Zen in any depth would know that's completely wrong. The Zen monks have tremendous discipline and ethics, and they also have great devotion for their teachers. But you can't write attractive Zen books unless they're just about meditation, and as a result Zen is often misunderstood.

We can also see a growing fascination with *Vipasana* or 'insight meditation', which is very popular at the moment. Like Zen practice, Vipasana as it's practiced in the West has been scissored out of a much bigger picture that also contains ethics, devotion and morality. It's been extracted from the Buddhist path as an isolated technique.

You could treat *Revelations* that way, too, reading it as a kind of sophisticated exploration of psychology without any religious, ethical or devotional elements; but that would be a disservice to the message that *Revelations* contains. If you treat it that way, you will never traverse the path. You simply won't. You will enter the Taklamakan Desert and you will never come out.

So we are now going to start down the road of looking at the path from the point of view of *Revelations,* which of course is from the point of view of the nature of mind. Nonetheless we must always bear these points in mind as we try to traverse this very difficult terrain. One might be tempted to read this second section as an extensive criticism of meditation, but this would be a misinterpretation. While the first chapters do contain criticisms for sure, they have been presented in order to inoculate readers who wish to develop a meditation practice free from the major misconceptions that make the path so difficult.

The first misconception is that meditation practice can stand alone without any other activity; the second is that meditation practice can be fully understood from the outset. The second is almost worse than the first—but they are both problematic. We have to have a degree of caution when entering a meditation practice.

You can develop meditation practice simply as a technique, and that's fine, as long as you know what you are doing. Many people will think you are denaturing a sacred activity, but actually you are not; rather you are being sophisticated about it because you recognize that you are not ascribing any value to it apart from being a technique. That's okay as far as it goes. But most of us enter a practice of meditation, or mental development, aiming to achieve some transcendental goal. If that is your intent, then be cautious about thinking you know what you are doing from the outset, or thinking that meditation can stand on its own without any other activity, because it can't. It needs to be embedded within a bigger picture.

There is one other thing to say about mental development that is helpful. The mind is like a universal hidden key. Like most seemingly omnipotent entities, it doesn't like being controlled; it resists it. It resists it for a very good reason. It's often called the 'monkey' mind, and like a monkey, mental activity jumps from one thing to another. From an internal perspective it appears to be doing that—there are all sorts of thoughts rushing around.

But on top of that, connected to this frantic activity but also distinguishable from it, there is a controller, a facet of mind discussed in the first section of *Revelations*. Remember, the controller thinks it has your best interests at heart. It has, after all, got you to this point in your life, so it resists analysis, understandably. It's a bit like a government: there are 'state secrets', things that you shouldn't know. There are also levers of power that the regime of mind will try and stop you from getting at—and for good reason. If people aren't prepared, when they get hold of these levers, they can do serious damage to themselves. There is a very deep intuition within our mental apparatus that we need to be protected from ourselves. So we have to be quite patient in order to truly engage in mental development.

Given this situation, many people, perhaps most people, make no progress whatsoever in mental development, literally zero. You can meet people who have meditated for forty years and are totally untransformed—exactly the same! They have just got this thing they do for an hour a day, and it doesn't do anything for them, nothing at all. That's because their mental apparatus never lets them get at the levers of power that would have caused transformation. They probably never even tried, because they didn't know what they were doing. So, one way or another, nothing happens; their meditation just becomes another activity about which they can then say, "Oh, I am a spiritual person and this is what I do for an hour a day." Even people who have apparently spent their entire life doing it are still pretty ordinary actually. In fact, you may find it very hard to tell them from anyone else.

That might seem a bit disappointing, but it's a demonstration of both how difficult mental development is, and how carefully controlled the overall mechanism of mind is. While the mind is turbulent at the level of what we are able to observe, beneath is a very deep level of control, and to access that level is difficult.

So to enter the Taklamakan we need a bit more than a bottle of soda and a T-shirt. To prepare, the first thing we need to do is to calm the mind. This means beginning to take the reins of the horse. Until we can show intent in that manner, we won't get anywhere. It's not only because all this turbulent surface stuff takes up our time, so we rarely have any attention span because we are always being dragged off of our feet by the next little turbulent thing! It's also because the deep controller won't take you seriously if you can't even corral this surface stuff properly. You've got to show yourself to be a serious contender. At the end of the day you have to persuade the regime of mind that you are a grown-up, that you actually know what you are doing. It's a negotiation. You come to realize that in many ways you are showing good faith to yourself by calming your mind. You are actually taking control, at least at the first level—and you are showing good faith.

In this regard the regime of mind can be described as a protector, but like most protective systems, it can be overprotective, and it can put protection above development. What we must do is make the case to the regime that we can be trusted with transformation, even though, by definition, if we are going to achieve transformation, we are going to lose its protection. There is a trade-off there, and for that to happen, a negotiation will have to occur.

The other thing to remember about practice is it's always provisional. If you develop a shamata practice, which is to calm the mind, it's always provisional, it's just a technique—don't go and hang your flag on it! Do a different practice next week!

one point

It's just a technique, so don't get hung up on one practice being better than the other.

There is view, path and fruit—always. There is a 'view, path and fruit' for the path, there is a 'view, path and fruit' for the view, and there is 'view, path and fruit' for the fruit. So, nine in all. With this in mind, as we are on the path, we are going to talk about the view of the path—just to set it up. We are going to consider how to approach the path. Of course, different traditions have different ways of doing this, because, as was mentioned, the path is deceptive and as a result there are many, many ways to approach it. It is said that the Buddha taught 84,000 techniques, although not all of them are recorded. But that's the idea, that for every mental affliction that we suffer from there is some sort of technique, and so there are said to be a very large number of techniques that could be used to develop the path. The important thing though is to understand the view of the path, because if you don't understand the view of the path, you've got nothing to rely on when you enter the Taklamakan Desert—you just enter this maze of experience.

Experience—we need to discuss this too. The reason the path is deceptive is because we are trying to traverse a system of transformation, self-transformation. As transformation occurs, we have experiences. Now even reading these words is an experience, but this is a mundane experience, a normal experience. However, you can relatively easily have extraordinary experiences—they are called *nyam* in Tibetan, or *nimitta* in Pali. These are experiences that you get in meditation when you do something unusual. Please bear in mind that such experiences are always deceptive. That is not to say they are not real, just don't go and build a house on them!

These experiences happen because we are shifting our perceptual frames; they are a byproduct of that change. That's why you get the famous Zen saying: "If you meet the Buddha on the road, kill him!" It's not because we are trying to kill the Buddha, it's because if you meet the Buddha on the road, if you meet the Buddha on the path, it isn't the real Buddha. It's just a reflection of your preconceptions of the Buddha evoked by changes in your perceptual framework. Because it is your preconception, this Buddha you meet is not going to help you, it's going to limit and mislead you. The real Buddha is beyond your conception.

In this regard there is a phenomenon that is a bit like beginner's luck, where new meditators can have amazing experiences and think they are enlightened—they get all kinds of ideas. These experiences can be somewhat problematic. They often happen when you first start a process of mental development, because the regime of mind has not yet got meditation categorized conceptually, and if the practice gets out of the bounds of normal experience, something really different can happen. It's a kind of 'Auntie wasn't looking' kind of thing. So when suddenly a weird experience happens, you grab it and think, "wow, look—I am enlightened!" That very statement is the regime itself reasserting control; "Oh, good, I've got him back in the conceptual box called, "Now I am an enlightened person!"

We can see what the regime does—it tricks us. It seems tricky to us anyway—but the protective instincts of the regime would prefer you to think you are enlightened and keep you in a safe conceptual box rather than have you get out of the box and into direct experience itself! The regime has neither a name nor a concept for direct experience, and that's extremely dangerous from its perspective. "Better to have the idiot think he is enlightened. At least we've got him in a box again. And then we can guide him around in the box, thinking he is enlightened, that's okay." That's because the regime doesn't care. It's not interested in what you think, it's interested in protecting you!

If experiences happen, they can show you that you are making changes to your perceptual framework, but they don't necessarily show you that you are making actual progress. Remember, this is the Taklamakan Desert—you can wander around in there forever, around and around, never really knowing where you are going. The scenery changes the whole time and there are lots of things that are very interesting to look at, but you never get out. You never cross the desert to the other side.

With this in mind, it's important to realize the difference between change and progress. We will come back to progress, because it comes up a lot toward the end of Revelations, particularly the question of how we can tell if we're making any. But as a general rule, you can tell you are making progress when you really are becoming more relaxed—less demanding, less paranoid. Funnily enough, "I am enlightened!" is not a very relaxed state. When you meet people who claim they are enlightened, they nearly always have this slightly edgy and uncomfortable energy. Often you have to kowtow in front of them because they are so enlightened, they can't stand it if you don't!

There is a famous example in Buddhist history about this, actually, when a Brahmin spat in the Buddha's face; there is a sutra that records it. All the Buddha's followers were really upset—it was an insult! But the Buddha was completely relaxed about it. He didn't care at all. Non-reactivity is a sign that progress has been made.

Another pitfall to look out for is fundamentalism, which crops up when people get a bit of experience on the path, and then they make it into the absolute truth. How often do we hear, "I've got this book, and I understand this book to mean this, and therefore this is how I will live." Because we know that we don't understand things clearly, we'd do well to remember that whatever the books might be saying, if we are really sure what it means, we are likely to be misleading ourselves. It's just the nature of what we are doing here—it will never be totally clear. So, those are all the caveats.

> PAGE 70, PARAGRAPH 1: *The ultimate role-player, mind has the power to create any object or image and report back to itself that what it has fabricated is real. Both steps in the process are necessary, for without them there could be no basis for further commentary or interpretation.*

When you pick up an object there is a process within perception. Say you look at a clock—there is the image of the clock, then there is the internal recognition, "Oh, it's a clock." That's a fundamental mechanism. It's like a game of tennis: there is a primary sense input, and there is an outgoing confirmation—it's in two steps. That happens when we are meditating as well—and that's the problem.

In this perception of a brown object with a white dial, there is a lot of mental activity: "Oh, it's a clock. Yes, I like that clock. No, I don't like that clock. Oh, look what time it is. Oh, I am late." Looking closely, we can see that 'I' turns up along with a whole bunch of associations. That 'I' is the frame upon which everything else hangs—self-identity, world identity, hang-ups, all of it. Self-reference is essential to the regime of mind as the anchoring point for networks of association.

So suppose we are going to meditate. We sit down, back straight, and say to ourselves: "I am going to meditate." Yes, 'you' are meditating. It's already begun, I am already in self-reference. I am meditating within self-reference right from the very beginning! The very act of you doing something is self-reference. You can see the difficulty. The problems presented by the Taklamakan start the moment we step across its border; we have deceived ourselves right from the very beginning. We may think that we are developing a great practice, but the practice is merely an extension of our regime—and it's been like that right from the get-go!

PAGE 70, PARAGRAPH 2: *We can see mind's genius for fabrication when we engage in any kind of silent practice with the mind—whether we call our practice 'meditation', 'contemplation', 'insight', 'silent reflection', 'prayer' or anything else. The moment we sit down, everything necessary for this process to unfold is already in place. Mind takes a position, setting the stage and supporting the central actor, 'I'. As 'I' watches, mind carries out its business, creating shapes and expressions that mind then comments on and interprets.*

There is the primary sensation, the reference and then the response, in which the internal voice says, "I am meditating." There it is: whether you name it as 'I' or just say "meditating," it makes no difference. That internal voice has created the whole metaphysical framework of 'you' 'meditating'. This is the first bit of the Taklamakan. No sooner do we step over the threshold of the Taklamakan than we get caught because we meditate within the concept of meditation.

PAGE 71, PARAGRAPH 1: *From its vast store of concepts, the mind in contemplation, the experience-seeker who yearns for total transcendence, brings up various expressions, moving with the 'I' to comment further, identifying, recycling, and validating its own interpretations and distinctions. When pleasurable sensations come up, mind interprets: "Yes, this is good, this is the way it should be, this is right," and we find ourselves thinking, "Now I am making progress." When the body becomes uncomfortable, mind says, "Perhaps I have been sitting long enough." Dialogues begin and interpretations and comments pass back and forth, weaving patterns through the mind that we relate to as real.*

In this situation, you might look like the perfect meditator from the outside. You might be sitting down to meditate, but actually you are in the idea of meditation, not meditation itself. You can be trapped there for a really long time, because the 'I' is already there. 'I' says, "I'm going to sit down and meditate with my back straight, ignoring the aches and pains, and watch my breath." It is completely within the structure. Actually, it is rare for meditators to escape the concept of meditation. As mentioned above, when people begin meditation, they sometimes have profound and extraordinary experiences precisely because they are beginners. These very experiences can lead people to be stuck in the idea of meditation, for having had those experiences, they will often try to recreate them. The memory of that wonderful experience is the very thing that traps you in the concept of meditation. You've barely started out, and the Taklamakan has already got you!

Taking these cautions to heart, perhaps we try to watch the mind. But this is another trick of the Taklamakan again. In all that dialogue, the meditator in meditation watching him or herself is all conceptual—all of it. The mind is watching itself, having created a watcher to do so! It's really tricky. And that is normally an impenetrable prison, because how do we ever escape from this self-reference that's happening all the time?

A very common technique is to say this: "Ok, there is all this noise, so I am going to settle into complete silence, and then, because it's totally silent, I will be able to overcome the whole thing." This is really seductive. The idea is that if all the mental chatter stops, we will be totally free.

PAGE 71, PARAGRAPH 2: *When pleasurable, ecstatic feelings arise, mind's commentaries continue, pointing out sensations and feeding back interpretations, associations, and meanings. Even when mind is lost and wandering, blanking out or following faint wisps of thought, its minding activity flows softly through awareness like a subtle undertow. We may even hear mind whispering in the calm—or even the deep peace—of contemplation.*

What is "chatter" & What is "thought?"

When we sit, even if we can develop enough concentration to settle into a calm state, unfortunately we are still within the regime. There is a famous story about the experiences of the great teacher Gampopa concerning this. In this period of Tibetan Buddhist history, there were still many strong Indian influences. Gampopa became a full bhikshu and he developed shamata, calmness meditation, to the point where he could sit for days in quietude. And famously, Gampopa came to see another great sage called Milarepa, and he said to Milarepa, "I don't know about you, but I can sit without a thought for a week at the time!" Milarepa famously replied, "My child, it's very lucky you came to see me, because had you continued like that, you would have been reborn as a formless god, and you would never escape samsara!" Milarepa was indicating that a state-without-thought is still *a state*; it's still within the jurisdiction of the regime. Even if you are reborn as a formless god, which is a god without the limitations of a body, you are still within the samsaric realm—you haven't escaped the mind at all. You are still within it. You are just in a totally calm place.

> PAGE 71, PARAGRAPH 2, CONT'D: *Shimmering in the background, immanent in silence, it is poised to intensify its minding the instant concentration lapses. Contemplation that unfolds this way is not likely to penetrate the closed shell of the mind.*

This can be seen sometimes in meditation retreats. Everything is very quiet as people meditate, then the bell rings and immediately chattering starts. The moment the bell rings—bang—mind can take over again. It hasn't gone anywhere at all; it's just waiting for its turn. And the moment the bell rings, oh, it's time to go back into the frame! This kind of experience is a good indicator that the meditation practice is being conducted within the regime. And effortlessly, the regime will re-establish itself: all mind did was give it permission, it didn't actually do anything else.

Now practicing meditation this way is not without value. The value is that the regime may take you more seriously. It has still got you fooled, but you are demonstrating a degree of control, because you can quiet down the trivial stuff. People who can do this have developed something of value. It's just not what they think.

> PAGE 72, PARAGRAPH 1: *Contemplative practices may in-*
> *troduce us to aspects of mind we never before experienced*
> *so directly. Observing mind in an open, relaxed way can*
> *reveal the essential insubstantiality of thoughts, the ur-*
> *gent promptings that arise spontaneously, and the ten-*
> *dency of thoughts to wander discursively among random*
> *themes and associations. The ability to recognize these*
> *patterns may clarify how we tend to engage problems in*
> *ways that fail to bring resolution. Sooner or later, contem-*
> *plation may lessen the hold of these patterns and brighten*
> *our outlook. Thinking we have found a key to a new and*
> *fulfilling way of being, we may be inspired by a fresh sense*
> *of meaning and purpose. But can we trust our discovery?*
> *Mind is deceptive and does not reveal itself easily; it tends*
> *to give us what we look for, and this can lead us on a path*
> *that entwines us in layers of confusion.*

By all means, if you can develop calmness, it is good and use-ful, but it is just a technique. Like any technique it improves with practice, and you can definitely cultivate the ability to observe your mental process and achieve a degree of detach-ment. Just do not think that you have escaped your regime, because you haven't, you are still within it—you just have a lit-tle more knowledge about the conditions in the jail, that's all.

One reads about Mindfulness Based Stress Reduction (MBSR) a lot nowadays, and the benefits it gives relate to stress reduc-tion, and importantly, an increased ability to take control of one's life. The MBSR techniques fall squarely within this cat-egory of in-regime practices.

CHAPTER 13

Watching the Mind

"Watcher all the way out..."
What's the difference between
infinite watcher)
one "+
NO watcher? -

PAGE 73, PARAGRAPH 1: *A common instruction for beginning meditation or contemplation is to "watch the mind." When we sit down to follow it, we may have a sense of facing forward, anticipating some sort of experience but not knowing exactly what to expect. We may be watching thoughts or counting breaths; we may be monitoring awareness, observing what arises in mind from moment to moment. Behind the watcher, there may be the sense of another watcher watching the watcher, protecting mind from disturbances and monitoring thoughts in the way a shepherd tends sheep.*

This is a bit like looking for the Loch Ness monster. We are told to sit down, watch the mind, and we are waiting for the Loch Ness monster to come, so we are sitting there, really trying to observe what's going on. Of course, what happens is that this thought drives all the other thoughts away, so we have the paradoxical effect of calming the mind while still being within it, because we've taken a big thought and pushed all the small thoughts away. And as long as we have enough willpower, we can keep doing that for quite long periods. But in the background, mind is shimmering, just waiting to get back in. The problem with watching the mind as a technique is that that thought, the watching thought itself, needs to be watched. So you can often get a sense of watching the watcher, which is like a thought within a thought. It can feel a little tense, but it is at the same time quieting.

> PAGE 73, PARAGRAPH 2: *"The way I know how to meditate is to have something to watch, something to do. So here I am, watching. The instructions say, 'observe the breath', or, 'observe mind', so that is what I am doing. But I have to do it very quietly and skillfully, so thoughts don't come up and distract me, I have to watch secretly, so my mind does not notice. If I do it right, something different will come up, some kind of feeling or possibly some unusual happening. I don't know what will happen, but it must be something different. If I just keep waiting, if I just keep watching. . . ."*

> PAGE 74, PARAGRAPH 1: *So we watch with a stealthy or sympathetic expectation, waiting for something esoteric to surprise us, something that has a different kind of flavor, something that tells us our contemplation is 'working' or suggests that we are 'getting somewhere'.*

This is why meditation experiences are considered so valuable by meditators. When you go and meditate in Thailand, the instructors always say, "What experiences did you have?" And what they want you to do is get your experiences out—"Oh, I saw the golden dragon!" "Oh, very interesting!" "And I saw this lake and . . ." They will listen patiently, and when you are done, they say, "Okay, let's go back and meditate again." They will offer you daily interviews where you get to talk about all these experiences with a guide. It takes a long time before you realize that none of it means anything much. It's important to get these things out of your system, though; otherwise, if you see the Buddha on the road, the danger is you are going to worship the Buddha. If that happens, you have stopped! They want to encourage you to keep on developing your capacity.

> PAGE 74, PARAGRAPH 2: *Perhaps thirty minutes pass, then forty or more. "My time is up, and I am still watching!"*

Then another day and another session that repeats the same pattern as before. Again watching, waiting, and looking, observing thoughts and feelings and listening to mind spin its stories. A sense of feeling arises; thoughts come, then possibly stirrings of emotion. Language comes in more strongly, interpreting these thoughts: "Now I see: contemplation means this, contemplation means that, I need to watch, I need to be aware . . . ."

As we are totally bound by language, we have experiences as our perceptual frames relax. "I saw the black-headed naga climbing up the temple steps!" We can get into a kind of metaphoric, mystical, weird language that we are excited about, but the fact is that these experiences are still about 'things', and we are still in the language construct. All that's happened is we've shifted our perception's sphere a bit so mind is producing some weird images for us—but it's still the same structure. That's the problem: we haven't actually escaped.

PAGE 74, PARAGRAPH 3: *Subtle currents of dialogues, sensations, and interpretations run through all this activity, rolling together and towing us along in a gentle yet mesmerizing flow that generates a sense of momentum. Words and comments bounce back and forth within mind, spinning out dialogues and interpretations and weaving them into stories. Using our own words, speaking to us with our own voice, mind relates its stories, telling us what is going on and responding to our questions as if addressing another person. It busies itself with inner dialogues: one mind talks and another mind responds, producing a stream of narratives that produce a comforting sense of continuity and intimacy between self and mind.*

Of course, writers know this. It's common to hear long-form writers report that at a certain point, the story starts generating itself, almost as if the story is writing itself. Mind can work with its own narrative structure in this way.

PAGE 75, PARAGRAPH 1: *Mind's dialogues draw us in, inviting participation. When they trail away, other thoughts drift by and more dialogues begin, back and forth, mind to mind. Some exchanges seem intense and serious, and we may find ourselves straining to listen, perhaps to identify who is speaking to whom and who is responding. Others are less energetic thoughts that tend to recycle the same bits of conversation over and over again.*

It's quite valuable to do this, although this is already quite an advanced level of noticing. We need a well-developed capacity for calm concentration before internal dialogues can be seen so clearly. But on the whole, most of us, when we begin to sit and when the chatter starts, will try to stop the chatter with the thought of silencing it. Don't! Listen to the chatter, allow the chatter, and if you do this what you are going to hear are dialogues going backwards and forwards, interpretations, experimental ideas, things that get triggered off other things—that kind of stuff. It is the association chains in action, the links that create the retinue that so amplify and muddle our responses in everyday life. It is good to hear them.

PAGE 75, PARAGRAPH 2: *This busy-ness of mind may dim at times, but it reemerges through periods of inner silence and blankness. It may seem as if someone were listening and judging in the background, ready to comment and interpret further or involve us in entirely new streams of thought. While we are quiet, mind is still observing and commenting: "Yes, I am meditating." "Now I am observing my mind." "Now I am watching out for thoughts." "Now I am watching myself watching out for thoughts." When our vigilance lapses, mind prompts us back to awareness: "Look here, look there, do this, do not do that." If it is drawn into a passing thought, it may elaborate on it until it discovers its distraction, corrects itself and regains its focus.*

Here is an effective meditation technique, if you can do this. Remember that we are just trying to watch. And if you do watch, if you set out with that intention, do so as if you were just doing an exercise. We don't have any intention of self-transformation by this—that's the point. We are doing this as an exercise before we enter the desert.

A thought carries you away and you come back to the meditation object. "Why can't I just sit without being carried away?" The reason is that your intention to watch the thought is itself a thought. It is like trying to dam water with water. It's always going to be swept away. You have to keep coming back again and again. The dam is impermanent; you can't make it stick. What you do develop is this concentrative ability to bring attention back to its chosen object. Once the object is internalized, this is called 'access concentration'. I am sure if you were to do it for a few years, and you were to take a PET scan before and after, there would be a change in your brain. You are exercising your faculties. This process of ruminating will never go beyond the level of thought however. Thoughts are watching thoughts. We're meditating within the concept of meditation.

> PAGE 76, PARAGRAPH 1: *So many times, so many sessions, so many weeks, months, and years, yet we may still be waiting, looking, and watching. There may be times when frustration breaks through: "I can't stand all this watching and waiting! I don't seem to be getting anywhere. But I don't know what else to do!" Exactly what am I watching? While we are waiting for something to happen, are we noticing what is actually happening? Mind is directing us, casting up thoughts, repeating instructions, ordering where to look and what to do. So are we watching mind, or is mind watching us? Who is watching whom?*

One of the things that happens is a sense of futility. If you meditate in this way you will never get further than when you started. You will develop concentration and restfulness, but it will never be transformative. We sit down to meditate. We

another dualistic description:
the act dualistic, n just the description.

give an instruction to our mental apparatus, "I now want you to sit quietly and I am going to watch you." The mind initially complies. All the time that the mental regime is creating that experience, it is operating without being examined. All we're looking at is its readout. We are in the readout looking at the readout. We're a thought looking at thoughts. The readout-maker is always hidden. It is never addressed.

Thoughts look at thoughts; mind looks at mind. Water builds a dam for water. Is that as far as we can go?

That's a really important question. The instruction 'be here now' contains within it the seeds of its own circularity. Who is this watcher who is going to 'be', where is 'here', and when is 'now'? If you try to be here now without any appreciation of these enigmas, it is a self-fulfilling prophecy in which ultimately the mind is watching you, while you think you are watching the mind. You are in a conceptual box called 'I am watching the mind'. The protective regime is actually happy enough with that—after all, you are off the roads, you are not going to kill yourself, everything is safe.

But if you ask who is watching mind, you are asking something quite different, and important.

> PAGE 77, PARAGRAPH 1: *Although practicing with these questions in mind offers a window into the workings of mind that would otherwise pass undetected among the distractions of daily life, within the stream of mental activity, its real purpose may be overlooked and its benefits lost. Mind keeps pointing ahead, deflecting attention from itself by holding out hope for the fulfillment of vague expectations that seem just out of reach. Despite ourselves, the focus of our watching shifts almost imperceptibly from watching mind at work to following its dictates.*

You can't watch mind like a wild animal in the garden. You can't hide behind the bushes and catch it working, because the looker itself is part of the readout.

So how do we make progress in this Taklamakan? We need to develop a capacity to concentrate. Then we have to use that faculty in a very precise way if we're going to be successful. We are watching the mind because we want to become enlightened. But enlightenment is just out of reach. Somehow, we think, if I watch the mind enough, I am going to be able to reach it. It's somewhere just there, like the Loch Ness monster. I've just got to find it, and then I am going to become enlightened!

You can see the trap here. It's a big trap, because what we are trying to grasp is something within the conceptual frame of our own experience. Once you see it, it's obvious, but it's very, very seductive, this idea that enlightenment itself is somehow within the frame of our own experience—you just have to get it, to do something: "This technique is going to do it for me, I am going to get somewhere." Of course, we will have experiences. We may even become more knowledgeable about our mental structure. But we will never understand ourselves, because we never ask that question, who is looking? We are always looking for something else!

> PAGE 77, PARAGRAPH 2: *Why does mind become bored? Because we are looking in the wrong direction—we are looking where mind is pointing, rather than looking at the source of pointing itself. Why? Perhaps we have not yet recognized that we could step back from mind and observe it in this way. Yet, that is what the instruction "watch the mind" is directing us to do: watch mind, take note of its tricks, and track its twists and turns. The moment language comes into contemplation, mind's regime comes into play, and that is the point where we should pay attention. We do not need to let this illusion-creating mind be the master. We might even ask, "Who is telling me to do this?"*

The first thing we have to accept is that mind is everywhere. That in itself is profound. Most people think that the world is

What is the evidence?

(everywhere, and the mind is in the world. Actually, the mind is everywhere, and the world is in the mind.)

The second thing is that language is the key. Why does language matter so much? This is because language lies at the base of the readout. Once you get a handle on language you can start to see the readout being made: this is where we need to look. If you just say, "I have to watch my breath," that is all within language. It's mind watching mind and thoughts watching thoughts. The frustration is that we aren't penetrating the readout-maker. We are just living in the results of the readout. We've adopted a new garb—that of a meditator.

When you look at the *New York Times* on Sunday, they have a regular article on meditation along with home cooking and decoration. It's regarded as just another consumer item. This is non-transcendental meditation! It is sad to think that we wanted to understand the whole of reality, but all we got was another idea we put up on the bookshelf. We meditate, do Tai chi, eat vegan and swim on Sundays—because we're still in the language bubble.

> PAGE 78, PARAGRAPH 1: *As watcher, mind still has a strong authoritative role to play. Even if we become highly skilled watchers, it is likely that sensing, or cognition, or mind itself is still playing subtly within the realm of mind. If so, mind is not yet free from its dualistic subject/object orientation. As long as we hold fast to this orientation, we will continue to play within the theater of mind, rather than observing mind itself.*

Now, that's the koan, if you like, the enigma, the paradox that meditation presents. How are we going to observe mind itself rather than playing in the theater of mind? How is that going to be done? And, if we could do that, then our meditation, our effort, would have a chance of transcendence. Otherwise, it's just going to be within the frame that we are already in— the theater of mind. Although we may look good and we may even sit nicely, if this isn't fully understood, it will always be a trap. There are many, many ways this is expressed within the meditation literature. Within Revelations the idea is this—how can we escape the 'theater of mind' to look at mind it-self? Is that even possible?

handwritten: maybe the theatre is the mind?

Exercise 8
Encouraging thoughts

Initially, it can actually be good to encourage thoughts. If you just sit there and say mentally, "Ok, I am going to meditate now," and just wait, initially the intention to meditate will shut everything out. Then that intention will fade, and then you will start getting internal questions such as, "What am I doing? Oh, I am doing that. Oh, yes, I meant to be watching!" You will start hearing a dialogue going on. This is quite interesting to hear, for those of you who have never heard it. It's like the mechanism, the mental structure, is extremely sensitive, irritable, to any kind of stimulus. It's ready to respond the whole time. The moment anything happens, it reacts to it and produces a dialogue; we have this incredibly sensitive and reactive system. When we first sit down to meditate you shut it all down temporarily with the thought, "I am going to meditate now." When that thought fades the shimmering activity of the mind starts up again.

Better initially start to think consciously, deliberately. For a few minutes, think about anything, everything, as hard as you can. Encourage one thought to run on to the next without a gap, really put effort into it. Then, after three minutes or so, just drop the effort and relax. Allow thoughts to idly come and go like clouds in the sky.

CHAPTER 14

Silence and Awareness

Right mindfulness is the last section of the eight-fold path in Buddhist teachings. The eight steps start with right view or right understanding; then comes right intention, which is trying to make good decisions for yourself; then right speech—not gossiping, slandering or lying; then right action—not stealing and deceiving; then right livelihood—not dealing in guns or drugs; then right effort; right concentration; and right mindfulness.

There are two key faculties to develop on this path. The first one is the ability to concentrate the mind, right concentration; and the second is the ability to apply the mind, which is right mindfulness. We need to make efforts to develop both of them. If we merely concentrate the mind without being able to apply it, we fall into trance-like states, which are states of pure concentration without any insight. On the other hand, if we try to meditate without concentration, we can get fleeting insights into who we are and what we are doing, but we can't maintain our focus because we haven't got the stability to hold them.

So there are these two aspects: the ability to apply; and having applied, the ability to sustain the application. In Pali they are called *vitaka* and *vicara*. In slightly broader terms, there are *shamata* and vipasana. Shamata, or calm state meditation, is about concentrating the mind; vipasana is the insight that arises from a calm and concentrated mind. Interestingly, vipasana isn't listed in the eight-fold path, even though the term is so widely known nowadays.

The main idea is that we have the capacity to be clear, but we are muddied by distraction. If we could just concentrate ourselves and become still, we would see clearly. We could apply that concentration. Muddy water is a good metaphor. If we have muddy water in a glass, we can't see through it. If we put it on a stable foundation such as a table and leave it alone, then it becomes clear. It's important to note, though, that once the foundation has stopped moving, the water settles all by itself. *water can't settle though it's own action.. needs the foundation to settle - non-action.*

All of us have extraordinary mental abilities, but they are distracted and dispersed; we need to allow them to gather together. Some remarkable examples of the power of concentration do exist: cases in which a child is trapped under a car and a young mother literally picks up the car in order to save the child. Where is that coming from? That's total concentration—the impossible that happens. We can see something similar occur in sports: good athletes can get totally concentrated and then they are able to do extraordinary things. This is the fruit of total concentration. Most of us only manifest that kind of concentration in extraordinary circumstances. Now we want to try and access that as a faculty so we could apply that clarity to our circumstance.

In this regard, meditation has an interesting history with regard to Western culture. Buddhist traditions during the early twentieth century were challenged by colonial Christianity. Westerners came with modern equipment and organizational skills and began taking over Asian countries. Naturally the local people looked at their own traditions and began to question whether they were effective. One of the reactions to colonialism was the development of vipasana meditation as a stand-alone technique in the 1930s. It came out of Burma in a movement led by a monk called Ledi Sayadaw. His idea was to downplay shamata, and all the religious overtones of Buddhist worship, and just stress 'clear seeing' or the so-called 'dry' vipasana practice. Coupled with this was an overt attempt to claim that Buddhist teachings are scientific, an idea promoted by an important Sri Lankan called Anagarika Dharmapala around the same period. This approach revolved around the claim that not only do Buddhist teachings get results, but that clear seeing is a parallel to scientific observation.

There is a lot of academic debate within Buddhist circles about what the 'dry' vipasana tradition is and whether it's canonical at all, because the Buddha was always recorded as teaching that we first need to calm and concentrate the mind through shamata meditation, and only then can we develop insight. So how can we generate insight without first calming and concentrating our mind? The way concentration is developed in the 'dry' vipasana technique is to stress the detailed awareness of everything you are doing. Such moment-to-moment concentration is claimed to be adequate to develop vipasana insight, even though there is no emphasis on sitting meditation to develop shamata first.

There is an important point here. Shamata itself is not unique to the teachings of the Buddha. In his search for enlightenment, the prince Siddhartha became a shamata master at the feet of two ancient Indian teachers, both of whom offered him leadership of their schools. He realized, however, that shamata alone was not enough, that it wasn't going to lead directly to liberation from suffering. The story is that following his shamata training he left his teachers to practice asceticism, and it was only when he abandoned that as well that he found the path to enlightenment. Something extra was needed alongside all the willpower he developed in his shamata and ascetic practices. We will also need to find that something else, no matter how much power we develop with a concentrated mind.

> PAGE 79, PARAGRAPH 1: *There are times when we are engaged in contemplative practices that we may experience periods of silence, when mind seems to let go of its usual way of minding. Directed to be calm and silent, mind may welcome the opportunity to slip into a relaxed, somewhat sleepy state. At first there may be a pleasurable sense of relief as tension melts and mind becomes quiet. For a time, thoughts may come and go peacefully, like soft clouds drifting through the sky. But if we sink more deeply into a blank 'not knowing' place, mind and senses can become so still and numb that thoughts and feelings simply cease to arise. At that point, we might enter the mental equivalent of a black hole, where nothing seems to be happening.*

Now, that is actually quite a common experience in meditation, particularly with the eyes closed. Technically, it's what the Tibetans call "entering the kunzhi." A lot of meditators think that it is deep meditation, because it is relaxing. A good example is after yoga; at the end of the class everybody lies down to relax, and then everybody enters a very calm, slightly blank state. It is often claimed that the purpose of meditation is to enter that calm state; your tensions leave you and you have a rest, essentially. And there is nothing wrong with it— it's in many ways very beneficial considering how much tension people have in their lives. However, it is not really what meditation is for.

When you concentrate on an object, there is often a tendency to zone out with the object in view, so you enter a kind of blank state in which the object is still there but you are in a blank state. It's almost like you have gone into aspic or gelatin.

not mind observing
not KUNZ Hi
not. what, then?

That state is also like this. But in concentration you need to look at the object! When you zone out, you cease looking. You kind of shut yourself off, shut down, so you become a bit like a camera with the shutter closed. There is a lens there but there is no one looking—you are absent. Just hanging there can't be a path to liberation, it can't be a path to transformation because nothing is happening, you are just zoning out. And so be careful of it because it's very tempting to think that's what meditation is.

> PAGE 79, PARAGRAPH 2: *We may rest in this sense of 'nothingness' a long while, immersed in a deep silence undisturbed by thoughts or any other kind of mental or sensory activity. There may be little or no awareness of our body or surroundings, not even a sense that time is passing. When we emerge from that state, however, what is the sum total of our experience? Nothing: a silent, negative nothing that seems the opposite of the awakened clarity we might have been expecting.*

This is an experience that one can generate quickly in meditation. It might not last long because something disturbs you or you get snapped out of it into reactivity. However, it is possible to calm the mind down until nothing but your attention is left. You are tentatively identified with it. It is just hanging there without doing anything. You are blocking the process of perception at its earliest phase, where impressions arise and the first movement of mind to identify them is occurring. Unfortunately, that phenomenon is not very valuable. Many meditators think it is voidness, but in Zen it is called false vacuity. Attention has stabilized at the very first movement of mind, but this is still within the regime of mind. It is just right at its very base.

> PAGE 80, PARAGRAPH 1: *Later, when we reflect on this experience, we may be surprised to find that mind has nothing to report, interpret, or even understand. Even so, we*

*may find ourselves thinking, "I was there, I was contem-
plating, and there was a flow of experience." Mind tracks
back, compares the experience with our expectations and
reports: "Yes, something was happening; there was a certain feeling—it was very deep, or maybe open, a sense of
something—something perhaps profound, but nothing I
can remember or describe."*

We have nothing to report about this state because the associative mechanism that the regime of mind uses to make
sense of the world requires the projection of a known label
onto an arising sensation. If you stop that process before dualistic consciousness has been projected, there is nothing to
be known. There is no possibility of association either because there is no point where associations can attach. Just
resting there in calmness does not in itself show a path to inner transformation.

> PAGE 80, PARAGRAPH 2: *Mind may take this further, "I must
> have experienced something—what was really going on?
> It was sort of—silent—dark—comforting, in a way, or
> warm. I don't have words for it, but I was meditating. I'm
> sure there was something happening."*

That kunzhi, the base, is sometimes mentioned in meditation manuals. This is the base we get to by deliberately developing calmness of mind. It is the base that begins the process
of projection. It is still part of the very mechanism we're trying to transcend however, for even this very deep experience
is still part of the readout mechanism of mind. It's not beyond it. It is calm, but not clear.

> PAGE 81, PARAGRAPH 1: *Quieting or calming the mind in
> this way is the basis for most meditative disciplines, es-
> pecially those practiced in the West. This kind of contem-
> plation eases the restless hunger of the grasping mind. It
> relieves the sense of need; it allows consciousness to rest in
> silence for extended periods of time, secure and protected*

from pain and emotion. Practitioners learn to detach from conceptual activity; if thoughts come, they are ignored.

This approach has benefits: it gives shelter, peace, and a sense of ease and confidence in one's embodiment. It offers some respite from the pressures of stressful lifestyles and promotes physical and emotional health. Practitioners become calm and relaxed, less driven by desire and anxiety.

Transcendental Meditation was very fashionable back in the 70s, when meditation was just coming into Western culture. T.M. is a very good example of hypnotic meditation that enters the base state of mind. The idea is that you calm the mind by chanting a mantra. You enter these very deep quiet states. People describe this kind of meditation as restful, that you can stop everything. For Westerners who are often stressed by work and expectations, this is a valuable experience. It is okay if you want to have a rest, but it will never lead to the readout-maker; it's within the readout.

PAGE 81, PARAGRAPH 3: *Those who practice for these reasons may see no purpose in analyzing the nature of their experience or investigating the possibility of accessing a more vibrant, energized state of being. But there is something static in this way of being, and practitioners could spend a long time in this dull, silent place. The mind's patterns of identity, recognition, and associations may be put on hold for a time, but they tend to regroup. All too soon, the back-and-forth movements of the dualistic mind revive the operation of self and other. The subject 'I' acts on the object, likes and dislikes come into play, judgments are made, and our mind-created reality unfolds as before. Unaware of possibilities for transcending these subtle deceptions of the dualistic mind, even experienced practitioners may not realize the outcome they seek.*

This quiet peaceful place is not the base of perception. It's part of the readout. The fundamental motion that causes the mind to grasp arising phenomena is based in fear, desire or indifference. These fundamental motivations are still present, but quieted. The actual readout mechanism has already been activated, but one is resting there. This resting state can be simply achieved by watching your breath, abdomen or an external object like a candle flame and developing the ability to watch without interruption. If you are able to do this for five minutes you will enter this state. You can then just concentrate on the state itself. You no longer need to watch; rather you hold the state of calm. It is very relaxing and nice, and many people who achieve this think that it is the final fruit of meditation. However, it doesn't really transform at a deep level.

We want to go further. We want to develop calmness as a technique, not treat it as an endpoint, for we will need to apply our calm and concentrated mind to something else.

In exactly the same way, the Buddha developed calmness meditation to a very high degree with his two Indian teachers, and then realized it wasn't going to liberate him. The moment of enlightenment was the application of calmness, those techniques, in the service of insight. The prince developed a capacity but was not taught the right use of it. He realized that for himself and was able to use that capacity to do something more that was far, far more important; that was the breakthrough.[24]

> PAGE 82, PARAGRAPH 1: *To ensure a different outcome, we need a completely different operation, founded on a mind that is clear and undivided, free of its present dependence on identity, perception, language, and the sense of self. But until there is a basis for understanding how this might work, the ability to introduce it is limited.*

---

24 See chapter 22 of the Lalitavistara sutra in new translation at www.84000.com; also Mahasacca Sutta 36 verse 34 in the Middle Length Discourses translated by Bhikkhu Nanamoli and Bhikkhu Bodhi, (Wisdom 1995).

Sometimes one hears that one has to find the gap between thoughts and then extend it. This is another path to the calm state. It will give a calm result but it will never penetrate the regime of mind. If you want to get out of a car that's going 100 mph, you bring the car to a halt. You've got the car stopped, but you haven't got out of the car yet. Even in the calm state we are not escaping the readout.

So how can we escape the readout? Once we understand what we're trying to do, we can make the transition from the still-ness of shamata, the skill of calming the mind, to the insight of using that calm mind to question our experience. Clarifying that questioning is the essence of vipasana. We all have a deep intuition that there is something else beyond the noisy mind. Every now and then we have experiences of it. We awaken into a sense of clarity that is not mind-made. We know it's there, but where is the path to it?

> PAGE 82, PARAGRAPH 2: *For some of us, contemplative practice may focus on becoming 'aware'. We give ourselves a very important task to accomplish through practice: "I need to work with my mind—I have to focus carefully, so my mind will not be distracted; I have to be aware and mindful." We proceed gently and quietly, feeling for what we sense is the right quality of contemplation, sensitively holding just the right position, as if we were balancing heavy jugs of water on our heads. "Be careful! Don't disturb the mind! Pay attention—maintain contemplation." Instructions take over, governing us, telling us what to do. Our minds become tense, compelled to echo these directives. "Be aware! Be sharp! Be clear! Focus on the instructions. Mastery comes through following instructions!"*

Mindfulness is often understood to be about grasping the present moment so as to be aware of it. Given that Nirvana is beyond grasping, one would think that one would realize that that couldn't be right, but if you read mindfulness writings you will often find statements to that effect. "The world is passing us by. We need to be aware of every moment of the day. We have to force our attention upon the smallest details, otherwise we miss what is going on in front of us. We're not mindful!" This view is sometimes associated with ecological, right living and political correctness movements. People try to control their manifestation to make it as mindful as possible. It leads to a really painful prison—like a feeling of constipation in which nothing can be spontaneous. One must be mindful—so how can anything possibly be spontaneous? Nothing is allowed to manifest that isn't held in this web of awareness.

This is the danger of technique and why techniques can be so problematic. In following a meditation instruction, it is important to be able to forget it. Being able to forget an instruction is much more difficult than being able to remember it. Often what happens when we receive a meditation instruction is we try to practice it and we get constipated. It becomes an obstacle to our entering the true state of meditation. We must learn to relax the meditation instructions so they cease to be a prison that forces us to do things.

> PAGE 83, PARAGRAPH 1: *Instructions are necessary to provide a certain level of guidance and encouragement. But since they arise within our familiar conceptual realm, they are readily appropriated by the operations of mind's regime, which repeats them at ever more subtle levels: "Be mindful! You will get lost! Be alert! Mind will fool you. Be vigilant! You may be doing the wrong thing." Even when mind seems to fall silent, it is subliminally whispering and admonishing: "Do this, don't do that, this is all right, you may do this." We do our best to stay aware, listening for whispers in the background. We become keenly aware of our senses, our ears very sensitive and alert, like deer.*

Here we have a classic problem. If you are following instructions, you are in a concept. So be cautious of meditation instructions that are complicated because the danger is that you will get yourself into this little bubble, where you are actually just doing your own thing—you are not actually doing *the* thing. In following those instructions, you may be reinforcing the very regime you are trying to escape. It's the ultimate subversion of intent. It is part of the enigma of trying to learn how to do something without the wisdom of knowing what it is. This is the reason why *Revelations* is critical of meditation practice in itself.

> PAGE 84, PARAGRAPH 1: *Some of us feel a strong need to adhere to this kind of approach. If we believe that awareness is the ultimate goal, we may tend to focus strongly on the need to be aware, even striving to be aware of being aware. Yet the need to be ready at all times to beat back intrusive thoughts and sensory perceptions holds us firmly caught in a subject/object orientation.*

This is really worth bearing in mind. When we concentrate the mind to the exclusion of all else, we are reinforcing the subject/object dichotomy with a great act of willpower and externalizing it onto the object of awareness. We should notice the contrast between concentration that is a state of tension, which is definitely "me against the world," and concentration that's relaxed, where the object of concentration is just the only thing present. The latter type of concentration is what we are seeking.

Concentration is subtle; it's not easy to concentrate in the right way, and most of us concentrate in the wrong way. Our very act of concentration is splitting the world into what we want and what we don't want, and that is by definition a state of tension. When we try to relax it, we are either so exhausted that we fall asleep, or all that distraction comes back like a coiled spring. The concentration we are looking for is to be just settled, like a mountain. We will consider the difference between these two types of concentration in the next chapter.

> PAGE 84, PARAGRAPH 2: *But it may seem we have no choice—we have to maintain the relationship between 'I' and 'my' mind. "Be aware!"... so we do not make mistakes. "Be aware!"... so no one can steal our concentration, so no distractions can come up. Some element of attachment, a sense of identity or possession, is at work, influencing mind and perceptions. We are still bonded, strongly tied to a mind that is functioning on the level of identification.*

The very idea that there is a right and wrong way is entirely based on judgment, the very mechanism we're trying to have insight into. It's a trap: the door to freedom turns out to be a dead end. When we open the door, it is just another corridor in the hall of mirrors. At the same time, knowing that calmness itself is not liberating is helpful; knowing that following instructions too literally cannot liberate us is also helpful. We know two important things now, and they are going to help us develop a genuine heart of meditation.

> PAGE 84, PARAGRAPH 3: *For those new to contemplation, this focused way of watching mind can be a useful training. But it is difficult to say whether it can actually lead toward liberating mind. The ability to trace the process of cognition and the interactions of thoughts and senses may not be sufficient to free ourselves of mental and emotional obscurations. To penetrate and eliminate subtle and persistent afflictions, it is necessary to take clarity beyond the level of possession so that it becomes indestructible.*

This sentence needs repeating. *"It is necessary to take clarity beyond the level of possession so that it becomes indestructible."* What are we talking about here? There is a little glimpse of something important. It is a very, very big statement.

> PAGE 85, PARAGRAPH 1: *Meditation, prayer, and contemplative practices can relieve pain and lessen our burden of suffering without being sufficient to quiet the business of mind. When we identify with our practice, we tend to project our own expectations and concepts into the meditation*

experience and set ourselves above or apart from it. Mind understands and supports this position, prompting us to take control. For instance, we find ourselves thinking, "I can tell the difference between a good practice and one that does not work for me." Again, mind may cast the self as the beneficiary of contemplation, prompting other thought experience: "Oh, I like this feeling! This is great! This is it!"

One goes from guru to guru, teacher to teacher and religion to religion looking to find authenticity. Knowing that authenticity won't be found just in calmness or in awareness gives us a real head start. It may enable us to avoid the common pitfalls that bedevil so many meditation practices. The fact that we see many images of the Buddha in meditation does not mean that meditation is the only path to liberation. Why don't we see the Buddha eating lunch or cleaning his teeth? Did the Buddha meditate all the time? This gives the impression that this is all there is to do. This is a misunderstanding. Meditation is a tool, and we need to develop the faculty of concentration. Using that faculty, guided by wise analysis, we may be successful in finding a way beyond the regime. We are not going to find it by just sitting quietly or by watching the mind however. It is necessary to take clarity beyond the level of possession so that it becomes indestructible! Suddenly we see the difference between mundane meditation that might calm the mind, that might even reduce thoughts, and a *Revelation of Mind*, which is transcendent beyond the level of possession.

Exercise 9
Internalizing stability of mind

Light a candle, and look at the flame in a concentrated manner. Really look at it hard and try to return to it whenever you get distracted. A thought may come along, and you lose it. The moment you lose it, go back and concentrate again.

Do this cycle ten times and stop, and only repeat the exercise the next day. After a few days, relax a little and try to feel the state of concentration itself. When you are really looking at the candle can you also feel that state of concentration? Can you feel what it's like to be concentrating? Do that ten times or so, and then stop.

When you become familiar with practicing shamata by watching a candle flame and developing the ability to concentrate and dwell in it, then just sit in that concentration. Your awareness will stabilize and settle. It doesn't matter what you concentrate on—a candle, your breath, your abdomen or anything. Concentrate firmly on it, then dwell on that concentration. For example, you can experience the whole body of the breath. By so doing, you are moving with the meditation object: instead of concentrating on it, you are experiencing it. Then start feeling what being concentrated is like and just hold that sensation. That internalizes the sense of concentration itself as the meditation object. One moves from the external object to the internal object, to the sensation of being concentrated. One can then just settle in that experience of concentration.

If you do this you've internalized stability of mind. The idea is to move from concentrating with an object to concentrating without an object. Once you realize that you can concentrate without an object, it is liberating. You can concentrate whenever you like. In the middle of whatever you're doing you can just concentrate. It's like doing pushups. Most of us find it challenging initially. As a faculty, however, it is useful to train the mind. By doing this you are beginning to take control of the reactive mechanisms that drive you to create the world of your experience. It's a first step toward going beyond the regime.

CHAPTER 15

The Problem with Ownership

Vitakka is the Pali word for fixed concentration, so it's the ability, the faculty of being able to hold the mind on something and not move. It's a very common meditation technique. In Hinduism it is called *trataka*, and it's widely practiced and very important. If you just practice fixed concentration, however, there is a tendency to narrow focus so much that a trance state occurs. This is a common mistake in meditation; if you concentrate on an object to the exclusion of everything else, you get into a trance-like concentration. You are concentrating the world down to one thing.

The other important term is vicara, the ability to appreciate a held object. Just practicing appreciation without concentration is to fall into distraction however, and that's another extreme. What meditation is trying to achieve is a balance between these two, vicara and vitakka together, so that you are concentrating, but at the same time you have a kind of global awareness, an appreciation. One way you can access this is by concentrating on an external object, developing familiarity with that feeling, and then relaxing the focus so it is not held exclusively on that single object. In Tibetan this is called 'relaxed' *shineh*, being-concentration. The idea is you concentrate and then you learn to relax that sense of concentration into global awareness. That relaxation in the Pali tradition is a balance between vitakka and vicara. So vitakka is like striking a bell, while vicara is enjoying the sound. Vitakka is hitting a post into the ground; vicara is the post quivering as it is struck. We are trying to train the mind to make it malleable, relaxed yet focused.

You often read in spiritual texts, "you must relax!" Relaxation is often associated with lying slumped in a deck chair, but that is not what is meant here at all! An accomplished musician embodies the kind of relaxation we're talking about here. That person has practiced scales for years and really developed the capacity to play a musical instrument; that is vitakka. But then, in a performance, the musician can totally relax and enter the music; that is vicara. Such a musician never forgets vitakka, but vicara is necessary for an expressive and musical performance.

A famous example of this is the recording of Bach's Goldberg Variations, played on the piano by the virtuoso pianist, Glenn Gould.[25] When you listen to his marvelous rendition, he is actually humming to the music at points in the recording! So that's his vicara—he is completely relaxed, he is having a good time, while he is actually playing a highly technical piece of music. But that's what makes it a great performance—it's exactly that. That's the union of vitakka and vicara together— that's what we are looking for. There is no single word for it. You could say 'mindful relaxation'.

Mindfulness, when it's practiced by beginners, can make them very tense, kind of uptight, as they are trying to be mindful all the time. Of course, that's definitely an extreme. In some traditions, such as the Thai, they encourage equal amounts of sitting and walking meditation; the idea is that in walking

---

25   Bach, Goldberg Variations, BWV 988, (Columbia Masterworks, ML 5060).

meditation you are going into movement to encourage a more relaxed attention, while at the same time remaining mindful.

We need to develop these faculties, not for martial arts or playing the violin, but to become masters of an incredible instrument, our own display of mind. But mental development, *bhavana*, is not an end in itself. We are not trying to beat ourselves up to get supernormal powers, or to break through to another reality, which again is a very common misconception of bhavana, unfortunately sometimes promulgated by a misunderstanding of Zen. Bhavana is an important faculty in the path, because through bhavana, we develop more and more insight, and we have more and more capacity to generate insight, because our mind becomes more and more focused and malleable.

Chapter 15 of *Revelations* centers on another obstacle that comes up, even if we have developed a balance between vitakka and vicara. This can be called spiritual materialism. We need to be motivated, but the danger of motivation is a sense of ownership of the result. It's a bit like balancing vitakka and vicara, but now at a more internal level. How do you generate motivation without falling into the trap of ownership?

Self-identification lies ultimately at the root of all our problems, but it's very, very, very deeply rooted, and difficult to access. On the whole, when we go and do something, we do it for us, even if we say we are doing it for someone else. We are doing it for someone else—for us! That's why we get frustrated when we are unable to achieve our aims, because something is being taken away from us.

If we were completely free of self-motivation, if obstacles came but we just kept on going without being upset, then that really would be something! But who is like that? Only in that state would we have truly achieved the overcoming of spiritual materialism. For us there is a different game, however: we can use our ambition to transcend itself. You could argue that's completely impossible, that you could never achieve it. But if we didn't have any ambition, it's hard to see how we would be motivated to do anything. So, there is a very deep enigma here, running through the spiritual path. The paradox is that we are setting out to transcend our setting-out.

> PAGE 86, PARAGRAPH 1: *Because the sense of ownership arises automatically as soon as mind labels a perception, it's difficult to avoid it, whether we focus on the inner workings of mind or on external objects. Awareness of an object activates the polarity of the dualistic mind, compelling mind to establish the object's position. Responding to a "longing to belong," mind posits a subject: the notion of 'I'. And in this single step, mind validates 'I' as subject and me as owner: "This object belongs to me," "this object is mine." Wherever 'I' manifests, ownership appears also.*

Something arises in our awareness, we name it, and then a little voice goes, "Yes, that's right." That naming is a subtle level of self-cherishing. Having named it, we come in as the knower of it. So actually, there is a double layer to the ego: there is operant ego, which is the knower and doer of everything which we examined in section one of *Revelations*, but underneath that there is an earlier sense of self, one who doesn't even speak, just a movement of inquiry. It is subtle, hard to get at, because that sense of identity has already been established in the earliest stage of knowing.

Even if we think we have completely overcome our knowing ego, this internal identity has already manifested. As we saw in the previous chapter, just resting there in calmness is not going to reveal it. We need something else.

We can develop bhavana and train our minds to be malleable and flexible, but this in itself does not reveal this fundamental volitional self. To do this we need the tools to be able to see it, the faculty called vipasana. That primary volition, that very first layer of volitional formation, that fundamental klesha, right down there at the very beginning, is active even in our meditation—that's why ownership becomes the issue. You can see its results when you become a practiced meditator: you have a feeling, "I can do this stuff." That's it, there it is—some sort of primordial feeling of self that's layered over the true nature of things, and swimming in that fog are volitional formations that happen before our senses even activate. Even though we may think we are having a pristine cognition, untouched by the human hand, actually that guide is already there, because that's the validator, confirming that our cognitions are correct.

> PAGE 86, PARAGRAPH 2: *Having created this product, mind tends to follow up as if we were customers it wished to satisfy. Encouraging thoughts may come: "I had wonderful insights—truly blissful feelings, I felt on top of the world! I can tell I'm getting into this practice; I can sense it in my body and my feelings."*

Our perception is conceptual. Everything we see we are conceiving as such, which is why we know what it is. As you begin to come to the level of the concept-maker, the concepts begin to change; they loosen, they become less fixed, and that creates experiences, the so-called *nyam*. They are very exciting: "I am really making progress now!" "Things are happening!" Always the advice is, "Be inspired by nyam, but never share them as if they are important!" The reason you don't share them is that if you share them, you are by default taking ownership of them, so you are reinforcing an unhelpful mental structure. Report them to a meditation guide, but don't share them as if they are valuable. It's a bit like a sugar fast: you say, I am going to go on a diet and I will stop eating sugar, then after a few hours you are desperate for a cup of tea and a biscuit! Ego is a bit like that. You get withdrawal symptoms. So sharing meditation experiences is like, "Ah, great, I'll have a biscuit now." "I have this experience, I have that experience, this happened to me, that happened to me." Sharing such experiences is just an expression of possessiveness, not different from saying, "I have this car, I have this picture, I bought this house." The great master Chogyam Trungpa wrote a book on this very problem, when Tibetan Buddhist teachings were just beginning to find a Western audience.[26]

Nyam do have some importance, though. They demonstrate directly that the perceived world is constructed. If we weren't able to demonstrate that to ourselves, then we would have a real difficulty with the classic outlook that regards the perceived world as absolutely real. The fact that you can demonstrate to yourself that your experience is actually a construct is an important element of the path. It's very motivating, because it shows, yes, at least something is happening here, I am not completely trapped in aspic, stuck with my concepts. So, in terms of strengthening intention, will, the wish to get on with it—nyam play a role. But if you share them, they reinforce ego possession.

> PAGE 86, PARAGRAPH 2, CONT'D: *I have a very satisfying sense of fulfillment. Before, I felt so conflicted and frustrated, but now I am feeling more confident and 'together'.*

One often reads articles concerning MBSR—Mindfulness Based Stress Reduction—making these claims. "I had this. I had that. This is good for me. That's good for me. This makes me better. This makes me . . ." There is now an entire industry based upon the benefits of meditating to the meditator. The whole point of meditation is to take you beyond the meditator. Here we've got an industry that advertises the benefits of being a meditator!

26 Chögyam Trungpa, *Cutting Through Spiritual Materialism*, (Shambala 1973).

PAGE 86, PARAGRAPH 2, CONT'D: *Thoughts are not pressuring me so much and my positive feelings are more intense. I feel less agitated, more relaxed, more in touch with myself. I am having many good experiences, so I must be making progress. This is definitely worth doing!*

While nyam can be inspiring, they don't indicate progress per se. Instead, nyam indicate that you have discovered the potential of progress. Progress occurs when you begin to relax into the thing that caused the nyam in the first place. So another reason not to share the nyam is that you risk turning these nyam experiences into a product that you are generating or consuming, and what that does is keep you at the door of the path—you never enter the path because the door is where these experiences are. You are so busy consuming experiences that you never go in, because the moment you go in, you can't share the product anymore. So, although nyam show you that you are on the path, they are not in themselves a guarantor that you are making progress.

Making progress comes from something else. Some people have a lot of nyam, some people don't have so many. Some people's perceptual frame is highly strung and consequently, when they relax, they have many experiences. Other people are less rigid, and so when they relax, it's not so dramatic. This means that the person who gets lots of experiences isn't necessarily making any more progress than the person who doesn't.

In conclusion, when we get experiences, they confirm our intuition that working with perception makes sense. But too much enthusiasm is itself problematic. That's why sometimes advice is given to make a routine out of meditation practice—to meditate at the same time every day for a fixed period of time, because that de-emphasizes expectation. But that, too, can create a problem. If meditation just becomes a habit, it ceases to work. Stability can easily turn into blankness, and if that happens you will want to break up the habit by suddenly practicing in the middle of whatever you are doing. "Meditate now, just now!" That's good, too, to break the habit that you formed by meditating at just one time during the day. We have to learn to play with the path, to master it, because we are always trying to find the middle ground.

If you regard meditation as a skill, it can be quite helpful. It makes it easier to get your head around the idea that it isn't something elevated and esoteric. The problem is that meditation has become synonymous in Buddhist teachings with 'spiritual practice'. Actually, it's not spiritual practice; you can meditate without any spiritual interest at all. Meditation is mental development; it's a skill, just like being able to juggle a football a hundred times. If you regard it as a skill, then you realize that just like with any skill you're trying to learn, be it meditation, violin-playing or soccer, the world doesn't help you—quite the reverse! It endlessly tries to distract you. You have to have that stubborn wish to do it and not get too hung up on an outcome.

All we are doing is developing a specific skill set. People seem to get very excited by scientific studies about monks with electrodes on their heads. Everyone is amazed when monks' brains are different from the brains of normal people. Of course they are different! They're meditating for hours a day—what do you expect? Similar studies show that London taxi-drivers have a big hippocampus because they have to learn every road in London—their brains change.[27] It doesn't mean anything, apart from that. Some say, "Ah, I've discovered the secret of meditation—it's in the frontal lobe," or something similar. It's because they don't understand that meditation is

27 Eleanor A. Maguire, David G. Gadian, Ingrid S. Johnsrude, Catriona D. Good, John Ashburner, Richard S. J. Frackowiak, and Christopher D. Frithl, *Navigation-related structural change in the hippo-campi of taxi drivers,* (Proc Natl Acad Sci U S A. 2000 Apr 11; 97(8)), 4398–4403.

just a skill. If you look at a wrestler, he has got big biceps. The only difference is that the skill of meditation gives you the capacity to do something else.

So to meditate well we have to learn how, having focused our attention, we can relax and yet our attention remains one-pointed and does not wander. That's a very, very specific skill. An expert meditator can just rest their mind on any object and be completely relaxed; their attention just stays there. That capacity leads to tremendous energy, because of the focus that can be bought to bear. For most of us, when we try to achieve focused attention, we think, "Ahh—now I have got to focus," and our mental energy becomes dissipated in effort. It's when the focus becomes effortless that it becomes truly like a laser; it's not being wasted on anything. That capacity is strongly related to the skill of a martial artist; in many ways they are identical. It's the ability to be completely concentrated and yet completely relaxed at the same time.

> PAGE 87, PARAGRAPH 1: *From this perspective, 'I' am not only the customer who collects and seeks to own experiences, but also the benefactor and recipient, the one who gives him- or herself the benefits of contemplation. 'I' am also the one who profits from it, the one looking for something better with every session. Many individuals engage their practice in this way: "This is my spiritual journey, my true home, and I am committed to it. I am getting tangible benefits, and I am proud of what I have accomplished. It gives me a sense of peace and fulfillment. Nothing else engages me in the same way. I have to have it."*

Many meditators have an internal commentary about their achievements, and this can be motivating. If they don't realize that the mechanism of mind is generating it however, it will ultimately lead them to a dead end. It will become a possession. Ultimately, the mind will say, "I am a great meditator," like being a great pole vaulter or being really good at yoga. Unfortunately, that's as far as they can go, because that sense of owner-ship is a limitation. Ownership itself is a cap on how far we can go from the house of concepts in which we live.

PAGE 87, PARAGRAPH 2: *Such thoughts motivate practi-tioners and encourage them with positive expectations. When an experience gives us pleasure or satisfaction, we tend to identify with the activity that produced it, so it seems natural to consider a spiritual practice as our per-sonal possession. In time, this approach to practice can take on a quality of compulsion—we have to do it. That is why the motivation is effective.*

So, developing meditation requires effort, but we need to be very skillful how to apply the effort. If you meditate at the same time every day, that's good, but it's also good to medi-tate without any warning. We have to be like this. Don't be like someone who does just one thing, and has to do it only that way; if that is how your practice has developed, you know you are getting locked into a cage. And that's not what we are about here—we are trying to get out of the cage. There are things we need to develop, without question—we need to de-velop one-pointed relaxed concentration. But the mind of the meditator should be pliable, like dough, able to conform to anything. It needs to be flexible, no lumps in it. A good medi-tator can deal with changing circumstances—they haven't got any issues, they just do that, do this. That's one of the ways you can tell you are making progress.

Progress doesn't come from experiences; progress comes when you find yourself more flexible, more relaxed, more able to deal with changing circumstances. You are not sleepy-re-laxed, you are just more flexible, and so change doesn't throw you off. If you find yourself saying, "Oh, I've got to get back to my shrine room—look at the time, I've got to get going!" it's worth remembering the famous yogi, Milarepa. Some of his most important songs came when he had been in meditation for weeks and weeks and somebody gave him a cup full of barley beer: and then, all these amazing songs came. Sometimes it is like that—it's when you break the routine that real insights can happen.

> PAGE 88, PARAGRAPH 1: *Ownership can also exclude and separate: "I deserve these rich feelings, because I have a long-standing investment in my practice. Others do not have the same kind of investment in their own path. I am more protected and secure, so I do not have to go through the same hardships as they do. I understand what they are going through, but I am not necessarily involved that way anymore."*

One can feel almost like a member of an exclusive club in which a skill has been developed, and that skill has been conflated with liberation. But if you really have a skill, like skill in carpentry, and someone else doesn't have that skill, there is no cause to feel exclusive. It's only when it comes to spiritual development that this can become a problem. The skill of shamata gets mixed up with the transcendental idea of liberation. That sense of pride becomes truly exclusive, a feeling that 'I'm further down the path toward liberation than you are'. These can be subtle feelings, because being inspired by one's progress can contain this dark side of pride. One has to be alert to this feature.

You will not overcome pride by merely suppressing it, however. That is not understanding it. If you are making progress, as long as you understand that it's within the regime, you will not have that pride, any more than a carpenter who is teaching a novice how to cut wood has pride. You know ultimately that the progress you are making is within the constraints of dualistic mind. That is the best antidote to spiritual materialism.

> PAGE 88, PARAGRAPH 2: *When these kinds of thoughts come up, it helps to realize that our positive results are*

being undermined by the mind's insistence that the bene-
fits 'belong to me'. That is the nature of mind; that is where
we are. We cannot yet stand on anything better.

Tibetans have a great metaphor. They say that seasoned practitioners can become like the leather bags that they use to
store butter. Gradually, the leather hardens and hardens with
the butter, until it becomes almost indestructible. You could
bury it and nothing would happen—it becomes almost like
rock. Long-term meditators can get like that because their
sense of ownership gets wound into their meditation and
they get totally cut off from progress. They've gotten as far as
they are going to go; they can't go any further. Often you hear
them say, "I know what I am doing, I have my way of doing it."
There we are—their ego has found a new home, a meditation
home; they are a 'spiritual practitioner'.

The Zen traditions are very much interested in this problem.
Recognizing that it is possible to deepen experience through
shamata, they then try to break up and challenge that stability. How difficult it is to forget the sense of self! It's almost impossible. There is the beautiful sunset and we just want to be
there, but somehow 'I' am there. This is annoying and difficult to overcome. It is spiritual materialism at its core. It manifests as accumulating initiations, becoming proud of one's
progress, becoming critical of others and becoming jealous.
Even if none of these things manifest and we are somehow
pure in our relationship to our practice, it is likely still based
on a sense of self. Even if we have a high degree of self-discipline, it doesn't alter the fact that it is based on a sense of self.
Even if we generate self-loathing and self-criticism, they are
still based on a sense of self. All of these things are still spiritual materialism.

PAGE 88, PARAGRAPH 3: *When 'me', 'myself', and 'my expe-*
rience' are central to our perspective, we may feel a strong
need to protect them. If we lack awareness of what is

happening, we may cling tightly to this me-centered realm, which wraps around us like an impenetrable shell. Now we have locked away everything that contemplation would normally nourish: a sense of the wonder of being, an open, receptive attitude, and awareness. Even after practicing various methods and techniques and taking many classes, programs, and retreats, even after a long spiritual journey, this may be where we end up.

This is a precise definition of what can be called 'spiritual' rather than physical materialism. It comes when one has taken ownership of the path. People often begin with a sense of openness and wonder, but too soon, that gets condensed into a technique; then they are trapped. Our best remedy for this situation may be to develop a beginner's mind, so that we can play in our practice; we should never allow ourselves to become expert at it. As soon as you become 'an expert' at it, it ceases to be fresh.

So here's our challenge: to avoid becoming an expert, while at the same time becoming completely proficient. This is another example of the middle way: we want to find the middle way between being an expert and being an amateur, always bringing that freshness to bear. If we try and do that it undercuts this sense of ownership, which otherwise becomes almost inevitable. We can then taste the true fruit of bhavana, fruit of insight, which is to catch sight of the knower itself who creates the ownership that limits us.

> PAGE 89, PARAGRAPH 1: *So sad and limiting, this sense of ownership that separates and isolates! Sad because we will have to struggle a long time before we can let it go. Sad, also, because we cannot manifest and share the true benefits of contemplation.*

There is a famous statement made by the Buddha: "If you have a mountain-like ego, it is easy to deal with, but if you have a sesame-seed-like clinging to emptiness, such as selflessness of ego, that is a far greater defilement to defeat." If there is this sense of ownership in our practice it is very, very hard to get to, because we cannot be surprised by anything; we know it all. So, when we meditate it's good to play around with our practice. It's just a skill, there is nothing special about it.

Often, we want to make special places, shrines to help support our efforts. If you are a magician, if you really know what you are doing, and you want to do magic, then having a shrine can be very powerful because you make it into a device that you can use to amplify your intentions. But having a shrine as a meditator can in some respects become problematic, because it produces a sense of ownership—"I've got this beautiful shrine. I have these lovely Buddhas. I've got all these nice statues I've collected. It's my thing." Shrines have an important purpose, but if you can meditate on the bus, it is probably better than in the shrine room, because the fresher the circumstance, the better.

> PAGE 89, PARAGRAPH 2: *However we name our method of practice, as long as it involves mind, tendencies toward ownership are likely to emerge. If we allow mind to nurture them, the result will most likely be misunderstanding and disappointment.*

The door we seek is hidden from us. In developing this skill, this flexibility, there will always be a tendency toward ownership. But as long as we know that, we are forewarned about it, it's not going to trap us. We can even harness the sense of ownership to motivate us. The great adept Shantideva said that the only illusion we can keep on the path is the illusion that we will become enlightened! The sense of ownership can be a great motivator as long as you can play with it. The trick is not to let it trap you.

Exercise 10
Concentrating without an object

Continue with the concentration exercise, a few times a day.
The core activity is developing concentration. Take any object, concentrate on it, and return to it when you get distracted. Having done that about ten times, if you can feel what
that state of concentration is like, try to hold the same sense
of concentration without an object for a few minutes. Then go
back to concentrating with an external object again. In that
way move from concentration with an object to concentration without an object.

You can do so many shamata exercises. It is not complicated
to develop these techniques. There are forty different ones
recommended in traditional Buddhist manuals. You can take
objects, colors and perceptions—there are so many things
you can use to concentrate the mind. Remember, though,
that the concentrated mind is a valuable tool, but it is not the
same as liberation.

CHAPTER 16

Getting What We Look For

As we turn to this chapter, it is time to fully define the second term: vipasana. Vipasana is normally described as clear seeing. That's because the term *pasana* means seeing. *Vi-*, on the other hand, has three meanings: it can mean 'discriminating', but it can also mean 'through', 'clear', 'intense' or 'total'. You could call vipasana strong, clear or intense seeing, although normally it is translated as insight.

The fruit of the combination of concentration and flexibility is right or clear seeing, vipasana. Because vipasana has been labeled as a meditation technique, people confuse vipasana as a path element, but it's really a fruit element—it's about clear seeing. And indeed, on the occasions when it is referred to in the Canon, the Buddha goes into states of concentration, the jhanas, then as he comes out of the jhanas back into waking experience, he sees clearly, he sees intensely—vipasana.

Vipasana is to see that we are in this readout, this amazing display created by our mental apparatus, structured by language in which we appear as an actor. The display is a seamless phenomenon—a memory we call the world. It might be only a quarter-second-old memory, but the known world of our experience is a memory. It is because we're unaware of this that we are ignorant of our true situation. No matter how much we know about black holes and neutron stars, we are ignorant if we don't know that our entire experience is a read-out made by our minds.

There are three fundamental obscurations we suffer from: anger, desire and ignorance. Ignorance is the hardest to see and the easiest to overcome—for once you see ignorance, you are no longer ignorant. In that sense, it's simple. But the read-out is very difficult to see. The readout is pervasive, it's both internal and external. It pervades so totally and with such seamlessness that it's very hard to penetrate it. Vipasana is the ability to penetrate through this veil of ignorance.

Just as the maker is invisible, so we are ignorant. This is 'primordial' ignorance, ignorance we carry with us all the time, whatever time it is. It is there as we live our lives—being successful or failing, getting or losing, loving, hating, wanting, not wanting. All the time we are suffering within a production whose creator, whose director, is unknown to us. Whatever we do, no matter what situation we are in, if we are unknowing of this creator, we are ignorant. That is the foundation of our experience that can't change, because we don't know where it's coming from.

Whenever we ask, "Who are you?" the question just echoes back; we can't directly confront the maker because the questioner is part of the maker's creation. We may have gotten that far conceptually, worked out that much, but now we are going to gear up, we are going to arm up with meditative power, with concentration and flexibility.

Don't forget that the maker is highly protective, rather like an over-protective maiden aunt who is trying to look after us, to guide us through the difficult world. Consequently, when we do something, the maker tries to make a success of it. One of the examples is in meditation. We sit down in meditation with huge expectations, and the maker provides exciting experiences! The mistake we then make is to think we are making progress; of course, we aren't. We are still ignorant, we are just ignorant in a specialized way, in an unusual way of being.

> PAGE 90, PARAGRAPH 1: *"But, wait! Before I started this kind of practice, I had lots of problems. Now I have had a peak experience—the ultimate, most blissful experience imaginable! My whole perspective has changed! I have truly opened to love."*

There are lots of meditators who say words like that, and lots of religions seek ecstatic states. From the *Revelations* perspective these states are viewed with a degree of caution, because statements made when experiencing them may not be reliable. The mistake is to think, "That's it, I've got there. I've got into some fantastic spiritual realm!" If we think we have a new possession, a new way of being, that immediately starts creating problems.

> PAGE 90, PARAGRAPH 2: *Yes, sometimes spiritual experience awakens a very deep devotion that can focus on our concept of God or spirituality, on humanity, on specific persons, or on symbols or other kinds of objects. We are enraptured, as if we had fallen deeply in love. We are totally convinced: "This is what I have been looking for! I am happy, I feel fulfilled. My life is perfect just as it is!"*

When we begin to meditate for the first time, we don't have any preconceptions or experience to muddy our preconceptions, so we can give very clear instructions to our minds. Often, we get a very big payback. The problem is, having got that payback, we then confuse our own expectations with that payback and consequently the mind is not quite as responsive next time around. Indeed it is easy to get stuck in a concept of what it was that we had in the first place, stuck in a loop of expectation.

As mentioned, many people say that their first meditations were deep, easy and oceanic. Then they lose that feeling. This is because their subsequent meditations seek to repeat the experience, so they are in the idea, the memory of that initial meditative state. Their experiences are second hand, and then it's a long slog. Sometimes people sit on their cushions for years waiting for that peak experience to come back again.

> PAGE 90, PARAGRAPH 3: *Many practitioners have peak experiences, especially in the early stages of their practice. But, this, too, takes place in the realm of mind. We may have been anticipating a certain kind of experience, and now our mind is accommodating us in a way we expected. While we may feel that we have attained what we were yearning for, what we have actually attained may only be a satisfying relationship with our own experience.*

We are not going to escape our minds' nannying enthusiasm for looking after us from within our minds. We can learn from our experiences of meditation and we can get an impression of how the mind works, but we cannot escape the mind from within mind. In many spiritual traditions there is what is called a 'crisis of faith' at this point, an invitation to start beating ourself up. The story of the Buddha's search for enlightenment contains just such a period, where he practiced severe austerities, having failed to liberate himself through shamata meditation with his first teachers. That doesn't work either, because actually, if you give the mind the instruction that you wish to starve yourself, it will go along with it: "If that's what you want . . !" So you are not going to escape the mind like that, either.

> PAGE 91, PARAGRAPH 1: *Mind has the power to express itself in many ways. From one moment to the next, it can arouse passion, love, or joy, or possibly their opposites—dullness, anger, crushing disappointment and dissatisfaction. In its positive modes, mind can congratulate itself: "Look! See what wonderful feelings I can give you! You could wish for nothing better! This is such a great method, such a powerful technique!" Yes, but we have to remember that all kinds*

of expressions—positive, negative, and neutral—are man-
ufactured by mind. The seller is mind, the customer 'I' is
mind, the expression is mind. And mind goes to negative
places as well as to happier ones.

Our customer 'I' that receives the fruits that we instruct the
mind to give us, and the fruits themselves, are all within the
regime of mind. They are just specialized parts of the readout—we haven't escaped it. You can become clairvoyant, see
previous lives or even see the structure of the universe, and
remain within the readout of mind. These skills do not mean
that you are enlightened. Often gurus and teachers have developed these powers, but it does not mean they are enlightened either. If you want to develop these powers, that's okay,
but it is part of the regime. It is not seeing the regime.

PAGE 91, PARAGRAPH 2: *The real problem is that this mind*
is not likely to go where it has not been before. However
ecstatic our experience, it is likely that we are still within
the illusion-making realm of mind.

This is key: you are never going to escape the inferential hall
of mirrors using the inferential hall of mirrors! Whatever
truth it is can never be something you are going to find, like
a pot of gold at the end of the rainbow, or a diamond lying in
the mud. The truth we seek is not within the inferential structure. More than that: it can't be. Ultimately, spiritual seekers
who are seeking the truth will always fail, because the truth
that they seek, if it's actually truly beyond their experience, is
beyond their experience. They'll never find it, because they
can't. It is not possible.

Most of us are literally like the drunk guy looking for his keys
in the dead of night under a lamp-post. When you ask him
why he is looking there, he replies it is because it's the only
place he can see! Once we realize that, we realize how stupid
we sometimes are on our spiritual quest. What we seek is not
going to be where we can see it!

PAGE 91, PARAGRAPH 3: *At any point, with any practice, if we become attached to our accomplishments and hold on to them, we may not be able to recognize and deal with the real enemies that are blocking our path. This is a serious obstacle. Whatever we may feel we have achieved, this is not the place to stop. Instead, we can take a fresh look at our observations of mind. Are we unknowingly falling into the very patterns of self-deception we had hoped to transcend? We can check to see if we are holding tightly to a position, or if there is a subtle—or perhaps even obvious—self-orientation.*

Even if our spiritual quest appears to be going well, and we are doing our yoga, and we are meditating, and we are eating healthily, riding a bike, yet we are still unable to recognize the real enemies that are blocking our path!

"Oh, dear! You mean the complete 'spiritual wellness' movement is a fraud? You mean, our real enemies are invisible to us? We don't know what they are?"

For example, that feeling of achievement when one finally gets success in one of these exercises is actually self-orientation. When you're doing well and you say, "Wow, I've done that," that's the moment to ask, "Who's done that?" The universe trembles when someone directly asks that question!

The way vipasana is usually taught is through skills such as stability and observation. But who experiences those insights? Who knows that you can watch the breath? Who knows that you are doing this? This is a huge question. We like to settle in to meditative states. They are very calming. We can sit quietly and feel happy that we've achieved something. It's calm and enriching. The famous Thai monk Luang Por Toon called this "sleeping on the cushion." You aren't really addressing the knower.

Asking "who knows this?" is a turning-within. This turning is essential if we are going to find anything new. As long as we aren't able to turn within, we are within our projections and all we are doing is changing the scenery in the projection from a non-spiritual to a spiritual version—but we are still within it. We have to ask the question; we have to take a fresh look and ask.

These are really valuable points of self-examination. Ideas about the goodness of our meditation, about the progress we are making, are self-orientation. They are cloaked in the robes of congratulation—but underneath the robes is 'me' doing well. Another aspect of self-orientation is when we become attached to things that 'work'. If we find that we are attached to things that work, we are undoubtedly holding to a position, and within that there is going to be a little 'me' who says, "This works. I am going to keep doing this, because it's really good!"

> PAGE 91, PARAGRAPH 3, CONT'D: *We can note whether we are observing in a detached manner or are rewinding and repeating our own experience. Are we experiencing just what we expected? If so, are we grasping the experience or feeling possessive of it?*

Grasping and feeling possessive are fundamental mechanisms by which we construct the world. If we have been able to develop stability of mind, vitaka, and mindfulness of experience, vicara, we are able to look at what we are doing and ask these questions. Otherwise, we can't even begin to turn around and look. It's too noisy; we just get swept away.

We have to keep turning toward the knower. The regime will always try to configure itself to be the questioner, but we have to question that questioner. This process takes a long time and lies right at the heart of the simplest meditation. Once you have developed the ability to concentrate on a candle flame and hold that concentration, then it is time to ask the question, "Who's doing that?"

It's a strange question. It almost feels like an impossible question because you're asking the question of nothing. You ask, "Who knows?" But there is no one there. We will have to spend time working with this. By doing this we are doing something totally different from many other meditation techniques. We've turned the tables. Instead of facing the readout, we are facing the readout-maker.

> PAGE 92, PARAGRAPH 1: *It is important to understand that we get what we look for, and our expectations of where to look and how to look may mislead us. Mind is only too ready to point in the wrong direction. For instance, when mind and body grow restless or cause trouble, we may escape for a time into the peace and silence of contemplation, and mind may support this move with a gratifying sense of accomplishment. But eventually we have to come back to the same situation. Have we looked in the right place?*

The assumption here is that we've developed some faculties of mind. Our meditation has stabilized to the point where we are having experiences—nyam. We are getting good feelings; we are getting insights. Those are accessible to us. With that, vipasana can start—it requires that kind of stability. It is not something you can just ask, because it's extremely difficult to ask these questions of ourselves. They are powerful questions if you can ask them. Without asking them you can develop deep shamata and vipasana within conventional understanding, and yet not escape samsara—unfortunately. And indeed, the history of Buddhist teachings is littered with monks who apparently were greatly accomplished, but who then started to fight over trivial matters. At the base of their practice there is a fundamental blindness: who is practicing? Who is developing these capacities? They are not an end in themselves, they are a means to a greater end that is hidden from you.

This is not suggesting that this sort of radical inquiry should be the dominant element of any meditation practice. It's really exhausting. The best way is just to do the shamata practice and suddenly without any warning ask, "Who's looking?" It's like the question pops out from behind the woodwork. It is an antidote to falling asleep within the practice.

Ignorance is pervasive, everywhere; we need to take care that 'who's looking' does not become a fixed practice in its turn. If "who's looking?" becomes a practice rather than an inquiry, the regime will reincorporate it, get behind it and hide.

> PAGE 93, PARAGRAPH 1: *The only way to be free is to clear our mind of all residues of grasping and identity. We can begin by taking advantage of opportunities to investigate what lies behind our anger, anxiety, frustration, guilt, and other manifestations of negativity. When these patterns come up, we lighten up the urge to escape and turn to face the troubling thought or emotion directly. We can pronounce its name, examine it, study it intently, and bring it closer and closer to us. When there is nothing between us and the perception, just seeing, with no associations or interpretations, the focus of our attention will open up, and its character will change.*

This is true vipasana. Vipasana is an attitude of mind, based upon a mind that is clear and calm; on the foundation of clarity and calmness, this sort of self-examination can occur. And the moment it does, things fall open because of 'vi' and 'pasana'. Remember: 'vi' means discriminating, intense, clear and thorough. 'Pasana' means seeing. In this self-examination, you divide, and you see.

We want to face obstacles directly. Without the armor of conceptualization, it is a very different and naked experience. Our words cover things up. It is almost like we have to become a child again, and find the experiences that are cloaked by them. But most of us cover our experiences all of our lives. We say we've solved a problem when what we mean is that we've conceptualized it. Actually, most problems are internal, and all that conceptualization is just pushing them away. To face a problem without pushing it away into concept is to experience whatever the problem is invoking—be it frustration, guilt or anger—really experience it, really explore what is happening.

It's very interesting when you do this. Emotions that start out as one thing mutate when you face them. For example, you might find behind the anger lies guilt. And behind the guilt, regret. And behind the regret, hidden memories of loss. The whole thing unpacks, like a series of Russian nesting dolls. That is what it means to face obstacles directly.

The external manifestation of the someone who annoys or angers us is a secondary cause. The primary cause of the obstacle is always within us. A lot of what we do in *Revelations* is working with this situation, because the external and internal are locked together. When we start realizing this deep and profound truth, we can turn and look, and the world changes. Everything starts mutating. This is vipasana. Now we are starting to see clearly.

This means that meditation can come off its cushion. One of the great weaknesses of shamata meditation is that it is stuck on a cushion. After we get up off the cushion, it's all gone. It's like we can only do it sitting still. There is no point just staying there longer and longer. What is more practical is to take a little bit of vicara and use that as a hook, so when we face obstacles directly, we can experience them, face the obstacle and pose, "who are you?"

When we do this, our meditation is totally freed from the cushion; that becomes the least interesting place to meditate. We are seeing clearly. We're not caught up in the display. We're starting to undermine the fundamental obstacle of ignorance. Ignorance is the display: it isn't real. That's the thing that's trapped us. This exercise in facing obstacles directly begins to dig us out.

PAGE 93, PARAGRAPH 2: *Since these patterns come up natu-rally within the operations of the dualistic mind, we may need to confront them many times.*

Because we are developing a capacity here, in its initial stages, problems are our friends. If we had no arising negativity, it would be very difficult to develop this capacity. Once we no longer push things away into the conceptualized memory we call the world, but rather accept them by facing them to see what they actually are, we find powerful forces of transfor-mation. Otherwise our whole experience is made from layer upon layer of conceptualization that in the end becomes a prison called the regime of mind. But a very simple thing un-locks something powerful.

PAGE 93, PARAGRAPH 2, CONT'D: *But eventually they will weaken, and in time may not come up at all. We might regard this as a way to immunize ourselves from the tyr-anny of mind's regime.*

The tyranny of mind's regime is that the mind, in giving us the world, isn't giving us control of itself. It gives us a world in which we can operate, but we are second-class citizens, if you like, because this world we are given is structured in a way we don't understand. But if we turn and face it, we can see it. We have that capacity. We can take ownership of our seeing.

We have always been the receiver of our seeing. Normally we are sitting there 'in the movies', watching the show. With vi-pasana it is as if we are saying, "No, I am going to see the mov-ie projector. I am going to take control." And the moment you do that, the movie ceases to be a movie and becomes your own expression. You are no longer caught up in the story.

The tyranny of the mind is not in what it does, but in the fact that we can't escape it. That's what makes it tyrannical. The moment we escape it, this tyrannical thing becomes an expression of who we are. It can even become enjoyable, because we've got control. It's the same display actually, but the very tyranny becomes an ornament, because we have taken control; we have generated vipasana.

> PAGE 93, PARAGRAPH 2, CONT'D: *As we gain confidence and certainty, the force of grasping and identity will weaken, and we will not be thrust so easily into painful situations. In time, we become stable, free of negativity, able to transform obstacles as they arise.*

Now, that is the practice of vipasana. It's a fruit. It's the result of being calm and clear so we have clear seeing. When we have developed the capacities that give us clear seeing, then we see clearly if we know where to look. The result of such clear seeing is that our problems begin to transform themselves, and we achieve freedom within our own experience.

> PAGE 94, PARAGRAPH 1: *For this we do not necessarily need a special situation, a complex system of practice, visualizations, or direction. Any time obstacles come up, we can be warriors, without fear. When we practice with this understanding, obstacles can become our partners, our friends, our energy, our wisdom, and our path, for we will have a different way to deal with them.*

Now, this really is the preface for the second half of *Revelations*. This is where we learn how we are going to transform obstacles into a path and how in so doing, they dissolve into wisdom. Obstacles, path, and wisdom are the very same thing—there is no difference.

We are not going through a series of different insights toward some mystical peak of enlightenment. It's right here in our present experience. But neither is it some revelatory breakthrough that happens suddenly. It is this inner turning, this turning within, that's the key to it. In developing concentration, we need to develop flexibility. If we don't have flexibility in our concentration, we are not going to be able to turn; we will be stuck with our spears pointing forward, even if our enemy is behind us. We have to develop the ability to be fluid and flexible, and once we have that fluidity and flexibility, then it's possible to make such an internal turning, if our inquiry is guided by the right understanding of our actual circumstance.

Exercise 11
White ball

Three times per day, imagine a white ball on the tip of your nose. As you breathe in, the ball moves away from you into the distance. As you breathe out, it comes right back to rest on your nose. Do this ten times. Continue with the concentration exercise with a fixed object, or the sensation of concentration itself, a few times per day if you have time.

Visualizing and concentrating on the white ball is vitakka, and allowing the ball to move as you breathe whilst holding attention on it is vicara. This can be an absolutely beautiful exercise, if you develop it. Imagine the ball moving away from you as you breathe out and coming toward as you breathe in. You can do it the other way around, it doesn't matter; the idea is that the ball is moving away and then coming toward the tip of your nose.

This exercise can be developed further. Imagine the ball goes further and further away with every breath, starting by going a few feet and back, then to the edge of the room and back, then to the front of the house, then to the local town, then the state capital, then the national capital, then the edge of the country, then right to the edge of the planet, then the moon, the sun, the nearest star, the galaxy, the next galaxy, further and further away and coming back with every breath until eventually it goes off the edge of the universe and into infinity before coming all the way back to you. Allow the ball's travel to expand steadily, a few breaths at each stage so it is stable there before moving on. This is combining both vitakka and vicara with an exercise of expanding and developing your sense of awareness.

CHAPTER 17

Cutting Through Mind-Business

Vipasana is often taught solely in terms of its result, which is seeing clearly, rather than the path to get to that seeing, which requires both stability of mind and the attitude which questions directly. We might understand this conceptually, but this questioning should be understood as a moment-to-moment inquiry, an attitude of inquiry, rather than a question one asks once that could have an actual answer.

This question does not go away with an answer, because we are continuously, moment-to-moment, being seduced out of direct experience into a construct containing fixed entities in time. That's the seduction the Buddhists call samsara. Samsara is not some 'thing' we are in, and vipasana is not seeing that 'thing'. Vipasana is to see the moment-to-moment seduction where we replace our actual experience with a reified entity that we've constructed, and within which we then make a life, with all its happiness and sadness, ups and downs, and endless confusion.

This is not to say nothing exists. It's just that the world that we know and whatever exists are two different things. The world that we know is a construct. Vipasana is the moment-to-moment seeing of that construct. And the circularity of life, this term called samsara, is the moment-to-moment ig-noring of actuality and the buying into that construct. It's a choice. It's an existential choice.

Some religious people have to crank themselves up into this kind of existential choice through self-denial and all kinds of extreme activities, like the anchorites in early Christianity who used to sit on top of pillars in the desert for days at a time. It's hard to understand it, but they actually did that. Lots of re-ligions have that kind of thing—very extreme—for people to push themselves into this existential choice. Indeed, in Bud-dhist teachings too there are practices called *dutong*, where monks do extreme things, like not sleeping for days. The prob-lem these practices address is that we are seduced—we are kind of sleepy, we are kind of comfortable in this illusion. We are just like cattle in a slaughterhouse that haven't realized yet that they are going to be killed. Many Buddhist writings are about being kind of asleep, not realizing that the end is coming.

Revelations is pointing to another way we can approach the same existential issue. The question is, what am I choosing? Am I choosing the sleepy world of things, beings, and times? This is a question we need to ask right now—not tomorrow, not after a meditation session.

But it's a catch-22 situation, in that the very tools that we think we have are the very things we have to overcome. We get caught out. We have to become very familiar with this some-what complicated terrain. We really need to generate genuine insight about how we make the world. If we really, really un-derstand that, then we have a chance. But if we don't have a real insight into how we make the world, all we are going to do is make a spiritual world, and call it vipasana. The demons would just laugh at us!

The word 'revelation' in the title of *Revelations of Mind* was very carefully chosen. A revelation is an ongoing process. One of the reasons why the term is used is because it is pointing to a process rather than a discovery. There is no thing beyond our concepts: things *are* our concepts, and that's the problem. What we are actually talking about is a way of living that's beyond our concepts, but it's not a thing, so we can't discover it! Furthermore, we can't achieve it and we can't live there—all these words are words that are constructed around the conceptualized world. Our entire language is constructed around a conceptualized world. But it doesn't mean that there isn't something to do.

We are looking for a right attitude of questioning. But anything we write down or think as an answer to such a question is wrong! It is the exploration that matters. We are on an interface, and that interface is very important. We are on the interface between our sensory inputs and the knowing of them—that interface called *nama-rupa*. And that's where it all happens.

Ultimately, we will have to generate a new attitude to confront the existential reality of being.

> PAGE 95, PARAGRAPH 1: *Contemplation is intended to free us from the pressures of self-image and obligations, from ego and emotions, and from the limitations and distortions that result from conceptualization. The aim is to allow mind to rest on neutral ground, free from assumptions and associations that support self-oriented views.*

We are not talking about getting anything; we are talking about taking things away. This is really important to understand. The whole idea of spiritual attainment seems to imply that there is something to get. Actually, it's what you get rid of that is the attainment, not what you get. For vipasana, unfortunately, one thinks, "Oh, I am going to be calm and clear. I am going to get calmness and clearness." No, you are not! Vipasana is to get rid of agitation and being muddled.

"investing in loss"

PAGE 95, PARAGRAPH 2: *If we have such expectations, we may be willing to work patiently with all the mind-business that drifts through our contemplation. But this is like cutting through a very thick jungle one tangle of vines at a time. We watch thoughts, wrestle with pros and cons, push and pull with likes and dislikes, notice weaknesses and needs for improvement, follow interpretations and trains of thought. Since such 'mind policing' interferes with contemplation, we may feel we need to intensify our efforts to concentrate. But the more effort we put into observing mind, the more active and agitated it becomes, so that pressure builds up. We may become frustrated and discouraged, either thinking that contemplation is too much work or else blaming ourselves when we sense we are not getting a good 'result'. But this frustration may be difficult to acknowledge. If someone asks, "Is your understanding of mind improving," the answer is likely to be, "Of course. I am genuinely involved with this practice, watching and analyzing mind."*

As an exercise, periods of introspection are actually quite valuable, although rarely done. But if you try to use introspection to break through to something that's calm and clear, you cannot. The very activity you are undertaking is guaranteed never to break through. . . . It can't break through itself, so you end up in this weird situation where you are watching, as if somehow by watching it's all going to disappear and lead to this calm and clear state—but how? When you actually think about it, it's hard to understand. All this does is create pressure, and the mind will respond to that pressure by raising the temperature, and so you get into these states of tension.

You sometimes see people who practice vipasana a lot who have a kind of tension about them. They can be quite shiny, but there is this sort of clipped cut-and-dryness about them. That's the attention that they are trying to cut through with. What they rarely have is a relaxed calmness and clearness.

There is always a sense of tension. They are trying to observe; they are doing what they have been told to do. "If you observe enough, something is going to happen." By observation you can generate a lot of mental power, so you will get a lot of intensity, but you won't ever break through, because that intensity is within the observational concept.

These insights show that our practice must ultimately be a not doing, at least from the perspective of our everyday mind. The importance of not doing cannot be emphasized enough. We always think of our mental work as getting, doing or achieving something. But vipasana occurs because of a not doing. It's our ability to let go in a very specific way that causes its arising. Vipasana, that clear seeing allowing us to cut through the obscurations that we suffer from, is the fruit of a not-doing, an elimination, not the fruit of an achievement or a getting. People often talk about achieving or getting enlightenment; all this language is wrong. Enlightenment, whatever that may be, is not an achievement. It's a non-achievement. It's about not doing. If you don't understand that, you go down a road of developing capacities that lead to more and more stress. That is not vipasana.

> PAGE 96, PARAGRAPH 1: *If we are frustrated and restless, preoccupied with right and wrong, shoulds and woulds, and other judgmental distinctions, we are undermining our own efforts.*

There is no right and wrong way to truly meditate. There *is* a right and wrong way to do the shamata exercises—those are mental exercises. But when it comes to developing insight meditation, right and wrong have to be abandoned. If we are still thinking that we are doing it right or wrong, we are not developing insight. We are still within the minding business. If we are able to develop a not-doing in a very specific way, the not-doing becomes like a scalpel. It can cut through the minding business. If we are unable to do it after watching our breath, developing momentary concentration, seeing the appearance of no self and impermanence, we are still within the kunzhi, the base of the regime of mind. We may end up stuck there for our whole lives, even as good meditators.

This is fundamental. Unless this insight is introduced right at the very beginning, meditation may be counterproductive. Indeed, you often find that there is more compassion and decency among people on the street than there is in Dharma centers, because people in Dharma centers are often confused about what they are trying to achieve. They are enmeshed in a form of materialism that is difficult to see.

These ideas of right and wrong are preconceptions, what Buddhist teachings call obscurations. Preconceptions come in different flavors, or different intensities. Overt preconceptions are things like trying to use a concept to break through a concept; in Buddhist teachings that is called a coarse obscuration. It's relatively easy to work that one out, as clearly you can't use a concept to break through concepts. That's obviously an easy one, a big one.

> PAGE 96, PARAGRAPH 1, CONT'D: *Instead of just allowing thoughts to come and go, we are watching and evaluating the process, absorbed in the details and making adjustments according to our understanding of the 'right' and 'wrong' ways to observe the mind. We are still playing the customer, engaging the business of mind. This too can be viewed as a form of understanding: understanding what practitioners do in tracking the business of mind, understanding how mind labels, how it makes meaning, and how it plays games. Both kinds of discipline—contemplation of mind and analysis of its mechanisms—have value. But they also have limitations.*

There are also subtle preconceptions, subtle obscurations, and this is a very good example. You think, "I am on a spiritual quest. I am doing a good thing, and I am trying to purify myself" and all these ideas, but actually at the heart of them is acquisitiveness. Right at the very center of the whole thing is a sense of self, trying to improve itself! And that's the subtle obscuration. It's difficult to eradicate, because it's totally hidden under good intentions. It's slightly less ignorant than someone who is completely non-analytical and has no self-introspective faculty, but it is still a false path.

The path of meditation should be without expectation, and without characteristics. We must embark on a journey without an expectation of getting anywhere, and without any overt characteristics to tell us that we are getting somewhere. We are trying to overcome that whole mechanism of doing and getting. Remember, the path is deceptive. Whatever spiritual practice you undertake—at the front of the book, it should say, "This is deceiving!" It should always say that. Otherwise, if you believe it, you are guaranteed to fail! You will create a concept of it, and you may even become quite radiant in your concept of it, but you will not have escaped the path.

The path is means to an end, so of course it's deceiving. There is a really good metaphor in one of the Suttas: you are on a path and you come to a river. You need to cross to continue and you can see the other shore dimly. How are you going to get there? You construct a raft, and you get on the raft to cross the river. When you get to the other bank you would normally leave that raft behind and walk away. But what we try to do is to put the raft on our back and carry it!

Just as we need to leave the raft, we need to be ready to let go of the path. If we don't give it up, we are never going to escape it; we are just going to be stuck all the time.

> PAGE 97, PARAGRAPH 1: *If mind eventually grows calmer and our outlook more positive, we may feel that we are getting the benefits we expected from our investment of time and energy in contemplative practice. If our practice also rewards us with pleasurable experiences, mind can*

become very attached to this seductive flow of feeling. This may trigger another round of expectations. We may be following instructions, proceeding correctly in our practice, but mind may anticipate some greater reward that is just out of reach, a prize that entices us to intensify our efforts. We do not necessarily know what it is, but we feel compelled to reach for it, because mind is telling us, "I need it, I want it." Mind's tendency to push toward resolution impels us to strive toward our goal.

Striving is valuable, but as you can see, within striving there is an inherent obstacle, a hidden preconception, that somehow by striving 'I' am going to get to the end of striving. To follow this path, we can only be allowed to strive if we also accept that we will never end striving—otherwise we are not allowed to strive. So we make a choice: either we are going to strive with the understanding that it will never end, or we don't strive at all. We are not allowed to think, "I am doing it so it will end." We have to strive without any expectation of result.

If we don't strive, how are we going to be able to do anything? That's the problem. But on the other hand, if we strive thinking we are going to get something out of it, that's an obstacle.

PAGE 97, PARAGRAPH 2: *Conceptual formulations that involve pointing out and naming—even the communication necessary to receive instructions—can take us far away from contemplation. The tendency is to take instructions literally, fixating on them in ways that are counterproductive. But until we understand in a way that does not involve concepts, until we can contact the flow of meaning that enables a more complete communication, we have no choice: we have to be obedient to the conceptual framework.*

It's important to be able to follow the path and to follow instructions, and at the same time it's important to see that following instructions, in the end, has to be overcome. This is like learning to play a musical instrument or learning a sport; initially you methodically work through scales and instructions, but in the end you must embody your training to move on from it and become an artist or a player. We have to go through this path to eventually transcend the path, to graduate. Right from the outset we need to understand that if we strive to get something, our path is fatally flawed. But nonetheless, at the end of the day, we've got to be able to take instruction, to listen and learn, and eventually embody that learning and enter spontaneity.

If we bear this in mind, we can see that the best way to view meditation instructions is as pieces of advice. It is like you are walking up a mountain and someone says, "Around the next bend there's a nice view." It's not really an instruction but more like a hint. You might remember to look that way, but it is not the end of the world if you don't. Try to receive whatever insights come from *Revelations* in the same way. These are hints, not instructions. If you try to meditate according to instructions, you will just activate the mental apparatus you are trying to escape. You are trying to find freedom in your own experience, and you cannot do that through instruction. You might even do something other than the advice because you are the master of your own experience. What we need to be alert to is the activation within us of our innate sense of getting 'somewhere'. That innate sense is entirely within the mental apparatus that we are trying to escape.

PAGE 98, PARAGRAPH 1: *This is why contemplation does not always work. We may move from a preliminary beginner's level to a higher level; we may exercise altruism and master the philosophical foundations of our practice, and we may have some blissful experiences from time to time. Eventually, at the highest philosophical level, we may understand that after all this time we are still caught up in pros and cons, wrestling with expectations and the unending grasping of our mental processes. Only then do we realize that we have been deceived by the fundamental orientation of our dualistic mind.*

Let's say that we become truly expert in spiritual practices but eventually get to a point where we realize we have been doing them for the wrong reason. It would be easy to misunderstand this sort of teaching and think that therefore we should do nothing, and just sit in the corner. That isn't going to work either. The advice is to "understand what you do." That's the advice for us as we walk up our personal mountain.

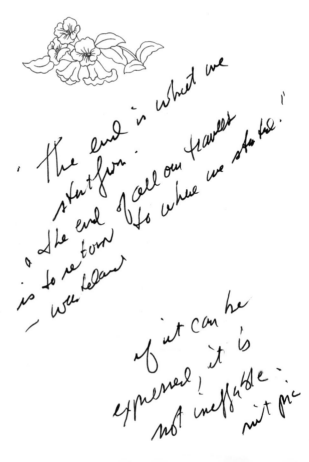

"The end is what we start from.
& the end of all our travels
is to return to where we started.'
 — will teland

if it can be
expressed, it is
not ineffable.
 — wit prc

CHAPTER 18

Obeying the Parameters

We all have an innate capacity to know directly—outside the casket of concepts with which we make the world. All our communication is inherently conceptual, however. Our words must have references that can be translated by others into their own experience or they mean nothing.

Hence, when someone talks, they are not talking to you. Moreover, you are hearing yourself based on the secondary cause of their talking. The primary event that is occurring in your experience is your own interpretation, not what their words are. If you realize that, there is a key in it. When we hear the word "dog," the concept "dog" comes up, so "dog" has been communicated. But once we realize that the words we hear are triggering our own concepts, and not the inviolable intention of the person who said them, we have a choice. We realize that our understanding is always free, always beyond the words that are being used. This is what poets recognize. They use words in ways that are evocative rather than attempting to express a precise meaning. A great poet is able to express the ineffable by using words in a very specific way.

We can all do that, and there is no time that this is more important than when we're talking about vipasana. When we have understood that, we have found a door to freedom from concept. Once we know directly that we are conceptualizing what we hear, that knowledge is not conceptual. It is direct. Have that in mind when you hear instructions, and the instructions will not be literal. Then we will become free of doing it the 'right' way or doing it the 'wrong' way—those terrible categories that trap us in the consumer mind.

> PAGE 99, PARAGRAPH 1: *Since the perceptual and minding processes of mind can only operate within established parameters, mind cannot go beyond the boundaries it erects between what can and cannot be known.*

In many ways our limitations are created by our preconceptions. Because we are trained in the belief that we can only understand things if we have conceptualized them, we can't go beyond concept into anything new. That's why inventors are so unusual—they go beyond what's known. Often with great inventions one thinks, "Well, that is obvious, why didn't I think of that?" Well, you didn't think of it because you were living in the known; that's why you never saw the possibility that gave rise to the invention. Because we are living within a bubble of what we know, and what we know we know well and it all works nicely, when someone comes along with something new, we put that in another bubble: we become consumers. We are progressing in that way, but we are not true inventors. A true inventor doesn't respect the limit of what is known.

> PAGE 99, PARAGRAPH 1, CONT'D: *It is as if the mind had established different zones marked with flashing green and red lights, designating where we can go and where we cannot. Strict rules of jurisdiction apply—there are laws that must be obeyed or some unnamed penalty will be exacted. In the area marked by green lights, the conceptual mind can perceive, identify, re-cognize, and interpret. Beyond are the red lights marking the area where these processes no longer apply. Within the green zone, mind can exercise its familiar patterns with relative comfort and*

ease. Beyond the green zone, it is unable to function in the same way. Mind knows the meaning of these signals and complies.

If you hear something that upsets you, you have hit a boundary barrier of your zone. Your upset is caused because there is an unnamed penalty that you think exists on the far side of the statement. It is really interesting to use vipasana to look and see what that is. It will almost always be some sort of memory, something that says, "You cannot say this. If you say this, terrible things are going to happen." When one realizes this one can dissolve the zone and get a bit more freedom.

There is actually a very good science fiction film about this— a great movie, for those of you who like Russian science fiction. In *The Mirror,* by Andrei Tarkovsky, the protagonists go into a zone that has gone beyond the rules of normality. It is an exploration of the interface between the internal and the external. It's about this very thing, that you can go beyond the known.

> PAGE 99, PARAGRAPH 2: *If we reflect on this, we may understand that our knowledge—even that gained through contemplation—is limited by its dependence on the conceptualizing aspect of mind. Of the fully open, 360-degree knowledge that is theoretically possible, we are accessing only a tiny arc, possibly no more than a single degree.*

If we are in experience and not concept, we are fully immersed; the field is open 360 degrees. We don't have a point of view. But our instinctive reaction to such an experience is to pull back, to recover the point of view that sets up a conceptual analysis of the experience in terms of named things. We have to 'get a perspective' on what is happening. Geometrically what that does is take the 360-degree openness and limit it to a point of view, a narrow slice. Instead of having a global awareness of everything that's going on, we have a narrow conception—perhaps only one degree of what is possible.

An example is to compare the behavior of older and younger people on a beach. The young ones are running around having fun. It doesn't matter if it rains; it doesn't matter if the sea is cold. They are living in the experience of it. Older people are saying, "I don't like this beach. It's too cold. I don't like the sand." They are narrowing the experience of the beach into a few known categories. We do that the whole time. Our global potentiality is turned into a little slice of pie that is known. We're exchanging totality for a known limitation. The known is expressed in terms of right and wrong, good and bad, nice and nasty, like and don't like. These are the categories of judgment by which we rule our lives.

judging

> PAGE 99, PARAGRAPH 2, CONT'D: *Until we become more attuned to the full dimensionality of mind, we have to confine ourselves to that tiny space and carry out our business within it.*

As we go from being babies to being children and then adults, we go from a globally immersed experience into an increasingly narrow set of things we're going to do as we grow up. Eventually we have a narrow slice of potentiality within which we live our lives. Most of us live within that slice, being successful or unsuccessful, rich or poor, happy or sad, without ever asking if there is more. If we think there could be more, we might decide to move—to another location, another relationship, perhaps even another teacher. Instead of looking at our own slice, we get another slice, and another slice and another slice. But ultimately, we have to look at the slice itself. This slice has nothing to do with the external world. It is made by us. The external world is an expression of the slice. Realizing that, we have the possibility of developing insight. This is vipasana 101. Developing this insight is the true path toward freedom.

All direct experience is non-conceptual. Actually, the totally sensuous is non-conceptual. The 360-degree view is non-conceptual; it is not nonsensical; it is non-conceptual. We might think that since everything we know is conceptual, something that is non-conceptual has to be beyond knowing and therefore somehow nonsensical. There's a very deep pre-conception in most of us that this is the case. But actually, it's not nonsensical; it's perfectly sensible.

The non-conceptual is more properly understood as the world of actual experience. ⟩Yes

We need to be comfortable that going beyond the known isn't going to lead to madness; rather it will lead us to experience. Conversely, if we don't go beyond the known, we are only ever going to have a very tight and narrow position.

> PAGE 100, PARAGRAPH 1: *What can we know of the zone beyond the 'red light'? We could speculate that the territory beyond concepts means a state where mind is 'empty' of concepts. But this is self-defeating. Now we are labeling this unknown territory with a known label: 'emptiness'. We are establishing it as a concept and pointing out how it is to be interpreted. We seem to be involved in contradiction.*

Some people say that it is not helpful to read books about what's beyond the known, because in attempting expression of it, in all kinds of sophisticated language, all such books do is encourage conceptualization of it in the mind of the reader. None of those words are going to help you get there! At worst, reading them is a waste of time, and probably more than that—it's going to stop you going beyond the known, because you are going to become very good at talking about it. A classic example is the Buddhist word sunyata, often translated as emptiness. Sunyata is a word that's used about what's beyond the known, but since all words are part of the path, ultimately, it is deceiving. No word—by definition—can express what is beyond the known. Words are used however, and sophisticated analytical work is done around them by thinkers, but ultimately all that work is deceiving. It's a little like a poison:

a little bit of a poison can be a very good stimulant, but most stimulants are poisonous if taken in large enough doses.

Once you see that, you realize that if you get a book on non-dual awareness, written by someone who knows what they are talking about, it's useful, but it's also poisonous. So you have to treat it with a bit of respect. You can read it, but read it with caution, because if you get into it too much, you run the risk of conceptualizing the very thing you are trying to get beyond.

Within the Tibetan tradition they have this idea of 'reading transmission', which is that advanced texts should be read to you by a teacher before you read them yourself. Your teacher gives you permission to read them. Actually, it's very wise. This approach respects the numinous nature of the contents of the text, so you don't just go, "Oh, it's just another book!"

You should treat books that are about non-duality with respect, because they are kind of special. If you have a book like that and you just shove it under the newspaper, you are not treating it with respect. It is not that the book cares—the book is just a thing—but the contents of the book will cease to be numinous and could well become poisonous if you treat it casually. The words will look normal—but they are not, because they contain all these seductive ideas that give you ways of understanding, and push the border between the known and the unknown further and further away from you. By reading them, you are extending your boundary of concepts, and so it becomes more and more difficult for you to get beyond the known.

There are many books written about sunyata. Such books are easy to find but realize that if you conceptualize sunyata as emptiness, it loses its liberative power and becomes just another concept for you. *What are other options*

for reading/understanding SUNYATA?

PAGE 100, PARAGRAPH 2: *Similarly, as we identify, name, and explain such spiritually significant words as enlightenment, wisdom, and realization, we fall into our familiar dualistic patterns of discourse. Intent on enabling mind to interpret their meanings, we accept the meanings mind provides, forgetting that they are simply concepts provided by a mind unable to function beyond its dualistic subject/object framework.*

In the discourse on enlightenment, which has been around in Western culture now since the Beat Poets in the 1950s, our culture has adopted words like karma, enlightenment, and Buddha that are part of our lexicon now. But they are not fully understood and this is problematic; it makes the job of becoming non-dual a little more difficult than it might have been when these things were truly new. We can use the incredible wealth of material that is now available to us, but need to realize that if it's about shamata, it's just about a technique, and if it's about vipasana, it's potentially toxic!

PAGE 101, PARAGRAPH 1: *As long as we focus on the objects that appear within the limited framework of mind, we are seeing only part of the whole picture. Knowledge based on this partial picture seems to be little more than a special kind of guesswork—guesses presented by language that has been constructed by mind. This is why, when we use concepts that point out an alternative to 'ordinary' mind, it seems especially important that we maintain an internal system of checks and balances. Instead of accepting what mind presents, we should remind ourselves to question: "Who is judging? Who is evaluating? Who is observing and pointing out?" Isn't it our 'ordinary' concept-bound mind?*

All words are guesswork, and what philosophers do is try and minimize the guessing by clarifying the meaning of words and concepts. But even fully clarified words are inherently limited.

This question, "Who?", when asked in this context, is very valuable. If you know that what you hear is inherently conceptual, you're on the way to non-conceptuality. You reinforce that by simply asking, "Who is hearing?" Who is hearing now? Who is hearing these words? Who? That question is incredibly powerful because it directly addresses the phenomena itself rather than taking it for granted. All the time we are seeing through our conceptual apparatus into the projection it has made which we call the world. If you say, "Who is understanding?" or "Who is seeing?", then what you're doing is challenging the presentation itself. The question, "Who is seeing this room?", is questioning the external display. The question, "Who is understanding these words?", is questioning the internal display. Both are a product; now we are turning from the products to their maker.

> PAGE 101, PARAGRAPH 2: *For our knowledge to be complete, we need something more. We need to know its origin and how it connects with the perception and minding processes that are facets of mind's regime. We need to be aware of the framework, the pointer, the act of pointing, and what is being pointed out.*

So, by all means become an expert, as long as you are asking these questions. When you do, your inner intelligence will guide you. You can understand with words, you can even elaborate them, extend and make their scope bigger; they can direct us to new fields of exploration. But always we should question what we are given, and ask, "Who is looking at this?" That question is always valid, because it puts us in the position of engaging the endless opening of mind.

Exercise 12
Who is looking?

As you look at something, ask, "Who is looking?" This is not to get an answer; this is more to experience the questioning attitude. As you look at something—you can do this three times a day if you want—you simply pose the question, "Who is looking?" If your mind responds, "Oh, it's a book" or whatever, you ask, "Who said that?" It's not that there is a right answer; it's more that we are becoming familiar with that questioning attitude.

CHAPTER 19

Closing Access to Awareness

The previous chapter described going beyond concepts. You can see immediately in that phrase "going beyond concepts" that the only way you can go beyond concepts is to not have a concept in the first place. To go beyond concept with a concept is to enter the 'beyond concept' concept, such as trying to become 'empty' of concepts, which is therefore to fail. This is why it is often said the fruit is the path, or perhaps that without the fruit there is no path. We are interested in non-conceptuality; we are not interested in conventional insights that you hear about such as 'seeing impermanence', or seeing 'no-self' or whatever, because they are conceptual constructs.

One of the reasons why we have fond memories of childhood is because there were fewer concepts and associations. There was more freedom and a feeling of freshness about experience that fades as we grow up. It is difficult to have a fresh experience if everything that you experience is conceptualized. As we mature, the concepts that are in play come from memory. Often one ends up with a feeling of being trapped in memory, which itself is an association point for further memory.

If this is a prison with layers upon layers of associations, then vipasana is the sword that cuts through them. Standing on the legs of flexibility and stability, to wield the sword of vi-pasana is to ask, "Who?"

"Who?" is a sword that cuts through concept because "who" is not looking for a conceptual answer. "Who?" is an existential question. When you ask, "Who is looking?" you are turning the conceptual apparatus around on itself. This causes interesting results. First of all, it causes a sense of mild confusion. It is an almost incomprehensible thing to ask. In these chapters, 19 and 20, we are going to develop this idea further and explore its ramifications.

> PAGE 102, PARAGRAPH 1: *In all aspects of our lives, we would benefit greatly from knowing the full context of our thoughts and actions. But mind's dedication to identifying and interpreting hijacks our awareness and robs us of the clarity we need to broaden our perspective in this manner.*

We know there is a problem when we try and take a step back to see the full context of what is going on; we get hijacked by our tremendous capacity to identify and work through conceptual forms. That tends to bring us back into a narrow perspective. We are embedded within a completely panoramic experience, but we are task-oriented, focused on the next job, which gives us a narrow perspective on it.

We come to realize that we're not going to analyze our way out of this predicament. We could possibly see our way out of it, however. But mind's process, mind's business, is to get on. It is quite difficult to stop and see because we get rolled into the next activity. The regime of mind is dedicated to getting on with things. We need to find a way of generating and preserving our clarity so the context of what we're doing will become apparent. Vipasana means exactly that: intense vi—and seeing pasana. It is intense, clear, bright, penetrating vision. It cuts through all those associations that so dominate our experience.

PAGE 102, PARAGRAPH 2: *Mind's need to identify and move on makes it impatient with questions that penetrate more incisively.*

We have to overcome a kind of itchiness to move on. This is absolutely true in meditation—one of the most difficult things to do in meditation is to do nothing! Everybody wants to accumulate mantra, do pujas or exercises, watch their breath—to do something. But meditations are not-doing. It is very, very difficult not to do, because we are absolutely conditioned to move on and do something.

Asking "who" is fine, but don't try to interrogate yourself for an answer. If you do, your mind will lead you into endless webs of self-reference. The mind finds it really difficult to turn around on itself in this way. It's not surprising because the mental apparatus uses concepts to analyze experience. If you try to turn your concepts on themselves with the question, "who," you are short-circuiting the very process by which the mind makes the world. But you can go deeper by just asking it directly.

PAGE 102, PARAGRAPH 2, CONT'D: *As a result, if we are asked to investigate this 'I' that is observing and pointing out, this 'I' that needs to establish connections, we may become frustrated, unable to grasp the purpose of such an unfamiliar kind of question. But we do have some options. If we observe our perceptions, noting the point where 'this is' shifts to 'what this means to me', we may see how quickly mind diverts awareness away from simple observation into meanings and interpretations.*

Interpretations begin when the focus shifts from what is happening, to what it 'means'. Meaning is a function of the narrative, the network of associations that attach themselves to the remembered actor, 'me'. "How is this happening" is a much more valuable question than "why is this happening," because 'why' personalizes the question, reasserting the whole conceptual structure.

The transition from "this is" to "what this means to me" is the beginning of thought. That's where thoughts begin. In time that's going to be a very fruitful place to direct our concentrated attention. We have the faculty, particularly if we develop shamata, to direct our attention to any appropriate object. Directing our attention to candles is great, and directing our attention to the breath is better, but best of all is to direct our attention to the point where "this is" becomes "what this means to me." Then you will be directing your attention to the very beginning of the concept association process. In terms of value added that must be a more powerful meditation object than merely watching a candle.

> PAGE 102, PARAGRAPH 3: *If we can sustain our focus on the questions that penetrate mind's constructs, we might find ourselves thinking, "That is an interesting perspective. I would very much like to know more about how this works." But this can be another point of deception. We may feel our mind waiting expectantly, gathering information, trying to point out what is happening, but not quite able to identify the concepts and associations that match it.*

Once you start developing a taste for asking these questions, you can get a kind of subtle feeling of self-congratulation that creeps in going, "Oh, this is interesting, I am enjoying this." That is your ego structure reconstructing itself around the back as 'you doing well'. That is being warned about here. We have to find a way of being direct in our experience so that what we experience does not carry with it the association web that ensnares us. This is the challenge of vipasana. This injunction to be careful about having strong ideas about what is right and wrong, good and bad is because if you base your meditation on the sense that "this is going well" or "this is successful," you can be sucked into a tidepool of wrong effort which is very difficult to escape.

> PAGE 103, PARAGRAPH 1: *At such times we may feel as though our mind is temporarily on hold. It is clearly active, but unable to formulate the concepts that would express what is happening. We may be trying to grasp a concept or experience a state of being that we have only imagined, heard, or read about. We may be keenly aware of straining after something, anxious to improve something or to present ourselves well, but something seems to be preventing resolution. If we pride ourselves on having a quick, responsive intelligence, we may be startled to note the dull, sluggish quality of inertia that has suddenly come over our mind.*

When we begin to embark upon the path of denying our own conceptual apparatus any purchase—when we won't let it do its conceptual thing—it can just go sluggish on us, just go dull. What can happen quite quickly is we become kind of sleepy, because we haven't got a hook to hold on to. The Tibetans have a wonderful term, *mugpa*, for this. The example given is like a mala, one of those sets of beads, and the idea is that the string breaks and all the beads just fall and bounce away into a random arrangement, because the string that normally holds the beads together is broken. That string is our conceptualization, and we have interrupted it with our questioning. The best approach is to directly experience those sleepy states by not resisting them, and then ask, "Who is sleepy?" As we experience them, they transform; they open up. Revelations is about putting experience first.

> PAGE 103, PARAGRAPH 2: *Even in contemplation, the business of the mind creates a jungle of complexities that fill the clear openness of mind with the anxiety of grasping and self-doubt. Pointing ahead, mind pushes us to keep going, but at the same time it piles up obstacles in our path. We may be yearning for clarity and a sense of respite*

from all this minding, yet the pressure to go forward only agitates the mind further. The dialogues continue . . . .

PAGE 104, PARAGRAPH 1: *"This is not what I am looking for. Contemplation should not be like this. I still have a problem, but I should not have a problem. Perhaps I should shift my position or try breathing differently. Just sitting here waiting for something isn't working for me. I'm feeling kind of sleepy, blanking out, getting a little cold and numb. Maybe I'll just lie down for a while."*

Anybody who has meditated knows these sorts of dialogues are really common. When you go against the grain of your own mind with its habitual conceptualization, you can end up in these situations where you feel both motivated and frustrated. This is why short sessions are often best at the beginning. Don't meditate just on your cushion in a shrine room; do it in a coffee shop, do it in odd places, break it up. It's a bit like writer's block. Often writers will go off and write in a cafe or in an unfamiliar place; it is the same phenomenon.

PAGE 104, PARAGRAPH 2: *When we reach such an impasse, our choices are limited. We can continue on in the same way as best we can, or we can give up. But neither one seems right. Searching for answers within its own realm, using the tools of language, words, and imagination, the mind comes back to the same place it began. Frustrated, we may ask ourselves, "Why is this happening?"*

PAGE 104, PARAGRAPH 3: *Mind has a way of recoiling back in on itself, gathering perceptions, concepts, associations, and meanings and feeding them back to mind.*

The way we normally work is in this self-referential loop. It is *nama-rupa*—name and form. Sensation arises; we reach out to identify and the meaning of that label is confirmed: "Oh, yes, that's correct." This self-referential process is the comfortable loop of normality we are always generating. What we are seeing is our own construct. Vipasana cuts through that construct, the ceaseless creation of a world with ourselves as the central actor in it, and sees beyond all the superstructure of associated meanings, memories, ambitions and judgments. The challenge is to be non-conceptual in the face of nama-rupa. In that sense, vipasana is a bit like standing on a cliff. There is a sensation of leaning into the unknown.

> PAGE 104, PARAGRAPH 3, CONT'D: *While we feel we are moving forward, looking for something that seems just on the verge of appearing, we may be experiencing a feedback system that is actually moving backwards, sideways, or inward. Perhaps we are simply listening to mind mumbling to itself.*

Another reason not to do practice too much is that we can end up being caught in a kind of feedback in which our effort to do things and our successes and obstacles in trying to do them become a kind of internal narrative. We don't want to become a 'practitioner'. All those ideas are an obstacle. We're trying to be free. It's simple. Learning to dance with our regime, learning to dance with auntie, is a really good way of thinking about it. We're dancing and playing around with our structured perception so that we will eventually become so familiar with it that we'll be able to overcome its control over us. Now *that* is a valuable insight.

> PAGE 105, PARAGRAPH 1: *Looking from this perspective, can we consider a different way to view what is happening? We can understand that mind is reading what mind presents; we know that mind is interpreting, then receiving back its own interpretations, which are once again presented, expanded, received back, and reinterpreted. If this insight arises in contemplation, it may indicate that we are becoming aware of the closed circuitry that governs the operations of mind.*

What we are actually seeing in that 'going against the grainness' is something very profound; we are seeing the closed circuitry. We are not immediately becoming engaged with it, sucked into the dialogues and urgings it inevitably encourages. Just by dancing with our own mental apparatus, we realize that it's a reality machine: a sense-maker able to create narratives out of all kinds of inputs.

The major narrative that we all have is the narrative called 'I'. Realizing that the sense-maker is interpreting experiences and putting them into a narrative called 'I' is a huge realization. It can turn you into a superb salesman or actor, because 'I' can be all sorts of different things depending on what inputs you wish to feed into it. More importantly, you are able to dance with your own psychology. You are in a real sense becoming free. This brings a lightness of touch and a recognition that what we are seeking is not to be found. It's such a relief when you realize that you can never find a non-conceptual thing, precisely because it's not a thing! That's what we're dancing with. Realizing that is very refreshing. It's like standing in an open window and feeling the breeze—it's actual rather than a bunch of words. We're really there, naked to experience itself, rather than wanting to "make sense" of experience. We're not wanting to make sense of anything. We can play and dance with the sense-maker; it can come up with all kinds of stories, but when we're playing with the sense-maker we are truly free of one narrative, the narrative of 'me' in 'my' world, and we are beginning to generate insight. We are starting to see the context in which our actions happen. We have found an opening into what seemed to be an impenetrable problem.

Exercise 13
Dancing with Auntie

Sit with the eyes open, bring your attention to the sensations of sitting there. Try to have your back straight so you are balanced and comfortable. Then say 'I', 'I', 'I', 'I', 'I', 'I', 'I', 'I', 'I', 'I', 'I', 'I', out loud. Notice the referent of 'I' gradually fading. What is left?

CHAPTER 20

Closed Circuitry of Mind

It is valuable to realize the historical dimension of this endeavor, our challenge to understand the regime of mind. It is now thought that tool-making among hominids goes back at least one million years. Now that we have DNA analysis and more sophisticated paleontology, it appears that humans were developing sophisticated behavior traits far earlier than we once thought. The regime of mind has been guiding us as walking apes for a very long time—yet our industrial civilization is only a few hundred years old. One can see from this history that the regime of mind is not to be trifled with. It is a well-established, tried, tested and substantial operation. It is a historical entity of real lineage, our human lineage.

The regime is a remarkable and intelligent device. It enabled a weak and puny ape to become a totally dominant force on this planet. There are many animals with more powerful bodies that are better adapted to living in the environment than we are. But what they lack is the ability to learn from experience through this powerful network of associations. The regime is not to be sniffed at as if it's some problem. It's to be negotiated with. It's not who we are, but it is a major element of who we have become. And dancing with it is what we're learning to do in *Revelations*.

PAGE 106, PARAGRAPH 1: *If we consider that anything cognizable must be processed through the regime of mind, we realize that all that the human mind can conceive of has had to evolve within the system that mind has been developing for many thousands of years. This system now operates like an efficient bureaucracy: the label department, the language department and the meaning department, with all reporting to mind at the head. Manifesting as mind's critical operations—sensing, identity, re-cognition, interpretations, discrimination, and all the variations of pain and pleasure that come through the senses—these departments, which may serve variously as factions, parties, and associations, shape our reality and direct every aspect of our experience. Whatever efforts we make, for whatever purpose—spiritual, psychological, intellectual, or materialistic—take their meaning and resonate within the framework that these operations have established.*

Seen in this light, the task of generating insight into the operating structure of the mind has a deep historical significance. Furthermore, we can embed our efforts within the insights given to us from cognitive psychology; there is no need to attempt something separate from these conventional spheres of knowledge. Our perspective is necessarily subjective, but can travel alongside the rapidly expanding knowledge of our own human species. Our efforts can be the personal partner to scientific knowledge, rather than some alternative to it. This can be of real value.

Because of the way Western culture has structured itself, although our scientific knowledge is growing exponentially, our self-knowledge is not. We are actually stuck; arguably we haven't moved for two thousand years. You can be spiritual. You can be a materialist. You can be psychological or intellectual. You can be a businessman or aspire to be a Buddha; but you are always within the regime of mind.

Recognizing the historical nature of this structure is valuable, for the endeavor as laid out in Revelations is quite different from spiritual development as it is normally understood. What we're trying to do is to understand the full context of all potential activity. Everything happens within this structure. If you renegotiate your relationship with it, everything changes.

If our culture is stalling, going around in circles; this is why. Everything we do is within a regime we don't understand. If we're able to understand it, it would have big implications. This is absolutely not trivial. It is not personal in the sense that people say, "I like the color red." It is really in a sense impersonal—because the regime itself is what determines whether it is personal or not, whether we like it or not. But in dancing with the regime, the dance has no opinion about right and wrong, good and bad, red and blue, like and dislike. All those opinions happen within the regime.

The regime makes decisions and judgments, and places us firmly in space and time. But in dancing with the regime, the dance is outside of place and time in a very real way, and outside judgments. It is just like asking, "Who?" That is a pointed question; it's also a 'point' question. There is no history to it. It is in a sense ending the clock. In becoming free of the regime, the world stops—the world of all that conceptualizing, "this-ing" and "that-ing", putting together and making sense. All that comes to a stop in the dance, because the dance of the question 'who' is outside of it. It is important to see it in that way—to see that human history in many ways goes around in circles precisely because it's within this mechanism of perception and association. In stepping outside it, history stops. The dancer moves in a direction that is completely unpredictable—not within that association set at all.

PAGE 107, PARAGRAPH 1: *These operations of mind conduct business in ways that on the surface look like a democratic, free-market society, but in controlling the course of our perceptions and thought processes, they are far closer in nature to a dictatorial regime. This semblance of freedom is insidious, for without our knowledge or consent they shroud us in illusion and collapse the pristine awareness of mind into a thin veneer of consciousness.*

We have this sense that we have lost our freedom, while at the same time being surrounded by glamorous images of freedom. The Marlboro Man on his horse in the desert, the Chanel supermodel on her yacht—these are such powerful metaphors. Somehow we've become urbanized with rules and taxes, and we've got to be careful what we say. Yet we yearn to be off into the wide-open spaces. There is something there that people feel very strongly, but they don't know what it is. There is a strong sense of nostalgia for some misty past where everyone was free. Actually, that never happened, because we always brought all our cognitive luggage with us; we never escaped it. But we have an intuition that there is something else that we have lost. It's because of the "thin veneer of consciousness," our wish to have everything conceptually structured, that we lose our primordial calm, the vast clarity that is our birthright. It's almost as if we have given one over for the other.

PAGE 107, PARAGRAPH 1, CONT'D: *A sophisticated propaganda machine keeps us in a state of distraction, while delineating what we can think and do in a way that effectively seals off alternate possibilities. Having established the framework of our reality, these operations now cooperate to weave the fabric on which we paint the landscape of our lives.*

We can all identify that feeling of clarity and freedom within our own experience. We all have had glimpses of it. But nearly always, when we have that glimpse, it is rapidly conceptualized. It's either named, "Oh, that's a beautiful sunset," or we feel the urge to try to capture it, take a photograph, or we can't sustain it without something dragging us away. We all know, we all experience that glimmering moment when we think, "Wow, look at that . . . ," and then it's gone, we can't hold it, it's too intense, too unusual. It's strange because it's non-conceptual. This is why it's so difficult to hold—it's non-conceptual. Our conceptual apparatus wants to get hold of it, grab it, capture it, but in so doing it loses it. Every now and then in a poem or a piece of music you can feel the poets and composers are touching this moment, and we need to treasure that numinosity, because that's the lodestone we are trying to get to. That's what's so disappointing about conventional vipasana, with all that talk about impermanence and lack of self . . . Actually, those are just words; it's this vastness that we are trying to get to, the trackless, unlimited, open freedom which we have lost.

> PAGE 107, PARAGRAPH 2: *Everything we know has to fit inside mind's framework. While we can extend our lines of inquiry and develop new branches of knowledge, any knowledge based on conceptual understanding can only expand within the boundaries established by the regime of mind. When our quests for knowledge meet the walls of mind, where the system no longer functions and our concepts do not apply, they are redirected back into more familiar, dramatic, and 'interesting' landscapes.*

How do we get trapped? This idea that we had access to clarity, but that clarity was stolen by an overprotective mechanism, is important to grasp. The regime is not being dictatorial in the sense that it is trying to be bad to us. It's overprotective. It's trying to be good for us, but unfortunately it's limited by its previous experience. The regime of mind is essentially historical. Like everything that is historical, it's going to be limited by its experience. The regime of mind is always going to react according to what has happened, not what is happening.

Our freedom gets stolen because the regime presents itself as reasonable, rational, sensible; often it's doing so before we have a chance to know what's going on. The very first moment of perception is already colored by the movement of mind reaching out, asking nice, nasty or indifferent—the very first moment. By the time 'I' have seen 'that', the process is already well under way. Our freedom is already lost. We've already become embedded within a network of associations. Every moment of perception is being taken away from us, and there are only choices already colored by preconception. This is exactly how what looks like a reasonable and responsive operation actually turns into a dictatorial regime.

> PAGE 108, PARAGRAPH 1: *It may be difficult to accept that the very structures that appear to support the basic sanity and competence of the mind can subvert its intrinsic urge for freedom and transcendence. Thus, when we discover these patterns through contemplation or experience the deflecting and re-directing tricks of mind's regime, we may find it difficult to investigate further. How else can we explain why we are so easily discouraged from venturing into fresh landscapes of mind, where its regime cannot function the same way?*

Our concepts are a labeling mechanism of understanding that can never reach beyond itself. We've reached land's limit. It is with that edge that we must become familiar. Most people don't like standing on cliffs thinking they are right on the edge of the known. "How can I be stable here? I've got to retreat, get back a safe distance!" So we develop a spiritual path and develop this skill and that skill. But ultimately, we have to go right to the edge. If we don't go to the edge, how are we going to find out if there is something else?

PAGE 108, PARAGRAPH 2: *Like victims everywhere, we tend to identify with our tormentors. We depend on them for our sense of reality—for our state of mind, our understanding, our relationships and interactions—for all that constitutes our being as we know it. We are totally, completely dedicated to the order they have established.*

If you get kidnapped, you often start identifying your kidnappers as friends—a phenomenon known as Stockholm Syndrome. Hostages may actually end up fighting alongside their kidnappers. In many ways the regime has the same power over us. People end up defending it violently when you tell them that you're thinking of leaving the club.

We don't become irrational in rejecting our reflexive rationality however. The guardian of the gates of our rationality might claim that is what we're doing, so we have to be clear about our intentions. We seek a way of being in which reflexive rationality does not limit our potential. It has to be a very sober and conscious choice. It's not a mystical choice. It is, perhaps, a religious choice, but not in the conventional sense. We are not reaching for something that's out there beyond us, some destination. We can feel that there is something else, something shadowed, hidden, clouded, covered by our rationality, and which is itself not rational. But it's not irrational, either: it's *a*-rational. Just like a majestic sunset is a-rational—you can't make sense of it. You could say, "That's a beautiful sunset because the yellow bit, the grey bit, they hang together . . ." But that's not why it's beautiful. You can't capture it in words and concepts: it is not a rational object.

PAGE 108, PARAGRAPH 3: *But do we understand what lies past the horizons established by the regime? Can we say how strongly the fabric is woven? Will it hold up under all experiences that life presents? What beauty, what fresh vistas might reveal themselves beyond the borders that now confine our being? These are the kinds of questions to carry into contemplation, to be asked every time we come up against the walls of mind.*

Inspired by such new vistas, our contemplation can rightly belong within our own culture and yet at the same time reach beyond it into something truly universal. Western culture has this incredible ability to understand—it's remarkable, it's truly without peer. But it's a prison, because of its dominant rationality. Once we start realizing we have access to this much greater faculty, even in small glimpses, it can start to inspire us, and we can start to develop a path based upon genuine intuition of what's possible, rather than just blindly flailing about in endless conceptions and ideas about transcendence.

There is a wonderful tarot card, card fourteen, Temperance. It is sometimes called "searcher reaches land's limits." The searcher reaches the edge of a huge cliff, and in the distance, over the ocean, are the pyramids, the holy land. There are these chains that go from the searcher across the water—"the gold and silver chains of speech"—to the pyramids. This is the same idea: you can't cross this chasm but somehow, by your aspiration, you *will* cross it. It's learning how to recognize that radiant clarity in our experience so it can reside stably: that is the path. It's already there, it doesn't need to be developed— it's already present within us.

It's a complete inversion of the normal idea. We don't have anything to find; we've already got it. If we didn't have it, we wouldn't have a chance. If we weren't able to intuit nonconceptuality we would have no chance of ever finding it; we could never find it, because by definition it is beyond our conceptual framework. Now we are going to turn back toward it again.

Exercise 14
Searcher reaches land's limits

Sit for a few minutes every day, and allow yourself to hold
the anticipation of "what lies beyond." Think about the last
paragraph of Chapter 20. If you can generate questions about
"what lies beyond," it will be a questioning beyond concept. We want to go off the map of the mind into true insight.
We want to leave the history of causes and conditions and go
beyond into genuine experience. Once a day, think, "What
would the world be like if I had no preconceptions? What
would the world be for me?"

would it be possible to function,
we?

like computer memory w/o
an operating system,
without windows
& Dos.

CHAPTER 21

Understanding the Inner Story

PAGE 109, PARAGRAPH 1: *Do we understand how mind knows mind? Have we any evidence that reveals how mind talks to mind? Mind talking to mind is a story, just as our life is a story.*

Historical photographs can be really interesting. If you go online and conduct a Google search for 'historical photographs', you will see amazing things. For example, there is a wonderful photograph of a large group of people on a stagecoach going on an excursion. It's called 'Old West coach Dakotas 1889'. They look so excited—all dressed up for an adventure. All those things they were doing, all the narratives they must have had about what was important to them, what was meaningful, are all gone now. This is worth contemplating. Soon we will all be a story as well, maybe tomorrow, or maybe in fifty- or sixty-years' time. We could leave behind a big story, like Alexander the Great. Or we could leave behind a small story, like someone ordinary that nobody's ever heard of. Either way, it's still a story.

It's good to think about this because we are living in a story right now. In that light, it's hardly surprising that we become a story after we pass away. We are all in a story now, a story told to us by our minds. Everything we do that makes sense to us is part of a story. That's why it makes sense. Although this is emphasized in the first section of *Revelations*, that simple insight is so profound that we forget it from moment to moment. We look at what is happening and say, "This is real!" Actually, it's a story.

> PAGE 109, PARAGRAPH 1, CONT'D: *What else could it be? A hundred years from now, no one will consider our lives as anything more than stories. Yet our lives are important to us and we take them very seriously. So why not pay serious attention to the stories that mind tells?*

Those people on that stagecoach had very serious concerns about what was right and what was wrong, who they were in the world and what their future would hold. That was very important to them. To us their concerns mean nothing: they have all been lost. This is an important clue.

If we were able to pay serious attention to the stories that mind tells us, we might be able to penetrate this veil that is so elusive. It is a veil that we call reality, even when we know from simple logical analysis that the reality that we think is there is not. It disappears and changes all the time. Moment to moment, what is real keeps disappearing.

Just think about what you were doing five minutes ago. All that is gone. You can't get it back. It's just a story. You can say that it happened, but you can't get it back. Because we are born into this situation, we rarely question it, but there is a profound sense in which the reality we feel we inhabit is deeply misunderstood by us. Where did yesterday go? You can talk about the past as if it exists, but it doesn't. This is a question that can lead to a profound insight into how we make sense of the world.

> PAGE 109, PARAGRAPH 2: *When we dream, especially if we have dreams that are vivid, do we think they are real? Or do we think that they are stories told by our mind? We could be imagining—recording various versions of a story with all manner of characters, qualities, and interactions*

that produce different feelings and emotions. Are our memories of dream-stories like that? Do we remember effortlessly creating such stories and living within them, as if we were taking a journey that had many interesting twists and turns? Now we are creating a similar kind of story—the story of our waking life—and relating to it as real. Could we be playing a secret trick on ourselves?

This is not trying to say that living is dreaming. Rather, living has strong similarities with dreaming—that's the point.

Imagine this: you go to bed; you sleep and dream of winning the lottery. Now you are super-rich and have everything you ever wanted: a wonderful husband or wife, fast cars, beautiful clothes and jewels, a huge house. Then you make some bad investments—and you lose everything. All of it is taken away. Finally, you are just a beggar living on the streets. From exaltation and wealth, you have gone to total poverty. And then . . . you wake up. All the time you were in your bed, yet all that happened. Was it real? That's the question.

In some respects, you can ask the same question about your life. Because all the events that happen to us move surely into the past: were they real? What was real about them? Our reactions to them were real, our suffering was real—that part was real enough. But the stories within which we embed ourselves were not; they were just stories.

Through storytelling, collective experience is embedded within a narrative to make meaning. This is a fundamental element of the regime of mind. Phenomena are named based on previous recollections of them, but the names themselves are arbitrary. The 'reality' of those names is given in a preconscious process before the ego actor enters the scene, and the ego actor itself acts as an anchor for a story—all the hopes and fears, ambitions and motivations with which we navigate our lives. That narrative, that story, creates the stage upon which the world actor, the ego, is playing.

That stage is called the world.

> PAGE 110, PARAGRAPH 1: *If our life really unfolds within the realms of imagination, our judgments and reactions to what is happening are equally imaginary. Yet that is not how we engage them. As our minds interpret our experience from different perspectives, we are happy, we are excited; we are apprehensive, fearful, unhappy. We record all the dramas and narratives that move through the mind. We hear them, we accept and establish them, and we live with them. These stories become part of our image of ourselves, our own personal history, and we respond accordingly. When they come up in memory, we say, "That's what really happened," rather than, "That is basically my imagination at work."*

We all have these dramas, things we want to do, things we get sucked into, arguments, whatever. We have to realize that these are narratives: that it's our imagination at work. The stuff we cared about when we were children we no longer care about as teenagers. The stuff we care about as teenagers no longer interests us as adults. We go from fighting over toys to fighting over video games to fighting over girls to fighting over positions of social importance to finally having an interest in doilies and collections of china! We get excited about certain things, but are they really important to us? What really matters? The job of vipasana is to try to find out.

> PAGE 110, PARAGRAPH 2: *Even if we cannot change them— they are still our stories!—we take our stories seriously and hold on to them, because without them parts of our lives would simply disappear. If we cannot hold on to them, perhaps because others do not see them the way we do, they become irrelevant.*

There was a film made in the 1960s called *The Manchurian Candidate* that was about brainwashing. The fear was that if you brainwashed people efficiently through isolation techniques, they could literally disappear; they would be unable to relate at all to their previous life. In a similar vein, soldiers who've been in war zones have great difficulty re-integrating when they come back, because the story of their life was interrupted so totally. It's not uncommon for these highly trained people to end up homeless because they cannot get back into the story they left when they went to war. The story of their life that made sense when they got on the plane to go to the war zone makes no sense when they get off the plane coming back. It is particularly difficult in this age of low-level, constant war where soldiers are in a small minority of the population. There is no one back home to share their experiences with, so their lives disintegrate.

These examples demonstrate how the meaning of life is the meaning of a story. And that's why history is so important: it's ultimately what gives meaning to human events. In this sense, understanding history is understanding the stories of our lives. Learning from our study of history, we can begin to take a 'historical' view of our own lives, by making a narrative, a timeline, to tell the history of 'me'. We can and should become historians of our own experience. Then, when we start generating true objectivity about our own experience, we will be able to say, "This is my imagination at work. I've seen this before—it's my story repeating itself."

> PAGE 110, PARAGRAPH 3: *Whether we experience our stories as a genuine account of our lives or consider them subject to revision, the framework, content, interpretations, and significance of these stories is taking place in the mind—nothing else is happening. We cannot necessarily catch it happening, but the story takes us over and becomes part of us.*

Phenomena arise. They are named. The naming process reifies them as real. In that reification process an 'I' and an 'it' are projected into a world. And that world is embedded within a narrative story. All this is happening in the mind—it's not happening in the world.

PAGE 111, PARAGRAPH 1: *Caught up in the movements of our mind, separated from our being, our life is a story. We live in a story. We are part of a story. We are the story. We contribute to it and take on its attributes. We are the one who orchestrates, responds, and interacts with it, accepting that this is the way our story goes. We have nothing else other than our story: our version of any experience is our story. Everything we receive and project is yet another part of the story.*

There is nothing we do that isn't embedded within a story. This is the reason why novels and movies are so involving: the stories they tell seem to be real as we engage with them. For example, it is interesting to watch TV and try to work out when you lose your viewer perspective and become embedded in the story. Initially you're just sitting there. Then suddenly you disappear and the story becomes real. Somehow you are there in the story, not on your couch in the sitting room. Once the film or episode finishes you go back to being your real self. We might think then that we are going back to the actual world, but we're not—we're going back to another story.

The things that grab you and pull you into the story are very subtle. The art of a dramatist is to sweep you off your feet so you're no longer objectively observing, but have entered the narrative. What we don't realize is that this is happening moment-to-moment in our normal experience. We're always being sucked off our feet into a narrative. A whole day can go by in which we are embedded in some story of what's going on. We lose ourselves, disappear.

PAGE 111, PARAGRAPH 2: . . . *We start to see certain patterns, and recognize them for what they are. Sometimes we get carried away with a topic and elaborate on it. At other times we do not remember exactly how we told the story earlier, but may decide we would like to revise it and present it in another way. Another conclusion to the story may accidentally pop up, or our memory may create a different story entirely. From time to time, we may experience a 'reality-check' made necessary by hearing someone else's version or interpretation of the story, and we may reinterpret the story to give it a new focus and believability.*

This is where creating a personal timeline of your life can be really valuable. Using recorded dates from diaries, ticket stubs, and so forth, you can create a framework with which to organize the narrative in a chronological order. As you do this, more memories will come up. You will be able to embed more and more memories into the timeline. A populated timeline begins to objectify the story of 'me'.

All sorts of insights will come out of this activity. When we track back, we can start to see the repetitive character of our behavior patterns. We will be able to notice how many of the things we do, even the ways we feel, are quite predictable. This patterned predictability is there because we live in a story, and the story has themes that keep coming back—themes of sadness, failure or kindness that repeat. Mistakes repeat, too; they are the consequences of these themes. We can relocate, change jobs, embark on new relationships, but as long as the themes within our story don't change, the outcomes will be similar. Perhaps we could change to another story, or perhaps we could become free of stories altogether. What would that be like? To be free of stories now is inconceivable. But at least we can see that identifying the regime of mind is a crucial task in order for vipasana to work. It's not enough just to sit down and watch your breath. Too often, that is just being fooled by another story.

> PAGE 112, PARAGRAPH 1: *So, are the fruits of contemplation part of our story? The structure seems very similar. We have an experience in meditation, or perhaps in prayer, and say, "I love it, it is mine, this is how mind is supposed to be." But the only thing we can accurately say is "I did not understand what was happening."*

All experience is a story—everything. This sets the stage for meditation. In the first chapters of this section, we were talking about shamata. It is useful to develop shamata as a technique because you can develop stability of mind. That is just a skill, like rope walking, except more useful. People who are really good at shamata can settle their minds on anything for a long time. Vipasana is the attitude of mind that uses that stability to pose the right question; here it is setting the stage for a question that we need to pose about our own experience. The danger is that vipasana also becomes a story—the asking of questions itself becomes a story; it becomes what 'you' do. Good experiences in meditation are great, but do we really understand what is happening?

> PAGE 112, PARAGRAPH 2: *This is not a criticism, but an important acknowledgement of reality. When we recognize that we have not understood, we also acknowledge that there is something to be understood. If we consider carefully what this means, we may glimpse the possibility of a new and creative way of understanding.*

There is the famous metaphor of the guy who wants a drink, but his cup is already full—you can't put anything in it. As long as we think we understand, we can't understand, because in our minds we have already understood. It's only when we begin to realize that we are not understanding the full picture that the possibility of understanding becomes open to us.

There is an important saying: "Truth cannot be fetched. It comes when you make demand of it." Until we get into that mindset of realizing that this experience is not exactly as it seems, we can't make demand of truth. We can elaborate our spiritual life with all kind of bells and whistles, become Tai chi masters and *pujaris*, travel to India and live with *sadhus*, and do all kinds of interesting things, but none of it makes any difference, if we are not making demand of truth.

You can make demand of truth here and now; you don't actually have to be a *pujari* to do it. However, until you realize there is something you don't understand, how can you make demand of it?

> PAGE 112, PARAGRAPH 3: *Our ordinary way of knowing, shaped within the regime of mind, is linear and flat, relatively devoid of the vital dynamic of creativity and revelation. When the mind points to an object and we recognize it, it is because we understand the labels and the meaning, all of which are products of the past. When all the labels and associations have been properly arranged, we may weave more thoughts about the object or experience into our story. While this follows the reality-rules established by mind, this is only one way of enriching our story. There are other ways we have yet to explore, and some have the potential to penetrate the all-encompassing envelope of mind.*

Let's review for a moment. Vipasana is about seeing clearly. To see clearly means that we don't have a story of seeing. Most of us are not meditating at all—we are just sitting within a story of meditation. There's the beginner's luck phenomenon where you start off by observing the mind and you get huge insights. But then it all stops. The reason it stops, remember, is because the mind has understood the new experience and has embedded it within a story. Then when you meditate again you are not meditating like a novice—you are meditating now within a story of meditation. It becomes a ritual with an expectation of a remembered result. The cup is now full.

But we have to empty that cup to have genuine experience; we must realize that we don't understand. The problem is that we can't imagine what life would be like without a story to give it meaning—yet it is that nakedness, that openness, that is the essential precursor to vipasana. We need the stability of shamata, but then we need to develop the courage to rest beyond the story. If we can rest there, we are resting like the searcher who has reached land's limits. We're resting on the edge of the known. Don't expect anything. It's not understood. The moment we expect anything, we've embedded it back into a story.

> PAGE 113, PARAGRAPH 1: *In this light, it is possible to reinterpret mind's signals to turn back when the borders of conceptual construction loom before us as an invitation to proceed. Acknowledging that we do not understand gives mind pause; its minding operations are briefly put on hold, allowing glimpses of a new, more liberated way of understanding—one that does not require that clever person in the background of our minds to take on the endless task of interpretation.*

Exercise 15
Listening with and without me

Just sit with your eyes closed, preferably next to an open window. Listen to the sounds pouring in. For three minutes, try to identify each sound, where it is coming from, and what it is. Use your hearing as a precise sensory organ like a blind person does. Really create as accurate a sound image as you can. In a second three-minute session, drop it. Drop all that identification totally. The more you have concentrated in the first half, the more for the next few minutes you can just allow sounds to happen. There is no outside, inside, left or right. Just allow sounds to happen. Experience the difference between the first and second sessions. Within that difference there is an important contrast. You may find yourself fantasying all kinds of ideas when you don't identify sounds. But just remain there, alert, resting in not-knowing. We have reached land's limits.

CHAPTER 22

Seeds of Separation

A major theme of *Revelations* is to deepen our understanding of perception. By having the ability to hold a specific element of perception in awareness, we can gain important insights. The ability to hold is called shamata, and the insights that arise are called vipasana. The key is the choice of the right meditation object. We can see this in the story of Prince Siddhartha. After all, he perfected shamata with his two Indian teachers, but left both of them because their guidance did not lead to liberation. There are key messages in this story.

The modern tradition seems a little hazy with regard to the choice of meditation object. *Revelations*, however, makes a lot of effort to find out exactly what it is that we need to know about, and then with this shamata engine that we've developed, we can rest our attention there. One of the great liberating realizations is to see that the knower comes after the known, not before the known. There is always an unknown arising there before the knower knows it. We always recall ourselves as knowers knowing things, but if we have the stability to look more carefully, we realize that the event had to be there for the knower to name it—so the knower came afterward. This is the key to why we are trapped—because we never get to what arises. We are trapped in a loop in which we are not first, but second—caught in a profound dependence of which we have no idea.

> PAGE 114, PARAGRAPH 1: *We are convinced we each have individual minds, but at a fundamental level, mind seems to be a uniform entity. It has certain properties that appear to be fixed, it makes use of the same basic systems of perception and cognition, and it plays the same games, no matter what individual happens to be operating it. However we might like to think that these systems and games do not apply to us, or that they apply to us in a different way, when we examine mind more closely, we find that we may be looking at the same fundamental entity, no matter who claims ownership.*

It's rather impressive how cognitive psychologists in collaboration with computer engineers have now made data algorithms that can predict people's behavior with alarming accuracy. Google probably knows more about what you do than you do! This shows that the operating system that we operate is uniform across human beings. We all have the same operating system. What makes us different is the content of that operating system. It is not that we are not individual. What we have to do is work out what causes our individuality. We come to realize that what makes us individual is almost completely accidental. Gradually we realize that our individual history is just a story among many, many stories.

> PAGE 114, PARAGRAPH 2: *Then why are people so different? Here we can offer a story. Imagine that a long time ago, no one danced. Then one day, one person, then a second and a third, began moving in a way others found pleasing, and more and more people began making the same movements. At first, dancing was all gesture and movement, but over time, someone began to beat a drum; the rhythm of the drum brought the group together and added meaning to the gestures. As others were inspired to elaborate and improvise, more and more people began dancing and*

playing drums. Specific styles developed, distinguished by different steps and rhythms and creative combinations. Perhaps strong preferences developed, or certain styles took on unique associations and were favored by specific groups, classes, or tribes. In time, many styles of dancing came into being in response to different contexts and purposes. Is it possible that the mental patterns that make us unique may have developed in similar ways?

The strange thing is that whereas there are billions of lives being lived and they are all individual, when you look at history there is a remarkable uniformity of activity. That demonstrates that the nature of our minds is essentially uniform. Read a little bit of Marcus Aurelius;[28] you will be surprised to hear such a modern voice coming from nearly two thousand years ago. That's because the nature of mind hasn't changed. The concerns and problems that people come up with really don't change much throughout history. Fashions and events change, but the structure that underlies them is relatively fixed. Our individuality is not trivial, but it is not our essential nature.

Whereas the content of the mind changes, the underlying mechanism doesn't. We have to learn to cut through the content to get to the mechanism. This is what we are doing in developing the right approach to a genuine meditation object. The cultural and social differences between us are not fundamental. At a fundamental level, we're all the same. It is that sameness that we need to get to if we're to truly understand the regime of mind.

PAGE 115, PARAGRAPH 1: *While we may have the same human mind and the same basic operating system, individual minds can run different programs that are not necessarily compatible. After all, when individual minds view the same picture, they do not necessarily arrive at the same understanding of what the image represents.*

---

28 Marcus Aurelius, *Meditations*, (Black and White Classics, 2014).

We have very individual conceptions of what we see. Much art is merely an individual expression and people's reaction to it can vary from loving to hating it—right across the board. Interestingly, Gurdjieff came up with the idea of what he called 'objective art'—examples in history of artistic representations that have broadly the same effect on everyone. It's the mark of a great artist that this is the case; the greater the artist, the more objective the art becomes. When you look at a Rembrandt self-portrait, for example, everybody is struck by it; it points to the fact that great artists are able to express something that speaks directly to the universality of our nature, rather than merely making individual expressions of it.

> PAGE 115, PARAGRAPH 2: *Since mind instinctively reshapes perceptions to accord with what has been identified previously, what is obvious and right from our perspective may not be true for others. If rigid patterns of reaction set in, with no way to accommodate opposing views, the result can be confusion, disagreements, heightened emotions, grudges, and peace-destroying hatred.*

Preconception colors perception, because when an object arises it doesn't have a nature, but it is then identified and categorized according to our previously established labeling, and on the basis of that label associations are made which can be wildly different depending on the history of the person who labeled it. This is how the same object or event can mean quite different things to different people. Chasms of misunderstanding open up as a result.

Recognizing that preconception colors perception is an important antidote to profound disagreement. It also explains how profound disagreement occurs.

> PAGE 116, PARAGRAPH 1: *Even when everyone uses the same words, the connotations of these words can vary widely. For a time, two individuals may seem to be thinking the*

same way, but eventually differences in meaning and valuation become obvious, and they sense the separation. Such differences manifest most strongly among societies and cultures, but they also show up between individuals, complicating communication, fostering misunderstanding, and sowing seeds of conflict.

Although words are universals in that they broadly denote classes of objects or events, nonetheless it can be very, very hard to truly understand what they imply to those who hear or read them, particularly across cultures. This is the hermeneutic problem; it persists not only across cultures and times, but also personally, in our own lives. How do we know what we know? Are we really sure we know it in the way we think we know it? We take this for granted as if we know what we know. But actually, we need to look again, and ask that question: How do we know what we know?

> PAGE 116, PARAGRAPH 2: *We can see from the state of our world today that such patterns of misunderstanding have universal significance to humanity.*

Our culture is advancing and our technology is advancing, but our human condition is not; and this is because our human condition is predicated on this lack of understanding. If we don't understand the hermeneutic problem, both between ourselves and inside ourselves, we have no chance of advancing. We are set up for problems. Even if we get to live to be 150 years old, with no wrinkles, we are still going to be fighting over misunderstandings.

It is striking when one appreciates that although our individuality is trivial and accidental, the suffering that we go through is real and absolute. This is true of everyone and it's true of every situation. The nature of mind is universal but the contents of mind are accidental. This is the case whether we are talking about individuals or societies. We must always remember that the suffering that people go through is real, even if the reason why they are suffering is because of accidental phenomena.

That's an appalling realization when you take it seriously. You suddenly begin to see that the tears that are being shed, the blood that is being spilt, the broken bones, the starvation and deprivation that's going on right now in many, many places in the world—all of it is entirely due to accidental causes. But the suffering is real. This is the basis for what Buddhists call 'compassion'. If the causes were real and the suffering was real, we could remove the causes and the suffering would go away; it would be a practical matter. If the causes weren't real and the suffering wasn't real, it would be like a dream. But what we have is that the causes are accidental but the suffering is real: the worst of all worlds. That's the basis of compassion. When you begin to realize the truth of this it provides strong motivation for wanting to understand how it happens. It seems that all this suffering occurs because of a fundamental misunderstanding.

> PAGE 116, PARAGRAPH 2, CONT'D: *If they take firm root in the mind, they can persist through many generations and give rise to countless forms of suffering. Unless we can understand how mind operates, so that we can defuse potential conflicts at their root, confusion will only increase. And such is the power of mind that the consequences of confusion are likely to become ever more severe.*

We have to ask the question: How do we know what we know? These misunderstandings arise within us because we never, ever ask that question. We refine what we know, we add to what we know, but we never ask the question, "How do we know what we know?" To answer that question, we have to stabilize the mind. Vipasana uses that calm as a platform from which we can ask the right question.

CHAPTER 23

Validating the Validator

"Where were you when I laid the foundations of the earth?"
God asked Noah out of the whirlwind. All cultures are interested in what began the beginning, how it all started. Modern
Western cultures tend to hold that the answer lies in some
obscure piece of physics to do with the Big Bang. We can take
a different view, however, for the foundations of our earth are
laid moment to moment to moment in our own perception.
What happened 13.6 billion years ago is of little importance
compared to what happened just now, now, now. The foundations of the earth are being laid *by us,* all the time.

We have to learn to question this process. If we can successfully question it, if we can make this process a meditation object that we can look at, then we will really start accessing the
nature of reality.

Reality is what occurs to us. If you talk about an external reality that doesn't occur to you, it's not a reality for you. The
reality that occurs to you is happening moment to moment
to moment. This is the fundamental process we want to question: to have clear insight into that is to have insight into how
we construct the world. Everything follows from it. If we don't
understand how we construct the world, then our perception is not being understood at a fundamental level. We may

understand the contents of our perception, but if we don't understand how its foundations are laid, then our knowledge will always be secondhand.

To use the metaphor used in the first section of *Revelations*, we live in a readout. We have to try and find out who makes that readout. Who is the readout maker? If we can find the readout maker, we can take real steps toward understanding the nature of our experience.

This Chapter 23 of *Revelations* begins with a statement: "There is." "There is" is a fundamental statement about reality. Think about that statement. If you can't say "there is" something, you can't say anything about your own experience. You're stuck.

> PAGE 117, PARAGRAPHS 1 AND 2: *There is. With these words we state that something is real, or exists in some manner. 'There' is a symbol pointing to something that has been established, and 'is' indicates that what is being pointed to exists. 'There is' indicates immediate recognition of a perception, thought, or fact that is now confirmed and validated.*

Our eyes fall on an object—let's say a gong. So we say, "There is a gong." Now, at the level of communication, it's obviously effective: there is a gong, we all know that's a gong. It was pointed out, no problem. But the process by which we state "there is a gong" still needs to be understood. And unfortunately, it never is; we just learn the word 'gong' and its associations in our childhood and we use the term, as something already fixed, already true: "There is a gong." No one has any argument about it. But remember, "there is" is a validator in action—it's called "there is." We will want to actively validate that validator; we will want to ask, "Well, how is that validator making such a strong assertion?"

As we consider this, we need to remember that the assertion "there is," and the assertion "I am," are the same. The process of validation works in both directions at once: it is double-pointed, validating the object and the validator at the same time. "There is;" "I am." This double-pointing is how we construct the world.

> PAGE 117, PARAGRAPH 3: *Prior to validation, the conditions for identifying a perception have already been established, but the entity is not yet recognized, like an egg that has been laid but not yet hatched.*

Suppose there is a clock in front of us. The impression of the clock comes into our sensory apparatus; before I know it's a clock, clock-ness has to be established. Remember the game of call and response? Clock-ness is established, clock-ness is ascribed to the sense impression. An inner process confirms, "Yes, that's the clock"—and now I see a clock. This play of internal call and response happens very, very rapidly in how a perception is re-cognized; and in the re-cognition of the perception, both the object and the knower of that object are produced together. Arising sense-impression, internal cognition, re-cognition and *boom*—the knower and the known are validated. The clock and me, me and the clock; me, myself and the world: the entire structure comes into being.

> PAGE 117, PARAGRAPH 3, CONT'D: *This 'prior' state is an unknown territory.*

The point before validation is unknown territory to 'me'. I cannot recall something prior to the process of validation. When 'there is' happens, 'I' can be recalled as being there. Before 'there is', though, there is no 'I'. This is why the point prior to validation is an unknown territory, and why 'I' can't recall anything beyond 'there is'. If you try to look, you just come up with a blank wall. 'There is' seems to be as far as we can go.

> PAGE 117, PARAGRAPH 3, CONT'D: *We do not know how it came to be or what conditions apply to it; we assume it exists, because in retrospect we know that a perception is immanent, but we have no way of knowing for certain. It*

would seem to be 'our territory', but we do not know how
to enter it or communicate with it. How can we validate
what we cannot grasp and recognize? We need a witness.

The statement 'a perception is immanent' in this paragraph
is important. If you introspect yourself observing anything, if
you slow it down enough, you will come to a point where the
thing-ness of an arising sense impression begins to glow. It's
immanent. That glowing property is as far as you can go with
your introspection. You can realize that there must be something that turns the sense impression into something that's
glowing, ready to be identified. But you can't know what it
is. This is the foundation of the earth and all that is in it. If
we don't understand it, we don't understand our own experience: our own experience is going to be a black box to us, and
consequently we are going to wander in ignorance of who we
actually are.

> PAGE 118, PARAGRAPH 1: *In response to this, the answer*
> *comes: "Mind can validate itself!" It seems that mind has*
> *a spokesman, an interpreter or intermediary who knows*
> *our language and reassures us: "The realm of mind is not*
> *chaotic or accidental; everything is in order and ready to*
> *go. There are labels prepared for everything conceivable*
> *and for their characteristics, associations, and history as*
> *well. There are senses endowed with sensitivity; there are*
> *perceptions, identity, labeling and recognition—a whole*
> *regime."*

The regime is the mechanism by which objects are perceived,
categorized, labeled, and confirmed; they can then form the
basis for associative webs of knowing. And this is a profoundly
important process, without which we could not survive. This
is essential to us. Furthermore, not only could we not survive,
we could not communicate, because the very ability to communicate relies entirely on the same mechanism. In this giant
web, knowing and communicating are linked together.

The mechanism by which we know is the same mechanism by which we communicate, because the objects we use and the words we use to communicate are constructed in exactly the same way. In a way, knowing is communicating—as messages go back and forth between what we identify as 'inside' us and the perceived 'world' we project outside us that we have learned to validate. Back and forth, from and to, perceiver and perceived, all are labeled up.

> PAGE 118, PARAGRAPH 1, CONT'D: ". . . *There are interactions and movement of meanings, feelings, and emotions. There is language to ensure that everything is correctly identified and that there is no mistake. Everything has been taken care of. There it is—there is reality. These are the tools for operating it. What you do with it from here is up to you."*

Our mental apparatus has been carefully constructed to understand the world. What we do from there is up to us. This is a seamless process: we identify objects with absolute certainty and speed. The classic example of this is the rope-snake. You are walking along a path and there is a coil of rope. You jump out of the way quickly when you see it; the appearance hits you like a shock. In that process of jumping, the whole chain of sensation, perception, identity, labeling and recognition has occurred. This process is very quick. But it's not just happening when we see special things like rope-snakes; it's happening with everything.

At every moment we are laying the foundations of the earth through this process of perception, labeling, identity and recognition, but we can't access it. We're trapped. We are trapped in a machine that's making the world for us. It's a vehicle, a chariot, a regime.

Our job as meditators is to see clearly, based on the shamata ability to hold the mind on a given object. Once we have that ability, it's a very powerful tool because we can then direct our attention to whatever object we like. Having shamata, we can then start looking at this immanence, this process of "there is," with our shamata-trained mind. That is the process of vipasana. We're now guiding our stabilized vision onto a valuable meditation object.

What we are going to find is that this immanence is very interesting. The moment prior to validation is fascinating. It's glowing. It's got a magical quality. By using this moment as our meditation object, we are beginning to get to the place where reality begins.

> PAGE 118, PARAGRAPH 2: *Every time we say, 'there is', we not only point something out, we also point out what we are doing: "I am perceiving, identifying, characterizing and possessing. I am connecting my personal, subjective awareness to the condition, quality, and meaning of my observation. I am acting on my need to establish connections and hold on to them."*

We ask, "Who is looking?" In the story of perception, we have a nice, comfy idea: we have the ego and we have the world. The world is the stage upon which the ego acts, which is constructed by the regime of mind; the ego is in the center of the story. That way of expressing it puts it all in the third person. We are very comfortable with the third person perspective, but it's missing something important. Actually, in the moment of 'there is', not only is something being pointed out, but the knower of that thing is also being pointed out: 'See a clock, clock is seen'. There, in that double-pointing, is the beginning of the story of 'me'. In every moment of the story of 'me', there is this same double-pointing.

I remember myself as an actor on a stage: I was there; I did this, I did that. 'I' is a tag, a locator used to point out what was remembered. As it happened, I wasn't there, but there was double-pointing as it was going on. The clock was 'known'.

Does that mean that 'the story of me' is not actually me? That's exactly what it means: as the story of me is being lived in real time, I am not there. The story of me is what I think I am, not what I am.

This is double projection: First, sensation; second, cognition; and third, the double projection of the thing and its knower. The double projection provides an anchor for a whole system of associations that then come into play. 'There is' is a point at which all kinds of memories and associations and ideas can start to be brought in, because 'there is' presents something that is firmly identified. As a result, the entire memory system can attach to it. Once the perception is validated, then all the associations connected to that object can come into play.

If you are able to take that process as a meditation object, all those projections would cease to have anywhere to attach to. Problems begin to mutate, fade and disappear because there is nowhere, no place, no geotag, no hook for them to attach to.

As it is, we struggle with our associations all our life. We have things we like, things we don't like, things that annoy us, things that we ought to do, things that we shouldn't do, things that went well and things that went badly. All this stuff, all this noise. All of it requires 'there is' in order to have a place to be. The moment 'there is' is undercut, there's nowhere for these associations to attach.

> PAGE 119, PARAGRAPH 1: *For instance, if mind's pronouncement, 'there is', points to a perception that accords with mind's pre-established notion of anger, mind will identify anger, call up agitation as the appropriate response, and embellish it with associations and feelings. Almost immediately, anger becomes real; body and mind respond, and we cannot stop emotion from flowing.*

We have all had this experience, where some frustrating event arises and the associations which that event triggers are signaled as a cause for an emotional response such as anger. For others it might be jealousy. Anger and jealousy are two dominant emotional forces. You get into a disagreement with someone and you can feel the associations rising as the disagreement gets more intense. If you have enough self-awareness you can feel yourself being triggered into anger by that association. It's not that there is actually anger or jealousy there in the disagreement itself. But if we don't base our awareness prior to the double pointing of validation—if we base our awareness after the double-pointed projection of 'there is', after the point where the knower and the known come into being—then we are completely at the mercy of emotional association. We have no control, because once the mechanism that associates a particular behavior with an emotion is triggered, the association happens automatically, and then 'we' are jealous, angry, sad or whatever. All we can do then is try and apply the antidote of self-control.

How different it would be if awareness were present before the emotional association was triggered! Then 'we' would not be angry or jealous; 'we' would not be sad or upset. 'We' would not be swept up by it.

> PAGE 119, PARAGRAPH 1, CONT'D: *As mind continues to identify and label each element in this unfolding chain of events, language comes more strongly into play, contributing reasons and justifications that spark more interactions, dialogues, and commentaries and summon memories that may carry a strong emotional charge.*

The regime of mind is not a computer program—if anything, it's more like a chemical reaction. The process of association brings with it products that carry an emotional charge, a long-lasting chemical event.

It is possible to measure those chemical changes in the brain. Once you have an emotion like anger, it gets smeared across every aspect of perception. Then all kinds of justifications and other cognitive processes get triggered to justify and give reasons why the anger is there.

Emotions, while they are very energizing and activate behavior in a very powerful way, are problematic because they color everything that follows after them for hours until the chemical results of those emotions have finally cleared away. A single argument can make you feel bad for the whole day. This is why a klesha can be considered a kind of coloration. Even if we want to be good, even if we want to be calm and even if we like to be flexible, we get sucked into things we don't want. Then all we've got is regret. But if we knew where the foundations of the earth were laid, we could in one stroke cut through all of these associations. We could be free of the entire mechanism that appears to trap us so totally and makes our lives so complicated.

> PAGE 119, PARAGRAPH 2: *From this point, mind could continue to spin out any number of stories that point in different directions. But now we want to turn mind around and track its stories to their origin instead. We want to know the history of this anger and validate for ourselves the reality that provoked it.*

We can only ask 'how' for real when we recognize that mind is double-pointing. As long as we keep the 'how' external to us, we are going to make progress, we are definitely going to become more rational, we are going to become better people, we are going to be less prone to negative emotions; there will be all kinds of good results—all from asking 'how' instead of 'why.' But truly when you ask how and see its double-pointing, it becomes transformative. Then you are really getting to insight—to how we know what we know.

> PAGE 119, PARAGRAPH 3: *Is there a structure we can trace that allows us to do this? Again, we meet the interpreter. "Mind has already created a history for you and the regime*

of mind is now presenting it to you in ways you can under-
stand. You have the appropriate responses, the thoughts,
expressions, and behavior expected of you. This is the pro-
cess that you have learned to engage and carry out. Be-
yond that, there is nothing that you can grasp or express,
so there is no point in analyzing further."

There are a lot of philosophers who take this view—that yes,
we can understand that we come into being with our perceptions, but beyond that, we can say nothing of any value. We
have to look at the so-called external world to learn anything
real. There's nothing in it for us. Suddenly we realize that
there is something profound here, however. We are all caught
in a double mirror. We're all being fooled. We have the question 'how' and our ability to introspect. Those two weapons
are like a sword that can cut straight through this presump-
tion that there is nothing to be found beyond the border of
double projection.

PAGE 120, PARAGRAPH 1: *We need to know more about*
what underlies this process, but we cannot seem to obtain
that information. We can only accept what mind has pre-
sented. If mind has interpreted what we are feeling as an-
ger, we can only hope that the anger, perhaps now escalat-
ing to rage, will not drive us to actions we will later regret.
But we are beginning to see how easily this can happen.

Once associations have taken hold, we become a passenger in
our own psychological process. All we can do then is mitigate
the unfortunate consequences. We no longer are able to stop
the cause, so we our only option is to attempt to mitigate the
effects.

The process has a momentum to it, like a cascade. There is
an initial object of projection, association or attachment,
then memories attach to that object. On the basis of those
memories, associations occur. Other memories start attach-
ing. Internal dialogues get engaged. All kinds of processes

get launched because of this fundamental element of our psychology.

> PAGE 120, PARAGRAPH 2: *How far can we investigate the significance of 'there is'? We can look to the senses, and we can give reasons for what we feel, think, and do. Sometimes we can connect cause and effect and arrive at explanations that provide some degree of satisfaction. But going deeper, we meet with a barrier we cannot penetrate. Beyond it is where the interpreter retreats when we ask who validates the reality of our experience.*

Self-examination is not going to cut it here; we are not going to be able to work this out by normal inquiry. A deeper way of inquiry is needed. "There is?" Who says there is?

We have to turn within and ask that question.

> PAGE 120, PARAGRAPH 3: *The realm beyond 'there is' appears to have a unique sort of system that we cannot see or touch. We can only accept the answer that the interpreter proffers: "Reality is validated by consensus. Everyone agrees to what it is." Pressed further, the interpreter balks: "Anything more is impossible to know or express. The question is irrelevant and of no consequence."*

It appears that we are now at a dead end. Is it so?

> PAGE 121, PARAGRAPH 1: *This is a very fruitful place to proceed with our inquiry. We would like to know how the mechanism of validation works, how it produces meaning instantly and coherently, almost magically, from whatever takes place in that 'prior' territory we cannot access. But our present understanding operates only from the point of recognition forward. We take birth in the realm of 'there is'. We live in that reality, placing great faith in 'the fact of the matter'. We own the whole operating system of existence—we wear it, we share it, and we carry it closely, playing it privately, rewinding it, then playing it again and again, as if listening to a favorite recording. But we are ignorant of its*

origin or composition. Wherever it takes our thoughts, feelings, and emotions, we have to cope with it. We cannot operate any other way.

We are now truly focused on the object of vipasana. By resting right at the point where 'there is' happens, there is something to be learned—because we know there was something that happened before. The whole structure upon which we build our lives is based on this moment. If we can see beyond it, we are going to find the foundations of the earth. We're going to find what makes the real, real. We're going to be able to cut through all our problems at a stroke. We're going to find freedom, true freedom, from the regime of mind. The prize that lies at the base of our own perception doesn't require us to understand the Big Bang or neurophysiology, or to be rocket scientists. What we need to do is turn within to face this process and understand it.

Exercise 16
Alert not knowing

Just three times a day, examine the certainty of identification with alert not-knowing. Alert not-knowing is the faculty of resting awareness at the point just before you know an object. The object is there but it's not yet an object of knowledge; it's merely an object of perception. Just rest there, looking at it.

An example: when a telephone or cell phone rings, try to see the double-pointing of 'there is' as it is ringing. When a phone rings, it is almost agonizing for some of us to not answer it! The phone sound arises, it's identified as a phone call, and the knower is associated with 'I must answer the phone'—they are linked together. "I've got to get that!"

That's the moment! Hang in there—there, at the arising of the phone call and the double-pointing of what that phone call represents. Just allow your alert not-knowing to rest there, because that interface between the arising sensation and your response to act on it is the key moment to examine. This can be true of any phenomenon, it doesn't have to be the phone, but phone ringing is particularly striking, because most of us run to get the phone.

That knowing is vipasana—knowing that you know that the phone rings and knowing that the demand to answer the phone is arising in you; knowing both aspects at the same time. You are understanding how the 'now' arises.

CHAPTER 24

The Reality-Realm of Mind

The last chapter dealt with validation, about how we come to say 'there is'. We talked about the double-pointing that occurs as an object is identified. The knower pops up with the known thing. It is easy logically to see that the thing itself has already been processed by our mental apparatus. Otherwise how do we know what it is? The original sense impression was processed and a label was ascribed to it before it became a recognized object. The knowing of it has another label attached to it—the label 'I'.

There is a lot of information that grows out of the recognition that the world is a construct. Much was written about it in the ancient philosophical schools of India. It is interesting to contrast their findings with what is found in the West. Western philosophers have only two tools, logic and analysis. The Indian philosophers also had those tools, but added to them insight gained through specific meditative techniques—shamata and vipasana. If you combine insight with actual experience, gained through meditation, you penetrate phenomena in a way that logic will never do. There is a huge body of literature, which gets subsumed under the title of Buddhist philosophy, which emerges from the insights that such philosophically minded meditators had.

PAGE 122, PARAGRAPH 1: *Sensing, feeling, and thinking, each person inhabits the realm of his or her own reality and plays very privately within it, thoroughly committed to it from birth to death.*

As was discussed in the first section of *Revelations*, it takes approximately 250 milliseconds to recognize a percept. We do not see this lag, because there are many sensory objects being processed at any moment and the result is integrated into a single display. Meditation enables us to isolate a single percept so we can see it being uploaded and producing a readout of a known event in the world. At the level of primary sensory processes, we upload the metaphysical structure of the world with 'me' in it, following which a whole series of associations attach themselves to that fundamental structure. "It's nice. It's nasty. It's sad. I've got to do this. Remember what happened last time?" All of these associations attach themselves to the primary upload of 'me' and 'it'. If there is no 'me' and 'it', there is nothing for the associations to attach to. If you're able in meditation to observe this, you will find there is no labeler and there are no characteristics—things are not nice, nasty, good or bad at all. All such characteristics are attached to the label by the process of association.

PAGE 122, PARAGRAPH 1, CONT'D: *A pre-established reality is projected as an outside world, and we perceive objects and attributes: grass that is green, sky that is blue.*

This pre-establishment is the past transmigrating into the present. The previous moment is recreating itself as the present; that's why it is pre-established. Our past experience provides the frame for new experience to inhabit. We then populate that preconceptual stage with entities, things which we identify and confirm, and then we enter that stage as a heroic actor, who then manipulates these objects for his or her advantage or whatever the story of our life happens to be.

So, whether you talk about pre-establishment in terms of genetics, or whether you talk about pre-establishment in terms of psychology, it is nonetheless pre-established. For this purpose, it doesn't matter much; we construct the world based on pre-established categories moment to moment. You might even say from life to life.

> PAGE 122, PARAGRAPH 1, CONT'D: *Since everyone operates with many of the same programs of mind, we share this reality in common, adapting its perceived qualities in accord with our individual faculties. We 'upload' the reality-realm program and watch it play out again and again.*

Moment to moment, we are moving through experience permeated by prior actions. This sense of movement is what is called *bardo* in Tibetan. All the bardo states described in the Tibetan tradition have this sense of moving on. The bardo of the moment of death is a bardo in which complete openness is momentarily present—just for a moment, experienced as a great light. If it is not recognized, it fades into associations, which is the next stage of the bardo. Our waking experience is similar. Moment to moment, we are initially without concept, and then concepts arise because we don't recognize that first moment of arising. If we can rest our awareness there, before the arising of labels, we can embrace freedom. If we don't, we enter labels and associations, falling forward because all that pre-conception has somewhere to land. The weight and momentum then propels us into the re-created world.

> PAGE 122, PARAGRAPH 1, CONT'D: *Running on a loop, the program continually comments on its own operations according to its own projections. Sense-perception operates as part of the program, but since we are not aware of that mechanism, we have not formulated the concepts and language that might enable us to see how it works.*

From moment to moment we are bringing with us a pre-conception that is then confirmed and known, and in that moment of knowing we live. Then we immediately die, and another moment of knowing arises, bringing all that pre-conception: it, too, is known, and we live, and then we die. And another moment of knowing arises. And that happens all the time, that process, continuously. So, the knower is flickering, and good and stable meditators say that they can actually experience this. If you become really, really still, you become aware of this flickering, and this flickering is that moment-to-moment knowing.

Of course, "who knows?" is the question to ask, which few meditators do. The knower of the flickering is not flickering; otherwise the knower wouldn't see it. There you can see that the mundane 'I' is arising and dying, arising and dying. So, arguably, we live and die many times a second, not once in a life. Indeed, neurologists speculate that the alpha frequency, one of the frequencies seen in the electrical activity of the brain, that beats between fifteen and twenty-five times per second, may be the 'refresh rate' that meditators are seeing.

PAGE 123, PARAGRAPH 1: *While this description of how reality unfolds seems to go against our usual understanding, consider what happens when we dream. Conversations and interactions in dreams are a kind of inner perception, but they seem just as real as outer perceptions. Although in a dream there is no object that we can actually see, hear, smell, feel, or taste, some kind of sensory functioning is going on, even in the absence of an external cause.*

If you can inhabit your dreams, again you have the same recognition that this is a construct. And you can use that construct to achieve things. Internal experience looks identical to external experience, and that's what gives the key to the realization that perhaps they are the same structure, the same mechanism; that the sensory inputs that arise in our everyday experience are absolutely the same as the inputs that arise in dreams.

PAGE 123, PARAGRAPH 1: *What we call cognition of 'outer' reality could be said to operate the same way. In waking life as in dreams, the flow of mental imagery, private thoughts, feelings, sensing, feedback, and identity gives rise to a unique, very convincing reality that we find attractive, perhaps even seductive.*

Now, that's very important, the word '*seductive*', because the external world we unconsciously infer based on inputs from our senses is very seductive; it's attractive or repulsive, but either way, it is seductive. And remember, most of us spend most of our time reacting to apparently external phenomena with either like, dislike, or complete indifference; and those three reactions are the basis of the responses we make to any incoming sensation.

If we were truly living in the knowledge of double-pointing, however, nothing that arose would ever shake our equanimity, because we would know it's double-pointed. Once we truly integrate double-pointedness, then every arising sensation has the same nature; when we really recognize that, we go beyond the eight worldly dharmas of gain and loss, fame and blame, like and dislike, pain and pleasure. We go beyond these illusions at a stroke. It isn't necessary to have an antidote for each one: they are cut off all at once, because they all require us to be seduced by an apparently external object to trigger them. The moment we are no longer seduced, they are gone.

PAGE 123, PARAGRAPH 2, CONT'D: *Yet, this is just the functioning of mind itself—for the mind, by the mind and of the mind—as it continually rewinds, interprets, and synthesizes its own sensing and cognitive processes. The dynamic power and magnitude of our mental imagery appears able to sustain a sense of momentum that validates the reality of what is seen.*

The momentum that we are talking about here is sometimes called 'the great eating'. Objects arise, we preconceive a reaction to them, we identify them, we recognize them, we know them and consume them, we die, we make a seed, a new object arises, we preconceive, we identify, we recognize, we know them, we die, we make a seed . . . all the time we are eating, eating, the great eating. This is mental food.

There is a famous image of Yama, the god of death, who holds a circular mirror inscribed with the Twelve Links of Dependent Origination. Those twelve links are a demonstration of this eating and dying, and Yama is holding it with his feet and arms and looking over the top. On the surface of the mirror, instead of the brilliant clarity of the mirror itself, we see reflections: the six realms of existence and the twelve links that drive them all. But if you were to wipe the mirror clean, if you could wipe all that covering away, then there would only be this brilliant mind, this pristine knowing that's always present.

> PAGE 124, PARAGRAPH 1: *But if cognition is the product of mind mechanisms, what is its basis? Something must provide the continuity that impels it to operate. Whether we call it the power of mind or the power of the will, or possibly the energy we identify as sensation, something must provide the continuity of feeling that brings our experience alive. We usually have a sense of the momentum that conveys the feeling of transition to a newly emerging moment, but this may only be a side effect of another dynamic—the motion of thoughts and feelings spooling out and rewinding. We could live forever in this familiar and comfortable place, playing our reality-tapes in continuing cycles of duplication. But do we have to settle for that? Is there a better way to understand the nature of mind and its relationship to reality?*

Here again we see 'the great eating', the momentum that's driving us from life to life, ever consuming. We are consumers in this desire realm whose motto is: Eat! That's what keeps things going in the desire realm. Eat! Grasp, cling, grasp, cling, grasp, cling, grasp, cling. From moment to moment to moment, driving round and round and round. That's what creates samsara; that's the wheel for us.

> PAGE 124, PARAGRAPH 2: *While the natural brilliance of mind has no foreground or background, or any other sense of place, mind seems to need some point of reference in order to receive and interpret meaning from the flow of sensory impressions.*

The natural brilliance of mind is Yama's mirror. It is covered with the slimy trace of our small mind that is eating, eating, going around and around. That brilliance is self-awareness, is always there, always shining—but it has no referent; there is the problem. That brilliance knows everything and yet it knows nothing, because it has no referent. The moment you create a referent by naming, the moment you point to a name, the whole mechanism of recognition and double-pointing starts. But in that initial moment, that luminous open moment, the natural brilliance of mind is seen like a shining orb: 360 degrees, all-encompassing, completely present.

And then, we know it, and in knowing it we start to consume, and then once again we start going around the circle, chasing our own tails.

> PAGE 124, PARAGRAPH 2, CONT'D: *Mind's way of accommodating this need has led to our dualistic way of understanding. Identifying through polarity and contrast, we focus on measurements that mark out the distance from here to there and create the distinctions we rely upon, using the language of our customer minds.*

> *Page 125, paragraph 1: When we are young, the distinctions we make may not be that complex, but as the scope of our experience expands, we add more specifics: concepts, private thoughts, memories, and personal habit patterns. Noting differences and relating to them as substantively real, we divide them into categories, assign them*

territories, erect walls to separate them, and place them within the walls in carefully constructed boxes. While we tend to trust 'our' experience, it is important to realize that every moment of that experience depends on such specifics. We know reality according to the way mind presents and interprets it.

PAGE 125, PARAGRAPH 2: *As we take our study of understanding deeper, we may question who put up the walls and divided experience into all these compartments and zones. Was it the senses, thoughts, and habitual patterns that created different categories? Or could it be that language evolved in that way?*

The book *Dimensions of Mind*[29] is a huge extension of these two paragraphs. It offers a detailed description of our internal space with all these zoning laws and territorial areas that we gradually accumulate as we develop our mental apparatus through our lives. The zones are created by this web of associations that we are moment to moment evolving, developing. Moment to moment we are living and dying, living and dying, and all the time we are elaborating and constructing an ever more complicated web of relationships. Of course, most people only ever experience such associative webs in emotional abreactions. It's quite hard to see them otherwise. But things that really upset you are quite useful in that you can follow their associative webs back and find out what constructed them; if you are scared of something, for example, that can trigger deep insights. When something really makes you jump back, then it's good to look at it. You will see there how the zones are made, how they are laid down by our regime of associations.

PAGE 125, PARAGRAPH 3: *If mind establishes categories as it scans our experience, isolating what seems relevant and shaping it into reality, any limitations imposed by that*

---

29 *Dimensions of Mind*, Tarthang Tulku Dharma Publishing 2016

*way of operation will mean that all our knowledge will be
limited as well. Unless we can find ways to operate mind
differently, we will continue to receive knowledge according to the structures mind creates to accommodate it.*

The categories and associations are klesha, formed by our actions and the impressions they leave behind, called karma.
Karma plants the seed, and klesha is the preconception that
has arisen due to the sprouting of that seed, which causes us
to act and create a new seed. Karma and klesha are happening
all the time in this great eating. Every moment of volition creates karmic seeds, so just think of the number of seeds you've
created, just today. Think about the number of seeds you create in one year. That's when you start realizing the infinite
complexity of our structure. We are massively complicated in
terms of what we actually carry from our past—it's huge! And
if you believe in previous lives and start adding them, then
you realize that this structure is truly infinite.

> PAGE 126, PARAGRAPH 1: *This is the challenge that faces us.
> We seem to have no way to investigate mind's limitations.
> However certain we may be of how and why we think and
> feel the way we do, without being clear on the full context
> of all the thoughts and beliefs that have arisen in mind and
> been developed through the ceaseless activity of mind's re-
> gime, it is more likely that we do not know. Few of us would
> admit to that depth of not-knowing, but is there another
> choice? Does our present level of understanding enable us
> to answer this question?*

One of the limitations of Western culture is that it has lost
its connection to inner experience, a process that began in
the collapse of the medieval world and with the arising of the
modern world view. Inner experience has been denigrated
systematically as being misleading; we hear all the time that
memory and personal accounts are unreliable, even though
evidence that memory can be reliable definitely exists. We

now live in a strange culture that denies the importance of personal experience and wishes to cast truth exclusively as an objective phenomenon. This objectivization of truth is a reason why so many of us feel alienated by modern conditions. This need not be the case, however. Once we understand the basis of our self-alienation, we are freed to find another foundation upon which to rest our subjectivity: a foundation that does not have to be written off as mere fantasy. This is the task, to build a new way of being based on the understanding of how our experience is sown and structured, moment to moment, in the tumult of our lives.

Exercise 17
All a dream

Revisit your experience by looking at everyday experience as just a dream. Three times a day, ask: "Am I dreaming?" Examine the arising of sensation and the process of recognition. Does that examination look any different whether we are dreaming or not?

This exercise is to try and come to grips with the idea of bardo, because the two bardos we have ready access to and can work with most easily are the dream bardo and the waking bardo. For those of you with stable shamata who can sit in meditation, you can ask that question in non-dual meditation in exactly the same way, because meditation is the third bardo we have access to.

So revisit the experience, looking at everyday occurrences as just a dream. Examine the arising of sensation and the process of recognition. Does that examination look any different whether we are dreaming or not?

CHAPTER 25

Turning Toward Clarity

In classic Buddhist parlance there are two obscurations, two ways that our natural brilliance of mind is covered over. Vipasana can see them both. The first is the obscuration of self, which is accessed by seeing emotions and the ego structure clearly. This is the result that people talk about when they say, "I got into my emotional stuff and I was able to work through it. I feel more relaxed and open."

Impermanence, selflessness and suffering, the famous three marks, if they are seen, are effective for overcoming the sense of self. We can see that the ego is a linguistic construct; we can see that a lot of the suffering that we experience is because we enter our life like a heroic ego, and we have a story in which we live. But that isn't enough. Ultimately we have to ask, "Who is the knower that knows that?" It's only when we see the storyteller that we have a chance of total freedom.

The danger of asking a question like this is that we might try to obtain an answer. But we are never going to see the story teller if we try and address the story teller directly, because the story teller creates the very knowing construct that we are trying to use. Conceptually we can never see the story teller, only the story the story teller has told. The knowing frame is invisible to the knower, and we can't know the answer to "who is knowing?" But that does not mean we can't access the answer. We have to see our question as an action. We can have an inquiry that doesn't conclude with an answer; we can learn just from the stance that poses the question.

The second obscuration, the obscuration of knowledge, is different. Breaking through this obscuration is about understanding the construction of the world, and seeing and knowing it fully. It is accessed by the question, "Who knows I am suffering?" This is not a question that is asked when working with the obscuration of self.

> PAGE 127, PARAGRAPH 1: *If a place is unknown, how can we go there? If something is inconceivable, how can we come to understand it? We can only work with things that are known, and for the most part this means the things that everyone knows and supports. We set out on the same journey as everyone else and extend understanding in the familiar ways. Like our fellow travelers, we label, name, identify, witness and sense; we experience feelings and make judgments. When mind decides, we accept its decision. This is the way our reality is constituted—normal, regular reality: common sense, truth. From all of these interactions, we draw conclusions that are logical, rational, and reasonable. That is our story—a story we all understand.*

This is why you can't talk about *Revelations* at dinner with people—because you are clearly leaving the tribe, and you get disapproval. What you are saying is that you are no longer going to fit in with the logical, rational world that's been made up from this basis. This will feel like subversion, and people may instinctively react with disapproval and distrust. Most people don't like it; and that's true from your parents on down. Your friends may be the worst of all, because someone who starts looking at their life like this isn't going to be a reliable friend in a normal sense.

PAGE 127, PARAGRAPH 2: *This may sound like a theory, but it is meant more as a description that you can validate for yourself. Any game we play—any story we enact—is based on the dynamic activity of mind. Mind establishes our view of time. Mind uses language to create different versions of what we know, and we understand them.*

Again, this is very subversive, essentially arguing that there is no fixed external reality. This idea can be confusing and alienating, because most people are living within the very fixed external reality in which they are getting on with life, being 'winners' and 'losers' in a zero-sum game.

PAGE 128, PARAGRAPH 1: *It is as if mind is dialoguing with its own internal editors, mind to mind, imagination to imagination: "So what is the problem? I understand what you understand." "All right, if you understand it, it is probably true. Do you understand it?" "Yes, if you want to say it that way, I suppose I understand what your version of the story means. Do you have any other versions?" "Yes, I may have another way to tell it." Back and forth, mind and imagination share stories with one another, adding perspectives and variations, shifting feelings somewhat as the drama unfolds.*

Plays written by the Greeks have this structure, perhaps because those plays were written when the dawn of consciousness was still glowing on the horizon. They have a chorus that acts almost like a commentary on the actions of the main characters. Dialogue in this regard can be very revealing.

PAGE 128, PARAGRAPH 2: *This kind of mind-to-mind interaction encompasses all of human history. It weaves the fabric of existence within the mind, giving rise to an imitation of reality held together by interlocking networks of emotional and mental patterns. Though each aspect of the extant world demonstrates its specific transitory and contingent nature, mind's story features a permanent subject—'I'—as its central operator. Otherwise the story would not work for us.*

So 'I' am the central actor in the story. The heroic ego is what holds the substantive projection of the external world together. The ego is the glue around which the world is made. And indeed, you can see little children constructing the world with the ego as the central part of that construct. This brings us back to the obscuration of self. If you can remove that obscuration, you've gone a long way in terms of going beyond construction.

> PAGE 129, PARAGRAPH 1: *Imagine that we are telling a story to ourselves. Only we know the story; there is no other audience, and our story is not relevant to anyone else. We are observing that our mind is identifying, recognizing, and creating our reality; it is commenting on our actions, arousing feelings we can now release and let go; it is bringing up thoughts that we know will aggravate resentments and we can smile as understanding dissolves them. We are now aware of everything that comes up in the mind, balancing easily in the flow of feelings and thoughts, with mind alert yet relaxed. We may feel we have arrived at the point where we have perfect understanding of mind. There is no mystery left, and we now think there is nothing else left to understand. But how do we deal with the background murmurings, the communication of mind to mind that only we can hear?*

The only success that life can offer you is within a story. We want to go deeper: our task is to understand the storyteller. The first chapters on meditation talked about how to calm the mind and begin to get beneath the surface; this makes it possible to have an encounter with the storyteller. If we could meet the storyteller, we could become master of all stories. We would understand how stories are made. We would have a deep appreciation for freedom because we would know how reality is constructed. We would have a choice.

But there's a problem. If we merely turn around, we just face inwards when we were formerly facing outwards. We still

don't see the storyteller. All it does is take the external projection of the world and project it internally into an internal projection. We are still 'subjects' looking at 'objects'—only this
time, we are treating our own inner lives as 'things to know'.
This in no way penetrates and reveals the storyteller. To see
the storyteller, we have to turn toward the inconceivable.

If a place is unknown, how can we go there? If something is
inconceivable, how can we understand it?

> PAGE 129, PARAGRAPH 2: *Is there anything that is not a sto-
> ry? So far, our minds do not seem to know of such a pos-
> sibility. When does the story end? It ends when we develop
> the habit of looking inward, at the 'from' of our experience,
> and seeing mind's mechanism at work. It ends when we
> realize that it really is just a story.*

This is turning within. The experience that mind creates is
mediated by language. Phenomena are Janus-faced: the object is known by a subject in a linguistic construct. Turning
within is universal. No matter what experience we are having,
we can always turn within. No matter what circumstances or
conditions appear for us, at every moment of experience we
can turn within.

> PAGE 130, PARAGRAPH 1: *Clarity arises through observ-
> ing mind. Observing the mechanisms of mind, seeing how
> they operate, what calms and what agitates them, leads to
> a potent understanding of mind's nature. To develop this
> understanding further, we can study the architecture and
> engineering of our mental patterns and observe how they
> play out in experience. Then we can see what we are in-
> volved in, how our patterns are constructed, how we as-
> sume roles and enact them, and how mind artfully posi-
> tions itself as director, knower, and leader.*

This is the way to overcome the first obscuration—the obscuration of self that results in a life ruled by emotionality.
Normally our emotions rule our behavior because we don't

understand the mechanism that creates the double-headed label that acts as a tag for associations to attach to and release emotional behavior. This fundamental unknowing makes us victims of our own experience. We are victims of our past preconceptions and memories.

It is sad to think that we normally have access to such a tiny percentage of our true potential. Overcoming this first obscuration will let us develop the skill to see how the mind constructs the world and how that construct acts as an anchor for emotionality, which establishes and perpetuates the same patterns going forward.

This loop doesn't just affect individuals. It can go on for generations—a kind of tribalism that acts like a prison. If you develop shamata, you can separate events from your reactions, allowing the emotional energy to cool off and the patterned response to lose some of its momentum. Your clarity increases. If you continue to practice, you will eventually get to a point where you are no longer ruled by emotionality. That's overcoming the first obstacle—already an enormous fruit.

This can have interesting side-effects; you may end up being recognized as a highly impressive and charismatic individual. More important, you are just not buying into the repetitive mechanism of emotionality and its results, which is the way most people live their lives.

> PAGE 130, PARAGRAPH 2: *Understanding this much, we can go more deeply into the fundamental question, to whom does this mind belong? Our inquiry pursues this question by asking further questions: Is mind the same as 'I'? Did 'I' create mind, or did mind create 'I'? Which is mind and which is 'I'? Do 'I' belong to mind, or does mind belong to 'I'? Do 'I' understand who owns whom?*

Now we enter the sphere of the second obscuration, the obscuration of knowledge. We've identified that the hero, the ego, the actor is the primary projection which arises in response to initial sense impression. "To whom does the mind belong?" is still a question to ask, however. This question starts going beyond the first obscuration and into the second. The first relates to the memories that attach to the primary construct of self. Those associations are the basis of all the judgments— nice, nasty, happy, sad, "want it," "don't want it." They get attached to the primary construct. But to whom does this mind belong? It is a strange question. Look at yourself in a mirror and ask, "Who are you?" You get a strong sensation; there is something interesting here. That is the deeper question.

> PAGE 130, PARAGRAPH 3: *If we have not yet developed a conceptual framework for this way of exploring, these questions may seem meaningless—like the babble of children learning to talk. We may feel we are long past the stage where we could ask such questions or find it valuable to do so. But they go to the heart of what mind is, and they offer us valuable opportunities to turn assumptions upside down and think in new ways.*

These questions about identity run deeper than the ego. It seems the concept-maker is still there even if we understand the ego. Who is this concept-maker?

This deeper form of questioning becomes the major subject of the second half of Revelations. We have more to do to fill in the perceptual structure. The more complete we can make this picture, the more penetrating this question becomes. We can work out what it is to be a human being by understanding how we construct the world. And by doing so exhaustively, looking at every single detail, we will realize that our picture is not complete. Who does my mind belong to? The stance from which this question emerges has a profound consequence. It reveals what lies at the heart of our being.

> PAGE 131, PARAGRAPH 1: *If we sense an inner resistance, or perhaps a willful reluctance to engage this line of*

questioning, we can use language and feelings to relax the regime of mind. We can dialogue with the mind. Even as mind reminds and directs us, we can encourage it to open and allow us to access deeper levels of consciousness.

There has been a witness to our whole life. That witness is the regime of mind. Every stupid mistake we made, every broken promise, every New Year's resolution that lasted twenty-four hours, every intention to do something we didn't carry through—all those things we did with nobody around so we could pretend to be rational beings—all of it is remembered by our psychology. Now we have to try to persuade our psychology that we can ask the question, "Who am I?" The regime of mind does not want us to ask such a question. We are so unreliable that our regime just wants to get us to bedtime! It's trying to protect us. We will have to negotiate if we are to get deeper than the first obscuration. The regime doesn't take us that seriously; that's why we have resistance when we meditate. We have to demonstrate sobriety. We have to demonstrate *to ourselves* that this is a serious undertaking. Otherwise the mechanism of mind that has been protecting us from all sorts of stupid behavior will not go along with it.

Essentially, we are asking permission to leave the protection of our mind—to take control. "I've graduated," we protest. "I don't need you to look after me anymore. I realize that your concepts are useful, but I want to use them as an ornament. I want to be able to choose to use them rather than have them limit my choices!"

Once we've developed a certain degree of skill in understanding that language is formative, we can use formative language to relax the mind. We will find that dialogue is actually quite powerful. And one of the most important things to say to yourself is, "Look, I am reliable, and if there are insights you give me, I will adopt them. I am not just going to ignore them. I am not merely curious; I'm not doing this just for fun. I genuinely want to understand the question 'who am I', I genuinely do."

Now, if there is one thing your mind is scared of, it is the idea that you could be truly free, because that means that it then would have no ability to control you—it would have lost control of the reins. So this may require a lot of persuasion. This dialogue—the use of language and feelings to relax the regime of mind—is actually a non-trivial activity. It's almost like psychotherapy, or rather like auto-therapy: there is a genuine wish to deepen our experience through dialogue. The dialogue referred to here is attitudinal; we are demonstrating good faith. We will not persuade our inner auntie with sophisticated arguments. In taking that attitude we must be a reliable party; if we are not, forget it. Do we really think a one-million-year-old piece of tissue is going to let us do something stupid, just because we ask? But if we are reliable then the regime can take a different stance: "Well, OK. You seem to be growing up now."

> PAGE 131, PARAGRAPH 1, CONT'D: *Just as mind uses language to remind and direct us, we can use language and feelings to relax the regime of mind. The more we understand the nature of mind, the more calmness and clarity we can offer the mind, and the more effectively mind can serve the whole of our being.*

What might this mean in practice? Suppose we get angry. We might normally apologize to the person we got angry with, but to take our understanding deeper, we need to apologize to ourselves. All the emotion we got swept away by damages us as much as it damages the other person. Our ability to be reliable is so questionable. We need to enter into this dialogue with ourselves, saying, "I want to grow up. I want to be free. I want to be a reliable, free agent that can use your assistance to navigate experience, without being dependent on your rules. I want to be able to use what you give me as an ornament to my freedom."

In a way, this is prayer, but not to God; rather, we are supplicating our own perception, the incredible, magical manifestation within which we have had the good fortune to be born. If we can become a reliable partner, then we can ask this question: "To whom does mind belong?" We're never going to get an answer if the regime of mind still needs to protect us. If the regime needs to protect us, it is not going to let us know anything about that!

This direct dialogue with the regime of mind is very meaningful. To undertake it is to practice true meditation. We are really engaging with our own perception: it's a negotiation, it's a relationship. It's not just "let's be calm" or "let's feel better"— although it might manifest that way to everyone else, as this activity can definitely help us develop calmness and clarity, bring us insight and change our behavior for the better. But these are mere side-effects, rather than the goals of our practice. The relationship with ourselves, with our minds, with our regimes—that is what's central.

This is about having a direct relationship with our own perception—learning to make contact with perception as a pure, magical display. To really understand, we will have to develop a relationship with this display. This is *lila,* sacred play; it is a dance, like the dance of Shiva.

Having gotten this far, we may feel strongly motivated. Now we want to deeply engage our experience, but this time, we'll do so as reliable, sober, sensible grownups—not as children, nor as curious, itchy, inquisitive 'Renaissance' man or woman types, interested in adding more arrows to our quivers of knowledge!

Exercise 18
Entering a dialogue with the mind

Sitting quietly a few times per day, enter a dialogue with the mind. Do not ask questions—that is mind asking mind. Rather, in the quiet place of alert not knowing, form the intention—"how do you make the world?" and "how can deeper aspects of consciousness become available?" Make an internal vow that you will act on any suggestions that come up. Be reliable. If suggestions are made available to you, use language and feelings to work with them, and if resistance emerges, go back into alert not knowing and form the intention again.

CHAPTER 26

Time to Understand

'Time' is one of the technical terms that has infiltrated common usage. Another couple are 'magnetic' and 'electric'. Time, magnetic and electric are words whose meaning has been redefined by modern physics, even though they have ancient roots within our language. As a result, when we use them we are often invoking something semi-technical without realizing it. Because of this dual meaning, the words become a little enigmatic—it's almost as if we can't work out what they mean. What has happened is that they have been redefined from a referent based in personal experience to a referent that is strictly technical.

In physics time is a metric: it's a locator. Modern physics locates everything with three space coordinates and one time coordinate, the four numbers that define 'space-time'. This definition has been very fruitful. Einstein developed equations that showed that time appears to pass at different rates depending on how fast you are moving. Although that seems pretty obscure, actually one way we use these equations is to correct the time signals that our mobile phones receive from satellites that orbit overhead. Naturally, because applications like this show us that space-time 'works', we tend to say it is 'true'. As we have discussed extensively in the previous two sections, however, such a statement is significantly inaccurate. We might better say: "Because it works, we can infer that it might be true." This small change is important, for it is entirely possible that some new theory will come along and provide a more accurate description of the passing of time. We would then infer that new theory to be true and Einstein's to be false. It is valuable to realize that all the statements we make about reality are inferences in this manner.

A second point is the definition physicists use for the measurement of time. Time is defined in a strangely circular manner: time is what clocks tell you, and clocks are devices that tell time. Clocks are devices that change in a regular manner, whether they be egg timers, hourglasses, wall clocks or atomic counters. The regularity of the change within these devices allows us to use them to base our measurement of time on a stable foundation. But this circularity in the definition of time reveals an essential truth—that time is change and change measures time. These two ideas are inextricably linked.

Although timekeeping devices were developed by very ancient cultures, including Egypt and Mesopotamia, it is fair to say that the modern conception of time really began to take off in the Middle Ages, with the invention of mechanical clocks. Before then, the cycle of the day was broken up into 'watches', periods of the day and night marked in both Christendom and Islam by regular calls to prayer. Shorter periods were called 'whiles' in medieval Europe, such as an 'eating while' or a 'pissing while'. Time was an experience: it was something you lived through. With the invention of increasingly accurate clocks, however, time began to take on its modern meaning, that of a metric or measuring system. Now most of us carry on our wrists or in our pockets devices capable of measuring time in intervals far, far shorter than we can actually experience. But the old meaning still lingers, which is what makes the question of time so confusing.

With these thoughts in mind, it is clear why we often get muddled when we talk about time. We say things like, "Things change over time"—as if time were some sort of medium and we are traveling through it. We ask, "What time is it?" as if time were some sort of thing. What these usages do is conflate two very different conceptions of time—namely, time as an experience, and time as a metric. The key that links them, however, is change. Indeed, it's almost a relief to see that time is change, and that change can be experienced. We might even say that change *is* experience. Once understood in this way, we can understand why time seems so enigmatic, and yet so intimately involved with our lives. Time is directly related to our experience, the most personal thing we possess.

If time is change, and change is experience, then time is experience. This linkage was well understood in ancient cultures. Time was understood as Maya, the great illusion, the all-powerful goddess who could control the entirety of our lives. Here is a wonderful example, extracted from Mircea Eliade's *Images and Symbols*.[30]

A famous ascetic named Narada, having obtained the grace of Vishnu by his numbers of austerities, the god appears to him and promises to do anything for him that he may wish. "Show me the magical power of thy Maya," Narada requests of him. Vishnu consents, and gives the sign to follow him. Presently, they find themselves on a desert road in hot sunshine, and Vishnu, feeling thirsty, asks Narada to go a few hundred yards farther, where there is a little village, and fetch him some water. Narada hastens forward and knocks at the door of the first house he comes to. A very beautiful girl opens the door; the ascetic gazes upon her at length and forgets why he has come. He enters the house, and the parents of the girl receive him with the respect due to a saint.

---

30 Mircea Eliade, *Images and Symbols* (Sheed and Ward (New York), 1961) 71.

Time passes. Narada marries the girl, and learns to know the joys of marriage and the hardships of a peasant life. Twelve years go by; Narada now has three children and, after his father-in-law's death, becomes the owner of the farm. But in the course of the twelfth year, torrential rains inundate the region. In one night the cattle drown and the house collapses. Supporting his wife with one hand, holding two of his children with the other and carrying the smallest on his shoulder, Narada struggles through the waters. But the burden is too great for him: he slips, and the little one falls into the water; Narada lets go of the other two children to recover him, but too late; the torrent has carried him far away. And whilst he is looking for the little one, the waters engulf the two others and, shortly afterwards, his wife. Narada himself falls, and the flood bears him away unconscious, like a log of wood. When, stranded upon a rock, he comes to himself and remembers his misfortunes, he bursts into tears. But suddenly he hears a familiar voice: "My child, where is the water you were going to bring me? I've been waiting for you for more than half an hour." Narada turns his head and looks: instead of the all-destroying flood, he sees the desert landscape dazzling in the sunlight. And the god asks him, "Now do you understand the secret of my Maya?"

> PAGE 133, FRONTISPIECE: *Why are we interested in understanding time? The simple response is: "Because the regime of mind as it now operates limits our freedom and leads inexorably to suffering." That regime has become unnecessarily confining, a product of an earlier age that the dynamic power of time may have rendered obsolete. Since the model that sustains the present regime developed from mind's interaction with time—the unit of experience that allows perception to take place—we begin by looking more closely at the relationship of mind and time.*

The first section of *Revelations* concerns the construction of perception; the second section takes as its topic how to stabilize the mind so it can become a good vehicle for self-observation. This third section begins to use the tool of self-observation to try and penetrate the act of perception as it occurs—of course, in time. The intention is to bring our focus of attention to the moment of initial sense contact, the point where mind interacts with time.

All this language can be misleading, in that it implies that time itself is some sort of entity. But clearly, mind is interacting, somewhere, and that 'somewhere' has a 'sometime'. That 'sometime' is what is being considered.

> PAGE 134, PARAGRAPH 1: *Perceptions, thoughts, and feelings are all aspects of a complex process that determines the nature of our experience and contributes to our sense of self, reality, and time. Since each aspect of this process powerfully influences the nature of our experience, it is important that we understand more precisely how this process works. Although mind moves too quickly for us to track these operations as they unfold, if we could focus at the point where perception begins, we could become more aware of the role of each element as sensory impulses give rise to shape and form. With practice, we might become able to see the entire process at once: the ground of perception, how mind develops it, and how mind's operations interact to construct our sense of reality.*

Initial sense impressions give rise to shape and form. This is called *rupa-skandha* in the Buddhist technical analysis of perception, the Abhidharma. *Rupa* is normally translated as 'form'. Unfortunately, Western metaphysics tends to creep into this translation through a conception of form as something that's separated out from us as an existent in an external world. In contrast, within Buddhist technical language, the term *rupa* is a referent for sensation. Initial sense impressions give rise to the inference of form rather than being form itself. So *rupa*, as it's properly described within Buddhist thought, is in fact initial sense impressions rather than an inferred 'physical world'.

We are interested in how *rupa*, initial sense impressions, underlie feeling, and then perception, and then volition. How does that happen? How is the inference of the world being constructed from our perceptual processes?

> PAGE 134, PARAGRAPH 2: *Since the system of mind is global, set up to take us seamlessly from a place of not-knowing to identity and re-cognition—step by step and picture by picture—understanding how it operates in any one situation would provide a pattern for resolving not only one problem, but many all at once.*

Now, this is really important. If we could inhabit that moment of contact, where sense impression first arises, we would solve all our cognitive problems at once, because every single event in our lives begins with that moment. If you can get to the origin, you would see everything that follows it, no matter what it is. And this is true of both internal and external phenomena—it doesn't matter whether the impetus is coming from within or without.

> PAGE 134, PARAGRAPH 2, CONT'D: *Using this pattern as a template, we could overlay it on the larger fabric of our experience and apply it effectively in different situations. Re-identifying and re-cognizing on a different basis, we would have a precious opportunity to release the knotted threads of our thoughts and feelings and weave patterns of far greater meaning and beauty into our lives.*

If we can inhabit this, we would have the power of Vishnu's Maya to weave any pattern we wanted into our lives rather than being a victim of the re-cognized patterns we already experience. Remember, cognition leads re-cognition, and re-cognition is a memory, so we are always in memory—that's why we are stuck. We go in circles, because memories reinforce themselves. Even if we start off going in a straight line, we rapidly end up going in a circle. So how can we become free of our circularity? By going back to the point of cognition and liberating it from re-cognition: then we have a choice. We can choose to go on and on in a circle if we wish, but we also have the freedom to move in another direction.

PAGE 135, PARAGRAPH 1: *While mind strongly protects our sense of ourselves as unique individuals, it does not seem to protect us from feeling pressured by time. We are easily disturbed by reminders of impermanence—situations, problems, and consequences that can arise unexpectedly to bring disappointment and close down opportunities. We know as well that time does not wait upon our convenience. It cannot be controlled, and it does not stop.*

What we are trying to do is to break the stimulus-response loop that causes us to be so pressured. Remember, what happens to us in our everyday experience is that initial sense impressions arise and we re-cognize them immediately. That immediacy creates a continual pressure to react, precisely because we don't inhabit that moment of cognition: we have no space and no time to stop before our reactions have set off another sensory loop. We can't stop the clock: we live in a world of continual change where there is always stuff coming at us. Because of this, learning to stop the clock is the secret of serenity. But you won't become serene by sitting in a cave and trying to shut off sensory input: that will not stop the clock. All that will happen is that your internal senses will start generating their own inputs and drive you crazy in your solitude. The way to serenity is by taking control of the sensory inputs: they can still be operating, but you are no longer obligated to react to them the moment they arise.

PAGE 135, PARAGRAPH 2: *Mind can only recognize what time allows. We could view time as a field of opportunity that mind enters in order to act. Immediately, as if suddenly enveloped in a gigantic hologram projection, we are presented with the whole context of our reality: the sense of being, the sense of surroundings, and the sense of movement 'from' and 'to'. Like a seed planted by mind in the field of time, this projection, developed and replicated throughout human history, is the model for each instant of experience. While the specifics change from moment*

to moment, the model is continuously replicated: it per-
sists, unquestioned and unquestionable, perpetuating it-
self through the power of its own dynamic. We participate
by embodying it and projecting into all we think and do.

So, we are now beginning to take a look at how the meta-physical constructs that we create are operating as they happen, moment-to-moment. In particular, we are focusing on the point where mind enters in order to act. This is the moment of contact. Every experience that we have begins here: this moment of contact is where the world begins. Accessing the moment of contact is a universal key. If it's accessible, it becomes the place where change is truly possible. Otherwise, change can only happen within a construct that's already crystallized, which limits what changes can take place. But at the moment of contact—the moment of conception—change is absolute. That's the difference.

The seed that contact plants in the field of time is re-cognition. A phenomenon arises. It is grasped: "What is that?" It is re-cognized: "Oh, it's a clock": and then it is recognized: "I saw a clock." And with the "I saw a clock," all the associations of 'I', 'clock', and where 'I am', all come into being together. The whole world arises like a magical display. I am in it, the clock is in it, everything else is in it. But right at the very beginning of conception, none of that was present—it was just a shimmering display.

That seed of recognition is planted, and its fruit is the whole world: and that's repeated again and again, from moment to moment, by every single sentient being.

PAGE 136, PARAGRAPH 1: *Senses, perception, identity, re-*
cognition, and labeling, 'I', me, mine, interpretations and
associations: Time enables mind to play all these roles.
This template for reality has worked for us throughout
human history. It now seems so reflexive that we may
never stop to think about how it works or to investigate

its implications to our thoughts and actions. It is as if we have received it as a sealed unit stamped 'do not open'. As its end user, we may be able to manipulate it to deal with some of the upsets and malfunctions that arise, but it would not normally occur to us that we could safely open it up and investigate a problem's point of origin. If such a thought were to arise, would we have the confidence to investigate mind in this way? Can we try?

Initial sense impressions give rise to the first moment of the regime of mind: rupa. "What's that?" Identity: "It's this!" Recognition and labeling: "I see it, it's a clock!" Interpretations: "That clock is 'mine': that clock belongs to 'me'!" Associations: "That's a nice clock," or "I remember when a clock like that upset me." This is the build-up. The initial sense impression arises: the mind grasps it. And in response to "it's a clock," "I see a clock" arises: ping-pong, now we have output! A seed planted in time. The dualistic world of "I see a clock" arises, and in that dualistic construct of "I see a clock," every other association then has a hook it can hang onto.

Memory only remembers "I saw a clock." Memory doesn't remember the first moment at all. It can't, because *the first moment has no hook*: there's no referent for the associative mechanism of memory to hang on to. There is nothing to remember. This means you will never be able to recollect this process by looking into your past experience. You'll only remember "I saw a clock," "I was in a room," "I went for a drive," "I did this, I did that." But as it is happening, in the moment of the events themselves, at the very beginning, there is nothing to do with 'I'.

'I' wasn't there, 'I' wasn't made yet, 'I' hadn't yet been brought into being by mind interacting in time. In that earliest moment, 'I' was not present! More than that: 'I' am *still* not present ever! But 'I' am *remembered* as present. This is Maya, the great illusion of time.

CHAPTER 27

Architect of Time

We all know that the world that we experience is constructed. There is an inferred world out there, but it's nothing we can experience. The world we experience is made by our minds. Time plays a fundamental role in that construct. Understanding how that works is important in being able to control the construct—that's why time is so challenging.

Time is not metrical in our experience. Whereas a clock moves steadily and smoothly, our experience of time is anything but smooth. It can flow quickly or slowly: it can stop entirely, or it can slip into non-awareness. An hour can seem to pass quicker than waiting five minutes for a bus. An incredibly rich daydream can seem to take hours, but actually take less than a minute. So it is not true that time flies only if we are not paying attention to it. Time is fungible: the reason for this is that our construction of the world is linked to time. As our constructs change, so does time.

Our experiences are 'whiles' of time, to use the medieval term, not the metric measurements of change that we've understood from the physicists. They turned time into something which is no longer an experience but rather the output of a clock. Whatever the technicians tell us, however, our experience of time is absolutely valid.

PAGE 137, PARAGRAPH 1: *If mind, time, and perception did not come together in some way, we would not have a sense of time or be able to know what is happening. In turn, perception itself is made possible by the nature of our senses and mental activity.*

The moment of initial sense impression, before conception has even occurred, you can liken mind to a mirror. It's merely reflecting something that's arising from sensory input. It's possible to be in this shimmery experience if you quiet yourself down and just allow your senses to dwell on something, without naming it. You begin to enter into the actual sensory input impression itself. The sensory input isn't fixed: it's as if it is waiting, shimmering. In classic mindfulness practice, this is what experienced meditators are accessing. When you become mindful of a sensation, and you allow your mindfulness to rest, it starts to go deeper than the labeling; it begins to access the sense gates themselves. Now, even if the input refers to 'pain', if you don't say "Oh, pain!", if you don't react, but just settle, you can actually approach the pain sensation: then the sensation may start to shimmer: it decoheres into something much less solid. This shows that the solidity of pain is a function of our reaction to it, not of the stimulus itself. Indeed, there are monks who can have major operations without anesthetic because of this. They are able to observe the pain itself rather than be dominated by the reaction to the pain: through this observation, the label of pain starts to disaggregate and the underlying sensation emerges.

The key point is that when we turn our attention toward a perceived sensation, it begins to decohere. Decoherence occurs because at the moment of contact, sensation is like a shimmering well of potentiality. It is then cognized and re-cognized. As it's recognized, it gets put into a box called a 'thing': it's made into something identifiable, known by a knower. It becomes a thing in the world. But right at the very beginning, it's shiny, shimmery. This is why a mirror is often used as a metaphor for the mind in this shimmery experience.

> PAGE 137, PARAGRAPH 2: *Prior to perception, we might think of mind as completely free of content, clear and reflective as a highly polished mirror. Then, in response to sensory activity, patterns of light and shadow begin to flicker. As they intensify and brighten into reflections, light reveals colors and texture, while other sensory impressions convert into forms, sounds, tastes, bodily sensations and fragrance. This sensory activity alerts the mind that something has presented itself for identification, and mind reaches out to grasp it, awakening the first stirrings of a quality of understanding.*

Pain can turn into pleasure easily, if you move your attention backwards down the flow of identification to the initial sense impression itself. If you rest there you can break through to where there is no object identified, and there is clarity in the mind. Every moment we are integrating multiple sensory streams into a smooth image of the world. That's what the brain does. Each element of that integrated whole that we call 'awareness' or 'the world' is in fact made up of cycles in which the mind is presented with sensory input. It then reaches out and identifies that input, and projects the result as a known entity in the world.

This happens all the time with multiple inputs, which is why we don't see it happening. In order to access this, it is helpful to limit it to one flow only. That's why it is often said in shamata, "Look at the sensation of the breath at the tip of the nose." Looking at just one thing and ignoring every other sense-door simplifies experience. As long as there are multiple sensory inputs happening, it is extremely difficult to penetrate and understand this process.

> PAGE 137, PARAGRAPH 3: *In order to identify the sensory activity, mind marks out and projects a tiny unit of*

experience, an instant in which recognition can take place. Let us call this instant a nanosecond, literally a billionth of a second, a unit impossibly small, but still large enough to allow for further divisions.

For recognition to occur, there must be a unit of time. Time measures change, the transformation of one thing into another. For perception to occur, it is as if time and space are tagged in order for experience to be known. Recognition identifies: it starts with this shimmering sensory input that has no time, no form, no place. Then the mind reaches out with its first cognition; whether to want, to avoid, or to ignore. The re-cognition of this primary movement confirms a label, but importantly that label is in space and at a time. It's been geotagged: "I saw the clock (then and there)." Then and there, the whole world has come into being.

For us, for our Maya, time is a unit of memory. We have a time-stamp on all our memories, which is how we distinguish cause from effect. Without time, we would become completely confused. Young children have this problem, because they haven't developed their time-stamp yet, so they sometimes have difficulty working out what is going on. They've just got stuff happening, but they are not sure where they are in it. Adults, on the other hand, live in a structured world where we know where we were an hour ago—intuitively, if not precisely—and we intuitively know that before that, we came from somewhere else. We know that, because we time-stamped it. We re-member. If we didn't time-stamp it, how would we know what came first? How would we have any idea?

> PAGE 138, PARAGRAPH 1: *Having projected the nanosecond, mind recognizes what the senses have presented, identifies the object, and applies a label that seals the object's identity. But this label is not based on the initial flickering of light and shadow, for the first point of contact is already past. It arises instead from reflections that continue*

*to develop from subsequent points of contact, as we be-
come involved in a secondary process of remembering, re-
reflecting and re-cognizing. We did not notice the point
at which reflections replaced initial impressions; in fact,
since the transition takes place before the label is presented and recognized, we would not even know how to notice
it. Already we are trailing behind, following reflections of
reflections as mind weaves the tapestry of our reality.*

The world we make is a step behind what we receive at all
times. It is a reflection. There is a process, an internal dialec-
tic that is going on all the time, in which initial impressions
are reflected and stamped in time, and then further associations are brought in, and the whole thing becomes populated
into a display, a readout. But it all begins at that initial moment of contact: that's the key to it all. If we can access that
initial moment of contact, the whole collection of reflections,
associations, memories, actions, wishes, likes, dislikes, opinions, etc. that come afterward is brought to light. Otherwise,
this huge cart of stuff acts as an envelope for us, a filter that
limits and controls what we experience.

PAGE 138, PARAGRAPH 2: *The instant mind recognizes an
object, the subject appears also, brought into being by
further reflections that bounce back and forth within the
mind. Subject and object accommodate one another, creating the environment for self and other, the dualistic perspective that characterizes our point of view and conditions our understanding of reality.*

This is double-pointing. In the initial sense impression, in
that shimmering moment when the senses provide the first
signal, there is no 'I', just unformed openness. The next movement is to reach out with a preverbal cognition: want, avoid,
ignore? There is no 'I' there either: nothing is 'known' yet. In
the third phase, however, comes the recognition: "Oh, that's
a clock." This is when the 'I' appears. In that recognition of
"that's a clock," boom, the clock and the knower come into

being, double-pointed. With the recognition of clock and knower come all the other associations, including all the memories of known clocks, all the information that the regime has assembled.

After that projection, everything that appears is double-pointed: everything is dualistic. Everything that 'I' knows must be dualistic because 'I' knows it. Thus there are always two parts to everything that appears: perceiver and perceived, 'I' and what 'I' know.

> PAGE 139, PARAGRAPH 1: *Reflections—mind reflecting to mind, mind feeding back to mind—provide the continuity necessary for sensory impressions to develop to the point where mind can generate a label that identifies the object and imprints it in memory. That label is now accepted as 'real': The object has a name, and the sound of that name can call up the image that corresponds to it. Thereafter, the identity of that object comes up instantly, because mind already knows the label appropriate to it.*

The name is pronounced: "It's a clock." That naming is very important. Before there was the word, there was nothing knowable: In the Bible this is wonderfully described as God's face upon the deep. Right at the very beginning there was just primordial experience. Then, the experiencer looked at experience and said, "What is that?" And it was known, it was named, and suddenly the experiencer had a self and the object had a name. "In the beginning was the word."

Understood in this way, this experience of 'I in the world' is actually a memory.

Called into being by sound, and acting as a frame in which all of our associations can be attached, this 'I in the world' is very useful if you are negotiating a dangerous place: it allows you to access your experience and map it onto your current experience. But the map is not the territory. It may well be that we have other faculties that we have lost because we are so reliant on the map. We may be living like tourists who go to Rome or some ancient city and walk around with their faces buried in their guidebooks. Are we missing the experience of something new? Are we missing the territory because we have a map?

> PAGE 139, PARAGRAPH 2: *Meaning and associations arise simultaneously with the label—this is red, this is soft, this is good, this is not good. Additional specifics, judgments, and interpretations follow. Instantly, we not only know the name of what has been perceived, but we can also point out the qualities and characteristics associated with that name.*

Actual experience is always neutral. But most of us don't live in experience: we live in memory. The memory itself can be manipulated and adjusted. That's what creates the glamorous cycle of consumerism. All the problems that we suffer from, our political differences, our religious differences and our territorial battles are all based on associations that have been constructed around labeled objects in memory. One can see the transformative potential of being able to get underneath the label to the actual experience. That has profound implications for the real.

There is an important point here. The qualities and characteristics that arise are associated with the label: they may not actually be present in the experience. The label is what we think should be present. This is why branding is so important. If you wear a famous product it's almost as if the label is as important as the thing itself. The logo really matters. Why? Because of associations. Advertising is trying to elicit those associations.

> PAGE 139, PARAGRAPH 3: *The point of recognition may be infinitesimally small, but without this small interval, mind cannot identify anything. Within a single nanosecond, there is observation, mind sensing an object, and thought identifying it; the instant thought is, meaning is. In the next nanosecond, as the senses grasp at the object,*

we may pick up a feeling and react: "I don't like this." But without the first nanosecond in which identity and recognition take place, that feeling and the thought that follows it cannot occur.

This first moment is the landing place of perception. Before that first moment, experience just shimmers. After it there are things and knowers of things.

Without that initial moment, the process by which memory can attach itself to experience cannot occur. The regime of mind cannot operate within direct experience: it has to project time in order to engage its webs of association. This is the Achilles heel of the regime of mind. Without that little bit of time right at the point of recognition, the regime can't work. This is why we want to look there very carefully. If it weren't for that little opening, there would be no escape for us from the prison of our own process.

PAGE 140, PARAGRAPH 1: *To generate the nanosecond, mind marks out units based on reflections. In much the same way that mind recognizes objects and establishes them as real, it points out, identifies, labels, and validates nanoseconds with the stamp of recognition. With each validation, mind reflects back to itself. It confirms, yes, that is a nanosecond; yes, that is a unit of time.*

So, up comes the sensory impression, the mind grasps, and in the confirmation that the grasped identity is a known thing, a small unit of time is laid out and the knower and the known appear: in other words, time and space. It all happens incredibly quickly, again and again and again. "This is Vishnu's Maya"—the creation of time.

PAGE 140, PARAGRAPH 2: *To see how this works, imagine a dialogue between Mind and Perception:*

Mind: I give you space/time.

Perception: How much?

Mind: The nanosecond.

Perception: Thank you. Now I have to act.

[Perception enters and begins to discriminate—'yes' to this, 'no' to that.]

Mind: I have provided this opportunity. I have projected the nanosecond and established time.

PAGE 141, PARAGRAPH 1: *Is Mind overstating its role here? No. For, if mind marks out the nanosecond, and this marking out initiates all the operations that follow, time as we know it is literally made by mind. Moreover, each subsequent operation of mind is implicit in the first nanosecond, for all the conditions are already present. The stage is ready, the script has been written, and each of the actors is ready to play the role that mind has assigned. Everything is prepared, awaiting activation at the instant of recognition. So, when mind pronounces, "I feel bad" or "I am happy," 'feel bad' and 'happy' are absolutely true.*

PAGE 141, PARAGRAPH 2: *Identity leaves no space for doubt, so it cannot fail. "I feel bad; I am happy." Yes, because these thoughts have been stamped into consciousness by the mechanism of recognition. The process unfolds automatically, because this is the way mind has set up the rules.*

So now we are restating the regime of mind from the perspective of time. Through the projection of a unit of time, the whole array—the known, the knower of the known, and what is remembered about the known—comes flooding into being.

PAGE 141, PARAGRAPH 3: *Projecting the nanosecond, mind also projects the time frame in which cause and effect can occur. It is as if mind takes two roles—mind as mind and mind as time—and collaborates with itself, saying, "I will give myself [as time] the opportunity to create the frame for an object to manifest. As soon as an object appears within it, I will provide the instant that allows me to capture and identify it." Given this instant, identity happens, followed by naming, recognition, associations, interpretations, and dialogues between mind and its retinue. As mind's regime falls into line, the process gathers momentum. All this takes place within the time frame created as mind projects the nanosecond. But we have no way to think about it before recognition takes place.*

PAGE 142, PARAGRAPH 1: *Where did this process begin? What caused it to begin? We can say that mind picks up sensory stimulations and generates thoughts in the process of cognizing, identifying, naming, and recognizing, but until we can trace the operations of mind to their origin, prior to the point of recognition, our knowledge remains incomplete.*

Think of the injunction familiar to so many meditators: "Be here now!" We are really explicating what 'here' and 'now' might mean. The here and now are recognized—they are concepts with an important role in our construct of reality. But what came before them?

PAGE 142, PARAGRAPH 2: *The point of recognition—the interval of the nanosecond—provides a kind of 'landing place' for mind, a point of reference for a segment of reality that mind builds upon and returns to for reassurance and validation. We see this process operating whenever we tell ourselves, "I have seen that. I have heard that. I thought it. I remember it. It happened. I believe it; it is true." But remember that, by the time we say "it happened," the first instance of contact with sensory vibrations is long since past. Only the reflections of the image are being recalled, re-cognized, and re-understood: we are far from direct contact with reality. What we have are but glimpses and assumptions, gleaned from reflections in the mirror of mind.*

This is the great enigma of our experience. We recall that we were present, but when we look, we are not. We can see that the 'knower' must come later. In our lives, we may react in ways that are stupid, even damaging, but the way to fix that behavior is to access what lies prior to our own arising, rather than blaming ourselves as if we were actually there and having to revert to repression to control our subsequent actions. The truth is we were not there when those actions were initiated. We might be part of the 'bad-thing-making process', but we were not in control of it: that is the problem. We were there as a passenger. We remember ourselves feeling it, because that's the earliest point of recognition that memory can grab hold of to remember, but we weren't actually present when the first impulse happened. We were looped in, born into actions that were already underway.

If there is no awareness before recognition fixes the world in place, then restraint is required after the fix is in. Hence the deep Freudian insight that civilization is essentially to be understood as repression. But can that repression and control be seen as a path to liberation—to freedom, or are we fated to continually repress our spontaneity?

>   PAGE 143, PARAGRAPH 1: *We experience this entire process as instantaneous; or rather, we experience only its results.*

The 'fix' is fake: we live in a readout. We experience the results of a process that's happening so fast, and so regularly, that we don't see it. We live in a second-order reality.

This conclusion seems surprising, even alarming, but upon reflection we realize it must be the case. If we use a very accurate clock, accurate to the millisecond, we know that we don't react at all until about a hundred milliseconds after any sensation—that's called our 'reaction time'. And we don't identify, cognize, for about a hundred milliseconds after that—so something like two hundred milliseconds passes between something arising and our recognition of it. We are behind events, working with the memories of what has just taken place. The regime of mind works in milliseconds here, not nanoseconds: a response takes that order of time to be processed.

PAGE 143, PARAGRAPH 1, CONT'D: *But if we could slow it down and observe its stages, we would know more clearly how perception works. We would understand the significance of naming, identity, and recognition. We would know how mind makes language, how language characterizes perceptions, and how mind uses language to interpret and comment. We might realize there is little or no opportunity to deliberate the stages of this process or to make informed decisions—all of the ingredients that make up experience already exist. They are prepared and ready to go at any moment, in any and all directions, and to any place. Mind simply assembles them and presents us with something 'understandable' that we can use and convey to others. This innate readiness to manifest experience instantaneously may be what the word 'existence' implies.*

If you ask someone, "How do you know the world is real?" they will always use the past tense to tell you why. In memory everything is geotagged, labeled up and identified. But if you ask them in the present tense—"Right now, how do you know the world is real?"— they will find it a lot more difficult to establish, because the whole structure requires the projection of time. It operates in the past. And that's how we live, all the time. We're living in a memory of the real.

Exercise 19 Listening to silence

The meaning of listening to silence is best explored in experience. Sound is a really good vehicle for the exploration, because the sounds we hear are clear, but they have a more obvious time-trajectory than the things we see. Take a gong, or a bell. First, strike the gong, and listen to the sound as it fades into silence. Then, try to inhabit the silence after the sound has faded away.

Continue in that silence before striking the gong a second time. Catch the moment when the sound begins. Can you be there as well?

CHAPTER 28

Labels and Identity

This chapter revisits the process of labeling, and shows the central role labeling plays in the outworking of historical events, whether national or personal.

> PAGE 145, PARAGRAPH 1: *For all phenomena we recognize, for everything picked up by the senses and grasped as an object, mind has a label pre-established and pre-formed, encoded with thoughts, feelings and associated patterns of emotional and physical reactions.*

The 're' of re-cognition is extremely important. Our common language has described it: we realize that first we cognize something and then we re-cognize it. At the moment of cognition there is no self, no identification of either knower or what is known. Re-cognition, on the other hand, is double-pointed—that is when the knowing self arises in the world.

If we look at the world, we see a landscape of known objects. They have been recognized. The actual data from which the known objects are inferred, however, are absorbed pre-consciously. By the time the known object is presented to us, it has been labeled in a process in which we as observer and it as labeled object come together. Encoded within the label we will find a whole range of emotional and cognitive elements.

Think back to how advertising operates: this is where the power of propaganda and advertising comes from. If you can engineer the association of a feeling or opinion with a label, then when that label is seen or invoked, all those feelings arise along with it. Since the process of association is preconscious, people often think those feelings and associations are personal; they feel very near and dear. We will vote for, purchase, defend or even fight for these images. While the rise of social media has brought this facet of human behavior to the forefront in recent times, this has been a feature of propaganda since the beginning of recorded history.

> PAGE 145, PARAGRAPH 1, CONT'D: *Stamped and sealed at the point of recognition, the label serves as proof of identity and a basis for interpretation. In using the label, we automatically affirm that we understand its connotations and associations.*

"Stamped and sealed": mind stamps a sense input with a label, and the recognition seals its identity as a known thing. That makes the known object both an object of memory and an object of association at the same time. The label, the name, is the tag upon which all the associations hang. In a single, almost mechanical process, the whole retinue of meaning wraps around the labeled object.

Labels not only provide identity in terms of recognition, they also provide identity in terms of self. We are confirming our own existence all the time. This is one of the reasons why the ego is so deeply rooted: everything we do confirms that we exist. Any action we take is labeled. The operation of identity is mixed up in the labeling process.

> PAGE 145, PARAGRAPH 2: *Like a coat that wraps around the body, concealing the specifics of what lies behind, labels conceal the true nature of what we perceive. In wearing a label, mind manifests the identity of that label and carries on its characteristics. Over time, labels take on a*

sense of reality that we are likely to hold on to for the rest of our lives.

The stickiness, the persistence of identity, is profoundly underestimated. Most of us, by the time we come out of school, are pretty much fixed in who we are. Even our accent and style of talking are fixed by that time. It can be very difficult to truly change, even in modest ways. On a fundamental level, most of us think that the structure constructed and guaranteed by labeling is real. For someone stuck in that belief system, change becomes virtually impossible.

When we recognize that in some sense our identity is constructed, one reaction is to become more and more educated, eventually arriving at a kind of stoic recognition of relative truth. There are educated opinions about both sides of almost any issue, and part of the liberal agenda is that there are many positions that can be taken. Normally if you scratch someone who holds such a position, however, underneath you will still find a strong ego structure.

Some of us get attracted to spiritual development because we realize that mere education, at least according to the Western model, isn't going to get us very far. Indeed, most religions encourage the faithful to take on a new identity, even to take a new name. All the monastic traditions, Buddhist, Christian and Muslim, require a name change. But to change your actual belief structure is really hard. Most of us, even after a long exposure to a new way of looking at the world, still find that our old labeling structure is still intact.

Spiritual development is not about changing your labels however. It's about understanding them. Many of us spend many years trying to be something else. Sometimes, Westerners try to become Tibetans: it would be preferable if Westerners understood their Western-ness. Picking up another set of labels is not going to liberate you! The point in Revelations is not to try to become something else, but to understand what we actually are. If we can do that, then we will make progress in ways we never knew were possible.

PAGE 145, PARAGRAPH 3: *Labels express meaning in a certain way; each has its own features, connotations, and associations, and each of these in turn has its own definition and description. Each description has a certain application, and each application has its set of meanings, all custom-tailored to express the nuances of specific situations, relationships, disciplines, and purposes.*

If you create a life history, you will begin to notice certain types of events that recur. Part of that recurrence is due to labeling, because when you identify a phenomenon and label it as a particular type, it brings with it all the associations of its previous occurrence. This reference to past experience is a strong influence, almost as if one is fated to repeat the same pattern. One of the most powerful labels, which operates in precisely this way, is "my character," which is expressed as "I am like that." This is the association base that informs the 'hero' who inhabits the story of our lives.

Furthermore, we assume that other people understand the world the way we do, that when we say something others understand it the way we said it. But listeners understand according to their own association networks, just as speakers speak based on their association networks. There is always a gap of comprehension between speaker and listener: one might almost say that listeners are listening to themselves. Perhaps that's why the Buddha said, "I never taught."

When it's understood in this way, it's clear that the labeling structure enables communication but also guarantees miscommunication. Whatever you say will only be partially understood. After the fascist catastrophe of World War II, there was an attempt to create languages that had absolute meaning, the so-called 'observer independent' languages of logical positivism, to overcome this difficulty. In the end it was realized that such an effort is impossible, that even the most technical descriptions that can be given still rely upon concepts that are derived from the point of view of the observer.

Fascist ideologies are deeply rooted in the idea that there is no such thing as 'objective' facts, and that facts themselves are malleable. Recognizing that there is no user independent language does not confirm this position, however. Facts do exist. It is just that we can only infer what they *mean*. When this is misunderstood, sometimes people will claim that they can believe in obvious falsehoods as a human right, as an expression of their freedom. In realizing that facts are the basis for labels, it is important to realize that the very existence of facts should not be a matter of opinion. Opinions relate to what facts 'mean', which is precisely the label and the associations that label has for any individual. Understanding this offers important insights into the difference between relative and absolute truth—the famous two truths of Buddhist philosophy.

> PAGE 146, PARAGRAPH 1: *Usage, repetition, and development through the centuries have shaped labels into the building blocks for language and civilization. Identifying, recognizing, naming, thinking and acting, human beings have migrated to all parts of the planet. Hunting, farming, weaving, establishing settlements, defining and playing social roles, they have developed large empires, civilizations, and systems of education, evolving countless languages to accommodate the continual expansion of information and the ever-changing needs of diverse populations.*

Once we have grasped the central functioning of labeling, it can be understood in the broadest historical sense. This is not to merely situate this activity of labeling within our own perceptual field, but to recognize that entire civilizations live by labels—that civilizations organize themselves based on the labels they have all agreed on. This is a very profound realization. Historically, ideas are more important than the behavior of great men or great women who act according to those ideas.

> PAGE 146, PARAGRAPH 2: *As beneficiaries of all that has come before, we tend to think that we stand at the highest peak of human development. But we all come from the same basic point, the unit of experience that allows perception to take place. From this unit comes our reality: the regime of mind that establishes subject and object, and with it, the way of seeing that distinguishes self from everything else and creates the conditions for separation.*

Whether we were born 2,000 years ago or yesterday, we, as actors in the world, arise from the same point. That means the point at which our experience arises is the primordial origin of all history.

In Buddhist and other metaphysical writings you will often read of this "primordial base." The primordial base is not something pre-established: it's emerging from moment to moment. It's where history begins. It begins where cognition becomes recognition. That's the primordial origin of everything, the moment before time begins.

This may be why human behavior appears to be surprisingly constant over historical periods. We can enjoy and learn from the plays of Shakespeare—now over four hundred years old, or marvel at the insights of Plato, written centuries before the common era. This surprising lack of change is because experience arises at the point where cognition becomes recognition rather than in the flow of time that is always after that event. The powerful processes that drive recognition shape us and make us fated to live in particular ways, which are then recorded as history. Phenomena such as famine and floods, economic downturns and territorial disputes will happen, but all the participants in all those events respond to them from this primordial point and continue to do so from moment to moment. In this sense, identifying that moment takes us beyond history. More than that, it explains history, in the sense that it provides a bigger context in which history occurs.

> PAGE 147, PARAGRAPH 1: *All of us live within the context of family, society, culture, and nation, but at an even more fundamental level, we live in a world of labels and concepts and we express our understanding through language. The rules related to our labels and the patterns of cognition that establish them are the most deeply imprinted of all. They prevent us from even conceiving of a way of thinking that does not depend upon subject and object, the contrasts of pro and con, and the continual pulling 'to' and pushing 'from' that characterize our dualistic orientation. Perception of subject and object is seemingly hard-wired into our being along with patterns of emotionality, desire, feeling-tones, and responses. All of these operate predictably without our conscious direction. All of them flow through mind and thoughts and find expression in our embodiment.*

It is possible to become 'well-adjusted': you can become very well adjusted to a labeled-up world. That's perfectly valid. You can become an expert in valid relative truth. You could argue that that's the aim of education—to create good citizens. Surely all of us who study *Revelations* should make sure that we're not just spouting opinions. We need to be good at what we're doing. Being ignorant is not a virtue. But such expertise is only the relative truth; there is something more.

One of the ways we know that is because of the extraordinary circularity that occurs both within our own lives and within the fabric of history. Ideas come back. This is a sign that there are fundamental structures within our mental apparatus that are not understood—and they doom us to fly in circles, like trapped insects. That's what gives us that sense of déjà vu, that ennui that we may often feel.

PAGE 147, PARAGRAPH 2: *We are bonded to ways of thinking and doing that have changed very little over many thousands of years, and our lives are constricted by the way these systems are set up. We have the master pattern, the rules to maintain the pattern and the roles to enforce it; and the players, ourselves, perfectly conditioned to apply and extend it. Everything is captured, from our environment and living conditions to our ways of participating in our culture and communities. Perceptions, thoughts, feelings, memories, and speech are perfectly integrated into the system, as if designed to support and perpetuate it.*

We have ended up in the perfect prison. It starts in the process of recognition in which subject and object appear as a perfectly matched pair. Onto that are added all our personal memories and associations, and all the cultural education and history that is received from our cultural institutions. Both family and institutions praise and blame us, make us a success or a failure and make us happy or sad. We end up within this perfect enclosure. You could say it's a perfect machine, in that such mechanisms should be a driver for human progress and an ever more perfect society. But our failure to make such progress demonstrates that recognizing our cognitive patterns and becoming conversant with them is extremely important. Only then can we see our limitations and ask whether we might find a better alternative.

PAGE 148, PARAGRAPH 1: *Everyone now plays the game the same way, and each of us reflects it to others. Within this framework, we endure a subtle, yet pervasive kind of bondage, lured on by promises of pleasure and hopes of success, and driven from behind by doubts, worries, dissatisfaction, fear, and the overpowering need to fit in.*

These are called the Eight Worldly Concerns—happiness or suffering, fame or obscurity, praise or blame, and gain or loss. People are looking to be happy; they want to be famous; they want to be praised; and they want to gain as much as they can get. At the same time they are afraid of suffering, afraid of being forgotten, terrified of being blamed, and afraid to lose what they have. These eight concerns are what drive the world.

When we consider the fundamental power of the Eight Worldly Concerns, the way they are built into our programming, it becomes easy to foresee tragedies in the making in the world around us. For example, in the South China Sea, America's idea of freedom is coming up against the Chinese idea of group identity, and this is very dangerous because neither side can back down. The Chinese can't say, "We don't own these islands. They really weren't part of China," because Chinese group identity is associated with their claim over them. The Americans can't say, "We're not free to sail the seas," because that is a central theme of American identity. This is how wars begin.

> PAGE 148, PARAGRAPH 2: *As we enact our roles, we feel compelled to satisfy expectations and desires—our own and those of others. We have obligations. We are busy. We suffer from frustration, mental and physical pain, and discontent, all of which drain the energy of body and mind until our very cells are exhausted. We cannot opt out or refuse. Everyone has to participate, which may help explain why we are so often tired and sick.*

The malaise that is affecting Western culture at the moment is a really graphic example of this. It's not just the adults who are exhausted. Everyone is exhausted. What we're putting our children through is appalling in terms of the competitiveness that is required to be successful. It's like the whole system is grinding people into terrible states. Something is profoundly wrong with a world that is so dominated by compulsion in this way.

> PAGE 149, PARAGRAPH 1: *Some might say that we do not have to continue on this way, but we do not know of any*

other. By naming, defining, and categorizing, collecting data and shaping structures that can be expanded infinitely, we set in motion the processes that now sustain our way of being in the world. Among them are identity and recognition, the back-and-forth of confirmation and validation, positioning of subject and object, observation of cause and effect, operation of the senses, awareness of feeling, discriminations and judgments, and the thoughts, ideas, and memories that comprise our human history and fundamental patterns of response.

Through naming and categorizing we set in motion the process by which the world is made. Back and forth confirmation and validation creates the base for the projection of self and the world as a matching pair. Experiences are ordered through the projection of time and related to one another as cause and effect. This structure provides the network of associations a framework through which to attach remembered feelings, discriminations and judgments. This progressive unfolding is the entourage that creates the structure of the world.

PAGE 149, PARAGRAPH 2: *At some point we became aware of a director with a decision-making function, an entity named 'mind'. As director, mind created the regime that now governs our thoughts and perceptions and developed language as its tool for communication. While our individual minds are specific to our being, they are not truly independent. Nothing is completely our own, not our thoughts, not our hopes and dreams, not our sense of right and wrong, not even our notions of self and reality. Everything has come down to us through the generations, recycled and updated, but fundamentally the same.*

Here is the final irony: we have a habit of thinking that our projected sense of self is unique, while the truth is that our self-projection is almost totally generic. There is almost nothing we do which is original. Consider fashion for example. Many of us choose styles unaware that these choices are completely bound by the labeling structure and the advertising industry that controls it. This is true of all of us. We are not unique. Google's predictive algorithms, sadly, have demonstrated this beyond a reasonable doubt. Using the patterns they identify, Google and other companies like it can predict people's behavior with efficiency. Machines can now predict what people are going to do.

Predictability occurs, because our mind is manifesting within a regime, and regimes generate and reproduce patterns. The regime itself is generic. The very thing we think is the base of our individuality is not. This is not to say that there is not something in us that is individual—it's just not what we think it is. The features we think are individual, the beliefs that many will live and die for, are not individual at all. They are constructs made by labeling.

> PAGE 150, PARAGRAPH 1: *Mind's regime manifests in the language that resonates in our thoughts and memories; the patterns it transmits surface in our sensory processes, reactions, and interpretations. As soon as our eyes open, we see and experience the reality mind has created—senses active and grasping, interpretations popping up, the pushing and pulling of pro and con, thoughts, feelings, desires, dislikes, frustrations, fears, doubts, ideas, and passions gathering speed and expanding like a snowball rolling downhill. But does this way of operating the mind truly serve our best interests?*

We are in a very real sense living in the readout. People can drive themselves to suicide. They can live in profound despair and self-hatred. Yet when you ask them if they are OK or if they would like to change, they say, "No. No. This is the way I am." Is that really in our best interest? But that's how the regime is. It's self-validating. It is as if there is no alternative. People can live in the most awful psychological states, and yet they think there is no alternative because that's the nature of the regime.

PAGE 150, PARAGRAPH 2: *People everywhere seek to in-crease pleasure and avoid pain and suffering, but mind does not always lead us toward those goals. Everything we view as positive has a negative corollary that tends to manifest however much we wish to suppress it. Striv-ing for pleasure sets us up for disappointment and loss. Our greatest joys can become occasions for grief and pain. Advances we view as improvements can make our situa-tion worse, and some forms of suffering are so persistent and universal that we tend to accept them as inherent in our human condition. Everyone suffers from rejection, self-doubts, and insecurity, conditions that arise through the dualistic operations of mind. If these can somehow be avoided, there still remain disease, the crippling infirmities of old age, and the inevitability of death.*

This is the question: how can we avoid suffering? Suffering appears to be inherent in the structure in which we live our lives. Realizing this, a common reaction is to become stoic. "That's the way it is. It can't be helped. Nothing can change. Too bad. Just grin and bear it. Do the best you can." Stoicism is the antidote to the extremes of either religious ideas of self-denial or hedonistic ideas of over-enjoyment. There is how-ever, a third way that doesn't boil down to grim stoic accep-tance. It is this: can we understand the structure in which we are embedded?

PAGE 151, PARAGRAPH 1: *In one way, we are innocent vic-tims of this process, but from another perspective, we have accepted it, participated in it, embodied it, and transmit-ted it through our thoughts and actions. While we dream of banishing pain and suffering from our world, we hold fast to the conditions that bond the human spirit to the most enduring, destructive, and debilitating forms of un-happiness. And however we may protest and complain, we are totally convinced of the fundamental rightness of our understanding of our own human situation.*

Everybody wants to end suffering, and yet we cling tightly to the causes of suffering. That's our human condition. Everybody says, "I want to be alive. I want to be happy." At the same time, our strongly held beliefs, ideas and objectives may be generating all the suffering in the first place. It's a bit like Stockholm syndrome. We're held hostage by the regime of mind, yet we become supporters of the very regime that imprisons us. We participate in the prison that entraps us. We do so by 'getting on in life'.

English is full of amazing words, and 'career' does not disappoint. A car careers out of control. The word implies inevitability. Someone says, "I have a stellar career": it's got momentum of its own, not unlike a car as it careers into a wall. In some real sense we understand that our future is out of our control. It's out of control because, in a sense, it's pre-ordained: it's been constructed for us out of pre-existing concepts.

> PAGE 151, PARAGRAPH 2: *Why has this happened? Because suffering, like everything else, has been appropriated and fused to our identity. Since our identity is our anchor in reality, we cling to it tightly, justifying it as part of 'the way things are' or perhaps as divine will, ennobled through atonement or martyrdom. In doing so, we blind ourselves to a major source of needless pain.*

There are inevitably going to be things that will happen to us, things that we can't control—not bad things, just things that we can't control. And the reason why things we can't control become sources of suffering is because our entire cultural structure tells us that we should be able to control everything. We are told that if we do this we will have a good life, if we do that we will get a nice partner and beautiful children. There is a whole structure we buy into and then, when it doesn't work the way we want, it becomes a source of suffering.

So, what's the alternative here? To sit in a box and look at the wall? Is that what's being suggested? No, it's not. You can be fully engaged with life and still recognize that things aren't going to go the way you expect all the time. If you engage like that, you get the benefits of engagement without the suffering when it doesn't work for you.

Now, of course, to do that, you have to understand labeling. You can engage with life without suffering if you use labels knowingly. As long as labels are used unconsciously, you can't engage with life with that crucial detachment, because the labels themselves won't allow it. You've got Stockholm syndrome: you've bought into the system that's imprisoned you, and consequently you will experience suffering you can't control.

> PAGE 152, PARAGRAPH 1: *Can we afford to ignore the suffering that this understanding of reality generates? Leaders among us have created impressive buildings, conquered powerful enemies, made millions in the stock market, gained power over many thousands of people, or become known throughout the world. But what do such accomplishments mean after we are no longer alive? Our lives and all our resources may have been dedicated to such activities, as have the lives and resources of countless others, generation after generation repeating the same model, building on what came before. But this way of living and acting has perpetuated the kinds of suffering that we have endured throughout human history. It has also nourished the seeds of separation and disharmony, cultivated from the outset in our patterns of perception and expressed in nearly every aspect of our language and culture.*

> PAGE 153, PARAGRAPH 1: *Since these seeds tend to proliferate, we might well wonder whether at some point they will crowd out our capacities to broaden and deepen our understanding of human being. As we depend ever more strongly on labels and concepts clouded by assumptions, judgments, and self-oriented concerns, at what point will awareness and clarity become sterile concepts rather than fundamental human attributes?*

Now, that's a very, very important question. Schools have reacted to the recognition of suffering by introducing mindfulness. Mindfulness is the panacea that somehow is going to protect our children from the appalling testing regime they are caught in. But of course it's not going to—sadly. We have to rediscover humanity in there somewhere, an education that is not exclusively goal-oriented: and if you don't do that then mindfulness is just another skill that you learn in order to be a better engineer at Google.

We are entering a world where in twenty years or so, something like forty percent of manual work will be mechanized. We are on the cusp of a true revolution in human society where self-knowledge will really matter, and seeking it will become a societal quest. Otherwise, we risk heading into a catastrophe in which huge numbers of people become completely lost. Already you can see the beginnings of this. If it continues to happen, there will be all kinds of toxic consequences, and large numbers of people will suffer from it profoundly.

> PAGE 153, PARAGRAPH 2: *Our present regime of mind may have become unnecessarily confining, a product of an earlier age that the dynamic power of time has rendered obsolete. Since this regime activates automatically once mind projects the nanosecond—the unit of experience that allows perception to take place—a fuller understanding of time might reveal possibilities for a different kind of regime, one able to lead us through the walls of mind and reveal the full beauty of being. To explore further, we need to look more closely at the relationship of mind and time.*

Exercise 20
Timeline revisited

As I've suggested before, it can be very valuable to make a timeline of the events in your life. The point of such a timeline is not to state your opinions about what occurred, but to use as many external sources of information as you can (old diaries, old passports, school reports, news or anything that is objective and identifiable) to create a catalogue of events.

The first step is to create a detailed history made up of events and dates. The next step is to enter those events using the time and date as fixed points in a sequence, and then begin to flesh them out. As you do this, you will find memories that were initially vague becoming clearer, allowing you to insert more events. Working in this way, you will gradually create a detailed record. This is a valuable base for beginning to look, as a historian of being, at your own life. This study reveals very clearly how patterns emerge, how certain events and behaviors repeat themselves. Those patterns are very significant because they point to fundamentally held beliefs.

There may be periods you can't remember, periods that appear to be blank. Don't gloss over these blank places, for they are very valuable. They are places where the mental structure has hidden away memories because often what's within them is traumatic. Those traumatic episodes are worth exploring. They have been suppressed and the cognitive consequences of the trauma are still operating. Opening up those traumatic episodes can cause rapid changes in the internal dialogue with which you make the world.

CHAPTER 29

The Forward Thrust of Time

I think it was the famous physicist Archibald Wheeler who said, "What is time? Time is what stops everything from happening at once." And it's actually quite an interesting insight, for through time we have the experience of an ordered world—a succession of events.

You could say time is a metric. But can you change time? Is time flexible? All of these questions start coming up. Westerners famously have 'no time'. This is really a problem—we in the West are living with painful time-deficits that seem to be getting worse the more 'efficient' our cultures become. If you know people from traditional cultures, you'll discover that they have all the time in the world.

> PAGE 154, PARAGRAPH 1: *We experience time as going forward, unfolding in a linear progression. As we move in time the past stretches behind us, becoming ever more distant history, while the future emerges, allowing opportunities for change and new experiences to occur.*

> PAGE 154, PARAGRAPH 2: *Morning gives way to afternoon. When nighttime comes, afternoon becomes the past and morning recedes further, becoming the more distant past. We organize time into units we can measure and manage, characterizing 'this time' and 'that time', morning, noon,*

and night. Relying on such observations, we mark out the segments of our days and give the name of 'time' to these segments, dividing up through language what we actually experience as continuity. In this culture, at least, it is universally accepted that time moves forward and can be divided into past, present, and future.

In this sense time serves as a psychological metric, a ruler or measuring stick, by which we sort out our experiences. It enables us to say, "Yesterday this happened to me." Through this we can see that personal time is indeed a construct of memory. Without memory there is no yesterday: without yesterday, no measurable time.

In ancient times, the largest of the early Buddhist schools in India, the Sarvastivada, took the view of the reality of the three times. The idea that the past, present and future all exist in some way is a common and longstanding trope. This way of thinking about time seems to make a lot of common sense. It is reinforced by the way popular culture has absorbed the scientific conception of space-time, as if time were some sort of terrain existing as a fourth dimension alongside the three dimensions of space. It corresponds with our feeling that the past is 'behind' us, and the future is 'ahead' of us.

The past exists definitively, insofar as the present is composed from it. Look at any object: things that happened to it in the past are visible now. It came into being at some point and is still here. Our character is of the same stuff: looking at our timeline it becomes apparent that our personal present is constructed on the basis of the past. We live our lives a bit like snails leaving a trail behind us, a trail of unfinished business, things that are unresolved, not fully worked out. Such things have consequences that can influence the present circumstances of some future time.

PAGE 155, PARAGRAPH 1: *Although we do not know the cause for time's apparent movement, we sense the passing of time and note transitions we consider significant. Our minds have endless stories that confirm this is true.*

If you ask most modern Westerners, "How are you positioned with regard to time?" they would say they are walking into the future. They are in the present and they are walking facing forward into the future. We see this attitude reflected in many of our metaphors and images of time. Interestingly, the ancient Greeks saw it the other way around. They said they were walking backwards into the future. I think this is a very profound recognition about the nature of our experience. What we actually have is the past, and all we can see is the past. We are facing the past and walking with our backs to the future. We're walking backwards, not forwards.

> PAGE 155, PARAGRAPH 2: *Time in this sense is not an object we can measure—it is the measurement itself, the yardstick devised by mind to identify, situate, and communicate experience, our own and that of humanity from its earliest origins. More accurately, it is the label we give to this measurement, a label that tends to distance us from the meaning of what it represents.*

We say time passes. What do we mean by that? There is no thing passing us. It's a term we're using to label a type of experience that's happening within us. We call it time. Everyone knows that time exists, but what is it? If you ask people, "What is time?" they generally are confused by the question and have difficulty finding an answer. Normally they fall back on high school physics with talk about clocks and Einstein and space-time. But none of those inferences are relevant to time as we've actually labeled it.

It is a fruitful insight to realize that 'time' is a label. It labels the passing of our experience. Underneath the label of time is an experience that it covers up—a detailed and specific phenomenon the label conceals. Realizing that 'time' is a label is extremely helpful. Otherwise we're searching about looking for a thing, and it's not a thing at all.

PAGE 155, PARAGRAPH 3: *What then, does the label 'time' represent? What does it point to? What is its meaning?*

We use the label 'time' often during the day. Yet this key element of our experience remains completely unexamined. What am I actually labeling when I talk about the past, present and future? When people say, "Be mindful" or "Be in the present moment," does that really make sense? If you ask them what they mean, or what is time, they will be confused. We have to penetrate time itself to find what to be mindful of.

PAGE 155, PARAGRAPH 4: *Every dimension of human experience—including culture, history, religion, faith, philosophy, psychology, and anything our imagination projects—is framed in the context of three dimensions of time (past, present and future) and experience: past memories, present feelings, and future-oriented imaginings that give rise to hope and expectations.*

Time is a major element of our internal psychological structure. It's a kind of yardstick that we have inside us to construct the world in which we live. We can catch a glimpse of its power when we notice how we are affected when it changes. Writers deliberately manipulate the tense of their writing to change the effect that the writing is having, for example. This works because the sense of time plays an organizing role in our experience. When we read a novel, we are pulled into the experience the author wants us to have.

PAGE 156, PARAGRAPH 1: *Within these three dimensions of time and experience, mind acts in the present. It identifies objects and relates them to the purposes of the subject 'I', much as a customer shops for items to bring home and enjoy. But what mind gives us is a reflection, not the genuine experience—a pale imitation already clothed in assumptions and interpretations. Fixated on the subject-oriented*

> *point of view, mind misses points of transition that could lead to a direct involvement with the dynamic unfolding of being.*

Ascribing date and location markers to sensory inputs as they enter memory is a central activity of mind. Any 'known' object consists of a set of these markers held in memory. In fact, any known object must be a memory, or it couldn't be known at all. Knowing what something 'is' requires memory—we can't know something without having the memory of it. When we think, "Oh, a clock," it's already a memory, because we know it's a clock.

So we are living in memory, in a very real sense. You could say it's a very short memory, for it's a memory of events that are approximately one quarter of a second old, which is the time it takes us to re-cognize a sensory input as was discussed in chapter 3 above. We are tagging everything: the labels associated with our sensory inputs are arranged on a matrix; that matrix is what we know.

Time is the warp on which we weave this seamless tapestry. In labeling sensory inputs as 'known' we also provide a time-'known then'. If there was no reliable sense of time, there would be no sense of continuity in our experience.

In mapping changing events, however, the readout is necessarily hiding points of transition. These points of transition are moments where the readout could potentially break down. But it doesn't! It doesn't, because it's got the strong metrical structure of time to hold it together. The warp of time is strong. We can go from morning to noon to dusk without ever feeling that we don't understand what's going on. Indeed, it takes a major discontinuity, such as a disaster, to break us free of that feeling of smooth normality. Anyone who has been through a catastrophe knows that during the catastrophe extraordinary things occur which demonstrate that we are papering over points of transition with our normal construct.

This is the reason that time is such a good vehicle for inquiry. Points of transition are places where we could break free, break through or find something else: but they are usually covered over by time, and consequently, we miss them. As we bring greater awareness to our sense of time, however, we prepare ourselves to notice these key moments in the smooth mind-made display in which 'I' have things that are 'mine' and do things to 'me' in what we call the 'world'.

> PAGE 156, PARAGRAPH 2: *Without realizing the treasury of potentials that mind has already overlooked or dismissed, we pursue pleasure and satisfaction as best we can, experiencing happiness, pain, well-being, suffering, misery, joy, and more, in no particular order.*

All of us live in a bubble in which we are pursuing goals that are essentially based on our memory. So, we want to be something because of our memory, and we pursue it in our memory even if there is something else going on in the underlying flow of events.

> PAGE 156, PARAGRAPH 2, CONT'D: *A shifting array of emotional and psychological states captures and occupies our attention. While mind tracks their rise and fall and responds to events that pop up from moment to moment, the operations of its regime obscure the emerging dynamic we call 'present' time, where all we most value—life, time, freedom, choice, and opportunity—is slipping away.*

A good many seemingly successful people end up regarding themselves as failures: this is why. They feel unsuccessful because their success can be found only in their memory: as soon as it's obtained, it slips away. As a result, even though they achieve what they set out to achieve, they end up out of touch with what really makes life worth living. They're left with little of value, and nothing to show for their efforts.

Making contact with dynamic becoming has nothing whatsoever to do with conventional measurements of success and
failure, however; it's something completely different. We see
great artists do it, at least in fleeting moments. In many ways
the function of an artist, poet or musician is to point to this.
But unfortunately, most people are taught to measure their
success by very conventional metrics, and those metrics don't
in themselves have any meaning.

> PAGE 157, PARAGRAPH 1: *Continually pre-occupied with rec-
> ognizing, identifying, and interpreting perceptions, memories,
> and thoughts, mind pursues, points out, and makes meaning
> out of everything that stimulates it to respond. From instant
> to instant, it generates a flow of interpretations, dialogues,
> and pronouncements. It recognizes, identifies, and speculates
> on the significance of specific characteristics: it pursues com-
> parisons and associations, analyzing and interpreting feelings
> and emotions. Easily bored, it may entertain itself by com-
> menting on its own imaginings. "Wonderful!" "Miserable!"
> "Beautiful!" "Horrible!" "Not healthy." "This is living!" "This is
> helpful." "This is happiness!"*

This auto-commentary is going on the whole time. Observe
yourself and others during the day—there is the continuous
dialogue. Once you have developed shamata you can watch
the auto-commentary that's generated by every arising sensation. It's almost as if there is a little voice continuously making sense of what's in front of you. It will never stop, because
it is a key function of the regime of mind.

Every impression that arises through any one of the six sense
doors is categorized, commented on and located within a
metric of the three times. This process of accumulation is
continuous. We call it 'time,' but underneath it there is a detailed experience of change. Realizing that time is a metric
and a label for something that underlies it, we can observe it
more closely, because now we know what to look for.

PAGE 157, PARAGRAPH 2: *Mind gives itself room to play and replay all manner of roles, going from place to place, reflection to reflection, moment to moment, moving forward toward identity and recognition and back again into uncertainty and doubt. Mind dictates, points out, gives feedback, and identifies and announces continuity. Each pronouncement is another expression of mind, validated by the perceptual processes that mind has established.*

So that is the regime of mind, the auto-commentary that makes continuity out of discontinuity.

This is how we make the world, and the world appears to be continuous, sensible: we have metrics for success and failure, we have past, present and future, and all the sense of time passing. It's essentially a classification of arising events, associated with past references and commented on in terms of praise and blame, fame and gain, and the rest of the conventional world.

PAGE 158, PARAGRAPH 1: *Cognizing, recognizing, memorizing and being aware, mind exercises its creative potential, shaping time—and our experience—into past, present, and future. In this way, it provides itself the stage it needs to play its roles and enact its version of reality. In accepting the limitation of the three times that mind sets up, we create the continuum that perpetuates identity— the continuum of our own actions, interacting, bouncing back, bounding forward, feeding back, filling the clear openness of mind with echoes, re-establishing reality instant by instant.*

This is the process of *reification*, 'thing-ifying' or making things real. It's very, very difficult to talk about what lies beyond that construct, because remember, any word you use is itself a construct. Whatever lies outside the construct can perhaps be evoked, but never truly described.

PAGE 158, PARAGRAPH 2: *If we are honest, we will admit that we are not fully at home in the realm mind has structured. From time to time, we sense that something is missing or is not quite right. If we were really secure in mind's reality structure, would we experience so much uncertainty? Would so many of our choices lead to frustration and pain? Would we lose touch with meaning and purpose, or be so easily bored or depressed? Too often, we hear the siren of an inner alarm system, saying "I am not happy. This is not fair. I should not have to feel this badly. This has been going on far too long. I don't know what it is, but something is wrong. Isn't there a better way?"*

If we were fully at home in the realm mind has structured, then examining it would not be worth doing. We're told about people who are well-adapted, to use the psychological term—people who are quite content to make a life within the box they are in. It seems they live happy lives: at any rate, they look happy on TV. Unfortunately, we never seem to meet these people in real life.

PAGE 159, PARAGRAPH 1: *This is the bondage of mind, the mind that forces us into servitude by the nature of its own operations. Ruled by this mind, we are sealed into the illusory reality-realm created by mind's regime, effectively locked out of authentic communication with the deeper currents of our being. Dependent on labels and interpretations assigned by mind, we cannot set aside notions of past, present and future and experience directly what mind presents.*

This is sometimes called the cry of *Tathagatagarbha*, the cry of Buddha Nature. It's as if our natural intelligence feels there is something wrong. Our natural intelligence gets seduced all the time, but we never totally forget that we've been seduced. That feeling of being seduced creates a persistent feeling that there is just something wrong. Often it leads people to become political, seeking ideals of external justice, because they think it's a problem in the world they have to fix. But we are being seduced from moment to moment, exchanging fresh experience for information. We have sold our birthright.

In seeing this basic discomfort, we are getting closer to understanding the construct. It is an amazing construct. It's not trivial at all. Furthermore, because it's refreshing itself from moment to moment, it can't be penetrated at a stroke. It will require some subtlety on our part to work with it successfully.

The point is not to reject the construct outright or to lament its presence as invariably damaging. In fact, the construct is valuable, because it's providing us with information. It's not the information that is problematic. It is the order in which the information is received that is problematic. If information gets in front of the openness of experience, it is limiting. We have to find a way to reverse this order, to make experience primary and information something that informs it. As things are now, we can be likened to an emperor who has been kicked off his throne by his chief advisor—a story familiar to us all. The evil Vizier takes over in *Aladdin*, or in *The Lord of the Rings*. But the chief advisor has no birthright. The emperor has to reclaim the throne, and then the advisor can advise him or her. That's what's happened to all of us. We were all emperors at one time, but somehow, when we were very young, our advisor suddenly took over and left us as strangers to ourselves.

Exercise 21
Review the day

Before you go to bed, run your memory backwards through the day to recall events and the times at which they happened. As you track back in your memory, notice that all experiences are organized along this timeline.

By doing this exercise you are giving an instruction to yourself to be conscious of time as a marker. When you run the memories backwards, you start from within your experience rather than watching it from the outside. You can remember the timeline from within, and see how one event arose from the one before it.

CHAPTER 30

A Seeming Continuity

The whole regime of mind is based on 'because'. It's making sense of the world, providing us with explanations for why things occur, and guiding us to take the most successful course based on prior information. 'Because', far from being obscure, is actually a central element of our mental structure. Arguably, it's *the* central element, along with the heroic ego. The heroic ego and 'because' are the two main products of the regime of the mind. If we didn't have 'because', we wouldn't know how to go forward from anywhere, or know where we came from to get to where we are now.

In our modern technological culture, scientists have become the new theologians of 'because'. It used to be priests who would give 'becauses'—they would tell you the meaning of life, they would tell you what to do, as they are still doing in some countries. Science has taken over that role in many parts of the world today. The attack on science that is so prevalent now is an attempt to wrestle that key authority away from scientific practitioners. That's why there is such a full-frontal attack on scientific truth. It's not so much because of any specific scientific insight, but because of the importance of truth as an anchor of authority.

✓ or conspiracy theories

Time plays a central role in the framework of causation. This is readily demonstrated in any simple machine, such as the Newton's cradle. This device has a row of five steel balls hung on an overhead bar. If you swing the ball at the end of the array away from its resting position and let it go, it swings back and hits the remaining four, causing the ball at the other end to swing away. When it swings back, it hits the other four, and the ball you originally lifted swings away again. This is a very simple demonstration of causation—one can easily see that the reason the ball at one end swings away is because the ball at the other end hit the array.

But let's do something different. If you put the cradle in an open-ended box or tube, so you can't see anything but one of the balls, and then lift the ball at the other end and let it go, the ball you can see swings out from the box and falls back in, then swings out again and falls back in, in a regular rhythm. Now, ask yourself, why is that ball moving? You have no idea! Is there a little mechanism in there pushing it? Since you can't see what's going on, you have no way of telling. What has happened when the cradle is partially hidden in that manner? What we have done is hidden what happened just before the event we are trying to explain. You could say we have hidden the past. When the cradle is partially hidden, the end ball swinging out just happens, in the 'here and now'. This shows us that if we really lived in the 'here and now', we would have no way of inferring causation at all.

When the entire device is uncovered, it's perfectly obvious why the ball at the end is moving, because the ball at the other end, that hit it just a moment before, is still visible. In other words, the immediate past informs our understanding of the present moment. However, once the other balls in the box are hidden, the immediate past is no longer visible, and then it's not clear why the visible ball is moving. This is a really simple demonstration of the close connection between time and causation. For A to cause B, A has to come before B. That means we must remember A even though B is actually happening 'right now'. It's because we remember A even though B is happening that we can say, A 'caused' it.

We don't realize it, but actually we are constantly calibrating time in this way. Through that calibration process, we generate causes. The moment we hide the past, the present becomes inexplicable, because that calibration cannot take place. So, not only do we live slightly behind the present, but it is only *because* we live slightly behind the present that we are able to infer causes to what is happening now.

Ultimately, our memory of what just happened before tells us 'why' things are happening now. Once this is seen, it is clear why time is such an important element of the world construct. We project a three-dimensional external display in which we operate, and we project a metric of time, and the time-projection enables us to say 'because'.

Memory, then, is a key element of our mental function in this additional sense. Just as memory allows us to know what things are, it also tells us when they are. You might even say that the regime of mind is memory plus projection. The regime has a memory bank full of ideas of what happened in the past, and it's got a labeling function which informs what we will do in the future in the light of current sense input. It is the perfect three-time machine. It is the regime of mind that took an insignificant ape living in Africa, and through its ability to learn from experience, enabled it to dominate every ecological niche our planet has to offer. There are many animals more powerful than humans, better adapted to their particular place in the world, but none have this ability to react to changing circumstances by modifying their future behavior in the light of past experience. If 'this' is happening now because 'that' happened, that means I can seek out or avoid 'this' by not doing 'that'. Now I have a map, a method for avoiding pain and getting what I want in the future.

Throughout the day we are accumulating a narrative of causes. While we may not realize how important this narrative is to us, we can get a sense of its role when we look at how children narrate their lives. It's very funny when you see children explain things. You can see their faces light up when they have a narrative that makes sense to them. If you talk to young children about what is happening, they will relate narratives before they have the faculty to know whether those narratives are real or not. Sometimes they will make up incredible stories about what's happening to them. The narrative works inasmuch as it's got 'becauses' in it, even though the factual elements in the narrative are invented. That shows you that the narrative structure-making, the 'because-ing' in our mental apparatus, is more deeply embedded than our common-sense experience shows.

The centrality of the 'why'-narrative would explain why storytelling is fundamental to culture. Cultures are held together by a collective narrative. Storytellers were very important people in many ancient cultures. In contrast, we've exported that storytelling function into the media business, which might help explain why we've seen a pattern of media celebrities becoming political players. Nowadays media-savvy politicians tell stories that create the narratives by which we live. In European pre-modern cultures, it was the priesthood that created the story of the culture. The culture of 'Christendom' was organized and unified by a narrative about the nature of life held largely by the church. One of the reasons why, in our time, entertainers have gone from being servants to being rulers is the collapse of the narrative structure of the Church and its associated social structures.

PAGE 160, PARAGRAPH 1: *Without the linear framework of time, there could be no causal connection between one event and another. Since it is the function of the cause to produce the effect, common sense and logic place the cause or reason for an event prior to its effect. If there were no past, there would be nothing that could be responsible for an event happening in the present. And if there were no future, the results of present events would have no opportunity to manifest: Cause and effect would be completely separate, with no connection between them.*

The question of cause is undoubtedly a central issue in philosophy. Certainly, if you go back to the great skeptical philosophers like Hume in the Western tradition, they argued that cause and effect was an illusion, just a supposition placed upon the flow of events. Another classic attack on causation comes from an Indian Madhyamika tradition founded by the great first century CE philosopher Nagarjuna. Nagarjuna's analysis throws the causal narrative into question by showing that the commonsensical idea of a linear relation between cause and effect is problematic.

When you consider it, there are an inconceivable number of events going on at once in parallel. Tolstoy considered this situation in *War and Peace*, pointing out that Napoleon never knew what his troops were doing in the battle of Borodino, so how could he have been described as having won the battle? Tolstoy describes him sitting on his horse on a hill as gunfire flashes in the foggy valley below him. Half of the time he couldn't even see what was going on, never mind influencing it!

In a similar vein, much of the narrative that we use to make sense of the world—this happened because of that, and that happened because of that—is largely illusory. There is a tide of events happening at all moments and at myriad levels, most of them beyond our awareness. It's almost inconceivably complicated. And so, to actually ascribe simple causation to anything at all is very problematic.

PAGE 160, PARAGRAPH 1, CONT'D: *What is moving into the past has to leave the stage of the present, otherwise the future has no place to manifest. But some 'current' continues on, linking the cause that is moving into the past with the future that will manifest the effect.*

The succession of events in a Newton's cradle is an effective demonstration of the flow of time and causation. As you look at the balls hitting each other and swinging out at either end, where is the 'present?' We have a continuity between past and the future here, in which past and future alternate as the balls swing back and forth. We would normally say this whole process is happening in the present, but importantly it is not, because we cannot register change without time. All change involves the three times, always.

The projected construct that we call 'the present' actually contains a bit of the past and a bit of the future. We've actually smeared out events to create this box called 'reality'. Otherwise it would be really quite alarming. If we were fully aware of our experience in which the past was disappearing all the time and leaving no trace, we wouldn't have any continuity in our experience: we'd be living on some sort of permanent precipice. But because we do not live in the present made like that, but always remember a bit of the past, we can categorize the present and project a bit of the future based on it. We can anticipate what will happen very comfortably based upon what is coming from the past into the present. We inhabit something like a slice of time—and that slice is what we actually call the 'present'.

PAGE 160, PARAGRAPH 1, CONT'D: *This continuation— what is happening now—is what we call the present. Thus we assume that cause and effect must play out in the context of past, present, and future.*

Page 161, paragraph 1: The present can be thought of in terms of a constant continuation that is vibrant and dynamic. Rhythm after rhythm, motion after motion, rising and falling like waves on the ocean, the present carries the motion of the cause, enabling effects to appear as the future comes forward to take the present's place. The momentum of the cause brings the effects to us in the present, which was the future when the causal event took place. We could say that the causal event is 'deposited' in the future, to mature, like a seed, in a future present.

Imagine how crowded the present moment is. Even if you just look out into your garden there are trillions of events going on in the present. It's not like there are just a few things happening. The more you look, the more there is happening in the present. Things get really crowded if one follows the idea that there is some causation happening in which things are clicking together in the present like the balls in a Newton's cradle.

When we allow ourselves to realize that our relationship with time is more immersive, more guided by the vast store of experiences each one of us carries, then our appreciation of cause and effect broadens.

PAGE 161, PARAGRAPH 2: *Cause and effect do not happen simultaneously, but at different times and at vastly differing intervals. We may not always be able to predict when the effects of a given cause will come: twelve months from now, thirty days, an hour, a minute, a second, or less. But even without knowing this, we accept as factual and real the ordered system that governs causation. Our reasoning reinforces the supposition that there is a causal continuity associated with time; there is movement, and that movement is toward a future that has not yet appeared. At the same time, the rhythms of the present move the continuum toward the past.*

Cause-and-effect relationships mature at different rates. So, depending on the complexity of the process, you may have instantaneous causes or what appear to be long-term acting causes. And this is true in physical science as well as in the psychological sciences. In this regard, we should consider the idea of karma.

Karma is a hugely important explanatory concept within Eastern culture. In the Vedic religion, the priestly caste, the Brahmins, using a magical language called Sanskrit, conducted ritual actions that were called *karmas*. These were ritual actions that obligated results, such as wealth, or prosperous marriages, or a particular outcome in a war or disagreement. In order to conduct a complete karma, the priests were paid to conduct a perfectly enacted ceremony, in which everything was done to the letter. These ritual actions or karmas still continue today in activities associated with some Buddhist and Hindu traditions.

What the Buddha did was take that concept of karma and ethicize it, emphasizing that the intention with which an action was carried out was an important component of the action itself.[31] Thus, in the Buddhist theory of karma, an action must be intended, undertaken, completed and rejoiced in for a full karma to be manifested.

This is similar to the Christian teaching of "As ye sow, so shall ye reap." If you plant rice, you are not going to reap oats. Although in this regard, you can see this teaching as a Christian interpretation of karma, it is not very developed as a concept, because there was obviously a conflict with the creative potential of God. It's difficult to have a fully-fledged karmic model if a creator God can turn up any time and change the rules!

The word 'karma' is becoming part of our modern vocabulary at least in part because scientific materialism can be understood to be karmic in the sense that it presents causes in the past that manifest as results in the present in a very predict-

---

31 See Richard Gombrich, *What the Buddha Thought* (Oxford Centre for Buddhist Studies Monographs, 2009).

able manner. What the Western position has more difficulties with is the idea that psychological states are also karmic: that they, in themselves, can be causal.

It's common for materialists to claim that consciousness is merely an onlooker to physical events; it is described as epiphenomenal, a secondary function that serves as a kind of display, like a TV screen, while all the 'real' actions are happening in the body. In this view, consciousness might be an effect (of neural activity, say), but it cannot itself be the cause of anything real.

Still, even within such a materialist model, it's possible to recover a concept of personal autonomy. If you have a complex collection of things, such a collection can do things that the individual components could, but don't. A good example is a cartwheel made of iron. The atoms of iron that make up the cartwheel don't themselves roll down hills. But if you put enough of them together in a circular shape, they will roll down the hill. That is an example of a so-called emergent phenomenon: the quality of rolling downhill has emerged out of a collection of things that don't individually exhibit that quality. And it's a real phenomenon—cartwheels really do roll down hills.

The reason that the quality of rolling down a hill can emerge at all is that it is a matter of indifference to the atoms of iron that make up the cartwheel—they don't care if they are rolling down the hill or not. Therefore, the phenomenon can emerge from the array of its components.

According to the materialist account of mind, in exactly the same way, if you get enough nerve cells together, you can get a phenomenon that emerges called 'consciousness'. And within that phenomenon there can be free will, as long as the willed action doesn't contradict the laws that govern its component parts. So, I can will any action that does not contradict the laws of physics. I can will myself to pick up a newspaper, and that can be a freely done action, but I can't will myself to fly out of the window, because that breaks the laws of physics. So you can get a model of free will within materialism quite effectively.

Is this, then, the causation that is being referred to in *Revelations of Mind*? It is worth pondering this point. Can willed actions in this perspective have consequences, as the law of karma predicts? Certainly the idea that materialism inevitably forces you to regard your own existence as irrelevant is not philosophically sound. Gaining freedom from the regime of mind is possible even if we hold a thoroughly materialist outlook. We can stay at the level of emergent phenomena and still end up, through understanding the regime of mind, coming to a far greater and more creative psychological freedom than we had before. To go further is also of course possible, but beyond the scope of this commentary here.

> PAGE 162, PARAGRAPH 1: *The only point where the cause could have a causal connection with the effect is at the exact point when the present is replaced by the past. To serve its purpose of linking cause and effect, this point where the past gives way and the present has not yet come would have to be almost inconceivably small, even smaller than the nanosecond.*

Now, this is a key point. Cause and effect must join—they must connect somewhere. Otherwise, how can a cause become an effect? There has to be a point of contact. However, when you start slicing time into smaller and smaller segments, you realize that that presumed point of contact becomes inconceivably small, and the more you slice it, the smaller it gets. Indeed, as one can subdivide time indefinitely, how does cause ever meet its effect?

Remember, the smearing out of the present that we found when we analyzed our reaction to Newton's Cradle is a psychological phenomenon. Now we are trying to understand the underlying physics here: where do the cause and effect actually meet?

Where is the moment where one ball on the cradle is hitting the next one? If I get a really, really, really fast camera, am I going to be able to find the moment when they touch? It seems that you can go on faster and faster, identifying smaller and smaller increments of time, but you will never quite get to the present. Whatever interval of time I have, I can cut it in half and find a smaller one.

With this in mind, let's conduct a thought experiment. *Where is the present?* Can you find it? It must be inconceivably small. Can everything that exists rest on such a small point?

PAGE 162, PARAGRAPH 2: *Imagine that nanoseconds are cylinders made up of slices of past, present, and future. Suppose there are fifteen such segments, each with its own specific character and role to play. Thus, in the past we can distinguish: 1) the very remote past; 2) the not so remote past; 3) the intermediate past; 4) the immediate past; and 5) the immanent past, just before the present arises. For the present, there is 1) the present poised on the verge of receding into the past; 2) the continuing present; 3) the present moment of experiencing (like the first two, already moving toward the past); 4) the present just beginning to manifest, freshly coming into view; 5) the still undefined 'cutting edge' of the present, moving to take its place as it emerges from the future.*

So, here is another thought experiment. We can slice up experience, making finer and finer distinctions, to try to work out exactly when an event happened. Can we actually divide time up in this manner?

PAGE 162, PARAGRAPH 2, CONT'D: *As for the future a similar fivefold progression could be said to operate, 'stocking' the future, but since the future remains unstructured and undefined,*

*it cannot be treated in the same manner as past and present.
We can only say that the future supplies the present.*

Now, this is problematic as well: can the future be modeled
in this manner? What's happening is we are realizing that our
concept of time is problematic, because there really isn't the
past, and there really isn't the future. Yet, without those two,
there really isn't the present either.

We are conducting this exploration of time in order to analyze this all-important word, 'because'. We use it all the time,
and we seem to have an uncomplicated idea that there is a
'because' of everything. But every 'because' involves time,
and when we look closely, we find it becomes very hard to
locate either past or future, except in the present. And then
when we turn around, when we try to look at the present,
we can't find that, either! Yet it is the fulcrum upon which
everything else rests. Without a present, where does a cause
become an effect?

> PAGE 163, PARAGRAPH 1: *By breaking each nanosecond
> down in this way, we might seem to be making progress
> in explaining how cause and effect might operate within
> the context of past, present, and future. But the proce-
> dure is not entirely satisfactory. While each of these fif-
> teen aspects functions in a certain way to connect cause
> and effect, the nature of the connection itself remains
> mysterious.*

> PAGE 163, PARAGRAPH 2: *Of course, there is no law stat-
> ing how nanoseconds are to be divided. For example, we
> can halve the intervals again, and then again, moving
> as close as possible to the point where existence begins,
> where 'not yet happened' becomes 'happening,' where 'not-
> exist' becomes 'exist'. Even here there is no reason to stop.
> We might envision the beginning or transition point as it-
> self an elliptical disk with many billions of points moving
> very fast along its forward edge. This would be the 'cutting
> edge' of the present moving to 'take place'.*

We tend to use a very narrow, billiard ball model of time, rather like the balls in the Newton's cradle we have been considering. The past 'causes' the present, as if the past bumps up against the present and gives it its current shape. Could a broader conception be possible? Could we at least begin to examine the presuppositions we have about time to see if other notions might work as well as the billiard ball model we learned in school and tend to believe is right?

Perhaps we're not living in a world of billiard balls, all bumping into each other in the present. Perhaps there are other ways we can envision time that don't require us to have a point of contact that apparently doesn't exist. Perhaps the present, rather than being a knife-edge, is more like a tide, with bits of the present slightly behind other bits of the present. Maybe the present isn't some really narrow place where one thing gives way to another. It could be understood to be more like a flow in which there is a disk of activity that moves. Parts of it might be flowing faster than others. Perhaps some of the edges are looping back. This is certainly a more relaxing conception of time.

> PAGE 164, PARAGRAPH 1: *But perhaps we are missing other possibilities. What if each of the fifteen units of each nanosecond were to move in a random, non-linear way. In that case, do we have any way to say with certainty which point connects with which, or even which unit is cause and which is effect? Can we tell which point provides each character and quality of the present, which provides quantity, or which influences a certain way of behavior?*

We can imagine the present as co-evolving in a complex way that doesn't necessarily offend our experience of causation, but still liberates us from this very narrow conception of a 'time-line', in which the past and present are connected.

> PAGE 164, PARAGRAPH 2: *Here is another possibility: Imagine, instead, the fifteen units within the nanosecond*

arrayed in a single horizontal line, with other nanoseconds flowing beneath them in their own horizontal array. The fifteen units arrayed along the top are the ones we have assumed carry the momentum of cause and effect from past to future. Yet suppose each of these fifteen units has fifteen additional units extending from it vertically. From each of these additional units extends a third generation of fifteen units, and from these a fourth generation, and so on through fifteen generations.

So here we reach a beautiful meditation on the present. Moments are arrayed, both into the future, and vertically, almost as if time flows in a spherical way, each movement at an angle to the last. This is very reminiscent of another famous meditation on causes—that of Indra's net in the *Avatamsaka Sutra*: there, the metaphor is a spider's web. If you look at a spider's web on a dewy morning, on every single intersection there will be a bead of dew. And if you look inside that bead, you can see the whole spider's web reflected. And if you have good enough eyes, you can look inside that reflected spider web and look at the dew there in every intersection, and in each individual drop of that reflected spider's web you see the web again reflected. So, it's a reflection within reflection within reflection, going on forever.

In this image of nanoseconds in array, you can see the same idea. You can imagine time flowing, but when you get down to micro-levels, it doesn't seem to flow 'forward' or 'past'. It has more of the feeling of a dance or cycle; it has more dimensionality than our plodding conception of cause and effect. Now, capturing this idea of dimensionality is very important, because the regime of mind, the prison, has a deterministic sense of 'going forward', moving along in one dimension. But the regime is built on the detailed specificity of actual events. When we step outside the box and enter that detailed specificity, when we access these events in a direct way, we sense that time is much bigger, much fuller, like a matrix.

PAGE 165, PARAGRAPH 1: *Or perhaps our nanosecond-units unfold in a circular way, not only on a plane, but in depth and into all directions. Eventually they would merge and become one like the elliptical disk described above.*

Here is Indra's web. It's reminiscent of the structure known as a tesseract, the four-dimensional structure in which all times are visible.

PAGE 165, PARAGRAPH 2: *Among all these possibilities, there is still no point of transition that goes beyond the fif-teenth unit, no 'landing place' where mind can initiate its operations so that the link between cause and effect can be established. Perhaps here, at the edge of beyond, before the next series of units, we could posit a smaller, sixteenth unit, the elusive point of transition. Invisible, unoccupied, and uncommitted, yet not stagnant or locked in, the point of transition is fluid and open, like a brilliant bubble of quicksilver, a window of opportunity that allows experi-ence to be.*

As we follow our word 'because' down into the realm of time, we can allow it to expand, while realizing that of course, the point of transition cannot be in time at all. It must be some-thing outside of time that activates time in some way. If it was within time, we would be stuck with the enigma of the unit of time—you could cut it shorter and shorter and shorter and never find the point of transition. The point of transition is there, but it's not in time itself. There can be no point of tran-sition within linear time.

Imagine you are standing in a steadily flowing river. You stand there and the water washes past you. It comes toward you, hits you and goes past you. Imagine letting go and just float-ing in the stream. The sensation of rushing past stops. You're in the stream—it is no longer moving past you. Everything becomes quiet and spacious. Can you be in time like that? It is not so much that the present is bumping into you and going into the past. It's more that you are in the present. The present is not moving at all. This has a very different narrative structure than the framework of past, present and future. If you frame events as present, the narrative structure that you create is contextual. Instead of seeking cause and effect, you become much more interested in the environment in which things manifest. Looking at causes that way is much more in line with the ancient Indian model of the four causes, in which the efficient cause is only one element of 'because'. This produces a very different appreciation of what life is and what life means.

> PAGE 165, PARAGRAPH 3: *In this realm of the infinitesimally small, points of transition remain mysterious, a kind of non-unit belonging neither to past or future. Time itself might behave in unusual ways, transforming itself into a different reality, possibly governed by different laws.*

Robert Grosseteste, a wonderful twelfth-century Christian mystic, said eternity is an eternal now.[32] The idea is that nowness, immanence, is actually not within time at all. We can access nowness, we can access immanence, but it's not to be found on a clock. It is like the moments we all experience when we see something very beautiful and time stops. We have a scent, a touch of something different. That is the sixteenth unit of time. It must be there, because we can see that change requires it. We can see there is something else. Furthermore, we all have fleeting experiences of it, which is reassuring. So it's not as if this experience of immanence isn't experienced: it's just that it's so fleeting—and it gets covered up, because the regime itself can't make use of it.

---

32 James McEvoy, *Robert Grosseteste* (Oxford University Press USA, 2000).

PAGE 165, PARAGRAPH 3, CONT'D: *In such a transformed reality, would mind be freed of the minding operations that shape our ordinary ways of being, rendering very different all that we know? If so, understanding points of transition could mean understanding the illusory nature of what we now view as unchanging and real. It could mean understanding impermanence and the whole context of life and death.*

When you begin to contemplate impermanence, you can discover something very magical in what appears to be a brute fact of life. Most of us refuse to accept that things are always changing; we reject impermanence by mapping permanence onto it. We reify the world into fixed objects, and navigate the map that such fixed entities comprise. However, if we can embrace impermanence, embrace the fact that everything is changing, and allow ourselves to enter into that changing world, right in its center lies this magical, multifarious jewel—the treasure of Indra's net.

Exercise 22
Finding the present

On occasions during the day, examine the present moment. What is this label of the present pointing to? From time to time during the day, just interrogate your stream of experience with that simple question.

It would appear to have a very simple answer, but as we can see, it doesn't. Right here, and here, all the time, every moment, we are passing over the present. We are in a sort of parallel stream. But if you can awaken to the immanence of the present, you will wake up in a very interesting way, and you will find the world is totally different. Instead of going from one task to the next in a linear way, all other directions are suddenly open to you.

CHAPTER 31

Opening the Nanosecond

Revelations of Mind begins by analyzing cognition and the constructs that we use to make the world. Then the second section looks at meditation, initially critically, and finally introducing a new stance of inquiry in the process of meditation itself. But where should we take this stance? This is what this latter half of the third section of *Revelations* is about.

One of the central features of *Revelations* is that it is very systematic in choosing a meditation object. When you meditate, you try to rest the mind on a single referent, a simple meditation object like a candle or something similar. This can be understood as a support for the practice of resting the mind on a chosen object. But rather than taking an external object, or bringing attention to an internal sensation such as the breath touching the nostrils, *Revelations* takes time as a meditation object. Although time seems enigmatic and difficult to grasp, we have gradually opened up some key features over the previous pages. Time is one of the two fundamental constructs we use to make the world, the other being place. But time is unusual, in that even when you are still and in a quiet place, time continues. This makes time very promising as something to relate to, because you can sit in one place and still look at time.

Normally, for Westerners, self-knowledge is exclusively concerned with knowledge of the 'I'—"know thyself" is the great Western thing. The idea is, if you are lucky, by the end of your life you will have a good idea who you are. There are many accounts about wise men, wise women, who understand who they actually are. But of course, at no time in that tradition is there any attempt to look at the stage upon which the 'I' is set, and consequently the value of such knowledge is constrained by a deeper layer of construction that is never analyzed—a construct we call the world. *Revelations* looks more deeply, however. Of course, it's worth looking at the 'I', but in *Revelations* there is a tacit understanding that getting to know the 'I' isn't enough. Even if you were able to be egoless, it wouldn't be enough. You would merely be egoless within another unexamined construct. And those of you who have had experience of spiritual centers full of people doing stuff like this know how true that is: you often meet people who have spent years trying to deconstruct their sense of self but somehow still seem totally stuck in some other prison that they never saw.

It is the nature of these constructs to be hidden. We know what we know within the construct: it remains hidden precisely because it's the framework within which knowing itself occurs. It's exceptionally difficult to discern, because even as we try to look at it carefully, we tend to recreate the framework in the very act of looking. All the time we are re-constructing the thing we are trying to see behind.

These last chapters are more experiential, however. Now, the experiential path is valuable and risky at the same time. It's valuable because it has the potential to conduct us beyond the construct: it's risky for exactly the same reason. So in becoming experiential we need to choose our meditation object with great care. In Buddhist teachings, that's called the view. The view is understanding precisely what it is that you wish to approach. It's a bit like docking a 747: you've got to be really precise. If you approach the meditation object in a random way, you can bring with you unexamined constructs, so the experience you get is conditioned. In Buddhist teachings that's called 'defiled cognition': this way of looking has been preconditioned by a construct that wasn't examined, and consequently it's not pristine, it's already constrained.

Ultimately what we are trying to do is get back into our own direct experience; you could say we are trying to get back into our own skin. We left our direct experience to explore the world, and we then used that world to understand our direct experience, so our own experience became something external to us. We are not trying to undo what we learned on that exploration however. Rather we are trying to undo that 'doing' and get back into our own experience again—our own skin. This is one way we could characterize the 'right view' of meditation: being in our own skin, and then acting accordingly. The ultimate purpose of meditation is to re-inhabit ourselves, literally to re-member ourselves. Meditation with right view on the right meditation object should enable us to re-inhabit our own skin, because what we do is undo the construct and start to inhabit the actuality that the construct is built on. We move beyond the construct into actuality.

> PAGE 167, PARAGRAPH 1: *Working with nanoseconds has the potential to open up the fields of the senses, allowing us to see wider dimensions of space and understand all appearances as projections of mind.*

In a way, that's a rather unusual sentence: "Working with nanoseconds," which is time, "has the potential to open up the fields of the senses, allowing us to see wider dimensions of space." This is because if you can enter the construct, you will see it all, the entire construct, time and space. As a result, you will be able to understand all appearances as projections of mind.

PAGE 167, PARAGRAPH 1, CONT'D: *Although this under-*
standing will not take us beyond the walls erected by
mind's loyalty to a subject/object perspective, opening up
our commitment to one single point may make it easier to
open others as well.

If we are able to enter time, the frame upon which the mind
projects the world dissolves. Going beyond the timeframe
immediately takes us beyond a subject/object perspective because it simply has no referent upon which to work. This is
the effortless consequence: although we are not addressing
such perspectives directly, taking time as a meditation object
dissolves the subject/object structure itself.

PAGE 167, PARAGRAPH 2: *Can we open up the nanosec-*
ond? While words are not likely to be helpful here, we
are free to experiment with our own minds. To start,
envision the mind as a camera taking photos in rap-
id-fire succession. Normally, our minds operate much
faster than any camera. But if we sit very still in a calm
environment without much external sensory stimula-
tion, we may be able to relax our senses enough to slow
down the shutter-speed of mind and let the nanosecond
become available.

This is shamata. If we choose a meditation object, we are limiting our sensory environment, and we are calming and allowing our mind to rest on that meditation object. Then we
can shift our attention from the object to the clicking shutter
of the mind. We shift our attention from the object in time
to time itself. The mind is making the world, clicking away
in little moments of projection. Each of the six sense fields
is clicking away. These little moments are integrated and result in a smooth experience of projection. Shamata narrows
experience down to one data-stream. Then, by relaxing and
settling, you gradually slow down and allow the shift of attention to time itself.

Whenever our attention is diverted, in that moment of diversion we're completely in that moment of mind. For example, I'm sitting in a room and then the door opens. Just for a moment as I turn around I'm in that moment of time. In the immediacy of that moment I am completely free—but then the next moment, conceptualization comes back as we grasp; "What is happening?" We're living in a conceptual continuity, a world. Every now and then something cuts across it. Just for a moment before a new stream starts we have a direct experience, and then it is immediately covered over by a new stream of known events.

Another example is listening to music. In a great performance, the audience is being attracted into a single sense field, and from there into experience itself. At the end of the performance, if it was good, then just for a moment there is complete, non-conceptual silence before everyone breaks out into clapping. Another example is going to sleep every night. There is a moment between being awake and going to sleep that is an entrance into direct experience. We may not notice, but our day is punctuated by these moments.

Can we make such experience a choice? When *Revelations* states, "We may be able to relax our senses enough to slow down the shutter-speed of mind, and let the nanosecond become available," that experience is what it is referring to. This nanosecond, this moment, is a fruitful meditation object. If we can bring this moment to mind and relax, we can enter the nanosecond. But to get there requires that we work with a precise meditation object. This is simple yet somehow secret, far from obvious. Yet the possibility is there all the time.

The word "available," as in "let the nanosecond become available," is interesting and worth commenting on, because, for most of us, time is no longer available. We have given away our time to engaging in the next event. *Revelations* asks us to bring time back and make it available. If you ever meet someone who's managed to do this, you will notice that they are never in a hurry. This doesn't mean nothing's going on. They may even be busy, but somehow they are not in a hurry. Time is available to them in a way that it is not available to us. We are always running and being pulled around by our sense of obligation. Yet from moment to moment, that gift of time is there for us. If we can make time available, we can experience this expansiveness for ourselves.

PAGE 168, PARAGRAPH 1: *Now imagine opening the aperture of mind very wide, a full 360 degrees.*

Have you ever used a manual camera with an f-stop? You have a lens and in front of it is an iris. The iris can open and close. As the iris opens you get a lot of light, but a narrow focus. If the iris closes you get a deeper and deeper focus, but less light. If you shoot a portrait you will need a wide aperture, so the face can stand out against the background, which ideally stays out-of-focus. If you want to shoot a landscape, on the other hand, you'll need a narrow aperture, so everything is in focus. The wide aperture shot is engaging, involving, which is why it is used for portraits. The narrow aperture is distancing, allowing a more critical analysis.

If we relax the mind, it is as if we are slowing time. We can then widen the aperture and enter time. Instead of being called back from time into a narrow little slice of experience, we are opening, opening and coming into the flow of time. Then the nanosecond becomes available.

This is a really important experience. We've all had it. Sometimes when we're truly absorbed in something it's as if time stops. I'm not talking about clock time, but time as a feeling of the flow of events. As mentioned above, the flow of events is like a steadily flowing river. If you stand in the river, the water pushes past you. You can feel time passing. If you float in the river, time stops. You're moving with the river: you no longer feel time passing. You have entered the stream.

PAGE 168, PARAGRAPH 1, CONT'D: *You may now be able to glimpse instants when raw sensing begins to take shape and form. You may even be able to pay special attention to the point in this process when mind grasps a form, and feelings, emotions, concepts, and streams of thought begin to arise.*

Remember, right at the beginning, a raw sense impression arises and the mind grasps it. In the grasping is an inquiry: "What are you?" This grasping, this focus, is the first movement of mind toward the sense gate. If you can relax your attention to the point where the time becomes visible, you can feel this initial response happening as the sense gates open. As you relax, time is becoming available. You are entering the present. It turns out to be not a narrow knife-edge passing by, but a vast spacious mansion that appears out of nowhere.

PAGE 168, PARAGRAPH 2: *Is this even possible? As you read and reread these chapters on mind and time, relax and open mind as widely as possible to what is being communicated, and the range of the possible may expand. There will be much that cannot be understood directly through words and meanings. But there are other dimensions that have not yet been explored.*

This is a meditation chapter, and here is a direct request. By allowing the aperture to open, we allow inputs from the gates to arise without focusing on them. We are not looking for meaning: we are looking to enter the experience. This is something to dwell on. When we are able to dwell quietly, we can just simplify our sense fields and rest there. One moves effortlessly from the object itself to the moment of time.

Once we enter the flow of time, there are many other dimensions to discover.

PAGE 168, PARAGRAPH 3:
Here I am, in the present. However I try,
however diligently I trace out the strings
of nanoseconds, I am still in the present!
I do not seem to be crossing over to the future.

It is almost as if someone were scolding:
"Are you still going back and forth among those
nanoseconds? How can you expect
to get to the future if you keep stopping here?
You have been playing here long enough!
Quit that!

If you are not playing around with
nanoseconds, why are you stalled
in the present? If you have no reason
for staying here, how can there
even be nanoseconds?"

No matter—even if nanoseconds
are not truly real, we can still mark out
units of time and call them nanoseconds.

We cannot argue with nanoseconds.
If we argue with the nanoseconds
we are arguing with time,
we are arguing with reality,
we are arguing with our experience—
we are arguing with our lives.

Time as a series of moments, and time as the continual present, are almost like alternatives. When you are present, there is no time. You can feel the nanoseconds: if you start going toward them, you leave the present to project back into the known world. But when you are present the world you are in is not the world of conceptual experience. Poets and artists can touch this. Look for example at Wordsworth's "Ode to Immortality":

Hence in a season of calm weather
Though inland far we be,
Our Souls have sight of that immortal sea
Which brought us hither,
Can in a moment travel thither,
And see the Children sport upon the shore,
And hear the mighty waters rolling evermore.

Develop shamata. Choose the right meditation object, time.
You're no longer being distracted from distraction by distraction, pulled this way and that, all muddled up. You're
calm. You start seeing clearly. You've begun to nose out of
the harbor into the vast open sea, the mighty waters, rolling
evermore.

> PAGE 169, PARAGRAPH 2: *The division of time into past,
> present, and future accommodates the notion of cause
> and effect, although it leaves the crucial operations of
> transition and continuity unexplained. But this division is
> only one way of considering time in relation to mind. Sup-
> pose that our conventional notion of time were upended,
> and we had not just three temporal dimensions to consid-
> er, but six, seven, or more. Could time still unfold as a lin-
> ear continuity, or would everything be in a state of chaos?
> Possibly everything would collapse, or perhaps nothing we
> know would have ever existed. For without past, present,
> and future, there would be no connection between cause
> and effect: cause and effect could not operate; they could
> not even exist.*

Looking again at the Newton's cradle, at one level we say
the movement of the ball on one side causes the ball on the
other to move. But that's an incomplete explanation. What
we're forgetting is the frame. All the balls are strung on a
frame—and without that frame it wouldn't work. The balls
are moving, so we notice them, but the frame is not, and so
it escapes our attention. This means that if we look at this
level of movement, at the level where time appears to be
passing, we leave continuity unexplained. When we project
the nanosecond to create the past, present and predict the
future, and say "because," we forget the continuity that lies
beneath it. We never realize there has to be a continuous
element for the discontinuous to be related by cause and
effect. The continuous element is the present from which
cause and effect are projected.

Always at the beginning of every instant of projection there is the ground from which causal continuity arises. Not only is that causal continuity present at the beginning of a projection, it's present through the entirety of the projection. We only get a chance to see it at the beginning, however. That's the door. But it never stops being there any more than the framework of the Newton's Cradle stops being there. There's the ocean that lies beneath the waves of phenomena that froth around on top of it. On top everything is noisy, hurried. Underneath is the vast body of the ocean, still, present, unchanging.

> PAGE 170, PARAGRAPH 1: *Let's try again. Imagine that we could mark out one given point that represents the center of existence. That point would have to be there in the first nanosecond, because without it, there would be no possibility of a future. There would be no character, no quantity, no physical forms, no realm of things and no things to populate a realm. There would not even be any place that is unoccupied, for there would be no borders. With no borders, there would be no place for cause and effect to manifest; there would be no universe, no existence, not even space.*

If we enter the present then time can be projected in many ways, because the present is always present. It can go in any direction—thus our freedom to experience events becomes multidimensional. Instead of being caught in a causal chain that only runs in one direction, from past to present to future, we may find that within the present, there are multiple ways in which things might manifest.

> PAGE 170, PARAGRAPH 2: *This imagining is not so far-fetched. In the remote primordial state before the universe and all its forms existed—the past of the past of the past—space was unoccupied and non-existent. This was a kind of first point, the center of all and everything. That once unoccupied point is now our realm of existence, our universe, the entire cosmos with its billions upon billions*

of stars, planets, and world-systems. How interesting to imagine this transition, from once unoccupied place to the fullness of existence manifesting in infinite variety, characters, and forms! Does this transition depend on cause and effect?

We are living in a golden age of cosmology at the moment: most Westerners know that current theory says the universe is expanding from a single point. There is a very interesting mental exercise we could do regarding this point, which is known as a singularity. The idea is that in the past of the past, there was no space and there was no time—there was just a single point.

Buddhist cosmology, not unlike modern cosmology, also talks about billions and billions of worlds—it has a very big vision. It talks about world systems expanding and contracting, expanding and contracting. While these writers also envisaged world systems collapsing back, for them there was always an underlying continuity. Cosmological ideas give us a vantage point from which to interrogate our own causal structure: they can help us notice that our own construct of cause rests on a basis that we never quite realize is there. There is something else that enables cause and effect to occur.

Cause implies continuity, but continuity of what? That's the question.

PAGE 171, PARAGRAPH 1: *We can go further: consider all forms that have or could possibly exist—all materials and manifestations imaginable and unimaginable, those that have disappeared in the past, those extant in the present, and those that will come into being. Consider them all appearing, exhibiting their unique characters, dancing in time and space, interacting, causing and effecting, producing in different ways manifold realms of existence. For such an array of forms to be established, cause and effect would seem necessary.*

PAGE 171, PARAGRAPH 2: *Before there was existence, before there was a universe filled with forms, before cause existed as cause, the cause itself had to manifest in a way that enabled it to become the effect. It had to 'take place', in order to bring about an effect. But this would mean there was something 'before' the cause. For, before the cause could arise, there had to be a functioning instrument that could transmit some kind of continuity. Before time, after time, continuation must therefore continue, transmitted by a process we can only call 'continuity'. But the instrument itself, along with its operation, goes unexplained.*

Now, this is true in our own lives as well. It's certainly true in our physical models of the universe. This is a fundamental problem of causation: what caused the beginning? There may eventually be a new synthesis in our cosmology that deals with this somehow. But in any event, in our own experience we have the same phenomenon. In experience, cause and effect are linked: we link them together through memory. As we see our causal structure arising, our sense of the present mutates: time ceases to be linear and becomes fluid. In entering the present, inhabiting it and living in it, we become free. We realize that continuity and the entire causal structure are rooted here, rooted in the beginningless beginning.

Exercise 23
Entering the present

The exercise this week is to enter the present twice a day. When you're in the present say, "Is time there?" It can be short. We're not talking about meditating for three hours. Just bring the attention down and enter the present.

Chapter 32

Ground of Illusion

Most of us are so trapped in a programmed response to things that arise before us that we have lost our sense of freedom. We feel as if our life is a funnel in which there is 'no time'. An important response to this is to begin to explore phenomena themselves. This is not necessarily because they are themselves of interest, but because it is beneficial to study how they emerge and disappear. When we examine the arising and cessation of phenomena, we have a chance to make contact with the ground. The ground is not arising or ceasing: it is there before, during and after. When we make contact with the ground, new opportunities open up: we have the potential to base our actions and understanding upon something other than instinctive reactivity. That alternative will manifest in a more relaxed, spacious and happy way of life.

In a sense one could say that this ground is the door to wisdom. Here we are going to explore how the time clock and the presence of time cover the ground of experience. Hopefully by exploring this we'll begin to open up windows or gaps in our causal continuity so that the ground of experience becomes more available. To make the ground of experience available is a virtuous habit that will take us a long time, but if we are able to do so it will be completely transformative.

PAGE 172, PARAGRAPH 1: *Before the universe existed, there must have been a 'before', a point, large or small, where the necessary conditions could converge and set in motion the process that allowed the universe to come to be. Mind requires a similar kind of 'before', a point from which its minding business can unfold our own mental universe.*

The big bang, as physical theory, was always problematic to people who thought about it, particularly in the early days when they were looking at it freshly. They asked how something could come from literally nothing, not just from formlessness, but from literally nothing. A number of current physicists still claim that the universe contains the seeds of its previous big crunch: what they're pointing to is the logical impossibility of a 'big bang' coming from nothing. You can't have an uncaused cause. It was recognized from antiquity that there is a major problem with having a beginning, a true beginning. Nothing really begins. Everything continues.

That's true of our lives too, in that we come from the 'causes' of our parents. We also appear to have a psychological beginning, the earliest memory we can locate. When we're born into the world, the world already exists. We forget how enigmatic this is. This has everything to do with the ground.

PAGE 172, PARAGRAPH 2: *With each such point—each new 'before', mind spins out a new illusion, like the rapid-fire camera imagined in the last chapter. The reflections of these illusion-images within mind create as well the illusion of movement and continuity. We sense 'time is passing', moving forward. Recognition by recognition, instant by instant, the mechanisms of mind give rise to a new reality based on each new 'before'. Reflecting on this, we might want to consider more carefully the nature of what came 'before'.*

These illusion images are a bit like the presentations of mind: in every moment of perception you get a phenomenon arising in the mind, containing the processes of initial grasping, rec-ognition and then the projection of a known world. We could call this projection of a known world the creation of a 'mind bubble'. The bubble lasts a certain amount of time. Then it dies and a new bubble begins, but they always occur in a se-ries, together. We call these bubbles 'thoughts'.

If you look up the word 'thought' you'll find that a thought is defined as an 'idea or consideration'. If you look up the words 'idea' and 'consideration' you'll find they are defined as a thought! We don't have in our vernacular language a precise definition of what a thought is. And yet we inhabit a world of thoughts. The perceptual world in which we live is made up of thoughts and most of us are thinking thoughts all the time. When we're asleep it's called 'dreaming'; when we're in our working day, we're either directly reacting to phenomena or talking about phenomena with one another. The whole time, we're making and re-making the world of thought. But always alongside thoughts, the time clock is ticking and marking events. That is how we make sense of our experience.

To look at this we need the faculty of shamata. We need to develop a basis of calmness from which such an investiga-tion can be made. If we aren't able to calm our mind enough to look without being bombarded by the stuff going on, we are never going to be able to look at the 'before', or see the bubbles arising.

Shamata is the simple ability to focus on a thing and leave the focus there, and then relax, so the focus remains. So shamata has two phases: the first is intentional, where you hold; the second is when you've developed the faculty of holding with effort and you relax the effort, and the object just remains. Both those elements of shamata need to be stable in order to start addressing something like 'before'.

PAGE 173, PARAGRAPH 1: *In order to arrive at a point before minding, a point that is clear and unoccupied, enabling experience to develop from a stable foundation, mind needs to calm down its restless jumping from thought to thought.*

Remember that shamata is about being able to rest the mind at will on any chosen object. When we attempt shamata, the first experience we will have is of incredible noise bombarding us all the time, and that's because we tend to ignore our own internal mental process. It's common in the initial experience of shamata for things to get more noisy, not less—you may even feel like you're going backwards.

As you enter this maelstrom of noise that you had no idea was there, as you enter it calmly and focus the mind, it begins to grow quieter, quieter and quieter, until eventually you are able to hold attention: and then you let the effort-element go. In this effortless quiet, the mind will just sit on an object without requiring any effort to stay there: that's when you have stable shamata.

PAGE 173, PARAGRAPH 1, CONT'D: *But if this were ever possible in the past, as the pace of change quickens and life grows more chaotic, it becomes increasingly difficult. Catastrophic events, new technology, and major social and cultural changes unfold ever more rapidly, challenging mind to make sense of these changes and to incorporate them into its processes.*

It's hard for us to imagine what it was like in the medieval world where there was no time as we know it. There were 'whiles' and 'watches', the day punctuated by bells calling people to prayer. The continual push toward events that marks our own lives seems to have been absent. Writings from that period reveal that people had a lot of time. Of course, they also had a lot of suffering and inconvenience. But in terms of being pushed by time, this 'iPhone phenomenon' of always having in our hand a little computer driving us toward activity—that is very much a modern development. It's something we have to actively resist if we are going to calm our energy down.

One very good habit to develop is to totally stop speaking, reading or listening for a specific period of time. You could call this meditation, and if you practice shamata, that is the effect. Another trick is to take deep breaths, concentrating on the outbreath. The mind rides on the breath, and you calm down, like a horseman calming his steed. Calmly breathing quietens down the nervous jittery energy that we all suffer from because of the pressure of our technological life.

> PAGE 173, PARAGRAPH 1, CONT'D: *Instead of calming down, mind is pressured to speed up. The result is that mind tends to communicate with the senses more roughly.*

As we get more jittery, more reactive, we make more pressured demands on our system. That tends to make the inputs into our system more jittery and reactive. We get caught in a vicious cycle of responsiveness, which results in feeling over-caffeinated, overwhelmed. One of the reasons to go to an art gallery or listen to music is to begin to calm down that interface between sense input and response. Beautiful things calm the mind; appreciating beauty can help to calm down reactivity. Because of this calming effect on the mind, beauty is a useful vehicle for touching the ground.

Do your best to make time to calm down the interface between mind and senses. It's all about developing healthy habits that enable us to reside in the ground, not in the phenomena that arise out of the ground.

> PAGE 173, PARAGRAPH 1, CONT'D: *Critical aspects of the perceptual process may not link up so smoothly with identity and recognition. Then mind, anxious for resolution, may grasp at incorrect interpretations, distorting the accuracy of thoughts and feelings and increasing the likelihood of misunderstanding.*

We are responsible for our minds. Although the perceptual phenomena in which we appear to live are a product of our mental operations, we are nonetheless responsible for our minds. We can deliberately engage that relationship to make it more harmonious.

This is not to claim that because there's a ground, we don't exist. What we're saying is that the 'we' we think exists is a product of something deeper, because it had a 'before'. Knowing this, we can begin to systematically explore it. As we arrange our way of living so that the relationship between mind and senses becomes more harmonious, we uncover more time. And with more time, we're able to begin to develop a relationship with the ground.

It's a bit like those martial artists you see in movies. Whatever is going on, they remain totally calm, and if anyone comes to attack them, they observe and then react appropriately. The roots of many of those martial arts lie, in fact, in disciplines developed by Buddhist monks to protect themselves on pilgrimage. Such techniques are full of teachings about meditation. If you can react to a rising sensation calmly it gives you a lot more latitude in your response. Normally, when something comes toward us, we see it, grasp it, name it, associate and react. This all takes place so quickly that we can hardly see the whole process happening. But that means our reaction is entirely 'historical'—it's based upon our memory of previous examples where we thought that same thing occurred. If we can control our sense-doors, however, then as the thing arises we can flow with it and have far more freedom to react to it appropriately. We won't be stuck in a fixed response.

> PAGE 173, PARAGRAPH 2: *This intensifying busy-ness of mind separates us even more from the instant before all minding activities, where mind functions in wholeness and clarity. To reach this point—to cross over the ocean of swirling mental activity—we would seem to need some kind of bridge.*

At every moment, we have phenomena arising in the mirror of mind, followed by the act of grasping to see what they are, and the projection of a world based on our memories of what the phenomena appear to be. We spend our entire life there in the product without realizing that it all had a cause that we can't see, because we are pointing in the wrong direction. We're looking at the screen, not at the apparatus that projects the images.

It is almost as if we are living on a horizontal line, collecting experiences that are good or bad, happy or sad, rich or poor, successful or unsuccessful. All the while, where we want to go is in a direction perpendicular to that line, but the perpendicular direction cannot be seen from the horizontal direction. Becoming aware of phenomena as they are reflected in mind's first moment is to face a direction invisible to the perceived world, which continues on its horizontal track.

The reason nobody finds it is because the direction is hidden from the sequencing of events as we experience them. But within every moment of experience there is the possibility of going in this other direction. We suddenly find time, time that does not seem to exist in the horizontal direction, the prison in which we live. The perpendicular direction is the hidden door toward freedom. No one else sees it. We won't be able to explain it to other people. However, only by entering it can we truly make change.

The horizontal direction is a career, an endless play of cause and effect. All of the results that you are going to get are written already. It is your character. It is 'who you are'. You may become successful at who you are. You may become a failure at who you are. But you won't really change. In the perpendicular, on the other hand, change is possible. This is a movement that is genuinely new.

PAGE 173, PARAGRAPH 2, CONT'D: *But we cannot even think about where that bridge might be found if our patterns of identity, labeling, and recognition are pointing us in the wrong direction by instilling a false notion of subject and object, and distorting our understanding of time.*

If we are living in the horizontal direction, mind and senses are all pointed toward the product, the readout that has already arisen in response to the fundamental movement of mind. We're never going to find within this any indication that there is something wrong. The only indication that we ever get is a sense of ennui, a sense of pointlessness. We can live our whole life on the horizontal, and it all looks wonderful—except it's going nowhere. And all the time, the other possibility is hiding within experience.

PAGE 174, PARAGRAPH 1: *Misunderstanding time, we relate to it wrongly and become caught up in illusions. Since mind and senses fail to alert us to the nature of these illusions, there is no incentive to understand and wake up to other possibilities. We take our point of view and all that follows from it to be incontrovertibly real, based on the observations of our senses and the rational processes of our minds, inhabiting what in some philosophic traditions is known as relative reality.*

Inside the bubble, it all makes sense. Here I am, and here is the world; there is nothing wrong with it all, it's perfectly OK. Why is that? Because it's a readout. It's obviously OK: it's a product, it's been ratified by the mind, it's got its passport, it must be legitimate. That's why from within the bubble, it's almost impossible to see the problem. The only thing that we are left with is a slight whiff of existential angst—that there is something wrong with this readout. Now, of course there are some people for whom the bubble is an unpleasant place, and some people for whom the bubble is a lovely place—but it's a bubble nonetheless. Inside, conditions are fixed, and causes are dictated in advance. Good or bad, happy or sad, it all makes perfect sense.

> PAGE 174, PARAGRAPH 2: *'Relative', in this sense, could be said to refer to whatever appears real within the scope of thought and concepts of past, present, and future. We know this territory and system from within. We know that it leads to restrictions and problems.*

Now, this term 'relative' is really very big in Buddhist teachings—relative and absolute reality is the two-truths teaching. Western culture has a similar idea. Western materialism for example would say that the everyday world of experience is an illusion, because underlying it are physical processes that are not revealed to it. So everyday experience is relative, and the real absolute is the physical reality discovered by physics and the sciences. That's an example of two truths. So Western culture has its own conception of relative and absolute. But there is an important difference: in the Western tradition, both the relative and the absolute are inferential, for reasons we have already explored.

What *Revelations* proposes, in contrast, is that the relative is the world created by our own pre-conception: it's essentially the world of our memory.

> PAGE 174, PARAGRAPH 3: *To free ourselves of these restrictions and problems, we need a different operation of mind, one that engages the dynamic of time more intimately. This would bring us face to face with impermanence, the continual falling away of the familiar and the emergence of the new.*

Now, impermanence is the most threatening element of our experience. You could argue the regime of mind is entirely predicated on the wish to ignore it as much as possible, because impermanence is truly threatening. All the time our experience is falling away from us, it's passing, and that process of passing is literally irreversible. It's as if we are on the edge of a waterfall where things are just dropping away from us.

An easy way to experience this is just to sit on a park bench in a public space and close your eyes. You may become scared by the extraordinary cacophony of sounds you hear and realize are happening continuously. What we do is create a box, a vehicle, a suit of armor, a carriage, a boat, which will carry us on this wave of impermanence. And that's how we live our lives. We may embellish the boat with education, with talent, with various achievements, but at the end of the day it's just a vessel. It's a boat, and our intelligence is within this boat being protected from what's actually occurring, which is this continuous dropping away. If we allowed ourselves to truly experience it, then we would realize that death surrounds us at every moment: everything is ending, all the time. The only reason why we appear to have a life is because our body is continuously renewing itself in the face of this always-dying, until eventually it doesn't, and then we die as well. Impermanence is our elephant in the room, a big secret that we all ignore, while living with it continuously.

> PAGE 175, PARAGRAPH 1: *Impermanence is the reality in which our lives unfold, a constant reminder of the change and loss that underlies our most persistent forms of suffering. Rather than attempting to dismiss in vain the implications of impermanence, it seems important to continue to investigate further mind's relationship to time, to cross the bridge to the instant before minding, to the clear, uncluttered landscape of mind prior to the instant from which all systems and 'mindings' arise.*

We will have to come to grips with impermanence if we are going to find the absolute truth of our experience.

Impermanence is scary. It's actually alarming when you realize that every moment is lost, and there's no way you'll ever get it back. But being patient in the face of impermanence is how we access the absolute truth of our existence. We have to be patient with impermanence in order to directly experience it. When we do, there is a strange exhilaration, because we realize that events are truly passing, but in a way we didn't expect.

The illusion-world is a protection, a bubble, a case, a suit of armor against actual experience. We need to break the illusion of the reflected world and realize that we are naked in front of change. That way, we can begin to open the door to something else.

From within the bubble, impermanence is death, because it's the end of the bubble. But if we live where the bubble begins, then all we have is mind, manifesting from moment to moment. Impermanence is life. It's a matter of the place we are looking from. Still, we have to see the impermanence before we can even begin to wonder how we are going to get anywhere else. If we can't accept impermanence, we are going to be stuck in the bubble, always running away from it.

> PAGE 175, PARAGRAPH 2: *In the process of perception, the interaction of senses and mind joins the physical and cognitive streams of our being.*

From moment to moment we have a stream of sense inputs, which we reify as the physical world. Remember that there isn't a physical world as direct experience—that 'reality' is an inference from sense input. Whatever the physical world may be, all we get is sense input. Then there is our cognitive stream that is grasping, inquiring: "What is this input?" When those two streams—one sensory and the other cognitive—unite, the result is 'me in the world'. In Buddhist teachings, this union is called *Nama-rupa*—name and form.

> PAGE 175, PARAGRAPH 2, CONT'D: *Sensory stimulation results in identity, labeling, and recognition, and we awaken within the realm of mind, our cognitive and intellectual*

processes fully operative. We are aware that we exist, that we are here in the present, that we arrived here 'from' some prior experience, and we sense we are going 'toward' some new experience that has not yet arrived.

We are aware that we exist, that we are here in the present, that we arrived from some prior experience, and we sense that we are going toward some new experience that has not yet arrived: but this sense of continuity is the product of a discontinuous process. It's as if we have a new dawn in 'me in the world' all the time. As long as we identify with 'me', with 'I', our experience will be discontinuous, because the 'I' is a product, and consequently it refreshes some twenty times a second with every mind bubble.

This is important to understand. Our sense of time is the consequence of our 'I', 'me', and 'mine' being products with time-stamps on them; that's where the intuition of time passing comes from. We know there is a 'before' and there is an 'after': we know that we've been made somehow, that we derive from somewhere. This intuition of time moving forward which we all have, which we think is continuous, is actually a little glimmer of understanding that we are inhabiting a readout.

Like all readouts, it's adequate for a short time—for a moment—but then we need another one, because something has changed. And then we need another one, because something else has changed. And each one of those readouts is a product in which I inhabit a world. We think, "Now I am moving forward through the world," without ever realizing that this forward motion is birth-and-death, birth-and-death, happening continuously all the time.

Now we have a mystery: what happens before, and what happens after the bubble? The easiest way to look at this is to take a thought as the object of our meditation. Like all bubbles, thoughts have beginnings and ends. So one of the interesting things to do as part of our shamata is to move our quiet attention to either the beginning or the end point of a thought, and try and catch what's happening. It's a very fruitful place to move attentiveness, to see if we can capture thought coming in or going out of being.

The ability to suppress thoughts to the point where we have no thought is still itself a thought. It's the thought of nothought. In Buddhist cosmology, were we to die in the state of no-thought, we would be reborn as a formless god, a being without any characteristics whatsoever. That's an almost perfect prison—nothing can reach us, until eventually the strength, the impetus of that no-thought thought dies away, and then we re-enter the world of samsara again. We haven't been liberated at all. Liberation lies in allowing thoughts to come and go, but in coming and going to see where they arise and where they stop.

> PAGE 176, PARAGRAPH 1: *Within this structure, every perception or thought must have a beginning and an end, a 'head' that is pointing toward what is coming up and a 'tail' as the perception or thought gives way, allowing another perception or thought to come up. We find ourselves asking: What was before the identity and recognition that brought us this thought or instant of perception? There must have been a before, but it is unknown. What comes after this perception or thought ends and the next one has not yet been identified and recognized? This 'after' is also unknown.*

As long as we have the ego within its nama-rupa bubble, we can never find out what came before and what comes after. After all, the ego is a product of this nama-rupa bubble. This bubble is the relative truth, and underlying it is another process altogether, which we could call the absolute truth. That's why from within the nama-rupa bubble we can't tell what came before or what came after.

What's really happening is this: an initial sense impression arises to the receptivity of mind and puff—we get a bubble. That bubble collapses. Then there is just the receptivity of mind. Then another sense impression arises and puff, we get another bubble. But before and after the bubble of consciousness, the receptivity of mind is visible. That's what we can't see from the perspective of the bubble. If we could find that, we would see the actual mind itself, the readout-maker hidden away underneath the process of a projected world.

> PAGE 176, PARAGRAPH 2: *Mind as we experience it is thus linked to identity. Before identity, we cannot recognize the existence of anything, not even ourselves. So we might also ask, where are we before we exist, before identity has summoned the subject into being and labeling has given it the name of 'I'?*

By holding your attention on the beginning of things, you are asking the most fruitful question there is to ask: where are we before we exist?

This is not a stupid question, for some continuity must have been there. All religions must accept this question.

> PAGE 176, PARAGRAPH 3: *For all we know, the 'before' of our present situation may well be an empty space. When perception happens, our present universe bursts into being, as if it had manifested inside of a gigantic bubble. We assume it is the same universe we experienced an instant before, but one perception had to end before the next could begin.*

What we discover when we ask this question is that we actually can't know what was going on before. We live in a construct that creates a sense of continuity, so we just assume that continuity is the case. Supposing you are talking to someone and the doorbell rings. They leave the room to answer it. If we ask the question, where did they go, we can't know; we can only infer that they went to the door. We can ask them when they return and they will say, "Yes, that's what I did": but actually even they don't know that anymore, because for them, too, what they did is an inference drawn from memory. We assume it is the same universe we experienced the instant before, but one perception had to end before the next could begin—so we cannot know directly.

> PAGE 176, PARAGRAPH 3, CONT'D: *Each instant of our conscious, waking life is bounded by a territory that is unknown, a 'before' and 'after' where identity, labeling, and recognition are not operating. The coming into being of our mind-universe is repeated instant by instant, perhaps hundreds or even thousands of times a second, perhaps even a thousand times in each nanosecond. What we perceive as continuity may be better understood as a series of discrete perceptions.*

This has important implications. Western philosophy is based on the Cartesian "I think, therefore I am," the famous *cogito*. What if it was realized that the 'I' that thinks is a product of something else? This shows the strange blindness of our culture in that we are unwilling to look at this, even though cognitive psychologists would agree that consciousness is flickering into and out of being from moment to moment.

All that we think we know of ourselves is based on inference arising out of an unknown foundation: all our knowledge of the world is based on inference drawn from sense perception or from scientific investigation. Can we have direct knowledge at all?

> PAGE 177, PARAGRAPH 1: *Even if we lack all access to the before and after, we can study this process by observing the beginning and end of thoughts. How a thought begins, how a thought finishes, and what lies between the end of one and the beginning of another: these are the places to be aware. This is what we wish to observe more and more closely.*

PAGE 177, PARAGRAPH 2: *Time goes forward—moving ahead to the not known. The 'from' is not known, the 'to' is not known. The 'before' of this present situation may have been only empty space.*

PAGE 177, PARAGRAPH 3: *Exercise every head and tail of perception! How much is unknown? How great is the gap between the known and unknown? Look not just once, but every second. How does it occur?*

Seeing this is true vipasana. This is what it means to direct inquiry onto a fruitful meditation object. And the meditation object is the construction of our own experience. You don't have to just use thoughts. If you can isolate a single sense, such as the sense of hearing, you can focus in the same way. A sound will arise, and you can ask, where did it arise from? And it will pass, and you can ask, where did it go? It is exactly the same meditation.

Working with sound can be a little bit scarier than working with thoughts, because sitting with your eyes closed, particularly in an environment where sounds are active, triggers other issues, particularly issues about vulnerability. Of course, the fact that we feel vulnerable when experiences arise is why we make a boat, a casket of concepts—to overcome that fear of vulnerability.

This is what can be called radical inquiry. Remember: the 'vi' of vipasana means 'to separate'; pasana means 'seeing clearly'. What we are doing is seeing clearly the beginning and end, because we know that in the beginning—before the beginning—is where the whole process of creation occurs. And where it ends is where the whole process of creation stops.

We can start to see that the beginnings and ends of thoughts constitute an incredibly valuable meditation object. And here we are, having this experience all the time—thought after thought after thought. We are continuously getting hints—we are being bombarded with hints. It's like the old Christian idea that the saints are knocking on our heads trying to wake us up, and we keep saying, "Where is God?" Wake up! It's exactly like that, except here we have the hints in our own perceptions. Our own perceptions are trying to wake us up, and we are in this illusion-bubble, thinking they are the world.

> PAGE 178, PARAGRAPHS 1, 2 AND 3: *Be aware: every ending. Be aware: every unknown place. Be aware: every beginning. See how the thought finishes and how the next one arises. Then observe closely how it ends.*
>
> *Learn to be aware. Pay special attention to how 'aware' happens. Is anything going on?*
>
> *Focus on that, then extend it.*

This is our next exercise. Having established the base of shamata, the flexibility of mind to be able to direct awareness at will, we can then generate vipasana by choosing a meditation object. The meditation object to use is the beginning or ending of thought. Become aware of how thoughts begin and end. Hold the awareness. Being aware of how thoughts end is particularly powerful. Thoughts die, and we can hold our awareness as the thought dies. Then we can extend it, and we'll find that as a new thought arises, we can see it arising.

Exercise 24
Thought bubbles

Set the alarm on your mobile phone to go off three times a day. When it does, watch where the next thought begins, and then watch where it ends—and repeat that for just thirty seconds. Then forget it and go back to your activities—until the next time the alarm goes off.

This is a wonderful meditation practice. It's effective because you can undertake it without warning, whenever the alarm goes off. Of course, as you develop the faculty of self-observation to the point where you can do it consistently and with stability, then you can make a regular meditation practice out of it. But until then it's quite helpful just to have the practice be interjected into your continuous series of thought-bubbles, this series we call a life.

Meditation without warning is more likely to be authentic than meditation that's deliberately undertaken. Having the thought to watch thoughts is like trying to build a dam out of water!

CHAPTER 33

Sensitivity of Mind

This chapter is about the undistracted mind, a mind that is not pulled into its own projection, distracted from its own nature. Remember, all the time we have been working through *Revelations*, the recurring theme has been that our experience is a projection, not real in the sense that what is presented to us is constructed. This is not making an ontological statement about reality, by the way. It is not to take the next step of saying that there is no reality. It is simply to say that what we are experiencing and seeing is a projection. That is the direct object of knowledge that we have, and it's because we forget that that we fall into the prison of pre-conception. We fall through our own projection into what we think is reality, which is actually our projection reified and projected as a real world.

> PAGE 179, PARAGRAPH 1: *Before perception, before thoughts, before consciousness, mind has a sharp, almost electric sensitivity. We might imagine it consisted of countless millions of electron-like particles moving randomly in all directions, backward, forward, up and down, poised on the sharp cutting edge of perception, radiating in all directions like beams of light.*

The metaphor here is that of the almost shimmering nature of mind before it is trapped in a fixed perception. If you—in a calm state, moving toward the cessation of thought—drop the intention to see the end of thought, what you are left with is a kind of potentiality, like a shimmering field that can be triggered at any time into manifesting as something. If you can calm down, you can feel the shimmering, that shimmering nature—waiting.

That shimmering quality is always there: it's just that we are caught by its projections, caught up in its display, distracted from distraction by distraction, continually taken away from our own nature.

> PAGE 179, PARAGRAPH 1, CONT'D: *Self-activating, moving at the speed of light, they attract whatever impressions come within range and immediately present them to the mind that knows. The linkage is instantaneous, with no interval between the attraction and the transmission.*

Before the process of perception makes the world, there is a sea of sensitivity that isn't going in any particular direction. It's just present and sense impressions trigger it into world-making, "I am"-making, and consciousness-making. What we're talking about is the very earliest phase of mind knowing where beginning sense impressions (rupa, to use the Buddhist term) are presented to *nama*, the mind, to know them. Rupa, the very earliest phase of experience, has this feeling of sensitivity.

If you go into a darkened theater and watch a movie, and after the movie ends you are walking down the street, you may notice that just for a short time, everything seems hyper-real. That's the feeling. It doesn't take more than a second or two before that sensation is gone, but just for a moment we have that feeling of brightness. Everything is a little different, and then it all becomes normal again as the conceptual box closes over. This electric sensitivity of mind is something that we need to understand, because it is unconditioned by sense inputs.

PAGE 179, PARAGRAPH 2: *These mind-beams would be what activate our sense perceptions, calling forth images, memories, imaginings, or fantasies, stirring up all manner of emotions and feelings. They would engage all the qualities of mind as well, even those that arise in deep meditation, which also develops within mind. Flowing below the level of our ordinary awareness, activated by receptors sensitized through prior experience and conditioning, all kinds of images could bubble up from imagination and dreams and blend into our thought processes, from where they could manifest in unexpected ways.*

In this way of looking at the mind, the sensitivity of mind is almost like an octopus—it's absolutely waiting for input. It's also, traditionally, been called 'monkey mind'. If our practice is stable, we can now take the mind back from its complete distraction in the world of things, back into its actual nature. Normally it's reactive, waiting, ready to react instantly to any stimulation. If we can get control of this monkey mind, we can open the door to freedom, true freedom, because it is the reflexive reactivity of mind that drags us into projection. It's through gradually disengaging from perceptions, from impressions, that the mind itself can be seen, waiting for stuff, wanting stuff.

Many meditators think that the goal of meditation is a calm mind, but calmness is just the foundation. The goal is to see this monkey mind. You can only see this monkey appear within calmness: you can't see it anywhere else. But if you reify a goal of calmness as your aim in meditation, what you do is give the monkey mind a place to go and hide.

True calmness has no objective. It's beyond any objective, even 'calmness' itself. True calmness has no label at all. It makes it possible to see the exquisite sensitivity of our nature. A very light touch is required—if any effort is applied, reactivity is triggered. This light touch is sometimes called equipoise—the lightest of balance. Let yourself remain balanced, light, calm.

> PAGE 180, PARAGRAPH 1: *An image in a mirror may appear three-dimensional, but on closer inspection we see that its dimensionality is only an illusion, created by light reflecting off a flat surface. Similarly, the image of the moon in a pond breaks up when the water is disturbed, revealing that there is nothing there—no moon, not even any image of the moon.*

This mirror metaphor is really valuable. It's actually good to spend time with mirrors: they are very interesting. If you spend time with a mirror, particularly a big mirror, you'll marvel at the mirror reflection—for it's a marvelous thing, an engaging thing. Of course, it's a total illusion. We forget that the mirror is just a flat wall, but the illusion is so total that it's as if we can fall into it; the mind can be completely caught in a projection that is merely a reflection of itself.

> PAGE 180, PARAGRAPH 2: *Suppose the images that appear in mind are similar, like holograms or projections. There is no 'basis' for a hologram: it has no 'from'. No one constructed it. It has no physical shape or form, nor any substance that could serve a function in time and space.*

Now, the idea of a hologram, remember, is that a three-dimensional display is projected when coherent light is transmitted through a two-dimensional image. In much the same way, the three-dimensional world we perceive is constructed from a two-dimensional retinal film on the back of the eyes, its soundscape is made from the canals in the ear, and within that three-dimensional display there is also a body image that's created. This map conforms with experience: we learn where our limits are—we calibrate distances and dimensions. But this map is not experience. In itself, none of it is functional.

PAGE 180, PARAGRAPH 3: *The images in mind might be much like this, arising from impressions shimmering on the sensitive, mirror-like surface of mind. Sensing, identity, labeling, re-cognition, interpretation, and imaginings weave narratives that feed back to our eagerly acquisitive customer minds. Reaching back to the past, scraps of narratives awaken memories and associations; moving forward, they unfold with their own sequential logic. Interacting, overlapping, looking back, moving forward, weaving stories that make sense, they convince us that they are real. But however real they appear to be, they may be projections that have no substantial foundation.*

Early in *Revelations* there was the metaphor of 'the customer mind'. This is the idea that the mind displays its wares as if it is seeking a customer. Our mental processes populate the display with known objects that appear as if in a mirror: "Oh, that's a clock", "that's a tape recorder", "that's a bell." The great protective cocoon of the known is being recreated moment by moment. Remembered narratives then offer feedback and reassurance in continuous dialogue.

PAGE 181, PARAGRAPH 1: *Misunderstanding mind's sensitive, shimmering quality, the regime of mind initiates the process of perception and shapes it toward existence.*

Our potentiality is always being limited by this key process of perception. Our reactivity shoehorns our 360-degree potentiality into an object of perception, and its functionality then is to gather up as much as it can about that object in terms of its associated memory set. What would happen if we could hold the object without the memory referent? Is our capacity to know greater than its recorded data set?

If we could do this, we would have the freedom of the sense array without the referent, and would suddenly be seeing something new that we didn't see before. This can only happen if we proceed soberly and with great care, because remember, the monkey mind is going to interfere! "Look, do you know what that thing is? Why are you playing around with this thing? What are you doing, it's dangerous—dangerous, dangerous. This could turn out to be something bad!"

We're always going to end up with that internal dialogue, because the monkey mind has basically done a good job: it's kept us alive this long. But once we have sober intent, we can enter this dialogue safely, because we are sober. If we're in it just for fun, the monkey mind isn't going to let go very much. It is not going to let us jump out of a window, thinking, "Oh, this is fun! It's just an image." No, it's not! There are real consequences to our actions, and sobriety is essential.

> PAGE 181, PARAGRAPH 1, CONT'D: *The 'cause'—identity and recognition—produces the 'effect', our view of what is. Now mind is ready for confusion and all manner of emotional obscurations. We do not have a choice in the matter: once the regime of mind engages sensory impulses in its characteristic mistaken way, we cannot choose not to suffer.*

We would normally say that the 'cause' is the world, and the 'effect' is our image of it. We have been taught that from our earliest education. The world is primary; we are secondary. Now we can invert that explanation. The world is a construct. We are the cause, and the world is the effect. It's that way around—a complete inversion of what we think is the case.

We suffer because our choices have been pre-determined for us, and within those pre-determined choices are real limitations that imprison us and leave us feeling profoundly discontented. "It's going OK, but it's kind of meaningless. What am I doing really?" That is a deeply-seated question that everyone has.

This is the 'ennui' suffering, which well-fed Westerners suffer from. No matter how hard we try, and no matter how many

Facebook followers we have, somehow life has become like a prison. Well, it is a prison in fact; it's not *like* a prison, it actually *is* a prison. It's a prison of pre-conception, and that's because we haven't got hold of our monkey minds. That's how suffering is made, that's its cause. That's where it comes from.

> PAGE 181, PARAGRAPH 2: *Perceptions seem to arise spontaneously and instantaneously, in a nanosecond or less. Each nanosecond in turn, occupied by images and energized by mind, engages the established patterns of perception that conduct mental energy into the programs set up by mind. Attachment arises along with grasping and polarity, the recognition of subject and object that sets up mind's dualistic orientation. All this happens whether the perception is painful or routine, or whether it happens in prayer, meditation, or visualization.*

We have this electric potentiality, but the moment anything arises, it is grasped as an object of knowledge. This is happening all the time in our everyday life, and sadly, it is also happening when we meditate, or try to change our ordinary behavior.

This internal stickiness is very difficult to control, because the monkey is always wanting to get stuff: it's always wanting to take and make. This is a very deep-seated process that's happening in our minds. When we sit down to do something, if we don't understand that, the monkey will just work in that arena, whatever the arena happens to be—it just goes ahead and does its thing. We never truly escape the prison in which we are living. And that's why the ennui gets really strong.

Imagine you go to the beach for a holiday, and you are sitting on the beach, and you suddenly think, 'nothing has changed, I am just on a beach'. There is always that slight sense of disappointment. For brief moments you might escape it, but you will drop back in again. Drugs provide similarly brief moments of respite. People love ecstatic experience, the kind of release you can sometimes get when you participate in extreme sports. We're grasping for any chance to break free, just for that brief moment, into something that's not known. "Ah, that's great!"—and then the normal world is back.

Those brief moments are what we call 'freedom', the taste of freedom that we all long for. That's what we go on holiday for, that's what we have adventures for, that's what the shiny new car gives us the day we get it—and then the next day it's just our car. It doesn't matter what it is; in the end, the novelty will fade, the window will close, and we'll be left with the same routine. As we get older, the routine gets more and more persistent, until eventually it's just like an ice cap on top of experience. Every time something arises, snap, the monkey has got it: there's no space, no matter what. "Oh, I know that. I know that. I've got that. I've got that." That's what's going on all the time.

Suffering is programmed into the process. It comes along with it, because we've never stopped being that shimmering freedom—but somehow, we got trapped. No wonder we end up with this feeling of "What's happening? Why am I trapped? I am stuck!" Of course we are, because our intuition is telling us there is something else that we might be, something that we already are: but we are trapped by this reflexive reactivity.

> PAGE 182, PARAGRAPH 1: *These processes are both incredibly fast and firmly interlocked. The senses grasp, initiating cognition; mind identifies, labels, and validates through recognition, stimulating thoughts, interpretations, meanings, characteristics, and discriminations, with emotions following close behind, like infantry divisions on the march. The heavy artillery follows, carrying an array of powerful weapons: desire, attachment, anger, ignorance, and more. In a flash this army has taken control of the field of our experience.*

There are two phases to it: the shimmering potentiality is initially grasped, and then it's fixed into a world of 'me and you'. That's called internal fixation: external grasping, internal fixation, grasping, fixation, grasping, fixation. On the basis of fixation, we get more grasping, triggering more fixation. On the basis of grasping, we get more fixation.

The grasping itself isn't dualistic, but it sets up the projection of the dualistic display that's the product of the fixation. The grasping is always involved in a process of selection and rejection: it says 'yes' to this and 'no' to that at the same time. Happening again and again, this process is ever producing this seamless experience that we call the world.

As meditators, we begin to look at the end of thoughts; we listen to the end of sounds. Instead of grasping the sounds of things, we allow sounds to arise, and then we listen for them to stop: and in that moment of stopping, just for a brief second, there is a potentiality before something else takes over. There are many, many places where this listening is possible; you can do this in any way you want. You don't have to worry about it: thoughts, sensations, anything will do. Sighing is a good one: *ahhh*, just for a moment, then it's gone.

PAGE 182, PARAGRAPH 2: *If it were possible to reduce the speed of our perceptual process, the first instance of recognition might be less likely to engage the regime of mind that propels us into confusion and emotional turmoil. This is why meditation, prayer, and contemplative exercises may provide some measure of relief. By neutralizing and stabilizing the ordinary activity of mind, calming practices slow the speed of sensory impulses, lessening their impact and diminishing the sense of time passing. But as long as the operations of mind unfold in a linear fashion, from one instant to the next, they will not enable us to transcend the temporal order of past, present and future established by mind. Our frame of reference will still be the illusory realm of cause and effect created by mind's regime. Within this frame, we can arrive at truth, but whatever truth we experience will be limited.*

If it were possible to reduce the speed of our perceptual process, we could perhaps disengage the process of reference. So you could say this is all about slowing and disengaging. But it's not about 'doing' anything, it's about not doing something.

Without clear seeing, if we merely concentrate on slowing down, we won't be able to put a halt to grasping-fixation. Slowing down will make things calmer, but there will still be a sense in which past, present and future continue to unfold. If, on the other hand, you truly get to the end of a thought, time stops: the whole thing stops.

CHAPTER 34

Engine of Mind

PAGE 184, PARAGRAPH 1: *We have been investigating how units of mind-perception—identity, name and meaning, sealed and validated by recognition—form unique chains of mental events that become the basis for our sense of what is true and real. We have seen how mind views this reality in a way that polarizes perception into a dualistic mode that gives rise to subject and object, self and other. Recognition engages the chain of cause and effect, and the momentum that results drives the programs of mind.*

These chains of mental events are likened to mind-bubbles— each one formed from input into identity, name and meaning. Something arises: it's identified, grasped and named: through this process it is fixed, recognized. That's the bubble. And in that recognition, it is known by a knower. The recognition is always two-faced, double-pointed. The recognition and the recognizer appear as a pair—and that is the display, the product that emerges from this underlying process that we never see.

We could also call this display 'cause and effect'—or 'because'. We think the display is the cause and we are the effect. But actually, once we realize this is a display, we realize that we are the cause and the display is the effect.

That's a really, really big change. Far from being an epiphe-nomenal side effect of the universe, we become its center. Or rather, we become the center of the multi-verse, because all of us are a cause. The regime of mind is a construct, it's being created, it is the result of a cause that is hidden at the base of our experience. Our task is to reveal that underlying element; only then can we make any change. The cause is unseen: all we see is the results of it. The underlying operator is what we are trying to uncover.

> PAGE 184, PARAGRAPH 2: *Some philosophies use the con-cept of cause and effect to explain the automatic and re-lentless way that mind's patterns continue, growing more complex over time. The more complex the patterns, the more variety we perceive, convincing us that something 'new' is happening. So we keep going on, hoping for some-thing that will awaken more interest and meaning in life, hoping that things will improve, hoping that tomorrow will somehow be different from today.*

Our internal commentaries lead to proliferation—the prolif-eration of views. Once the associated web is activated, every association proliferates more association. As we get older, the structure becomes deeper and denser. In actuality all these views increasingly constrict us, until the freedom of youth is just a distant memory. That's the proliferation of associations occurring as we continue generating experiences within the context of grasping and clinging.

> PAGE 185, PARAGRAPH 1: *Since our observations confirm that there is indeed change, our hopes continue.*

So we think, well, I learned French: that was change. I painted the house: that was change. I got a new job. I moved to Aus-tralia. Some people go through serial marriages. Most of us, when we feel like we need a change, change our location—in the language of addiction and recovery, it's sometimes called 'doing a geographical'. We get kind of stuck in a place, so we do a geographical to another place. And then we stay there for a bit, it's new for a bit, and then it gets kind of boring, and so we do a geographical to somewhere else. That's a common technique: young people do it a lot. And then they eventually settle down and marry someone and then they are just stuck, because they've got kids in school so it's not so easy.

We all know that somehow we grew up, but perhaps all we did was grow old. It is a good question to ask: "Am I growing? Or, am I just growing *up*?" Because most of us just grow *up*, we just become adults, but we don't actually grow in the sense of actually changing, developing, maturing. Look in the mirror, and you may still see that nineteen-year-old—because you didn't actually grow, you are still the same person, only with gray hair.

> PAGE 185, PARAGRAPH 1, CONT'D: *But the patterns governing experience go on as before. The endless cycles of cause and effect they create lead us through varied landscapes of mind that range from ecstasy and bliss to extremes of loneliness and confusion. Yet, behind all this movement is a sense of dullness and disconnection, a product of the essentially repetitious and aimless activity that characterizes much of our lives.*

Soap operas are about this, aren't they? They are about endlessly cycling emotional ups and downs. And they are amazing to watch in many ways, as the stories cycle round and round, in a gyre going nowhere. The landscape changes, so the story can be engaging, yet it is going nowhere. This leads many of us to a world-weariness, once we see through to the basic circularity of the story.

> PAGE 185, PARAGRAPH 2: *The engine driving these patterns is the process of perception, and perception in turn seems driven by a certain kind of anxiety.*

Perception is driven by grasping, which is anxious by its very nature. Remember, grasping is all about "What is that?" so it's very difficult to be grasping in a relaxed way. Almost by definition, grasping is paranoid. When you don't grasp, the first emotion that rises is fear. Until you can live with fear, you can't stop grasping. In the course of a day, we grasp and fix thousands, perhaps tens of thousands of times. That's why it's really difficult to sit and enjoy the sunset, because somehow, the feeling creeps in: 'I've got to do something, I can't just be here!' We can see how perception is driven by anxiety.

We are not merely a camera, recording external events. In a very real sense, we are making them.

> PAGE 185, PARAGRAPH 2, CONT'D: *The senses are alert, actively searching for something to perceive, while mind is poised in readiness to identify and recognize what the senses present. There is an underlying tension, experienced as a deep, subliminal urge: "Have to get there: must have it." As the urge grows stronger, we become more aware of the subject: we have to get somewhere, we have to have something.*

There are three fundamental drives: fear—which is to reject or push away; greed—which is to want or pull towards; and ignorance—which is indifference. Here we are looking at greed. One could just as easily write this paragraph and talk about fear: "I've got to hide away from there: I've got to get that away from me." It's exactly the same mechanism in reverse. These three roots are the fundamental drivers at the base of our responses. They set up the very first movement in the mirror-like sensitivity of mind, in that very first moment of time.

> PAGE 185, PARAGRAPH 3: *Perception pushes for identity and recognition, which resolve uncertainty and allow mind an instant to relax. But even this limited resolution does not always progress smoothly. When the push toward 'have to get' is blocked by 'cannot get', internal pressures tend to activate patterns of agitation and frustration.*

Lots of people think, "Oh, all I've got to do is to shut everything down and I will become calm." No, you won't, that's the problem—you won't become calm. If external inputs are shut down or blocked, the internal inputs at the sixth gate of the mind take over. The display is made from identity and recognition: there can be no calm there. The patterns of frustration in not getting what we want, and agitation in being unable to avoid what we don't want, can only be overcome if both of them are seen and accepted. That's why we should meditate with our eyes open, because the objects that arise are all teachers to us. In fact, we should welcome them, because they are showing us the display. They constantly offer us an opportunity to see the display.

> PAGE 186, PARAGRAPH 1: *Committed to a dualistic orientation, mind manifests in ways that can be contradictory and confusing. Sometimes mind displays the persona of a sympathetic friend or a practical business person; another moment it may turn on us, undermining our self-confidence and filling us with apprehension and fear. Depending on the conditions and circumstances at work, mind and its regime can call forth an array of emotions and attitudes, from lonely and despairing to rich, healthy, and joyful. One moment we may feel confident and in control. On the downswing, the story is very different. As soon as we get settled in one place, mind moves to another, then another, and yet another.*

These are all programs. The regime of mind is a massive parallel processor in which there are thousands of subroutines, which in totality construct our behavioral responses. We are full of subroutines and loaded vectors that are constructed by our experience to give us appropriate behavioral responses.

Some of these behavioral responses can be triggered by external events. If we're having a good day and something suddenly goes wrong, we might hear a critical voice saying, "You're no good. You always fail." That's a learned behavior. We carry legions of learned behaviors like this with us. Some of the voices tell us how well we're doing, and others nitpick, saying, "You're doing it all wrong." We accumulate these behaviors in the face of problems, most of them experienced in childhood. Gradually, as we enter middle age, they start confining us and herding us into a smaller and smaller box.

> PAGE 186, PARAGRAPH 2: *Wanting and not wanting, wishing and dreading, waiting and hoping, always needing more—the shadows of this dualistic mind keep rising up and we simply live with them. So boring, so repetitive, yet also so magnetizing! For some, this back and forth, up and down rhythm brings a sense of drama into ordinary routines that cuts through boredom and makes them feel engaged and alive.*

What we often call 'society' is inseparable from this process of magnetizing. Our town, our school, our clubs, our politics: they are all magnetizing. Reinforced by news media, linked through advertising to the primary economic engine, nothing much changes. You will see this if you read old newspapers. With surprisingly little editing, they could be current editions. There is nothing new happening: we are just being sucked and spun around in a vortex. This magnetizing is the process by which we are dulled and fooled into not dealing with anything in our lives. This could account for the attraction of soap operas: something happens, it's exciting, we have something new, and then gradually we fall back into just going round and round and round in circles—whirling and twirling in the widening gyre until some other new thing happens.

To see more clearly, we will have to cut through this apparent continuity, this continual transmigration, this continual succession. Recognizing that this is a display cuts the continuity. Suddenly, we are the stranger in the soap opera. Everyone else is talking about the display, what's in it, but we are talking about the display itself—we suddenly left the story.

> PAGE 187, PARAGRAPH 1: *It is not surprising that fictions based on this familiar rhythm are nearly guaranteed to hold our interest. Reading a novel or watching a film, we can experience strong emotions without exposing ourselves to the consequences of events because we know that in fact the words or images we are encountering are not 'real'.*

It's incredible how engaging stories are. Try this sometimes: watch TV and try to see how and when you get caught up in the story. It's really interesting to see what position you adopt when you become engaged with it. Remember, your own display is like a big interactive TV, and you are getting sucked into the story all the time. And so, watching a small TV and trying to work out how you get sucked in is in many ways the same as watching the 'big TV' of your experience. If you can watch and yet not watch, that could be very useful practice for looking at the display.

It's equally interesting to watch the TV with the sound off. Sound is very important in creating a story, yet we don't usually realize how important a role it plays, because hearing is often treated as a secondary sense in our normal awareness. Sound plays a fundamental function in reifying the display, making it real. If you mute a TV show, it becomes just a series of images. Put the sound back on, and you get sucked back in. In this regard, radio and podcasting can actually be more immersive and evocative than TV. Creative programming on the radio can create complete soundscapes that engage our reality-motor. It's the very thing that we get fooled by.

> PAGE 187, PARAGRAPH 2: *We could experiment with viewing mind's programs in the same way. If we knew that we could change the focus of our minds as easily as we can turn the page of a book or change a television channel,*

how might that understanding transform the 'locked-in' quality of our lives?

There is a great saying: "Alter your gait and meet a stranger." If you alter your behavior, you're going to meet completely different people. We live in a world that is a reflection of what we present to it. Present a different face, and you will meet different people. If you wear a suit, for instance, some people will look at you and some won't; meeting a stranger is easy. This is a simple demonstration of how the world in which we live is actually a small slice of what's possible, and that slice appears the way it does because it is a reflection of what we present to it. We only know about the bit of the world that we reflect. The whole challenge is to become free of that fixed reflection. As long as our reflection is fixed, we are a prisoner of our appearance. However, with awareness, we can magnetize our appearance so we can change it at will.

That quality produces a sparkle. On occasion, you'll meet people who have a certain twinkle, and you know by that magic that they are not embedded in the story of their life— they are somehow a little bit outside the story.

On that note, when we make the shift from being stuck to recognizing the nature of the display we call 'the self', we don't necessarily have to become wild performers, calling dramatic attention to a 'big act'. We don't need to behave outrageously in order to realize that we are *acting* being ourselves. Some really small change might be all that's needed. In fact, the change could be so small that other people might not even notice we are making it. We could be performing the 'self' act while appearing totally normal. We tend to assume that seeing through the act will lead to 'crazy wisdom' and unconventional behavior. Yes, if you are an enlightened being, and you want to shock people, you might display outrageousness, but just to realize that this is the display does not require any special kind of behavior.

PAGE 187, PARAGRAPH 3: *Understanding mind without being locked in to its regime, we would see more clearly the patterns that drive the ups and downs of our lives: the blissful happy times, the anxious and devastating times, and the lost and hopeless times.*

The three drivers of experience are right here: greed, fear, and ignorance.

PAGE 187, PARAGRAPH 3, CONT'D: *We would understand that the convoluted coding in the programs run by mind's regime developed in response to conditions that may no longer apply to us today. This understanding would free us of the impulse to respond automatically and give us pause to take a more appropriate direction. Aware of the futility of replaying or justifying each twist and turn of our stories, we might find ways to develop a more original approach to our own lives, based on a mind free of confining walls and fixed positions. Processed differently, less constricted by past emotions and stale expectations, experience might reveal more purely the beauty and dynamic power of mind itself.*

Experience itself is a great teacher. Experience experience—that's it. We can be aware of awareness, we can experience experience—it's the same thing. It's about realizing that whatever we are experiencing is just one possible iteration. There are other iterations available to us. Formal meditation gradually identifies the display, recognizes the display as constructed, and then rests awareness on the process of construction. That's the formal meditation in three phases; but the actual story is what we are experiencing all the time: the play of the display that is happening to us continuously. And that's what we are working on.

Exercise 25
Seeing the display

Remember the alarm-clock practice for examining the beginnings and ends of thoughts? Try it here, with the display. Two or three times a day, stop and ask: "Am I seeing a real world, or is it a display of my own perception?" It's important to break the continuity of the display. When the alarm goes off, right then, ask that question.

We need to get familiar with asking that question, so that the question doesn't become an end in itself, but is instead a little wake-up call to make a very small change that is also very profound. If we are able to do this, the rest of *Revelations* becomes true revelation, and we suddenly start seeing this as a real path. The key to unlocking the path comes from breaking the continuity of the display. Unless we can do this, the door to the path won't unlock. It will just be a nice story, another story in a library's worth of stories that we carry around in our heads.

CHAPTER 35

Another Kind of Mind

We may recognize intellectually that our perception is a read-out, a display, but actually confronting that and directly addressing it as a product of mind takes practice: it's not necessarily something that we can just know. The reason is this: because we don't recognize our perception as a display, we don't realize that our awareness is double-pointed. For example, the Tibetan word for perceiving actually glosses as "perceiver-perceived." It's double-pointed, whereas we in the West always talk as if perception is one-pointed toward the object, so there is always the assumption that perception has entirely to do with the object, and not the perceiver. Western theories of perception tend to leave out the perceiver. This is intensely important. Because of that omission, we can easily forget ourselves and become blind to our own process.

The first half of *Revelations* is largely about this view: much of the analysis that it undertakes is attempting to demonstrate, again and again, that the whole process of perception is double-pointed. It's only when we come to grips with double-pointing that the path to freedom opens: for if you can't appreciate double-pointing, you're always going to project the path within the construct you have unconsciously created. In so doing, you fall into endless illusions of progress, which eventually always double back to the perceiver, who remains unknown. As long as the perceiver-side of perception remains hidden, the regime of mind will remain in force.

If we can come to grips with being in and part of a display, then we can begin to open up a relationship with the displayer, the original creator of that display. And that process is fundamental. The most beneficial place to do this is either at the beginning or the end of those periods of display we call thoughts, because in those moments, which are often fleeting, there is the possibility of seeing the display either start up or end.

Of course, the entire bubble in which a thought occurs is also the display, so it's not as if those places, the beginnings and ends, have anything special about them. They are just where the display starts and where the display ends—that's all. Once we see that clearly, then the whole process of the display is ultimately fruitful: there is no need to think, "Oh, I've got to get to the end," or "I've got to get to the beginning." The challenge is just in looking at the display at all.

> PAGE 189, PARAGRAPH 1: *We can imagine that, prior to perception, mind is a radiant arc open 360 degrees in all directions, and suffused with laser-like beams of light. If we could enter such a prior dimension, we would see a world not yet shaped by the operation of cause and conditions.*

Again we are presented with the idea that behind our perceptual display, there is a possibility of something that hasn't yet been fixed in that way. Conditioned experience is conditioned by something. It follows that if we could have experience of our mind prior to the process of recognition, experience would be unconditioned. Indeed, it seems the only way we could ever escape our conditioning would be if we could access our mind prior to conditioning. As long as we rely on the double-pointed, conditioned experience of the knower and the known, no escape is possible.

Everything that happens in the realm of the knower and the known is by definition conditioned. This immediately points us toward a fundamental question. Can we know not-knowing? Is there a way of entering a profound open or unconditioned state? If we could do that, we would have an anchor in the unconditioned to guide us.

Of course, if we were just robots, there would never be such a point to guide us: there wouldn't be a prior unprogrammed experience. The fundamental truth being pointed out here is that we are not machines. We cannot be merely programmed up. There is something prior to the programming that is actually there. Because our present double-pointed way of knowing precludes true, open access to the unconditioned, for the moment this will have to be an article of faith. But if we recognize that there may be something else, that opens the possibility of true development.

Recognizing that there is something else but not immediately believing in it, however, is important. If we immediately believe in it, the danger is that it becomes reified as the 'God within' or 'the ultimate', or some similar anchoring idea. Then we've just gone from not believing to believing—from nihilism to eternalism. Instead, let's *imagine*: prior to perception, we can imagine this radiant arc of the unconditioned.

This is the final bit of the view. We've examined the regime. In this final chapter we are talking about the alternative, a new possibility, this unconditioned mind prior to experience.

PAGE 189, PARAGRAPH 1, CONT'D: *In this pristine realm, the view from wherever we stood would be the same. Surrounded by light rays moving rapidly and randomly, it would be hard for us to distinguish a center, an end, or a beginning. We might even have to let go of the notions of center, end, and beginning—even the notion of a 'present'. Yet in this brilliantly luminous realm, labels, associations, and expectations would fall away, revealing different qualities than we have experienced up to now—qualities that mind has never learned or been taught, has never been exposed to in any way. Experience unfolding within this unbounded vista of mind might find expression in new forms of art and new possibilities for language.*

The knowing faculty referred to here is not the same as what we know. Once we are able to relax our obsession with the display, the knowing faculty itself is released to new possibilities.

You could say we have a small mind and a big Mind, a regime of mind and a revelation of mind. The regime and the revelation are closely connected. Their relationship is what's at issue. If we can stop our obsession with the small mind— the regime of mind, which is full of judgments and ideas and concepts—then the big Mind can operate. The big Mind is something quite different, because it doesn't rely on concepts or judgments. Our task is to learn to rely on the innate intelligence of our big Mind before it gets seduced into concepts.

If our innate intelligence is only able to access pre-digested concepts, then it is trapped in the past. But what would happen if our innate intelligence were free to experience the present? Perhaps it could use all those associations, words and judgments as ornaments to express itself, yet not be trapped by them. Once all the conceptual labels and associations fall away, different qualities become visible within the freshness of the perceptual field.

PAGE 190, PARAGRAPH 1: *In such perfect openness, free of obstructing forms, mind itself would become one-pointed, with no content, nor even thoughts.*

We have been talking about shamata, the ability to concentrate the mind. Ultimately, total mental concentration arises when the knowing faculty is freed from the double-pointing of the known, and rests within itself. That's the only time real calmness can occur. As long as we are trying to do something, that very effort is itself a disturbance. Concentrating the mind is a process of relinquishing activity, not doing anything—exactly the reverse of what we normally think. One-pointedness is the fruit of total detachment. Once we are completely detached from activity, what's left is one-pointed concentration, with nothing to disturb it.

If we just rest in perfect stillness, then there is an increasing gap between thoughts that feels almost timeless. The view says that that mind underlies all experience, like a ground upon which all experience rests. Because thoughts muddy everything, we tend to ignore the ground and get excited by all the associations triggered by the thought process. But when we develop calm meditation, gradually it all settles. Then we find ourselves in a state of knowing not knowing, which is full of qualities we can rely upon and rest within.

> PAGE 190, PARAGRAPH 1, CONT'D: *Clarity would expand infinitely, allowing understanding to take place. All-encompassing, with duality revealed as unity, mind would become singularity, with nothing 'in between'.*

This is again both a review and a pointer to the rest of *Revelations*. There is a term in the Tibetan system called 'relaxed shiné', which is the idea that one-pointedness can be taken into such a state of ease that it becomes completely stable. It simply becomes part of our manifestation. On occasion one meets people who embody this, who are always concentrated, because their innate faculties are no longer wedded to a box of concepts.

Watching the mind, which is what 'mindfulness' is normally thought to entail, creates a strange tension. The whole illusion of a knowing self, an *Atman*, some kind of internal knower, is a complete projection based on this watcher. Preoccupied by this knower and its known, we are separated from our experience in a very profound way. Yet if we calm the mind down, we can get to a place of openness where we are not watching the mind. Rather than watching, we are the mind. We have entered experience. Once we have entered experience, it becomes infinite. Time stops. Instead of being a watcher in time as time ticks past us, we enter the timeless experience of openness. This is a fundamental experience upon which we can build a path.

> PAGE 190, PARAGRAPH 2: *How could mind experience such an all-encompassing understanding? Here we could refer back to our reflections on the structure of the nanosecond. When the artificial barriers of past, present, and future dissipate, mind enters the sixteenth moment of the nanosecond, the unit of transition completely freed from mental regimes, without borders, open 360 degrees. No longer separate from crystalline clarity, mind becomes a shining array of points of awakened awareness that bear the seeds of all possibilities, immanent in what we might call a perfected understanding.*

This beautiful language referring to immanence—a very important word—reminds us that once we begin to take back our experience, our awareness, we suddenly enter something that can expand infinitely. It's as if we were in a cone, and as we come back to experience, it suddenly expands and expands into openness, and suddenly there is a very different experience of mind: clear and calm, and always concentrated, for that is the nature of mind.

When the mind no longer grasps sense impressions as they appear, there is no time. All there is, is the manifestation of the sensation itself, and the mirror of the mind. A state of timeless openness occurs. This is something we can understand as we complete the view.

This is not to say that this mind knows nothing; we could say that this mind knows everything. This is the knowing of first impressions that never lie, the knowing at the beginning of every thought, experience or movement of mind, the immanent potential of all knowledge.

Normally this experience is fleeting because our reactiveness is so fast. Although it is difficult to rest in this experience, we have to learn to trust it and become familiar with it. We have to learn to inhabit this state. As we do so, it becomes more and more reliable, and we are able to rest there more stably. All kinds of insights then arise spontaneously, prescient and accurate. Experience becomes numinous. This is the field that opens to us once we rest in the timeless present prior to perception.

> PAGE 190, PARAGRAPH 3: *How can a single point of transition—smaller than the smallest unit of space/time imaginable—display the seeds of all possibilities? When the point is known to be totally single, we understand effortlessly how this is so. We experience the power of awakened view, which suffuses the operation of mind with pristine, positive qualities and immunizes us against the poison of illusory existence. We bring peace to mind and enable it to expand.*

This is the awakened view. Having developed a view of the regime of mind, we can now develop a view of the absolute mind, which is totally subjective—yet because it contains all potentiality, also totally objective. It's both together. It's of time, but not in time. In its openness and clarity, it purifies all the reactive responses of conditioned existence and floats like a healing balm through our mental system, leaving peace and potentiality in its wake.

Most of us live in a maelstrom of fragmented experience, constantly obliged to respond to all kinds of demands and events. Yet the absolute mind is completely calm. It does not have to do anything; it is not obliged to launch into action; it is not triggered into reactivity by a misunderstood problem. When it does act, it acts knowingly, deliberately, free from stress.

Residing there, we can transcend a fundamental source of the anxiety and agitation in which most of us live from day to day. A mind like this immunizes us against our reactivity and heals us from the stress that reactivity brings.

We see this big Mind sometimes in the middle of a great performance. When we look at musicians or sports players in the middle of a performance or game, what we see in them is calmness. Even though they can be in the middle of the most complicated activity, they are completely calm because they have entered the present through their art. That's why we want to listen to them or watch them. That's the nature of a great performance. We can almost smell it; we can feel its magic.

Such experiences do not need to be relegated to an unattainable realm; they are within our reach. We too can become great performers, masters of our own perception. This is our birthright as human beings.

> PAGE 191, PARAGRAPH 1: *Clear and direct, the open dimension of mind is untainted by self or personality. Inherent in its undisturbed nature are the innumerable variations in the shapes and forms of our ordinary reality, revealed in the feeling-tones, thoughts, and images that flow through our minds during meditative contemplation. Open concentration allows full access to these shapes and forms, and its power enables us to attune ourselves instantly to what each moment offers.*

Imagine that our nature, our characteristics, thoughts, doubts, ideas, ups and downs all become something that mind can express as magical displays, as ornaments, freely and without any compulsion. Mind itself is free of them—they are merely places it can go.

> PAGE 191, PARAGRAPH 2: *As long as we work within the parameters of the dualistic, concept-dependent mind, we have no choice but to experience each situation in*

> *whatever way the regime of mind presents. Yet when understanding deepens, we can choose to use these appearances as pathways to more comprehensive understanding. This is not a matter of playing games; it is a way of coming to understand how not to play games and how not to hold on to roles.*

If we live in the regime of mind, then we have a limited menu in front of us. Whatever the regime of mind thinks something is, we have to choose; we have to say 'yes'. But when we reside before the regime has activated we have an infinite array of possibilities. We suddenly find we have freedom in situations that seemed to imprison us before.

The regime of mind is literally putting the cart before the horse. The cart of concepts acts as a prism as well as a prison: it's a barrier through which we experience the world. We feel imprisoned by the conceptual nature of our experience.

By accessing this prior big mind, we put the horse before the cart. The turning that puts the horse before the cart is an internal turning within. Knowledge ceases to be an obstacle to overcome or a treasure to obtain: instead, it becomes an organ of expression. We still have the concepts, associations and experiences, but we can choose to use them instead of being trapped by them. Instead of the associations and concepts being like a box in which we are trapped, they become like an instrument with which we can express ourselves. The prism becomes a generator of rainbows.

Almost all of us have the yearning to go back to a state of innocence, like the wonder of childhood. Yet in that state, we would not know how to express ourselves. But when we put the horse of being before the cart of concepts, we have the ability to express ourselves fully, for our entire life experience is at our disposal.

PAGE 192, PARAGRAPH 1: *From within such understanding, we may now be clear on how mind uses language, how mind points out, how mind interprets, how mind constructs meaning, how mind structures what we view as reality, how mind names and philosophizes about existence and truth, and more. Seeing this, we may be ready to recognize that the human mind does not have to be based on the ordering of concepts, an order that leads us into a no-choice regime.*

PAGE 192, PARAGRAPH 2: *As long as mind is bound to its present orientation, our intellect will keep playing games, but now we may understand that it is possible to explore mind from a different point of view. Attentive to the processes that drive our responses, we can understand the proud, game-player mind, the creative, imaginative story-teller mind, the behavior-carrier mind, the knowledge-holder mind, and the mind that gives us language, interpretations, and meaning. The more we understand, the more options we have and the more informed will be our choices. The options presented by understanding will be ever freer from the delusions constructed for us by our ever-creative role-playing mind.*

We are no longer observing mind: we are occupying the mind prior to experience. And from that position we're observing how conceptualization arises. This is not a change in content, not an addition of some new component: rather it is a change in the focus of our awareness, a focus that opens into a re-occupation of the center of our being. It is not that we have to eradicate any part of our normal behavior, it is that we can choose whether to occupy that normal behavior or not—that's all.

PAGE 193, PARAGRAPH 1: *This understanding works for everyone: no special knowledge or skills are required. It shows us that mind is flexible, that our way of being is not cast in concrete. We do not have to be great thinkers, or spiritually oriented, or practitioners of meditation to open up alternatives and take advantage of them.*

There are extraordinary capacities that can be developed through focused meditation, without question; there are amazing things that certain yogis do. But none of them are necessary. Ultimately, all that's necessary is that we take control of our awareness—that's all. This is why no special knowledge is required. You don't have to be a deep thinker, you don't have to be particularly religious, you don't have to be a great practitioner to transform in this manner. This is something that anybody can do. And when you realize this, you realize that you can do it anywhere, at any time.

So it's not that you have to make some incredibly special preparation for this understanding to occur, or have a special place where it happens, or anything like that. Just engage for a few minutes a day, wherever you are, because understanding is always available to you. It is a true refuge. Remember, our minds are our true refuge. *Revelations* is about recognizing that refuge, and relating to it.

> PAGE 193, PARAGRAPH 2: *So open your mind wide to possibilities and allow yourself to engage them. Let the processes of minding and mind-dialogue begin. Let it uncover and feed back alternatives. Think about knowing, think about mind's way of interpreting, look at the programming that comes between 'I' and mind, leaving us no opportunity to know who we really are. Ask how to connect with mind at the outset, when all is still open and luminous.*

Some people may not understand this. They may think that *Revelations* is trying to encourage a kind of self-inquiry, an examination of how the mind works. But this is not about conceptually dissecting experience. Rather it is to know the mind when it's open and luminous, to get on the horse of direct experience, to rest in the ground before experience is grasped, and from there to be the master of the conceptualized and projected world.

Exercise 26
Movement in presence

Just for a few minutes a day, try moving your arms while being totally present. All you are doing is entering the display while being present. Babies do this a lot, actually: babies lie in their cribs and look at their hands. Before they start conceptualizing, they are enjoying entering the display. It's a really good exercise to do. But to begin, just move your fingers in front of your face while being fully present: see if you can inhabit the movement.

It's not 'I am' moving, with 'I' mental, and 'moving' physical. Rather, inhabit the movement. In movement, there is no sense in which 'I' am 'moving'. I am in the movement: I am inhabiting the movement: I am totally still.

APPENDIX 1

Introduction to Revelations of Mind

Looking back on the millennia of human history, we may marvel at how far we have come to attain our present ways of life. Over the past two hundred years alone, the age of reason and scientific exploration has opened entirely new avenues of understanding ourselves and our surroundings, from the far reaches of the universe to the microscopic realm of atoms and particles. Advances in technology and medicine continue to improve living conditions for people in many parts of the world. Each season brings new fashions, new products, new devices for communication and electronics. Even social attitudes and economic patterns, as well as occupations and lifestyles, are continuously in flux.

Yet, in fundamental ways, human beings remain much the same. As children, we are educated by parents and teachers to fit into social roles and occupations, and trained in the patterns and behaviors expected of our status and position. As independent adults, we exercise the views, priorities and attitudes with which we identify, while earlier influences continue to shape the fundamental orientation of our minds, manifesting in thoughts, feelings, language and emotional responses.

As in ages past, we still pursue pleasure and seek to avoid pain; we still strive to accomplish and be successful in what we do. We still follow our senses, our thoughts, and our imagination and rely upon judgments of right and wrong, good and bad that have not changed substantially throughout the course of human history. Our attitudes and views are shaped by patterns of language that have come down to us through our families and culture, and we connect sound and gestures with meaning in characteristic ways to establish our reality. We respond to the need to make ourselves acceptable to others and fit in with what has been established.

Within the established structures for thought, communication and action, there is little room to develop another understanding of reality or to generate a new vision. Even philosophers, religious leaders, artists, and other creative individuals continue to track along well-worn paths, unable radically to change the patterns of language or the rules that govern the prevailing logic. From time to time, conditions shift, clearing the way for new forms, styles and movements, but a certain continuity underlying the fabric of ordinary life inhibits even the most visionary and creative among us.

Outworn conventions may be challenged and even overturned, but fundamental assumptions go unquestioned. For example, we still see reality from the perspective of the self— the self that announces "I am" and claims ownership of everything that can be thought or perceived. As soon as we grant this sense of identity primacy in our lives, what 'I' believe, what 'I' want, what 'I' possess and what 'I' think become the operating principles of our lives.

Once the dichotomy of self and other is accepted, the logic of this assumption is automatically reflected in patterns of thought and speech. Language conveys the sense of sequential actions related to past, present, and future, reinforcing

our perception that this is the way time operates. Vocabulary and grammar enable language to express the polarities
of pros and cons, subject and object, pain and pleasure, and
various degrees of good and bad, right and wrong. Each noun
has its associations and connotations, each adjective expresses shadings of meaning and enables finely detailed compari-
sons. Shaped by syntax into interlocking units of meaning,
these tightly woven patterns support a dualistic view of reality based on unquestioned distinctions of self and other.
Imprinted in mind, the patterns of language become the
structure of our identity and the framework of our thoughts,
where they strongly influence what we accept as real and true.
Expressions that do not accord with them are often dismissed
as meaningless.

If we were fully attuned to the creative unfolding of each moment and all that this unfolding potentiates, our lives could
manifest like chapters in a deeply engaging book; we could
savor experiences while their flavors were still alive with the
freshness of immediacy. Line by line, page by page, our book of
life would relate a meaningful journey, satisfying in the present and rich in memories to be treasured and revisited. As
one chapter closed, the next one would begin, revealing open
fields to populate with new thoughts, ideas and experiences.

Yet very few individuals use their life experiences in such em-
powering and energizing ways. Focused on the future or
sorting through memories of the past—planning, worrying,
imagining what may or may not come about and speculat-
ing upon how best to respond to endless "what if's"—our
minds are far away from the immediacy of the present. We
tend not to notice what our eyes are seeing, our ears hearing, and our bodies sensing, or even what is going on in our
minds. Of all that we do every day, we remember very little,
and the quality of our experience is dulled by mind's lack of
attentiveness. In this situation, it can be difficult to enjoy

the full measure of our life experiences, and even more difficult to learn from them. This is deeply unfortunate, since
the ability to learn from experience is among the most precious benefits life offers.

Our experience is more than the thoughts, emotions and
events that stand out in memory. What happens when we
turn our attention inward to observe and listen? Very quickly
we become aware of a nearly constant mental activity that
manifests as internal dialogues. We may not have paid much
attention to these dialogues before, dismissing them as mind
idly playing with thoughts, or as part of our efforts to think
through and resolve issues that are unclear. But if we focus with awareness on this internal chatter, we may notice
that mind is playing two distinct roles. One aspect of mind
is noticing, another is listening. Further, the noticer is making statements that the listener is receiving and interpreting.
There is mind that perceives, cognizes, and identifies, and
mind that acts upon what has been cognized. Moving back
and forth, sealing and validating cognition through recognition, mind creates the continuity it requires to sustain our
view of reality.

Looking more deeply, we find that within this inner realm,
many activities are in process simultaneously. There are
thoughts and imagery that entertain and project as visualiza-
tions or fantasies, reflecting back to mind and stimulating
imagination and trains of thought. There is a judge who as-
sesses good and bad, right and wrong. There is a discriminator
who determines what to like or dislike, what to accept and what
to reject. There is the self that we express as 'I', 'me' and 'mine'.
There are followers and influence-peddlers, collectors of data,
memories and feelings, reminders and prodders and monitors
of causes and effects. We present ourselves to the world as a
single being operating rationally from a single perspective and
point of view, but inside, a whole society or regime is active.

Accustomed to looking at objects from an 'outside standing' perspective, we may never have thought to look at the subject, to take into account the speaker's voice, the thinker's mind, the decision-maker's activities. We have been taught, or have assumed, that we are the ones who are feeling and thinking, determining meaning and making decisions. But when we look through the magnifying glass of awareness, we learn that the mind is not just 'I, me, and mine'. We begin to see that mind is far more complex than we may have thought, and the process by which it translates perceptions into meaning is not necessarily a clear and orderly progression. While we have a sense of meaning that comes through thoughts and senses, feelings and thoughts themselves are not necessarily organized in a logical sequence, but combine and find expression in different ways.

We might imagine that just as the rhythms of speech shape sound into words, our decision-maker mind shapes meaning sequentially from awareness to consciousness to words and concepts. If our awareness were fully open, 360 degrees, we might be able to observe how this process operates. Until we can do this, however, we can say only that we experience reality through the filters of mind. We depend for meaning on mental processes that do not seem to connect in predicable ways. No wonder we are vulnerable to confusion and the problems that come in its wake.

For thousands of years, a question has plagued humanity: why does life have to have so many problems? Must we continue to experience frustration and confusion? Must we waste much of our lives in coping with emotional upheavals? Since it has always been this way, we may think we have no choice: "That is the way it is," we say. But can we question if this really has to be?

Problems are situations that we cannot resolve. They seem completely real, yet the circumstances we experience as a problem are conducted to us by mind. We can only think about the problem in the ways that mind allows, and mind operates through rules imprinted on its ways of perceiving and presenting reality, leaving us very few alternatives or solutions. If mind's way of operating blocks off all conceivable alternatives, there is nothing more we can do. We become fused to the problem as it has been set up by mind. For the most part, people just accept that is the way things are. Yet, it seems important to give this matter serious thought and do what we can to resolve it. The need to initiate such a process inspired the idea of understanding presented here.

We are fortunate to be the beneficiaries of knowledge gathered through many centuries of inquiry into every conceivable subject, but mind itself has seldom received the depth of attention necessary to ease its burdens and enable it to operate in happier and more creative ways. Mind has incredible power and flexibility, but uncared for and unguided it becomes a despot, limiting the ways we can know and respond, and subjecting us to confusion, anxiety and despair. If we wish to free ourselves of problems, we must become more aware of what mind is and what it needs.

We need an intelligent, creative, innovative way to study mind, one based on a gentle, detached observation that does not reinforce mind's tendency to grasp and concretize experience. This realization has inspired me to share my thoughts on mind with friends and associates within our Nyingma community. What began as informal exchanges developed into a more focused effort to express my way of thinking about a subject central to the quality of every human life.

In 2006, I met regularly with several senior students over a period of several months for talks and discussions intended to reveal where more detailed explanations were needed. In the course of these talks, I adopted the approach I felt would best illustrate important, but unfamiliar points which traditionally require a substantial context for understanding. Transcribed by Elizabeth Cook, these sessions were combined with earlier talks to provide a working manuscript. During the review process, this material was edited further and shaped into a more integrated presentation by Pema Gellek and Richard Dixey. After a third major review, the manuscript was brought to completion by Elizabeth Cook, Robin Caton, and Jack Petranker. All five editors are members of the faculty of Dharma College in Berkeley, California, where I had determined that this new form of understanding could be presented.

Although these talks were not intended to constitute a systematic presentation, the organization has taken on a certain order that reflects the unfolding quality of understanding itself. Since mind hears and expresses according to its own understanding, I have monitored the progress of this manuscript and intensively reviewed its contents with the editors several times. While I expected the editors to correct my dictated thoughts to standard English, some unusual uses of language have been deliberately retained.

There is no stopping point, no end to the unfolding dynamic of understanding. As areas of misunderstanding are recognized and acknowledged, understanding manifests as necessary to resolve them. Each manifestation is a fresh revelation: While one may appear to contradict another, ultimately there are no contradictions, only different points of reference. All meanings are the unfolding of understanding, and all serve to dispel the negativity that shadows the human mind.

When understanding replaces misunderstanding, misunderstanding releases its hold and disappears, like the coils of a snake vanishing into its lair. With nothing left to act upon or correct, understanding quietly merges into the body of knowledge that informs our actions. Nothing remains that can be grasped; nothing remains that the self can appropriate and use for its benefit.

I realize that the approach I adopt here is unusual and that its perspectives may seem odd, even startling. Yet, from time to time I have been encouraged by glimpses of understanding in those who have given these thoughts serious consideration. These glimpses reveal that mind afflicted with problems can engage understanding in ways that dissolve these problems at their roots. Such understanding may be preliminary, with much more remaining to be understood. But it is my view that developed and fully extended, understanding can go far toward liberating the human mind.

May this volume benefit
all who seek understanding.

Sarvam Mangalam

Tarthang Tulku
Odiyan, Sonoma County, California
2013

How to Read this Book

from *Revelations of Mind*

Revelations of Mind is neither a traditional presentation of mind nor a philosophic or psychological system. My aim has been to introduce a universal approach to mind and mental processes rather than focusing on any specific viewpoint, system, or discipline. While *Revelations* touches on topics that readers may associate with philosophy, religion, psychology, or science, its orientation is more experiential and its style more impressionistic.

The whole of *Revelations of Mind* is an exercise for the mind, an unfolding of our mental experience intended to invite understanding that each person can access individually. Although practitioners of meditation may benefit in special ways, this book is addressed to any individual who appreciates the importance of developing a clearer understanding of his or her mind.

To activate this flow of understanding, you as the reader must be prepared to do your part. As you read, let go of the impulse to react too quickly to the points presented. Instead, just keep reading. Hear what is being said before you generate your own saying. If you can let your mind walk down this road without stumbling over a stone here or a crack there, you will soon find that you can stride more broadly and exercise a more innovative way of reading.

If you would like to explore in more depth, I suggest you read this book several times. The first reading will let you become familiar with the concepts and gain an overall orientation to the major points presented. A second reading allows the mind to engage the topics on a more experiential level. I hope you will note a deeper sense of meaning as the words connect more directly to your own observation and intelligence. After this reading, you could perhaps say, "Now I recognize what is being pointed out."

The third reading moves deeper, toward seeing specific self-interpretations and readouts in action in your immediate experience. At this point, you could say, "Now I see what I am doing."

By the fourth reading, you may find yourself actually applying this way of understanding and gaining confidence through direct experience. Here you could say, "Now I understand what I am doing." Understanding can begin to reveal its own way of manifesting, its own way of commenting and pointing, and its own way of releasing.

When you have read the book four times, you may wish to make time for a two to four week retreat. This will give you a valuable opportunity to integrate this material and stabilize understanding on a sound foundation. Then you will be in a better position to take understanding to a higher level, where it becomes clear and inalienable.

To benefit most fully from what you read, contemplate it as if mind were hearing its own thoughts. Let mind read and feed back within itself, mind to mind, until clarity comes and mind understands. This is how mind naturally works, once we know how to give it the opportunity.

Since this book presents no system or doctrine, there is nothing to be gained from grasping at understanding when you sense it arising. At whatever level you are reading, mind is reading mind—generating mind interpretations and mind meanings, not final, fixed truths. Mind remains free to inquire into the source of each interpretation or to ask who is reading each level of meaning.

As you read, it is important to find your own individual way of looking, seeing, and tasting, your own way of viewing yourself and your journey. All the negative expressions of mind, from inflexibility and moodiness to self-centeredness and ego solidity, are based on perception of your own fixed ways of juxtaposing. When you understand how this works and how it confines the mind and limits its natural brilliance, you can liberate yourself. When you act, your understanding will be different. One who knows the self and one who does not know the self will conduct themselves differently, because understanding and not understanding have different outcomes. The benefits and the virtuous power of the merit that action brings are different as well.

When you reach this stage, you will start to sense that you are gaining leverage of a new kind over your life, leverage that comes from knowledge. Whatever discipline you may practice, such as meditation or philosophy or education, you may have the increasing impression that creativity and protection are both coming your way. With a little understanding, mind has tools for working with the raw materials of mind's expression. It has a supportive friendship with itself, a shield against anxiety that allows new possibilities to emerge.

As you feel freer to engage your life experience in new ways, you may have a sense of something unfreezing deep within you. This indicates that your being is becoming more whole and your action more able to bear the power of virtue. This is more than self-improvement at the psychological level: it is genuine self-accommodation, like a pledge of unconditional friendship that is reliable and operates in all situations.

Whether at a given moment you understand or you know something more remains to be understood, you are increasingly liberated from the fundamental anxiety that arises from having no understanding. As understanding unfolds, you see with new eyes, and you feel with a heart healing from the wounds of misunderstanding. In a way uniquely your own, an understanding of mind is emerging that can be applied in any time and any place.

Once you have useful tools for understanding mind and self, the knower and the subject who experiences, you will be prepared to realize the benefits that understanding bestows. You will not be so easily influenced by the strong opinions of others or become lost trying to find your way. Understanding will support whatever you wish to accomplish, extending your journey, enlivening your contributions, and bringing depth to your vision.

Tarthang Tulku
Odiyan, 2013

Notes for Teachers

General description

Revelations of Mind (*ROM*) is a book arranged in six sections with a substantial introduction and postscript. It was collated from a series of talks Tarthang Rinpoche gave to a small group of students over a five-year period at Odiyan between 2007 and 2012. The material was extensively edited before publication, a process that included the re-ordering of paragraphs and the insertion of chapter and paragraph headings.

Because of how it was compiled, some readers have observed that it appears to be repetitive. Some themes are covered many times, but a close reading reveals that the positions expressed in *ROM* are steadily developing a new 'operating system' for mental processing. In the introduction *ROM* is described as 'the mind hearing its own thoughts,' as so much of the material deals with mental operations themselves.

By way of overview, it can be helpful to view the book as falling into two major parts. Of the six sections following the introduction, the first three sections deal with the conceptualized construction of perception and the important role of language; how the construct can be explored through the development of mental stability; and how the construct can be understood through the projection of time. The second three sections deal with how to develop non-conceptuality through an explanation of the path and an exploration of the result such a path can bring. Broadly speaking, the term 'understanding' used in the first half of the book refers to conceptual understanding, and the term 'understanding' used in the second half of the book refers to nonconceptual knowing. In a similar manner, the term 'mind' used in the first half of the book refers to experience arising from conceptual construction, and the term 'mind' used in the second half refers to innate radiance and clarity. In these notes the latter use of understanding and mind are capitalized as Understanding and Mind.

The book can also be analyzed in terms of view, path and fruit. The first three sections deal with the view of how conceptualization arises, its consequences, and the means to penetrate it; the fourth and fifth sections deal with the generation of a path towards nonconceptual knowing; and the final section explores the fruit of such development, the Revelation of Mind.

The first and third sections of the book describe a non-technical Abhidharma, a unique achievement among writings of Buddhist masters in English. Strong parallels to the points made in these sections can be drawn from the findings of neurophysiology and cognitive psychology, as well as Yogachara Buddhist teachings.

Teaching ROM
ROM has a strong internal logic and can be taught chapter by chapter. With sixty-eight chapters and a long postscript, this takes seventy weeks, but creates a satisfying two- or three-year course for those interested. In the notes below, one potential trajectory through the entire book is laid out, first by section, and then in brief notes, chapter by chapter, and finally, paragraph by paragraph.

In working with the original instructor group, however, Tarthang Rinpoche made it clear that there is no 'right' way to teach *ROM*. Each person will bring their own experience in guiding readers through the text, and the liberating effect of working through the book finds expression in many different ways.

The pedagogy of the book can be likened to an incoming tide gradually making new highs on a beach; new insights are reached based on previous discussions, and then those steps are partially retraced before further discoveries are made. This backwards and forwards movement can seem confusing to the reader, but what is being established is literally a new way of being, not merely another object of knowledge. The careful back and forth has the effect of construction rather than just explanation.

OVERVIEW OF THE MAIN SECTIONS

A. INTRODUCTION

The introduction contains a brief synopsis of the major themes explored in *ROM*. It is stressed that *ROM* is not 'about' anything—there is no doctrine or system to be grasped. A first reading will give initial impressions, but readers are encouraged to re-read the book four times as the mind gains insights that feed back into what was understood from the printed words. After such prolonged exposure, a brief period of retreat is suggested both to stabilize the foundations of a new way of being, and to begin the exploration of what lies beyond language itself.

B. SECTION ONE — A FRESH LOOK AT MIND

The first section contains eleven chapters and covers the central theme that the totality of our experience is mind and the 'external' world is an inference we make based on such direct experience. In our day-to-day living, this process of inference is largely unconscious, and the chapters deal with how 'reality,' including our sense of the real and our sense of selfhood, is constructed through language. As *ROM* points out, we are living in a 'readout' generated for us by our mind. It further explores how our failure to understand this construct dooms us to instability, and stresses the historical requirement to understand it and so break the endlessly repeating cycle of human suffering.

C. SECTION TWO — WORKING WITH THE MIND

The second section contains thirteen chapters and covers conventional models of mental development, including meditation and mindfulness. If practitioners are unaware of the pervasive character of the mental construct, however, meditation and methods of mental development are of limited value. These limitations are explored. The section then describes how we might go beyond our constructs, and develop a path of genuine insight through direct inquiry into the moment of experience.

D. SECTION THREE — MIND AND TIME

Section three contains nine chapters and examines one of the central elements of our mental construct, time. The process by which units of time (called 'nanoseconds' in *ROM*) are projected is explored, and how that process of projection is the ground on which the other elements of the mental construct are based. This insight opens the door to the identification of a fruitful meditation object, namely what lies before the first unit of time is projected moment to moment in our mental experience.

E. SECTION FOUR — GROUND OF UNDERSTANDING

The fourth section contains ten chapters and explores a new path of mental transformation, where genuine renunciation of constructed experience is developed along with the capacity to abide before unit time is projected. The insight and action that arises from this capacity is called 'Understanding,' and forms the major theme for the rest of the book.

F. Section Five — Ladder of Understanding

The fifth section contains eleven chapters and explores the potentiality of a life lived from a totally new modality, that of Understanding. There is a detailed examination of how the intrinsic brilliance of our natural intelligence is hijacked by our mental constructs, and how making the firm intention to resist fear-based conceptualization opens a path that can cut through all our problems and disease at a single stroke. Mind becomes our friend and Understanding a true refuge, a reliable capacity within us that allows for the ceaseless unfolding of knowledge.

G. Section Six — Revealing Understanding

Endlessly deepening and broadening, the final nine chapters are both a celebration and an exploration of a totally new way of being, the Revelation of Mind.

H. Postscript

Revelations ends with the transcript of a talk given by Tarthang Rinpoche for the opening of Dharma College in 2012. Acting as an auto-commentary on *ROM*, the talk explores how our knowledge and language are intimately related, and how understanding this relationship is of historical importance to the human condition and the freedom of the human spirit. This new class of knowledge opens the door to creativity and joy, an artistry of manifestation described in Indian and Tibetan writings as lila or rolpa, the Dance of Creation. A description of the importance of these ancient Dharma teachings and their relevance in modern conditions completes *ROM* itself. The book ends with a complete listing (as of the date of publication) of all of Tarthang Rinpoche's publications and activities.

APPENDIX 3

List of Exercises

A Life Devoted to Dharma Activity

Tarthang Tulku, also known as Kunga Gellek Yeshe Dorje, was born in Golok, Eastern Tibet, in 1935. He is one of the last surviving Tibetan lamas to receive a comprehensive traditional education in Old Tibet.

As a young tulku, he studied intensively with more than twenty celebrated masters, traveling widely throughout Eastern Tibet. His root guru was Jamyang Khyentse Chokyi Lodro, one of the most remarkable Tibetan masters of the twentieth century. In 1958, Tarthang Tulku followed this master on a journey to Sikkim, just escaping the annexation of his country by the Chinese. At the young age of 23, he became a refugee in India.

After a short stay at the Young Lamas Home School in Dalhousie, he was asked by H.H. Dudjom Rinpoche to represent the Nyingma School at Sanskrit University in Varanasi. There he established Dharma Mudranalaya to print Tibetan Buddhist texts. In 1968 he left India for the United States, becoming the first Nyingma lama in America.

In 1969, Rinpoche founded the Tibetan Nyingma Meditation Center (TMMC), a California corporation sole, as the nucleus of his activities. He established Padma Ling as the residential headquarters of TNMC, and in 1972-73 founded the Nyingma Institute, where he taught publicly until 1978. During these years, he published the first of his nearly three dozen original books in English. He also founded the Tibetan Aid Project to support Tibetans in exile; Dharma Press and Dharma Publishing, which have now printed and produced hundreds of art reproductions and more than 230 books in Western languages; Nyingma Centers, to guide the growth of four international centers, in Amsterdam, Köln, São Paulo and Rio de Janeiro, with a new center, as of 2020, emerging in Porto Allegre; and Odiyan Retreat Center, a mandala of temples, stupas, and libraries, including Vajra Temple, Cintamani Temple, the Enlightenment Stupa, and Vairocana Garden. Consecrated in 2019, Odiyan's Dharma Wheel Mandala surrounds the Mandala's central temple complex with 2,016 18-inch-tall Prayer Wheels, each of which contains the entire Tibetan Buddhist Canon; it is the largest monument of its kind in the world.

Ratna Ling Retreat Center, established in 2004 as an adjunct to Odiyan, offers retreats to the general public on topics that encourage the integration of mind and body and emphasize many forms of wellness. A special facility to house and support elder members of the TNMC community is in development.

In 1981, Rinpoche published the *Nyingma Edition of the Tibetan Buddhist Canon* in 120 atlas-sized volumes, followed by an eight-volume Catalogue and Bibliography. The Yeshe De Text Project, founded in 1983, produced *Great Treasures of Ancient Teachings* in 641 volumes, and has printed and distributed to the Tibetan community an enormous treasure of sacred books, including six editions of the Kanjur and three of the Tanjur. Its most recent edition, the *Yid Bzhin Norbu Kanjur*, may be the most comprehensive Kanjur collection ever assembled. In all, more than 10,000 sets of the Kanjur have been offered to the Tibetan Sangha.

In 1989 Rinpoche founded the Nyingma Monlam Chenmo (World Peace Ceremony) in Bodh Gaya, India, where

8,000-10,000 monastics and lay faithful gather annually. He also provided seed money to the other major schools of Tibetan Buddhism for Kagyu, Sakya, and Gelug Monlams. Through the Monlam, Rinpoche was able to make extraordinary text offerings to the Sangha. Yeshe De's recent offerings include collected works of great masters like Jigme Lingpa, Patrul Rinpoche and Lama Mipham. As many as 100 unique volumes of texts can be offered in a given year, with thousands of copies of each volume being provided free of charge to the libraries of Dharma centers throughout the Tibetan diaspora. A participant who received books every year of the Monlam would now have a personal Yeshe De library consisting of more than a thousand volumes.

Since 1989, along with more than 5 million sacred books, TNMC has distributed 3.25 million sacred art images and 176,250 prayer wheels to more than 3,300 Dharma centers in India, Nepal, Bhutan, and Tibet. Thousands of bronze reproductions of authentic ancient sacred images created at Odiyan have also been offered to the Sangha. A total of 67,285 copies of the precious 8,000-line Prajnaparamita—including 414 granite plaques engraved in Sanskrit, Tibetan, and English, 100 large hand-sewn victory banners, and six important editions in traditional Tibetan format—have been offered to the Sangha.

Other offerings for Bodh Gaya include eight butterlamp houses; hundreds of prayer wheels; golden lhantsa and Tibetan Prajnaparamita plaques; financial support for the restoration of the Mahabodhi Temple spire; site beautification; fabric banners, hangings, and umbrellas produced at Odiyan; and year-round offerings of butterlamps.

In 2002, to support the restoration of Buddhism in the land of its origin, Rinpoche founded the Light of Buddhadharma Foundation International (LBDFI). In 2006, TNMC and LBDFI jointly sponsored and organized the first annual Tipitaka Chanting Ceremony by the Theravadin Sangha in Bodh Gaya—the first gathering of its kind in more than 700 years.

As this annual ceremony continues to be held, additional Tipitaka Chanting Ceremonies are being organized and held around the world, including Berkeley, CA; representatives from 11 countries now participate. LBDFI's work has been embraced by the Indian government, which enthusiastically supports initiatives like the Dharma Training Wheel, bringing venerable monks on an extended pilgrimage to the Eight Great Holy Places of the Buddha.

TNMC and its mandala organizations have installed seventeen 2½-ton World Peace Bells at holy places throughout Asia, and have supported renovation projects at numerous sacred sites, including the historic renovation of the Swayambhu Stupa in Nepal. Other major restoration projects include the refounding of the practice center of the great twentieth century renunciate master Khenpo Chokyab, and the restoration of Adzom Gar, the seat of Adzom Drukpa and Rinpoche's own teacher, Adzom Drukpa's son and heir A-'gyur Rinpoche.

In 2005, Mangalam Light Foundation was established. Operating through four "daughter" foundations, with LBDFI being joined by the Ananda, Prajna, and Vajra Light Foundations, Mangalam Light's mission is to revive, preserve, and support the heritage of the Buddhadharma in Tibet. The Tibet-based Light Foundations have given substantial support to many diverse projects, including construction at Tarthang Monastery in Eastern Tibet. Ananda Light Foundation has funded repairs and construction at numerous monasteries and nunneries; it has also built primary schools serving 800 children throughout Eastern Tibet. Vajra Light Foundation has provided ceremony support throughout Central and Eastern Tibet, particularly sponsoring large Monlams at Larung Gar and Yachen Gar, respectively the largest Buddhist monastery in the world and the largest nunnery in Tibet. Prajna Light Foundation has made great efforts to restore Tibetan libraries: more than 1,000 sets of the Kanjur and 10,000 sets of the collected works of the great Nyingma master Longchenpa have been distributed to monasteries throughout Tibet.

In 2009, Rinpoche founded the Mangalam Research Center for Buddhist Languages in Berkeley, CA. Partnering with a distinguished group of international scholars, MRC has received several prestigious grants from the National Endowment for the Humanities, enabling it to develop the highly innovative Buddhist Translators' Workbench data tool for researchers. It also offers many conferences, colloquia and seminars, as well as numerous programs open to the public. In the same period, Rinpoche founded Guna Foundation, a documentary filmmaking unit that has produced three well-received documentaries on Tarthang Tulku's Dharma activities, including the award-winning film, *The Great Transmission* (2016).

In 2012, Rinpoche established Dharma College in downtown Berkeley to serve as a site for the exploration of dynamic and synergistic new teachings on the nature of the mind, expressed in recent books like *Revelations of Mind, Dimensions of Mind, Keys of Knowledge,* and the *Lotus Trilogy.* 2013 saw the inauguration of Sarnath International Nyingma Institute (SINI) in Sarnath, India, founded by Rinpoche in order to bridge the gap between Eastern and Western modes of knowledge, to foster the study of the earliest period of Tibetan Buddhism (embodied in Khen Lob Cho Sum, the Founders of Tibetan Dharma), and to host the annual Tibet Peace Ceremony. SINI is also home to the ecumenical Kanjur Karchag Project, which gathers Tibetan scholars from all major schools in a deep study of the origins and structure of the Tibetan Kanjur. As the TNMC mandala continues to unfold, the Nyingma Association of Mandala Organizations (NAMO), incorporated in 2012, helps guide and protect the work of its seventeen distinct member organizations.

In 2018, Rinpoche published *Caring,* an accessible exploration of the power of compassion in healing ourselves and the world around us. New programs based on *Caring* are being offered throughout the TNMC mandala. As of 2020, online programs for the public on a wide variety of topics are available from the Nyingma Institute, Dharma College, Ratna Ling, Odiyan, and the international centers.

Rinpoche has dedicated his life to the work of preserving, protecting, and distributing the Tibetan Buddhist heritage. All his books and projects are efforts to manifest the sacred forms of Kaya, Vaca, Citta, Guna, and Karma—enlightened embodiment, speech, mind, qualities, and actions—for the sake of the entire world. More information about these activities is recorded in more than 45 volumes of the TNMC Annals, copies of which can be found at the Nyingma Institute and the International Centers. Now in his mid-eighties, Rinpoche continues to preserve and distribute sacred Tibetan texts, to write books for Western audiences, and to energetically direct large, innovative and inspiring Dharma projects.